International Comparisons
of Prices and Output

NATIONAL BUREAU OF ECONOMIC RESEARCH

*CONFERENCE ON RESEARCH IN INCOME
AND WEALTH*

International Comparisons
of Prices and Output

Edited by D. J. DALY

YORK UNIVERSITY

Studies in Income and Wealth
VOLUME THIRTY-SEVEN
*by the Conference on Research
in Income and Wealth*

NATIONAL BUREAU OF ECONOMIC RESEARCH
NEW YORK

Distributed by COLUMBIA UNIVERSITY PRESS
NEW YORK AND LONDON 1972

Printed in the United States of America

*Relation of the National Bureau Directors to
Publications Reporting Conference Proceedings*

Since the present volume is a record of conference
proceedings, it has been exempted from the rules
governing submission of manuscripts to, and
critical review by, the Board of Directors of the
National Bureau.

*(Resolution adopted July 6, 1948,
as revised November 21, 1949,
and April 20, 1968)*

Prefatory Note

THIS volume of *Studies in Income and Wealth* is devoted to a discussion of international comparisons of prices and real product. It contains seven papers presented at the sessions of the Conference on Research in Income and Wealth held in May 1970 at York University in Toronto, together with comments of participants. The Program Committee consisted of Solomon Fabricant, Irving Kravis, Barend de Vries, Abram Bergson, Richard Ruggles, Nancy Ruggles, and D. J. Daly, who served as program chairman and conference editor.

Funds for the economic research conference program of the National Bureau of Economic Research are supplied by the National Science Foundation.

Contents

The Role of the Price Structure

Price and Cost Differences—Industries and Commodities

International Comparisons
of Prices and Output

Introduction

D. J. DALY

YORK UNIVERSITY

AS we enter the 1970's a large number of countries, both developed and developing, produce national accounts and national income data with varying degrees of detail and of varying levels of quality. The presentation of the accounts and the uses to which they are put are heavily influenced by J. M. Keynes's *General Theory of Employment, Interest, and Money* [1] and by the heavy emphasis, in subsequent discussions of both a theoretical and an applied variety, on factors affecting the levels of demand.

However, in the history of economic thought, the early work on national income emphasized its use in appraising differences in living standards and the efficiency with which resources were used in different countries. In current terminology, Adam Smith's *Wealth of Nations* [2] would be called the "National Income of Nations." Much of it concerned the factors contributing to differences in standards of living between countries. Alfred Marshall's *Industry and Trade* [3] provides a comprehensive appraisal of some of the factors contributing to the differences in national income, productivity, etc., for some of the major industrialized countries, such as the United States, the United Kingdom, Germany, and France. *Industry and Trade* contains insights on many aspects of these intercountry differences that are relevant to this conference volume. The general emphasis of this volume is on the use of national income concepts and data to appraise the supply and output side of national economies and some related aspects of international trade.

[1] J. M. Keynes, *General Theory of Employment, Interest, and Money,* London, Macmillan, 1936.

[2] Adam Smith, *The Wealth of Nations,* New York, Modern Library, 1937.

[3] Alfred Marshall, *Industry and Trade: A Study of Industrial Technique and Business Organization,* London, Macmillan, 1920.

Earlier conference volumes have dealt with the conceptual and practical problems of achieving international comparability of various countries' national income estimates that are calculated in their respective currencies.[4] The work of the United Nations and the Organization for Economic Cooperation and Development in national accounts and of the International Monetary Fund on the balance of payments have facilitated a broad measure of international comparability for a large number of countries. However, the considerably more difficult task of comparing the levels of prices and real national product between countries has received much less attention in past conference volumes. To some extent this reflects the primary interest of the membership of the conference in economic developments within the United States, but it also reflects the relatively limited amount of resources going into this field in the world as a whole.

Volume 20 in the Income and Wealth series, *Problems in the International Comparison of Economic Accounts,*[5] contains several important papers relevant to this volume. Among them are "Measuring Comparative Purchasing Power," by Dorothy W. Brady and Abner Hurwitz, and the comments on it; and Irving B. Kravis's "The Scope of Economic Activity in International Income Comparisons," the comments by Everett E. Hagen and Jacob Viner, and the reply by Kravis.

Volume 25 in the series includes a paper by Milton Gilbert and Wilfred Beckerman on "International Comparisons of Real Product and Productivity by Final Expenditures and by Industry."[6] It reviews the conceptual basis of such comparisons, discusses the possibility of differences in taste between developed countries, and reviews the statistical features of the two approaches, using comparisons between the United Kingdom and United States.

---

[4] For example, T. C. Liu and S. Fang, "The Construction of National Income Tables and International Comparisons of National Incomes," in *Studies in Income and Wealth,* Vol. 8, New York, NBER, 1946, pp. 75–118; Edward F. Denison, "Tripartite Discussions of National Income Measurement," in *Studies in Income and Wealth,* Vol. 10, New York, NBER, 1947, pp. 4–22; Morris A. Copeland, Jerome Jacobson, and Bernard Clyman, "Problems of International Comparisons of Income and Wealth," in *ibid.,* pp. 136–59; and Hans Staehle, "The International Comparison of Real National Income: A Note on Methods," *Studies in Income and Wealth,* Vol. 11, New York, NBER, 1949, pp. 223–72.

[5] New York, NBER, 1957.

[6] *Output, Input, and Productivity Measurement,* Princeton University Press for NBER, 1961.

An interest in international comparisons is also reflected in Hollis Chenery's discussion in Volume 31. He comments that

I suspect that a comparison of the growth of the several inputs and corresponding output in the United States to comparable estimates for other countries may be the best way to acquire better insight into growth policy for the United States itself. The case for intercountry analysis becomes even stronger when we consider substantial departures from patterns of output and mixtures of input that have been experienced in the past. Intercountry analysis therefore becomes essential to the design of growth policies for underdeveloped countries, whose own experience is of very limited value for this purpose.[7]

In planning the present conference, the program committee wanted not only to have papers on theory and measurement, but also to move further in two other directions—to provide papers and discussion on the *uses* of the basic data in economic analysis and public policy and, also, to go below the level of the national aggregates into more *disaggregation*. A number of the committee members working in the area of international comparisons are impressed by the implications of price-quantity interrelations below the aggregative level for analyses of resource allocation, international trade, economic development, and economic growth. A further factor contributing to a program going beyond the primary emphasis on measurement was the limited amount of resources going into the measurement area, compared to the magnitude of the problems, at the time the conference was being planned.

The conference covered in this volume was a lively one for participants, partly because the problems discussed were important and relevant to current problems. At various times the discussions below deal with such topics as problems of economic growth and income differences between countries, economic problems of developing countries and the scope for relative prices in planning for such countries, international trade and specialization, economic integration in Latin America, and comparative productivity levels in the United States and Soviet Russia. Many of these topics are high on the list of relevant and important issues in international economics and public policy.

A second factor in the lively nature of the conference was the

[7] Hollis B. Chenery, "Comment," in Murray Brown, ed., *The Theory and Empirical Analysis of Production*, Studies in Income and Wealth, Vol. 31, New York, NBER, 1967.

diversity in viewpoint of the conference participants. Professor Andreas G. Papandreou, as chairman the first morning, distinguished three viewpoints in the discussion: the classical line of thought, reflected in an interest in and concern for productivity, a contemporary reflection of the historical concern for the struggle of man against nature; the neoclassical viewpoint, reflected in an interest in individual utility and welfare and its relation to social values and a social welfare function; the planners' viewpoint, expressed in the quest for numerical materials in a variety of applied economic problems. These three points of view emerged and were presented with varying intensity at the various conference sessions. The published volume catches some, but not all, of the spirited discussion from the floor.

In the remainder of this introduction, I will briefly outline the main topics treated by the various authors and discussants to convey a little of the flavor of the contents. The papers cover a wide range of topics, and the summary may prove a useful guide, especially to the reader who wishes to pick and choose.

The papers fall roughly into three categories. Sidney Afriat's paper concentrates on the theory of price index comparisons. Dan Usher's comment on Bergson's paper also concentrates on the classical index number problem in the context of both welfare and production comparisons. A second group of papers provides new data on international comparisons. Abram Bergson provides data on comparative national income in the USSR and the United States. The Grunwald-Salazar paper is a progress report on a project for making a comprehensive comparison of prices and national product in Latin America. Barend de Vries provides data on prices of a number of capital goods in the developing and developed countries. A third group of papers concentrates rather more on the uses of national income and price comparisons. This group includes my paper, on the relationship between such data and international trade for industrialized countries, and the paper by Gus Ranis, on shifts in emphasis in the use of relative prices in planning in the developing countries. Both of these papers introduce some disaggregation and deal with the structure of relative prices within the national totals. The Kravis-Lipsey paper also concentrates on disaggregation in relation to substitution between countries as suppliers of goods.

SUMMARIES

Sidney Afriat's paper provides an articulated mathematical exposition of index number theory, starting off with utility theory. His contribution is useful, since it is one of the few at the conference reflecting an explicit emphasis on mathematical reasoning and exposition. It is worthwhile to be reminded of the assumptions made in such comparisons.

This paper led to an active discussion from the floor, not all of which is reflected in the published volume. Ulmer and Kravis discussed the degree to which the key assumptions made in index number comparisons are applicable to both place-to-place and time-to-time comparisons of prices and real income. A number of participants supported Kravis's view that the real differences between these comparisons were empirical, and that there was no essential difference in index number theory between the two sorts of comparison.

The paper by D. J. Daly surveys some of the main uses to which intercountry comparisons are put in economic analysis. Special emphasis is given to its applicability to international trade, and the extent to which the data point up differences in production conditions between countries. The evidence on comparisons between the United States and Canada is used to illustrate the significant contrast in output in relation to labor and other factor inputs beween the two countries. The role of tariffs in the two countries and the degree of variation in effective tariff rates in Canada contribute to the productivity gap by encouraging product diversity and short production runs in Canada. The same points are applicable to other countries as well.

The discussants, Balassa and Bhagwati, agree on the empirical importance of different production conditions in different countries, but there were unresolved differences of opinion about the tests of the Ricardian view of trade using United Kingdom–United States data. The discussants extended the international trade discussion in a number of directions.

Bergson provides comprehensive estimates of comparisons between the United States and the USSR, drawing on some of his own earlier work. The statistical estimates are based partially on the theoretical framework of Moorstein's 1961 *Quarterly Journal of Economics* article.

Bergson concludes that the level of real national product per capita in the USSR in 1955 was about 23 per cent of that in the United States in rubles and 38 per cent in dollars. This would make the Soviet per capita level roughly similar to Italy's in real terms.

In the discussion, Usher argued that the Paasche and Laspeyres index number formulas provide inside limits for price comparisons, and that there is a much wider range of indeterminancy in such comparisons than suggested by Bergson and the prevailing view in the literature. Kenessey considers how comparisons between the USSR and the United States would look if approached from the Soviet viewpoint, and is reassured. Greenslade discusses some of the institutional differences between the two countries and their influences on the problems of measurement.

The Grunwald-Salazar paper is a progress report on their project on Latin American economic integration and on the cooperative research program of comparative studies being coordinated at the Brookings Institution. The differences in prices between countries and the contrasts with official exchange rates are explored, and the methodological questions are discussed. The paper also contains preliminary results.

In their comments, Williams and Mason raise some questions on the scope of the paper and discuss the representativeness of the data, because it pertains to urban areas. They also question some of the interpretations drawn in the paper.

Gus Ranis's paper concentrates on some of the choices facing developing countries, particularly the possible conflict between growth and efficiency. He argues that the efficient allocation of resources over time and space is not the key problem in developing countries. Key questions rather are "how to introduce technological change, how to broaden participation, how to create entrepreneurs, how to create institutional change, and how to induce minimum mobility." In dealing with these questions, he distinguishes between a typical import substitution phase and a subsequent shift from import to export substitution. He illustrates his themes from the experience of Korea and Pakistan.

Although the Ranis paper is short, it created a lively reaction both at the conference and in some comments submitted subsequently. In this volume, Ruggles points out that it is difficult to achieve income redistribution and efficiency simultaneously. Eckstein argues that there is little conflict between the objectives of basic growth and efficiency and gives examples of countries that have grown continuously and rapidly with broad participation in the world market. Bhagwati suggests that the waste from inefficiency can be very large and that the costs of import substitution have sometimes been too high, rather than that import substitution is inherently harmful. Stolper is very critical of the early parts of the Ranis paper, and argues that sound price policies are required for economic growth and the development of an entrepreneurial group.

De Vries's paper moves to price comparisons for a particular industrial group rather than, as in most of the earlier papers at the conference, for the economy as a whole. His paper concentrates on selected capital goods industries, and points up the large contrasts between prices of identical items in the developed and developing countries. Some of these differences can be reduced by changes in government policy, but other factors contributing to higher manufactured goods prices in developing countries are expected to persist, including scarcity of skills, management, and capital; lagging technology; and short production runs.

Felix feels that de Vries's diagnosis of the problem of developing industrial exports is too optimistic. He expects serious adjustment problems if protection is lowered on competitive imports, and deals rather fully with economic developments in Argentina as illustrative of his position. Dorothy Walters also comments on some of the policy implications, including the need to minimize economic loss while recognizing the high priority of job creation and employment.

In the Kravis-Lipsey paper, the authors use new data from *Price Competitiveness in World Trade* for four industrial countries to assess the elasticity of substitution as a variable in world trade. They find the elasticities of substitution lower after 1961 than before, and they identify and discuss a number of explanations for those differences. Some of the possible explanations relate to the recapture of more traditional market shares, factors affecting elasticities of supply and price and income elasticities of demand, and the effect of market shares upon elasticities. In the Comment, Stern raises a number of questions about the theoretical foundation of the measurement procedures, and makes a number of suggestions on future research.

SUPPLY AND COST OF INTERNATIONAL COMPARISON DATA

A number of papers in this volume show how data on international comparisons of prices and real incomes can be and have been used in the economic analysis of a number of applied problems. However, even for developed countries, such as Europe and North America, the range of high-quality and reasonably recent comparisons is still quite limited. When one moves to comparisons between the developed and undeveloped countries, the problems are even more acute, as Dan Usher has illustrated in his comparisons between the United Kingdom and Thailand.

During 1969 new work was initiated by the United Nations on a selected group of developed and developing countries, new resources are being put into comparisons for Europe, and this volume contains new results for Latin America and the Soviet Union. All of these projects have moved forward considerably since 1965, when this conference was first discussed. However, the extent of resources going into such intercountry comparisons is still small, compared, for example, to the regular surveys of price changes within individual countries. Many countries have monthly wholesale and consumer price indexes and quarterly and annual GNP deflators. In many countries indexes of stock prices are recomputed frequently throughout every day, even though the value of stocks traded over a month is typically minute in relation to the total value of stocks outstanding.

What are some of the reasons for the relatively limited range of data on intercountry comparisons? Three considerations seem to be relevant to this question. First, data on intercountry comparisons are *difficult* to obtain. Issues are encountered, including, for example, theoretical aspects of comparability of tastes, practical problems of commodity specification and comparability, and index number problems, that are of far greater quantitative magnitude than anything encountered in time-to-time comparisons for individual countries. Work in this area almost inevitably involves cooperation and coordination of statistical agencies and/or research groups in a variety of countries; and whole new problems of interpersonal, intercultural, and intercountry relations inevitably arise. All of these problems require a substantial amount of professional expertise, time, and patience to resolve. A second general consideration is that the resulting intercountry comparisons can fill a variety of *general purpose uses*. However, many national and international agencies have much more specific interests, and their priorities on data development and analysis reflect this. Third, the intercountry comparisons provide a basis for considered views on *basic and long-range problems*. However, many governments and international agencies get more heavily involved in short-term topics. Even though short-term economic crises, both domestic and international, grow out of longer-range problems and vulnerabilities, resources are frequently not put to the study of longer-range topics ahead of time, and when a short-term crisis develops, it is too late to do the appropriate basic study.

If the conference and this volume widen and deepen the range and degree of support for further work on international comparisons of prices and real incomes, they will have achieved one of the objectives of the conference organizers.

Theory and Uses

The Theory of

International Comparisons of

Real Income and Prices

SIDNEY N. AFRIAT

UNIVERSITY OF WATERLOO, ONTARIO

1.0 CONCEPT OF COMPARISON

1.1 *Framework*

Two or more countries have similar commodities. But prices and quantities differ, and it is required to construct indexes which express a comparison. For a theory of such construction, it is essential to have a prior concept of the intended meaning of the comparison. From such a concept, together with a scheme for the data and a principle by which the data are related to the concept, the theory of construction should follow.

Comparison between two places in a single period is to be viewed in the same abstract framework as comparison between two periods in a single place. Though variables might occur in time and have a corresponding designation, temporal priority has no role. It makes no difference whether the distinctions be of time or place. What is in view is a variety of locations, temporal or geographical or possibly both, where prices and quantities differ, and which, when combined by analysis are to indicate differences of economic situation.

Let there be some k references which are to be compared and are indicated by $t = 1, \ldots, k$. But if there are but two, these can be indicated by $t = 0, 1$ and distinguished as the *base* and *current* reference.

NOTE: This work has been supported by the National Science Foundation under Grant GS 2195.

The distinction between references can be taken to be as between different countries, or different periods of time, or both in conjunction. But in the question of international comparison, there often are k, or in particular two, different countries during the same period.

There are assumed to be some n goods involved. With n as the nonnegative numbers, Ω_n and Ω'' are the spaces of nonnegative column and row vectors of n elements. The basic element of the data is a pair (x, p) formed by a vector $p \: \varepsilon \: \Omega_n$ of prices p_i and a vector $x \: \varepsilon \: \Omega''$ of quantities x_i. Such a pair describes the *demand* of quantities x at prices p. The associated expenditure is $px = \Sigma_i p_i x_i$, and, with $M = px$, $u = M^{-1}p$ defines the associated *budget vector*. It forms with x the pair (x, u) such that $ux = 1$, which can be called the *associated budget*. Often an observed demand is meaningful only through its associated budget. Then discussion is simpler in terms of budgets rather than original observed demands.

By an *expansion set* (S, p) is meant a set of demands $[(x, p) : x \: \varepsilon \: S]$ all associated with the same prices p. The set S could consist of a finite set of points, or it could be a path, in which case (S, p) indicates an *expansion path* associated with prices p. Inherent in the price level concept is the assumption that expansion paths are rays through the origin. In that case, the data for a demand (x, p) amount to data for an expansion path (S, p), where S is the ray $[x\lambda : \lambda \geqq 0]$ through x. A more general model for an expansion path is the linear model, where the paths are lines not necessarily through the origin. In a common special form of this model, the expansion lines associated with different prices converge in a single point, not necessarily the origin.

For a basic scheme, it is postulated that the data consist of a set of demands (x_t, p_t) or, more elaborately, a set of expansions (S_t, p_t), associated with each country $t = 1, \ldots, k$. But in fact a single demand determines an expansion when analysis is based on the concept of a price index and hence on the assumption of homogeneity, which requires that expansion paths be rays through the origin, each determined by any one of its points. Thus again it is expansion data that are available, either explicitly or implicitly.

1.2 *Nature of Comparison*

It is understood that the comparison is to be in real terms. This means; in the first place, that its reference must be exclusively to quantities of the basic goods, independent of the accident that money and prices are part of the data by means of which the comparison is made. The role of money and prices is just to express limitations of opportunities for possessing goods. But these limitations are of no significance if what is limited is not valued. Also value is meaningless if it is not pursued to a maximum within the limited opportunity available. With such optimality, data on choice under limitation communicates information about value which is relevant to comparisons. But value is an attribute of the chooser, and the chooser must therefore be clearly identified. Thus with national measurements it should be decided whether value derives directly from individuals or from the nation as a whole. In the latter case it should be asked in what sense, since national wants are not easily discovered and stated, and have dimensions which are without counterpart for the individual.

Some significant yardstick is presumed in making comparisons between situations. A yardstick that refers to bundles of goods is an ordering of them which expresses their relative value according to a system of wants. This immediately shows an obscurity in the meaning of comparisons between countries where wants are manifestly different, whether this be for the wants of the individual inhabitants or, in any sense conceivable, for that different type of individual represented by a single country. To speak of real national outputs or incomes implies a presupposition of national value, that is, a system of wants described by a utility relation. If this relation is not already on record and available in a form suitable for making the required comparisons, then it can only be inferred from price-quantity data, under the maximum hypothesis. Concerning the mechanism which provides this maximality, and there is only what Schumpeter termed the "maximum doctrine of perfect competition," which is an early concept. It was first criticized, seriously but cautiously, by Marshall and has now altogether lost its suggested meaning. Some such doctrine seems necessary if prices and price indexes are to be relevant to the measurement of a national output that differs from the summation of individual real incomes seemingly permitted by the assumption of homogeneity of utility which underlies the use of price indexes. Such a summation would appear to be permitted mathematically by the homogeneity assumption, but it would have no significance unless called for by some theory. Investigation of real national measures and comparisons seems to have little opportunity for development except for those that refer directly to individuals.

1.3 General Principles

A problem to be considered is that of establishing a correspondence between individual incomes in different countries which represent the same real income or purchasing power, that is, which in choice of goods at the prices that prevail would obtain the same real output or utility. Such correspondence is to be established on the basis of a utility order $R \subset \Omega^n \times \Omega^n$ which compares bundles of goods $x, y \in \Omega^n$ according to value, or output of utility, so that the priority xRy signifies x is as good as, or produces at least as much utility as, y. The problem in such a comparison arises because though it is based conceptually on a utility scale no actual scale has been identified. However, the scale is validated by the holders of the incomes themselves. It is with that same scale that they are assumed to make optimal choices under limited budgets. The obverse of this is that data on choices impose a limitation on the scale that is to be applied. With fragmentary observations, this is a loose limitation, but essentially it is all there is with which to proceed.

So far as the idea of a definite structure of wants can be applied at all, it is recognized that wants are related to circumstances and differ between individuals, times, and countries. But the comparisons under consideration essentially involve the notion of a want structure that is common for all, and this universality is what makes the comparison intelligible. Such a yardstick is therefore a purely statistical concept. In such a case, complete generality of the basic model makes no sense. Indeterminacies can just as well be diminished, and in cases even removed, by imposing a special structure on the model. The structure most commonly imposed is homogeneity, which underlies the concept of a price index and with it almost the entire traditional theory of index numbers. It is an important form because it greatly simplifies procedures, and its lack of elaborate overrefinement is appropriate to some applications. But in other applications it effaces structural features which are of crucial significance.

In section 2.0, below, the basic analytical concepts bearing on index number construction are described. A special branch of this subject evolves from the homogeneity assumption, and leads to the theory of price index construction treated in section 3.0. Homogeneity of utility is equivalent to a homogeneous linear form for the expansion functions. Certain objections will be made to this in the present section, and to linear expansion in general. However, a limited generalization of the price index concept will be developed. This is the theory of marginal price indexes, which is presented later. It too is vulnerable to a serious objection, and it is shown how a further extension can overcome this, without sacrificing the practical features that belong to the earlier methods.

1.4 *Analytical Formulation*

The basic concept of index theory is the value-cost function

$$(1) \qquad \rho(p, x) = \min\,[py : yRx]$$

which derives from a utility relation R (see section 2.3). It determines the minimum cost at given prices p of a bundle of goods which ranks in R with a given bundle x. Since xRy, because of reflexivity of R,

$$(2) \qquad \rho(p, x) \leq px$$

for all p, x. Certain minimal properties are assumed for R (2.1), which in fact are not at all restrictive for the questions considered, with finite data (2.5), but give a simpler basis for discussion. While $\rho(p, x)$ derives from R, nothing of R is lost in it even when it is prescribed just for one value of p, since then as a function of x it is a utility function representing R:

$$(3) \qquad xRy \iff \rho(p, x) \geq \rho(p, y).$$

Such a particular utility function could be called a *cost gauge* of R. Any one can be constructed from any other:

$$(4) \qquad \rho(p, x) = \min\,[py : \rho(p_0, y) \geq \rho(p_0, x)].$$

These are the natural yardsticks for the comparisons under consideration, since they deal with value and cost simultaneously, one of them being associated with any price situation; but they all represent a single system of measure by virtue of the transformations between them.

If R is specified for consumers (in practice, it is not), then $M_{10} = \rho(p_1, x_0)$ is the cost at current prices of living at the standard represented by the base consumption x_0. It goes without saying that the notion of costs has no meaning, and the equation has no unique determination, unless the calculation is at *minimum* cost. By (2),

$$(5) \qquad\qquad M_{10} \leqq p_1 x_0,$$

that is, the "true" cost M, which is true in so far as R is the true utility relation, does not exceed the Laspeyres cost $p_1 x_0$. This is reassuring for traditional doctrine, which has proposed the Laspeyres index to be an upper bound of something. If more is intended than has just been said with (5), which is a vacuous consequence of definition, then it is necessary to be explicit.

Observed demands (x_0, p_0), (x_1, p_1) for the base and current periods, or countries, being available, a formula for M_{10} is required, traditionally in the form $M_{10} = P_{10} M_0$, where P_{10} is a "price index," and $M_0 = p_0 x_0$. Thus with the Laspeyres price index $P_{10} = p_1 x_0 / p_0 x_0$, $M_{10} = p_1 x_0$ as just remarked. But first the question will be considered without regard for the proposed significance of this form. What has mostly been lacking is an explicit recognition of a principle which relates the data to the question. One such principle is that R be such as to show observed cost $M_t = p_t x_t$ not to exceed minimum cost for the value obtained, $M_{tt} = \rho(p_t, x_t)$, that is, the observed demands must be expressed as satisfying a condition which is necessary for optimality, when R is the prevailing utility relation. Then

$$(6) \qquad\qquad \rho(p_0, x_0) \geqq p_0 x_0, \qquad \rho(p_1, x_1) \geqq p_1 x_1.$$

With (2) this is equivalent to

$$(7) \qquad\qquad \rho(p_0, x_0) = p_0 x_0, \qquad \rho(p_1, x_1) = p_1 x_1.$$

Any R for which (6) holds can be said to be *compatible* with the data. The further logic of the compatibility relation is shown in section 2.4. Possibly no compatible R exists. If any does the demands can be said to be *consistent*. (A more general theory of consistency is developed in section 2.5.) Then it can be asked, What is the range of values of $M_{10} = \rho_{10}\,(p_1, x_0)$ for all such R? The range of M_{10} appears to be an interval, which always includes the upper limit $(M_{10})_u$, but not necessarily the lower one $(M_{10})_l$. But the question of attainment of units is unimportant. What we really want to know is whether these are the proverbial bounds of index number lore. The Laspeyres value is identical with $(M_{10})_u$, but the Paasche value not only has no connection with $(M_{10})_l$, but even need not lie in the interval, presumed nonempty since the data are consistent. But it is evident in all arguments involving the Paasche index, and generally whenever the peculiar concept of a price index is dealt with, that an implicit special assumption has been made, namely, the homogeneity of utility. (It is examined in the next section.) Since there are serious objections to that assumption and, also, to limiting the data to base and current demands only, it is interesting to go outside the traditional framework and investigate the determination of $\rho(p_1, x_0)$ in a more general way.

It is simpler to discuss demands (x_t, p_t) through their derived budgets (x_t, u_t), where $u_t = M_t^{-1}p_t$, and $M_t = p_t x_t$, so that $u_t x = 1$. The requirement $M_{tt} = M_t$ for compatibility of R with any set of demands for $t = 1, \ldots, k$ is then

(8)
$$\rho_{tt} = 1, \qquad t = 1, \ldots, k$$

where

(9)
$$\rho_{rs} = \rho(u_r, x_s), \qquad r, s = 1, \ldots, k.$$

The next step is to determine the range of any ρ_{rs} for all R such that $\rho_{tt} = 1$ for all t. Again the range is an interval, whose limits can be determined. Let

(10)
$$D_{rs} = u_r x_s - 1,$$

and define a relation D by

(11)
$$rDs \equiv D_{rs} \leqq 0,$$

and Q by

(12)
$$rQt \equiv rDsD \ldots Dt \text{ for some } s, \ldots$$

and let

(13)
$$(\rho_{rs})_u = \min \, [u_r x_t : tQs]$$

$$(\rho_{rs})_l = \min \, [u_r x : sQt \Rightarrow u_t x \geqq 1].$$

The condition for the consistency of the demands can be stated in three equivalent ways,

(14) $D_{rs} \leqq 0, D_{st} \leqq 0, \ldots, D_{qr} \leqq 0 \Rightarrow D_{rs} = D_{st} = \cdots = D_{qr} = 0$

for all $r, s, \ldots, q$ or

(15)
$$rQs \Rightarrow u_s x_r \geqq 0$$

for all r, s or

(16)
$$(\rho_{rs})_l \leqq (\rho_{rs})_u$$

for all r, s. Then, subject to consistency, so that the interval will be nonempty, $(\rho_{rs})_u, (\rho_{rs})_l$ are the desired limits. Consistency of the data implies the consistency of these as upper and lower limits, that is, that the one be not less than the other, for all r, s. In fact, by the equivalence of consistency to (16), the converse also is true.

In the special case of a pair of demands $(x_0, p_0), (x_1, p_1)$, the consistency condition becomes

(17) $p_0 x_1 \leqq p_0 x_0, \quad p_1 x_0 \leqq p_1 x_1 \Rightarrow p_0 x_1 = p_0 x_0, \quad p_1 x_0 = p_1 x_1$

evidently implied by the Samuelson condition

(18) $p_0 x_1 \leqq p_0 x_0, \quad x_1 \neq x_0 \Rightarrow p_1 x_0 > p_1 x_1$

which can be stated more symmetrically as

(19) $p_0 x_1 \leqq p_0 x_0, \quad p_1 x_0 \leqq p_1 x_1 \Rightarrow x_0 = x_1.$

Further

(20)
$$(\rho_{10})_u = \min \, [u_1 x_t : u_t x_0 \leqq 1]$$

so that, if $u_1 x_0 \leqq 1$,

(21)
$$(\rho_{10})_u = \min \, [u_1 x_1, \, u_1 x_0]$$

$$= \min \, [1, \, u_1 x_0] = u_1 x_0$$

and if $u_1 x_0 > 1$,

(22)
$$(\rho_{10})_u = \min \, [u_1 x_0] = u_1 x_0.$$

Therefore, in any case, $(\rho_{10})_u = u_1 x_0$, which corresponds to the Laspeyres index, as already stated. Also

(23) $$(\rho_{10})_l = \min [u_1 x : u_0 x_t \leqq 1 \Rightarrow u_t x \geqq 1].$$

Therefore, if $u_0 x_1 \leqq 1$,

(24) $$(\rho_{10})_l = \min [u_1 x : u_0 x \geqq 1, u_1 x \geqq 1] \geqq 1,$$

and if $u_0 x_1 > 1$,

(25) $$(\rho_{10})_l = \min [u_1 x : u_0 x \geqq 1]$$

$$= \min [u_{1i}/u_{0i} : u_{0i} > 0],$$

so certainly $(\rho_{10})_l$ is not related to the Paasche index.

This approach, general though it is in that it depends on no special properties for utility, is nevertheless too rigid. Data may not satisfy the required consistency condition, and in that event the analysis can proceed no further. But the model is in any case unrealistic because there is no provision for error. An extension is shown in sections 2.4 and 2.5 where deviations are explained as error, measured in economic terms of inefficiency. No real economic agents have exact and invariable wants. But assuming any did, none would accurately allocate their expenditure down to the last penny. There would be perhaps a rough tendency toward equilibrium until any effort and cost for improvement would seem to outweigh any plausible benefit. Equilibrium in the larger framework, which takes into account the value and cost of every movement, its sacrifice and gain, would leave disequilibrium in the narrower framework to which analysis is confined. Since the wider framework is unknown, the method must be essentially statistical, dealing with fluctuations in a hypothetical model. Since economic error has the nature of inefficiency, it is appropriate that distance should be measured in an inefficiency sense, instead of, for instance, by a Euclidean sum of squares. A Euclidean distance, however vast, but which corresponded to a difference of a negligible penny would nevertheless be negligible. This argument, which is in opposition to some classical and other statistical techniques usual in econometrics, in particular in production and consumption analysis, is related to the argument in favor of approaching statistics from the viewpoint of decision theory.

To return to the demand consistency condition, in addition to the three equivalent conditions (14), (15), and (16), there are two further equivalents

$$(26) \qquad \lambda_r D_{rs} + \lambda_s D_{st} + \cdots + \lambda_q D_{qr} \geqq 0, \lambda_r > 0$$

for all $r, s, \ldots$, for some λ_r, or

$$(27) \qquad \lambda_r D_{rs} \geqq \phi_s - \phi_r, \qquad \lambda_r > 0,$$

for all r, s for some λ_r, ϕ_r. Moreover, for all λ_r and ϕ_r, (27) implies (26), and for all λ_r, (26) implies (27) for some ϕ_r. With any λ_r, ϕ_r let

$$(28) \qquad \phi(x) = \min_t \phi_t + \lambda_t(u_t x - 1).$$

Then (27) is equivalent to the compatibility of the utility function $\phi(x)$ with the given demands, for it is equivalent to

$$(29) \qquad \phi(x_t) = \phi_t, \min [u_r x : \phi(x) \geqq \phi_s] = 1$$

for all r, s, t. Thus, whenever the demands are consistent, that is, compatible with any utility function at all, then they are compatible with a utility function of the form (28), corresponding to a solution of (27). This method, as extended in sections 2.4 and 2.5 to allow different degrees of efficiency and approximation, shows how the utility hypothesis, which is basic to index numbers, can be given constructive realization with any data.

Any utility order R between consumption bundles determines an *adjoint utility order* S between consumption budgets. Thus uSv means there exists x such that $ux \leqq 1$ and for all y if $vy \leqq 1$ then xRy; in other words, there exists a consumption attainable within the budget u which is as good as any attainable within v. Also, any utility function $\phi(x)$ determines an *adjoint utility function*

$$(30) \qquad \psi(u) = \max [\phi(x) : ux \leqq 1]$$

and if $\phi(x)$ represents R then $\psi(u)$ represents S.

Compatibility of R with (x_0, u_0), where $u_0 x_0 = 1$, is equivalent to $\phi(x_0) = \psi(u_0)$, and to

$$(31) \qquad u_0 S v \cdot \Longleftrightarrow \cdot vy \leqq 1 \Rightarrow s_0 S y.$$

Given this,

(32)
$$\rho_{10} = \min \left[u_1 x : xRx_0 \right]$$
$$= \max \left[\rho : u_1 x \leqq \rho \Rightarrow x_0 Rx \right]$$
$$= \max \left[\rho : u_0 S\rho^{-1}u_1 \right].$$

Hence, with $\psi(u)$ representing S, it follows that $\rho = \rho_{10}$ is the solution of

(33)
$$\psi(u_0) = \psi(\rho^{-1}u_1).$$

Equivalently, $M = M_{10}$ is the solution of

(34)
$$\psi(M_0^{-1}p_0) = \psi(M^{-1}p_1).$$

With $\phi(x)$ concave, $\psi(M^{-1}p)$ is a concave function of M, so that, for some P_0,

(35)
$$\psi(M^{-1}p_0) - \psi(M_0^{-1}p_0) \leqq (M - M_0)/P_0$$

for all M. If $\psi(u_0)$ is differentiable at $u = M_0^{-1}p_0$, this implies

(36)
$$(\partial/\partial M_0) \, \psi(M^{-1}p_0) = 1/P_0,$$

so that P_0 appears as the marginal price of utility at the level of expenditure M_0 when commodity prices are p_0. Correspondingly, $1/P_0$ is the marginal utility of money. The average utility of money, or the reciprocal of the average price of utility, is $\psi(M^{-1}p_0)/M_0$. Identity between the average and marginal prices of utility, that is,

(37)
$$M\partial\psi(M^{-1}p)/\partial M = \psi(N^{-1}p),$$

implies that R is homogeneous. Conversely, if R is homogeneous, it can be represented by a linearly homogeneous utility function for which (37) holds. In fact, a necessary and sufficient condition that R be homogeneous, that is

(38)
$$xRy \Rightarrow x\lambda Ry\lambda \qquad (\lambda \geqq 0),$$

is that the utility cost function be factorable thus:

(39)
$$\rho(p, x) = \theta(p)\phi(x)$$

and with this $\theta(p)$ is identified simultaneously with the average price and the marginal price of utility $\phi(x)$. The factorability of utility cost underlies the concept of a level of prices, and hence also that of a price index, which compares levels. There appears to be a lack of explicit recognition that the meaning of a price level, and therefore of all price indexes, depends on homogeneity of utility. Index constructions which depart from this, and which, so to speak, belong to a family which is one rung up the ladder of generality include the "new formula" of Wald (1939), and the "constant utility" index of Klein-Rubin (1947) which, appropriately put, exhibit utility price which is linear but not at the same time homogeneous. They can be seen as extensions of the Fisher and Palgrave formulas, respectively, and have corresponding limitations. Also the Paasche and Laspeyres indexes have correspondents in this family.

With $\phi(x)$, the utility function given by (28), and $\psi(u)$, its dual, compatibility, implied by (27), is equivalent to $\phi(x_t) = \psi(u_t)$. It appears, in (29), that $\phi(x_t) = \phi_t$. Thus ϕ_t appears as the utility at x_t, with a compatible utility function $\phi(x)$. Equivalent to (35) is

$$(40) \qquad \psi(\rho^{-1}u_0) - \psi(u_0) \leqq \lambda_0(\rho - 1),$$

where $\rho = M/M_0$, $\lambda_0 = M_0/P_0$. Thus λ_t/M_t appears as the marginal utility of money for $\phi(x)$.

It is curious that (27) holds with $\delta_{rs} = \rho_{rs} - 1$ substituted for $D_{rs} = u_r x_s - 1$. For

$$\phi_t = \phi(x_t) = \psi(u_t), \qquad \psi(\rho_{st}^{-1}u_t) = \psi(u_s),$$

which, with

$$(41) \qquad \psi(\rho_{st}^{-1}u_t) - \psi(u_t) \leqq \lambda_t(\rho_{st} - 1),$$

gives

$$(42) \qquad \lambda_t \delta_{st} \geqq \phi_s - \phi_t.$$

Since, by (2),

$$(43) \qquad \delta_{st} \leqq D_{st}$$

(27) is recovered from (42). A certain duality between the D's and δ's becomes even more specific in further developments. The D's correspond to crosscosts which apply to quantities, essentially Laspeyres indexes, which derive directly from data, and the δ's to crosscosts which apply to their utility, which are the concern of index construction.

1.5   *Concept of the Price Level*

The price level concept has its origin in the arithmetic of the market place, where the product of price and quantity equals exchange value in money, and in the notion that such a scheme of arithmetic can apply just as well for many goods treated as one, so that a product of price and quantity levels, determined from many prices and quantities, equals total exchange value, that is, the sum of products of individual prices and quantities. Thus, by simple market arithmetic

$$(1) \qquad p_0 x_0 = M_0, \qquad p_1 x_1 = M_1$$

and then it is postulated that also

$$(2) \qquad P_0 X_0 = M_0, \qquad P_1 X_1 = M_1,$$

where the P's and X's correspond to levels of prices and quantities. Then

$$(3) \qquad P_{10} X_{10} = M_{10},$$

where $P_{10} = P_1/P_0$, and so forth. The idea is then taken further, and it is assumed that the composite price ratio P_{10} can be "approximated" by some kind of average of individual price ratios p_{1i}/p_{0i}. All standard price indexes are apparently expressible as averages—arithmetic, geometric, harmonic, and mixtures—of these, with various weights and exponents. Fisher examined about two hundred of them, and found that their divergences from each other were small compared to the errors inherent in the data. With P_{10} thus "approximated" by almost any formula, it is possible to "deflate" a money ratio M_{10} to determine $X_{10} = P^{-1} M_{10}$ as its "real" correspondent. This is the intelligible scheme for almost any index construction which has had application, starting with Fleetwood in 1708. The Laspeyres index has the merit of almost irreducible simplicity, and the theoretical distinction of being an "upper bound," though of what and to whom requires elaboration.

The essential concept here is that a utility relation R prevails and that its utility cost function $\rho(p, x)$, that is, the minimum cost at prices p of attaining the utility represented by x, can be factored:

$$(4) \qquad \rho(p, x) = \theta(p)\phi(x).$$

But this is equivalent to the homogeneity of R, that is

(5) $xRy \Rightarrow x\lambda Ry\lambda$ $(\lambda \geqq 0)$,

and implies that both the price and quantity functions $\theta(p)$, $\phi(x)$ are linearly homogeneous,

(6) $\theta(\mu p) = \mu\theta(p)$, $\phi(x\lambda) = \phi(x)\lambda$,

where λ, $\mu \geqq 0$. Clearly all functions which can appear in the factorization (4) can differ only by a constant positive multiplier. The function $\phi(x)$ is fixed entirely by taking $\phi(x_0) = 1$ for any x_0. Thus the pair of *antithetic price and quantity functions* are, to this extent, uniquely determined. While R is represented by a wider class of utility functions, equivalent under increasing transformations, homogeneity in the sense of (5) requires there to exist a subclass of linearly homogeneous utility functions that are equivalent under multiplication by a positive constant; and these are the ones which are relevant.

From (4), and 1.4(2),

(7) $\theta(p)\phi(x) \leqq px$

for all (p, x) and the condition for equilibrium is

(8) $\theta(p)\phi(x) = px$,

which holds for a demand (x, p) which is compatible with R. Since for all p this holds for some x, it follows that the adjoint of $\phi(x)$ is

(9) $\psi(u) = [\theta(u)]^{-1}$

so that

(10) $\psi(M^{-1}p) = M/\theta(p)$.

With $X = \psi(M^{-1}p)$ as the utility of money M at prices p, and the average price P of utility at that level given by

(11) $X/M = 1/P$,

$P = \theta(p)$; so P is fixed when p is fixed and is independent of M. This implies that also

(12) $\partial X/\partial M = 1/P$,

that is, the fixed average price necessarily coincides with the marginal price, which is then also fixed. But even if the average price is not fixed, it is possible to have a fixed marginal price. This shows the direction of the first step in generalizing the traditional price index concept, while preserving part of its practical simplicity.

The elementary prices, when they are taken as given in a perfect market, are themselves conceived of as fixed average prices coincident with marginal prices. The traditional price index concept corresponds to the idea that the average price of utility is fixed when elementary prices are fixed. It allows every unit of money to be treated separately and uniformly, aggregates to be treated by simple addition, the utility of a sum being the sum of the equal utilities of the equal units that compose it. Any unit of money in the base period is equivalent in general purchasing power to P_{10} units in the current period, and any M_0 base units are equivalent to

$$(13) \qquad\qquad M_1 = P_{10}M_0$$

current units, since this is the condition that $X_{10} = 1$, in (3), and $X_0 = X_1$ in (2). It does not matter who or what the money is for; it could be a part or the whole of an individual income or a national income. All amounts of money have only to have a multiplier uniformly applied to them for a general correction for price change to be effected. Such a scheme has great statistical and social convenience because it is put into operation by publication of a single number. However, when the implications of the assumption which underlies the scheme are examined, it appears that no care in the choice of that number can overcome the radical defects. There is a similar, though more favorable, situation even with the next more general scheme, where it is required only that the marginal price of utility be fixed, as will be examined later.

Homogeneity of the utility relation brings about the cost separation (4). Then any x, p in a compatible demand have the relation E defined by

$$(14) \qquad\qquad xEp \equiv \theta(p)\phi(x) = px.$$

Since then

$$(15) \qquad\qquad xEp \Rightarrow x\lambda Ep \qquad (\lambda \geqq 0)$$

for all p. Equivalently

$$(16) \qquad\qquad x \varepsilon Ep \Rightarrow x' \subset Ep$$

where $x' = [x\lambda : \lambda \geqq 0]$. It appears then that the expansion locus Ep for any price p is a cone, since if it contains a point then it contains every point on the ray it determines. If, for instance, $\phi(x)$ is quasi-concave then Ep is always a single ray if and only if $\phi(x)$ is strictly quasi-concave. Then, when prices are fixed at p, and as incomes vary, all consumptions lie on the ray Ep through the origin. That is, when prices are fixed the *pattern of consumption is fixed*, that is, the propor-tions between the goods which enter into consumption are fixed. But it is an overwhelmingly significant fact of experience that the rich, whether individuals or countries, have things that the poor do not have at all, let alone in corresponding proportion. Deliberately to overlook this in a system of calculation that seeks to make general comparisons leaves the significance of such calculation quite obscure, even as to the locus of injustice.

1.6 *National Measurement*

The application of prices and price indexes to measure national output seems to be supported if not by arguments then by urgings from two sides, both objectionable. One is more straightforward and will be remarked upon first. The other has something to do with the "maximum doctrine of perfect competition," so called by Schumpeter, or Adam Smith's teaching of the Invisible Hand, and whatever is to be made of such doctrine.

The homogeneity which is the essential characteristic of the stand-ard index method based on the price level concept pictures a ray in the commodity space, determined only by prices, along which lie the consumptions of all individuals according to their different in-comes. Hence the sum of all consumptions, since these lie on a ray, is also a point on that ray, and the income needed to purchase it is identical with the sum of all incomes, since $p\Sigma x = \Sigma px$. It is possible therefore to picture the sum of these incomes, or national income, as the income of a fictitious individual who has the same preferences as all other individuals and who, at the prevailing prices, would there-fore spend it as would any others, that is, at the point on the ray cor-responding to the consumption bundle that that income would pur-chase. Thus the nation is to be treated as an individual, and national income as the sum of individual incomes is to be treated like an individual income. National income deflated by a price index, determines the base period income which has the same purchasing power, and it gives a measure of current real national output. This seems to be the logic of the uses in the third category referred to by Chase (1960) in listing the major functions of price indexes, that is, the "deflation of [a] value aggregate to estimate physical quantities." Value means money value at prevailing prices, and physical quantity means quantity level in the utility sense of output.

Again, the average of all consumptions, since these lie on a ray, is also a point on the same ray, and moreover this average, or per capita, consumption corresponds to average or per capita income because $p(1/N) \Sigma x = (1/N) \Sigma p x$. Hence it is possible to picture an "average individual," whose income is the average income, who again has the same preferences as any other individual, and who, at the prices given, would spend it as any one else would, that is, at the point on the ray corresponding to the consumption it can purchase. This puts average or per capita income, like total income, on the same footing as individual income. This seems to be the implicit logic of average comparisons.

The accident that permits individual incomes, average income, and total income all to be treated in the same fashion depends on both linearity and homogeneity. More explicitly, an average of points on a line is on the same line, but so also is a sum of points but generally only if the line passes through the origin. Thus it is necessary both that the locus of consumptions be a line and that the line pass through the origin. Should the locus of consumptions be a line but not pass through the origin, the argument for the "average individual" still holds, but that for the "total individual" loses the basis of its meaning.

This is not a general rejection of comparisons of totals but a description of the implicit logic of a standard procedure. If the concept of the procedure is still acceptable when this logic is made explicit, there can be a requirement that practical procedure be more strictly in accordance with it. There appears to be a reversion to the old concept of general purchasing power in a sense which does not even allow for the plurality of purchasing powers recognized by Keynes (1922). It asks that the economy resemble a molecular structure composed of homogeneous atoms, with reference to which the purchasing power of every penny, described by a particular bundle of commodities, is uniformly determined. But, as Ruggles (1967) says: "The concept of a price index as a measure of the level of prices no longer has significant support among economists." After dealing with the application to real national income, he adds: "Despite this disillusionment with the concepts of price level and economic welfare, the use of price indexes flourishes."

Overall comparison in terms of an "average individual" holds up better conceptually. Moreover, a description of the fictitious average individual, together with a statement of the number of individuals in the national population, conveys all the information that could be communicated about a "total individual," plus something more, namely, population size, and in a form which may have a more direct meaning.

The second approach to the relation of prices to national welfare measurement reinforces this first one, but is more objectionable. The first can be seen to be misleading because it requires that points for individuals lie on a ray and that a sum of points on a ray also lie on that ray, an event which could occur only by chance. It is compelling to view that sum point as associated with an individual, but without a theory to encourage such a summation, to make it conceptually and not only mathematically natural, it is meaningless. Here the Invisible Hand might come to the rescue. According to that doctrine, the freely operating adjustment mechanism of the competitive market automatically brings the economy to a state of maximum welfare or utility output. The prices are therefore proportional to marginal welfares, just like individual marginal utilities. Therefore, with homogeneity granted, the same indexes are applicable. This doctrine could have power beyond index numbers. But it is without quantitative content. Newton's second law of motion—that the force on a unit particle is identical with its acceleration—would be equally meaningless were there not separate ways for determining force and acceleration, such as gravitational or other force theory and kinematics. The maximum doctrine has no separate theory about the determination of welfare, whose maximum must then coincide with the position determined by the market. Its starting point seems to be in the observation that "we owe our bread not to the benevolence of the baker but to his self interest" (Adam Smith), so by adding nonsense to a truism an influential contribution has been made to an economic philosophy.

2.0 ANALYSIS OF VALUE AND COST

2.1 *Utility*

A relation $R \subset \Omega^n \times \Omega^n$ is reflexive and transitive, that is, it is an order in Ω^n, if

(1) $$xRx, xRy \ldots Rz \Rightarrow xRz$$

Equivalently

(2) $$xRy \Longleftrightarrow xR \supset yR$$

where $xR = [y:xRy]$, and similarly with Rx. It is complete if $xRy \vee yRx$, and continuous if it is a closed set in $\Omega^n \times \Omega^n$. If R is a complete order in Ω^n then it is continuous if and only if xR, Rx are closed sets in Ω^n. An order R is quasi-concave if the sets Rx are convex.

Any order R in Ω^n can be a *utility relation*. In that case, xRy means that consumption x is as good as, that is, produces as much utility as, y. The *law of disposal* for a utility relation is $x \geq y \Rightarrow xRy$. An x appears as a point of *oversatiation* if yRx and $y < x$ for some y, and the *law of want* excludes such points. If R is complete and continuous then this implies the law of disposal.

For simplicity, in the present discussion a utility relation is specifically limited to be a complete, continuous order in Ω^n subject to the law of want. It is distinguished as a *normal utility relation* if, moreover, it is quasi-concave.

Any function $\phi(x) \; \varepsilon \; \Omega$, where $x \; \varepsilon \; \Omega^n$, represents a complete order R in Ω^n where

(3) $$xRy \equiv \phi(x) \geq \phi(y).$$

It is a *utility function* if R is understood to be a utility relation. The law of disposal for R requires

(4) $$x \leq y \Rightarrow \phi(x) \leq \phi(y),$$

and that $\phi(x)$ be nondecreasing; the law of want requires

(5) $$x < y \Rightarrow \phi(x) < \phi(y),$$

and that $\phi(x)$ be semi-increasing. Any complete, continuous order in Ω'' admits representation by a continuous function. An order R which is quasi-concave requires that any function which represents it be quasi-concave, having convex level sets $[y : \phi(y) \geq \phi(x)]$.

A *normal utility function* represents a normal utility relation and thus, beside being subject to the usually understood limitations, is quasi-concave. A utility function is concave if

(6) $$\phi(x\lambda + y\mu) \geq \phi(x)\lambda + \phi(y)\mu \qquad (\lambda,\mu \geq 0,\ \lambda + \mu = 1).$$

This implies that for all $x_0 > 0$ there exists $g_0 \geq 0$ such that for all $x \geq 0$,

(7) $$\phi(x) - \phi(x_0) \leq g_0(x - x_0),$$

and $\phi(x)$ is differentiable at x_0 if and only if such g_0 is unique, in which case the g_0 is the gradient $g(x_0)$ of $\phi(x)$ at x_0. Now a classical utility function is defined by the existence of such $g_0 \geq 0$ for all $x_0 \geq 0$. This implies it is expressible in the form

(8) $$\phi(x) = \min_{x_0} [\phi(x_0) + g_0(x - x_0)]$$

where a $g_0 \geq 0$ is determined from any $x_0 \geq 0$. It is therefore continuous, semi-increasing, and concave, and thus also a normal utility function. A *polyhedral classical utility function,* which is the most important type for empirical analysis, is expressible in the same form, but with x_0 ranging in a finite set, usually corresponding to finite observations, instead of possibly throughout Ω''.

A utility relation R is *homogeneous* if

(9) $$xRy \Rightarrow x\gamma Ry\gamma \qquad (\gamma \geq 0).$$

A utility function is homogeneous if it represents a homogeneous utility relation. Such a function is equivalent, under transformation by an increasing function, to one which is *linearly homogeneous,* that is, such that

(10) $$\phi(x\gamma) = \phi(x)\gamma \qquad (\gamma \geq 0).$$

A function with this property is concave if and only if it is quasi-concave.

2.2 *Adjoint Utility*

A *budget constraint* $px \leqq M$ ($x \; \varepsilon \; \Omega^n$), associated with an expenditure limit $M > 0$ at prices $P \; \varepsilon \; \Omega_n$, is equivalent to a constraint $ux \leqq 1$, where $u = M^{-1}p$. The budget constraints in Ω^n are thus coordinated with the points of Ω_n. Let the relation $W \subset \Omega^n \times \Omega_n$ be defined by $xWu \equiv ux \leqq 1$. Then $Wu = [x : xWu]$ is the *budget set* associated with any $u \; \varepsilon \; \Omega_n$. In such association u can be called a *budget vector,* and otherwise an *exchange vector.* The *primal* space Ω_n has a symmetrical relation with the *dual* space Ω^n, a point of which is a *composition vector* which describes the composition of a consumption, each space being the space of nonnegative homogeneous linear functions defined on the other.

For any $x \; \varepsilon \; \Omega^n$, $u \; \varepsilon \; \Omega_n$, x can be said to be *within, on,* or *under u* according as $ux \leqq 1$, $ux = 1$ or $ux < 1$, or, in a dual sense, the same can be said with x and u interchanged. Thus beside the within-relation just defined there are further relations (I, V) defined by $xIu \equiv ux = 1$, $xVu \equiv ux < 1$.

Any utility relation R in Ω^n has associated with it an *adjoint utility relation* $S = R^*$ in the adjoint space Ω^n, where

$$(1) \qquad uSv \equiv (\vee ux \leqq 1)(\wedge vy \leqq 1)xRy,$$

that is, uSv means there exist x within u which are, according to R, as good as every y within v. Thus uSu means there exists a consumption within the budget u which is as good as any other, that is, which is R maximal. This is always the case if $u > 0$, because of the compactness of Wu and the continuity of R. Thus S is reflexive at every point $u > 0$. Also, because R is a complete order, S is a complete order in the domain where it is reflexive. Thus S is a complete order at least in the interior of Ω_n. Because R is semi-increasing, S is semidecreasing. From the form of the definition of S from R, regardless of properties of R, uS is a closed convex set. By this convexity the order S is quasi-convex. The order R is quasi-concave if Rx is convex, and a necessary and sufficient condition for this is that $R = S^*$, where S^* derives from S by the dual of the formula (1) by which R^* derives from R, that is, the identical formula where budget and composition vectors exchange their roles.

Let $\phi(x)$ be any utility function representing a utility relation R, that is,

$$(1) \qquad xRy \iff \phi(x) \geqq \phi(y).$$

Then the *adjoint utility function* $\psi(u) = \phi^*(u)$ is given by

$$(2) \qquad \psi(u) = \max [\phi(y) : uy \leqq 1],$$

for u wherever this is defined, which is where S is reflexive and is at least in the interior of Ω_n, by the compactness of Wu, if $u > 0$, and the continuity of R. Then the adjoint ψ of the function ϕ, where it is defined, represents the adjoint S of the relation R represented by ϕ, that is,

$$(3) \qquad uSv \iff \psi(u) \geqq \psi(v).$$

The function $\psi(u)$, which thus determines the maximum of the utility $\phi(x)$ attainable in the budget set Wu, is continuous, semi-decreasing, and quasi-convex. Since, from the definition

$$(4) \qquad vx \leqq 1 \implies \phi(x) \leqq \psi(v)$$

it follows that

$$(5) \qquad \phi(x) \leqq \min [\psi(v) : vx \leqq 1],$$

for all x, with equality if and only if

$$(6) \qquad \phi(x) = \psi(u), \qquad ux = 1 \text{ for some } u.$$

But this is true for all x if and only if $\phi(x)$ is quasi-concave and thus a normal utility function. Thus a utility function, subject to the given limitations, is quasi-concave, and thus normal, if and only if

$$(7) \qquad \phi(x) = \min [\psi(v) : vx \leqq 1]$$

for all x. The pair of relations (2) and (7) shows the reciprocal relation between a normal utility function and its adjoint. But in any case

$$(8) \qquad \phi^{**}(x) = \min [\phi^*(v) : vx \leqq 1]$$

is normal, even if $\phi(x)$ is not, and has the same adjoint $\psi(u) = \phi^*(u)$ as $\phi(x)$. It defines the *normalization* of $\phi(x)$. Any demand observations that admit $\phi(x)$ as compatible with them will also admit $\phi^{**}(x)$. Hence if a utility function is admitted, so also is a normal utility function. In this sense there is equivalent empirical scope between utility functions and normal utility functions and no empirical content to the assumption that a utility function be quasi-concave, that is, have concave contours.

The *profile* corresponding to exchange prices $u \geq 0$ of a utility function $\phi(x)$ with adjoint $\psi(u)$ is the function $F(\rho) = \psi(\rho^{-1}u)$, which is increasing since $\phi(x)$ is semi-increasing. Since a utility function and its normalization have the same adjoint, this is also the profile of the normalization. *A necessary and sufficient condition that a utility function be concave is that its levels and profiles be concave.* If $F(\rho)$ is concave, as when the utility function or its normalization is classical, then there exists a $\lambda > 0$ such that

(9) $$\psi(\rho^{-1}u) - \psi(u) \leq \lambda(\rho - 1)$$

for all ρ; also $F(\rho)$ is differentiable at $\rho = 1$ if and only such λ is unique, and then $F'(1) = \lambda$. But, with $u = M^{-1}p$, $M(\partial\psi/\partial M)(M^{-1}p) = \lambda$; so λ/M appears as the marginal utility of money M at prices p, and $P = M/\lambda$ as the marginal price of utility.

Since, with p fixed, $\psi(M^{-1}p)$ is an increasing function of M, $t = \psi(M^{-1}p)$ has an inverse $M = \sigma(p, t)$, which determines the minimum cost at prices p of attaining the level of utility t. Then, with p fixed, $\Delta M/M \geq \Delta t/\lambda$, or $\Delta M/\Delta t \geq P$.

It follows immediately from the definition that $\sigma(p, t)$ is linearly homogeneous as a function of p. Therefore it is concave if and only if it is quasi-concave. But it is quasi-concave, because $\psi(u)$ has this property directly from its definition. Thus $\sigma(p, t)$ is a linearly homogeneous function of p. It is a convex function of t only if the normalization of $\phi(x)$ is concave.

Now setting $t = \phi(x)$, the function $\rho(p, x) = \sigma[p, \phi(x)]$ is obtained. But this function is most basic and is properly introduced directly from the utility relation R, without the auxiliary functions ϕ, ψ, and σ as intermediaries.

2.3 *Utility Cost*

For any utility relation R, with the given limitations,

(1) $$\rho(p, x) = \min\ [py : yRx]$$

exists for all $p \ \varepsilon \ \Omega_n$, $x \ \varepsilon \ \Omega^n$ and defines the associated *utility cost function*. It gives the cost at prices p of attaining the standard of utility represented by x. From its definition, for all x, it is a linearly homogeneous concave function of p, determined by the set of homogeneous linear bounds py where yRx. Its linear supports at $p \geqslant 0$ are pz where

$$(2) \qquad\qquad \rho(p, x) = pz, \qquad zRx.$$

It is differentiable at p if and only if such z is unique, and then the gradient is

$$(3) \qquad\qquad \rho_p(p, x) = z.$$

From the properties of R as a complete, semi-increasing, continuous order,

$$(4) \qquad\qquad xRy \iff \rho(p, x) \geqq \rho(p, y),$$

showing that, for all p, $\rho(p, x)$ is a utility function which represents R. Since R is reflexive

$$(5) \qquad\qquad \rho(p, x) \leqq px.$$

For all p the equality holds for some x, and for all x the equality holds for some p if and only if R is quasi-concave.

A necessary and sufficient condition that R be homogeneous is that $\rho(p, x)$ be factorable, that is, that

$$(6) \qquad\qquad \rho(p, x) = \theta(p)\phi(x).$$

Then $\phi(x)$ is a linearly homogeneous utility function, unique but for a constant multiplier, which represents R, with adjoint $\psi(u) = [\theta(u)]^{-1}$, and cost function $\sigma(p, t) = \theta(p)t$.

The functions $\theta(p)$, $\phi(x)$ can be called *antithetic price and quantity functions*. Both are linearly homogeneous, and $\theta(p)$ is concave. If $\phi(x)$ is not concave, its normalization is concave and has the same antithesis, and is compatible with every demand that is compatible with $\phi(x)$. Hence nothing essential is lost if $\phi(x)$ is replaced by its normalization, or simply assumed to be concave, so that it is identical with its normalization.

From (5) and (6), antithetic functions satisfy the functional inequality

$$(7) \qquad\qquad \theta(p)\phi(x) \leqq px$$

for all p, x where the equality holds for all p for some x and for all x for some p. It follows that

(8)
$$\theta(p) = \min_{x} px[\phi(x)]^{-1}$$

$$\phi(x) = \min_{p} [\theta(p)]^{-1}px.$$

It follows from (8) that $\theta(p)$ and $\phi(x)$ are both linearly homogeneous and satisfy (7).

2.4 Compatibility

The condition $H = H(R; x, p)$ for a utility relation R and a demand (x, p) to be *compatible* is the conjunction of conditions

(1)
$$H' \equiv py \leqq px \Rightarrow xRy$$

$$H'' \equiv yRx \Rightarrow py \geqq px$$

signifying "maximum utility for the cost" and "minimum cost for the utility"; so H is the Pareto condition as applied to the competing objectives of gaining utility and saving money. But, with R semi-increasing, $H' \Rightarrow H''$, and with R continuous, $H'' \Rightarrow H'$. Thus, with the given limitation on R, H' and H'' are equivalent to each other and hence to H. A statement of H'' is

(2)
$$\rho(p, x) \geqq px.$$

But by 2.2(5), since R is reflexive, this is equivalent to

(3)
$$\rho(p, x) = px.$$

Then, if there is differentiability,

(4)
$$\rho_p(p, x) = x, \; \rho_x(p, x) = \lambda p,$$

where, if there is homogeneity, $\lambda = 1$.

More generally, e compatibility, or *compatibility at a level of cost efficiency* e is the condition $H(R, e; x, p)$ given by

(5)
$$\rho(p, x) \geqq epx.$$

Thus 0 compatibility is unconditional, 1 compatibility coincides with compatibility, and e compatibility implies e' compatibility for all $e' \leqq e$. With the *cost efficiency* $\bar{e} = \bar{e}(R; x, p)$ of (x, p) relative to R given by

(6)
$$\bar{e} = \rho(p, x)/px,$$

e compatibility holds if and only if $e \leqq \bar{e}$.

From the demand (x, p) is derived the budget (x, u) with $ux = 1$, where $u = M^{-1}p$ is the associated exchange vector, $M = px$ being the expenditure. With this,

(7) $$\bar{e} = \rho(u, x).$$

2.2(5) is equivalent to

(8) $$\rho(u, x) \leqq 1.$$

The compatibility condition (3) is

(9) $$\rho(u, x) = 1,$$

which, if there is differentiability, is equivalent to

(10) $$\rho_u(u, x) = x,$$

and implies

(11) $$\rho_x(u, x) = \lambda u$$

where $\lambda = \rho_x(u, x)x$, so that $\lambda = (u, x)$ if there is homogeneity, in which case (9) is equivalent to (11) with $\lambda = 1$,

(12) $$\rho_x(u, x) = u.$$

Therefore, in this case, conditions (9), (10), and (12) are equivalent.

Consider a *demand configuration* D whose elements are demands $(x_t, p_t) : t = 1, \ldots, k$, and the derived *exchange configuration* E with elements (x_t, u_t), where $u_t = M_t^{-1}p_t$ and $M_t = p_t x_t$. Compatibility of a utility relation R with D is defined by simultaneous compatibility with each element of D and is equivalent to compatibility with E. Thus it is the condition $H(R)$ given by

(13) $$\rho(u_t, x_t) = 1, \qquad t = 1, \ldots, k.$$

More generally, the condition $H(R, e)$ of e compatibility of R with D is

(14) $$\rho(u_t, x_t) \geqq e, \qquad t = 1, \ldots, k.$$

If

(15) $$\bar{e}(R) = \min \bar{e}_t(R),$$

where $\bar{e}_t(R) = \rho(r_t, x_t)$. Then

(16) $H(R, e) \Longleftrightarrow e \leq \bar{e}(R).$

Thus $H(R, 0)$ holds for all R unconditionally, and

(17) $H(R) \Longleftrightarrow H(R, 1) \Longleftrightarrow \bar{e}(R) = 1 \Longleftrightarrow \bar{e}_t(R) = 1.$

2.5 *Consistency*

A demand configuration D or, equivalently, its derived exchange configuration E, is *consistent* if there exists a utility relation which is compatible with it, which is to say the condition H that there exists a utility relation R such that $H(R)$. More generally, e consistency, or consistency at the level of cost efficiency e, is defined by the existence of an e-compatible utility relation, that is, the condition $H(e)$ that there exists a utility relation R such that $H(R, e)$. Thus $H(0)$ holds unconditionally and $H(1) \Longleftrightarrow H$, and $H(e) \Rightarrow H(e')$ for all $e' \leq e$. The *critical cost efficiency* is defined by

(1) $\bar{e} = \sup [e : H(e)],$

so that $0 < \bar{e} \leq 1$. Then

(2) $H(e) \Rightarrow e \leq \bar{e}$ $e < \bar{e} \Rightarrow H(e)$

and

(3) $H(\bar{e}) \Longleftrightarrow \bar{e} = 1 \Longleftarrow H.$

Let P denote any property for a utility function, such as homogeneity, or having a certain separation structure, or being on any special model. In particular, C can denote the classical property. Then let $H_P(R)$ be the condition that a utility relation R both have the property P and be compatible with D, and let $H_P(R, e)$ be the same with e compatibility instead. Then the condition H_P of P consistency is defined by the existence of R such that $H_P(R)$, and similarly for $H_P(e)$, or P consistency at the level of cost efficiency e. The P *critical cost efficiency* is defined by

(4) $e_P = \sup [e : H_P(e)].$

Thus, for any P and e,

(5) $H_P(R, e) \Rightarrow H(R, e)$

so that

(6) $H_P(e) \Rightarrow H(e),$

and hence $e_P \leqq \bar{e}$. The same things are defined in particular with
$P = C$. Though obviously $H_C(R, e)$ is not implied by $H(R, e)$, it is
nevertheless the case that

(7) $H_C(e) \Longleftrightarrow H(e),$

and hence $e_C = \bar{e}$. In other words, the classical restriction does not
affect consistency. In particular $H_C \Longleftrightarrow H$, that is, consistency is
equivalent to classical consistency.

   In fact these results essentially are stronger than is apparent in this
formulation. They are true when a utility relation is understood to be
any order relation in Ω^n without any further restrictions whatsoever,
specifically without dependence on assumptions that R be continuous
and semi-increasing. But in that case the basic condition $H = H(R;$
$x, p)$ is not equivalent to H', since now H' and H'' are independent, but
must again be identified with the conjunction of H' and H''. The same
is true with the modification which permits a partial cost efficiency
$e < 1$.
   Defining *cross-differences*

(8) $D_{rs}{}^e = u_r x_s - e$

and *e cyclical difference consistency*

(9) $K(e) \equiv D_{rs}{}^e \leqq 0, D_{st}{}^e \leqq 0, \ldots ,$

                    $D_{qr}{}^e \leqq 0 \Rightarrow D_{rs}{}^e = D_{st}{}^e = \cdots = D_{qr}{}^e = 0$

it appears that

(10) $H(e) \Longleftrightarrow K(e),$

and thus $K(e)$ provides a finite test of e consistency. It follows then that

(11) $\bar{e} = \min_{r,s,\ldots,q} \ \max[D_{rs}, D_{st}, \ldots , D_{qr}].$

But $K(e)$ is necessary and sufficient for the existence of $\lambda_r > 0, \phi_r > 0$
such that

(12) $\lambda_r D_{rs}{}^e \geqq \phi_s - \phi_r.$

Then with

(13)
$$\phi_t(x) = \phi_t + \lambda_t(u_t x - e)$$

$$\phi(x) = \min_t \phi_t(x)$$

it appears that $\phi(x)$ is a classical utility function, and that it is e-compatible with the demand configuration D. A consequence is (7), namely, that e consistency is equivalent to classical e consistency. The adjoint of $\phi(x)$ is

(14) $$\psi(u) = \max [t : t \leq \phi_t + \lambda_t(u_t x - e), \, ux \leq 1].$$

Numbers $\rho_{rs} = \rho(u_r, x_s)$ are determined as solutions of

(15) $$\psi(\rho_{rs}^{-1} u_r) = \psi(u_s)$$

and equivalently as

(16) $$\rho_{rs} = \min [u_r x : \phi_t + \lambda_t(u_t x - e) \geq \phi_s].$$

Then $1 \geq \rho_{tt} \geq e$, demonstrating e compatibility. In case $e = 1$, it appears that

(17) $$\phi(x_t) = \phi_t = \psi(u_t)$$

and

(18) $$\psi(\rho^{-1} u_t) - \psi(u_t) \leq \lambda_t(\rho - 1).$$

With $\delta_{rs} = \rho_{rs} - 1$, it appears from (15), (16), and (17) that

(19) $$\lambda_r \delta_{rs} \geq \phi_s - \phi_r.$$

But since $\rho_{rs} \leq u_r x_s$, also $\delta_{rs} \leq D_{rs}$, λ_r and ϕ_r having been chosen only so that $D_{rs} = D_{rs}^1 = u_r x_s - 1$ satisfy (12).

Analogously for homogeneous e consistency, which can be denoted $\dot{H}(e)$, with *cross-ratios*

(20) $$L_{rs}^e = u_r x_s / e,$$

and e *cyclical ratio consistency*

(21) $$\dot{K}(e) \equiv L_{rs}^e L_{st}^e \ldots L_{qr}^e \geq 1$$

which is necessary and sufficient for the existence of $\phi_r > 0$ such that

(22) $$L_{rs}^e \geq \phi_s / \phi_r.$$

It appears that

(23) $H(e) \Longleftrightarrow \dot{K}(e)$

and, with ϕ_r as given,

(24) $\phi(x) = \min_t \phi_t u_t x$

is a linearly homogeneous classical utility function which is e-compatible with the given demands. A consequence is that homogeneous e consistency is equivalent to linearly homogeneous classical e consistency. Also it follows that the homogeneous critical cost efficiency is

(25) $\dot{e} = \max \ [e : u_r x_s u_x x_t \ \ldots \ u_q x_r \geqq ee \ \ldots \ e].$

The antithetic price function for $\phi(x)$ is

(26) $\theta(u) = \min \ [ux : \phi_t u_t x \geqq 1],$

so $\theta(u)\phi(x) \leqq ux$, but it appears that

(27) $1 \geqq \theta(u_t)\phi(x_t) \geqq e,$

as required for e compatibility. In case $e = 1$, then moreover $\phi(x_t) = \phi_t$, $\theta(u_t) = 1/\phi_t$.

3.0 PRICE INDEXES

3.1 *Theory of the Price Level*

The idea of the existence of a *level of prices* is made intelligible by assuming that utility cost can be factored into a product of price and quantity levels,

(1) $\rho(p, x) = \theta(p)\phi(x),$

which is equivalent to assuming that the utility relation R is homogeneous. Then for all p, x

(2) $\theta(p)\phi(x) \leqq px,$

and for utility cost efficiency of a demand (x, p),

(3) $\theta(p)\phi(x) = px.$

Hence if (x_0, p_0), (x_1, p_1) are a pair of demands compatible with R, say, corresponding to a *base* and a *current* observation,

(4) $$\theta(p_0)\phi(x_0) = p_0 x_0, \qquad \theta(p_1)\phi(x_1) = p_1 x_1$$

and

(5) $$\theta(p_0)\phi(x_1) \leqq p_0 x_1, \qquad \theta(p_1)\phi(x_0) \leqq p_1 x_0.$$

Then

(6) $$P_{10} X_{10} = M_{10}$$

where

(7) $$P_{10} = \theta(p_1)/\theta(p_0), \qquad X_{10} = \phi(x_1)/\phi(x_0)$$

and

(8) $$M_{10} = M_1/M_0,$$

where

(9) $$M_0 = p_0 x_0, \qquad M_1 = p_1 x_1.$$

Also

(10) $$p_1 x_1/p_0 x_1 \leqq P_{10} \leqq p_1 x_0/p_0 x_0$$

and

(11) $$p_1 x_1/p_1 x_0 \leqq X_{10} \leqq p_0 x_1/p_0 x_0.$$

From (6), $\phi(x_0) = \phi(x_1)$, that is, $X_{10} = 1$, if and only if $M_1 = P_{10} M_0$. This is the condition that an expenditure M_1 at prices p_1 be equivalent in purchasing power to an expenditure M_0 at prices p_0. All that must be specified to establish this purchasing power, or real value relation, is the *price index* P_{10}. Any current money M_1 can be *deflated* by the index to give the base equivalent $M_0 = M_1/P_{10}$.

In terms of derived budgets (x_0, u_0), (x_1, u_1) where

(12) $$u_0 = M_0^{-1} p_0, \qquad u_1 = M_1^{-1} p_1,$$

so that

(13) $$u_0 x_0 = 1, \qquad u_1 x_1 = 1$$

and with

(14) $$U_{10} = P_{10} M_0/M_1 = \theta(u_1)/\theta(u_0)$$

the foregoing relations are equivalent to

(15) $\theta(u_0)\phi(x_0) = 1, \qquad \theta(u_1)\phi(x_1) = 1$

(16) $U_{10}X_{10} = 1$

and

(17) $1/u_0x_1 \leqq U_{10} \leqq u_1x_0,$

                            $1/u_1x_0 \leqq X_{10} \leqq u_0x_1.$

The condition for equivalent budgets is $U_{10} = 1$ or, equivalently, $X_{10} = 1$. But compatibility of a budget (x, u) with a homogeneous utility relation implies the compatibility of $(\rho x, \rho^{-1}u)$ for all $\rho > 0$. Hence the condition that $(\rho_0x_0, \rho_0^{-1}u_0), (\rho_1x_1, \rho_1^{-1}u_1)$ be equivalent is that $\rho_1/\rho_0 = U_{10}$.

3.2 *Laspeyres and Paasche*

From 3.1(17), for homogeneous consistency of the given budgets, that is, their simultaneous compatibility with some homogeneous utility relation, it is apparently necessary that the Paasche index not exceed that of Laspeyres. Equivalently,

(1) $u_0x_1u_1x_0 \geqq 1,$

and in fact this is also sufficient. Also, if a homogeneous utility relation is constrained by compatibility with the budgets, then U_{10} is constrained to lie in the *Paasche-Laspeyres interval* defined by 3.1(17), which is nonempty by (1). In fact, the constraint set is identical with that interval. Without imposition of further constraints on utility, such as compatibility with further given budgets, or possession of special properties, there is no sharper specification of U_{10} than this. Various price index formulas single out various special points in the admissible set, which is nonempty subject to the homogeneous consistency condition (1). Thus the Paasche and Laspeyres formulas single out the extremes, and the Fisher formula singles out the geometric mean of these. But no principle is explicitly available here for discriminating between admissible points.

3.3   *Fisher*

Buscheguennce (1925) remarked that with the assumption of a homogeneous quadratic utility function the Fisher index is exact. In translation to present concepts, and with appropriate additional qualifications, given a pair of budgets (x_0, u_0), (x_1, u_1) where x_0, $x_1 > 0$, if R is compatible and homogeneous and has quadratic representation in a convex neighborhood containing x_0, x_1 then

$$(1) \qquad U_{10} = (u_1 x_0 / u_0 x_1)^{1/2},$$

and reciprocally, and equivalently,

$$(2) \qquad X_{10} = (u_0 x_1 / u_1 x_0)^{1/2}.$$

By *homogeneous quadratic consistency* of the pair of budgets can be meant the existence of such an R. Immediately, this is at least as restrictive as homogeneous consistency, which is equivalent to 3.2(1), and appearances suggest it is more restrictive. Therefore, there is some surprise that *for a pair of budgets, homogeneous quadratic consistency is equivalent to homogeneous consistency*. However, for more than two budgets, it is more restrictive.

Such a utility relation R corresponds to an antithetic pair of price and quantity functions of the form

$$(3) \qquad \theta(u) = (uBu')^{1/2}, \qquad \phi(x) = (x'Ax)^{1/2}$$

where $BA = 1$, in a region where they are defined and satisfy the functional inequality

$$(4) \qquad (uBu')^{1/2}(x'Ax)^{1/2} \leqq ux,$$

which is to say in the convex cone where $x'Ax$ is semi-increasing and quasi-concave, equality holding in equilibrium. Though such compatible R, if any, exist and are not unique, they all determine the unique value of U_{10} given by (1). But, as just remarked, a compatible homogeneous quadratic R exists if and only if a compatible homogeneous R exists. It follows that the Fisher index, where it is capable of interpretation at all, which is in the case of homogeneous consistency, is identifiable with the value of U_{10} determined with respect to a locally quadratic compatible homogeneous relation. Thus *the Fisher index cannot be divorced from the quadratic utility hypothesis.*

3.4 *Palgrave*

A demand (x, p) has a total expenditure

$$(1) \qquad M = \Sigma_i p_i x_i = px$$

which is a sum of individual expenditures

$$(2) \qquad M_i = p_i x_i$$

which represent a distribution of the total in shares

$$(3) \qquad \sigma_i = M_i/M = p_i x_i/px = u_i x_i$$

where $u = M^{-1}p$. The Laspeyres index is expressible as an arithmetic mean of price ratios between the base and current period with the expenditure shares as weights. For

$$(4) \qquad (U_{10})_u = u_1 x_0 = \Sigma_i u_{0i} x_{1i} = \Sigma_i u_{1i} x_{1i}(u_{0i}/u_{1i}) = \Sigma_i \sigma_{1i}(u_{0i}/u_{1i}).$$

The geometric mean which corresponds to this arithmetic mean, in which the same weights become exponents, is

$$(5) \qquad (U_{10}{}^p)_u = \Pi_i(u_{0i}/u_{1i})^{\sigma_{1i}}$$

This is Palgrave's formula, translated into present terms. By the general relation of an arithmetic mean to the corresponding geometric mean,

$$(6) \qquad (U_{10}{}^p)_u \leqq (U_1)_u.$$

Similarly the Paasche index $(U_{10})_l = 1/(U_{01})_u$ has associated with it the companion to the Palgrave formula

$$(7) \qquad (U_{10}{}^p)_l = \Pi_i(u_{0i}/u_{1i})^{\sigma_{0i}}$$

It is obtained by replacing the current shares by the base shares as exponents. Similarly

$$(8) \qquad (U_{10})_l \leqq (U_{10}{}^p)_l.$$

Just as the Fisher index cannot be divorced from the homogeneous quadratic utility function, so the Palgrave formula cannot be divorced from a quantity function of the extended Cobb-Douglas form.

$$(9) \qquad \phi(x) = \Pi_i(x_i)^{w_i}; \qquad w_i \geqq 0, \qquad \Sigma w_i = 1.$$

The antithetic price function is

$$(10) \qquad \theta(u) = \Pi_i(u_i)^{\sigma_i},$$

It is noticed that then, with $ux = 1$, $\sigma_i = u_i x_i$,

$$(11) \qquad \theta(u)\phi(x) = \Pi_i(u_i x_i)^c = \Pi_i \sigma_i^c \leqq 1,$$

with equality if and only if $\sigma_i = w_i$ (as can be verified by the Kuhn-Tucker argument). The equilibrium conditions

$$(12) \qquad \theta(u_0)\phi(x_0) = 1, \qquad \theta(u_1)\phi(x_1) = 1,$$

therefore require

$$(13) \qquad \sigma_{0i} = w_i = \sigma_{1i}.$$

The consistency condition for this model of utility is therefore

$$(14) \qquad \sigma_{0i} = \sigma_{1i}.$$

If this is satisfied, the companion pair of Palgrave indexes coincide, and, along with the Fisher index, provide just another point lying between the Laspeyres and Fisher indexes. However, the consistency conditions thus associated with Palgrave are more stringent than those associated with Fisher, which have been seen to be identical with the basic homogeneous consistency.

When Palgrave consistency is not satisfied, a Palgrave critical cost efficiency $e_P \leqq \dot{e} \leqq \bar{e} \leqq 1$ can always be determined, and, for any $e < e_P$, a Cobb-Douglas utility function can be constructed which is e-compatible with each of the given two budgets.

The Laspeyres, Paasche, Fisher, and Palgrave formulas appear to be the only traditional price index formulas involving base and current budget data which have a supporting utility theory.

3.5 *General Price Index Construction*

Ordinarily, the elements that are to enter into a construction of an index between a base (0) and current (1) location are regarded as data for the locations themselves. The conceptual basis for a price index is a homogeneous utility relation. Here it is understood that the purpose of budget data is to impose a constraint on the utility relation, by the compatibility requirement, and thereby to place a constraint on the admissible values of the index. There are two reasons why this framework is too simple. Any available budget data are pertinent by the same principle that the base and current data are pertinent. Therefore calculations should apply to a more general scheme of data, with two budgets as only a special case. This is particularly important and even essential when simultaneous comparisons are required between more than two locations. Then, with two or more budgets, there might not exist a homogeneous utility relation, or any other utility relation, with which they have simultaneous compatibility. That is, they might not be homogeneously consistent. In any case, exact consistency is too limiting a condition to insist on in practice, even if it is a basic theoretical requirement. Any budgets are homogeneously e-consistent, for some cost efficiency e, where $0 < e \leqq 1$; and with this limitation, homogeneous consistency is just the special case of homogeneous 1-consistency. Thus a simple way of accommodating inconsistency is to permit partial cost efficiency. (The method is stated in section 2.5.)

Let $(U_{rs}{}^e)_u$, $(U_{rs}{}^e)_l$ be upper and lower limits of the interval described by $U_{rs} = \theta(u_r)/\theta(u_s)$ when determined with respect to all homogeneous utility relations which are e-compatible with a finite set of budgets (x_t, u_t), $t = 1, \ldots, k$. Then

$$(1) \qquad e' \leqq e < \dot{e} \Rightarrow (U_{rs}{}^{e'})_l \leqq (U_{rs}{}^e)_l \leqq (U_{rs}{}^e)_u \leqq (U_{rs}{}^{e'})_u.$$

The intersection of all these intervals, for $e < \dot{e}$, is an interval with limits which coincide with $(U_{rs})_u = (U_{rs}{}^1)_u$, $(U_{rs})_l = (U_{rs}{}^1)_l$ if there is homogeneous consistency. Then in the special case where the available budgets are just the pair for $t = 0, 1$, these limits for U_{10} coincide with the Laspeyres and Paasche indexes,

$$(2) \qquad\qquad (U_{10})_l = 1/u_0 x_1, \qquad (U_{10})_u = u_1 x_0.$$

But more generally,

$$(3) \qquad (U_{rs})_u = \min_{ij\ldots k} u_r x_i u_i x_j \ldots u_k x_s, \qquad (U_{rs})_l = 1/(U_{rs})_u,$$

so

$$(4) \qquad\qquad (U_{rs})_u (U_{st})_u \geqq (U_{rt})_u,$$

and

(5) $$(U_{rr})_u \leqq 1$$

since $u_r x_r = 1$. A necessary and sufficient condition for homogeneous consistency is that

(6) $$(U_{rr})_u \geqq 1;$$

equivalently $(U_{rr})_u = 1$. In that case

(7) $$(U_{rs})_u (U_{sr})_u \geqq 1.$$

Equivalently,

(8) $$(U_{rs})_l \leqq (U_{rs})_u,$$

which generalizes the homogeneous consistency condition of 3.2. t requires that the generalized Laspeyres and Paasche indexes are con, sistent as upper and lower limits, the one being at least the other. Since

$$(U_{rt})_u = \min_s (U_{rs})_u (U_{st})_u$$

it follows that (6) holds for all r if and only if (8) holds for all r, s. Let

$$U_u = \min_v (U_{rv})_u$$

$$= \min_{r,s,\ldots,q} u_r x_s u_s x_t \ldots u_q x_r$$

so $U_u \leqq 1$. A necessary and sufficient condition for homogeneous consistency is $U_u \geqq 1$; equivalently $U_u = 1$. With U_u^e denoting U_u with each $u_r x_s$ replaced by $u_r x_s / e$, so that $(U^1)_u = U_u$, a necessary and sufficient condition for homogeneous e consistency is $U^e \geqq 1$. Since U_u^e is a decreasing function of e, the homogeneous critical cost efficiency $\dot{e}$ is determined as the unique e such that $U_u^e = 1$.

3.6 *Extrinsic Estimation*

Consider k countries and m levels of income in each which are judged by extrinsic criteria, that is, not on the basis of value and cost analysis of demands, but so as to correspond in purchasing power, at respective prices. Thus let M_{ti} be the ith level of income in country t ($i = 1, \ldots, m$; $t = 1, \ldots, k$). If the prices in country t are p_t, $P_t = \theta(p_t)$ is their level, and X_{ti} is the utility of M_{ti} at those prices, then a cost efficiency level of at least e requires that

(1) $$M_{ti} \geqq P_t X_{ti} \geqq e M_{ti}.$$

But it is judged that, for all i, the X_{ti} are the same for all t, say, equal to X_i. Thus

(2) $$M_{ti} \geqq P_t X_i \geqq e M_{ti}.$$

The value system and the efficiency being undetermined, it is proposed to determine P_t and e satisfying (2) with e as large as possible.

For $e = 1$ to be admissible in (2), equivalently for

(3) $$M_{ti} = P_t X_i$$

to have a solution for P_t and X_i, it is necessary and sufficient that M_{si}/M_{ti} be the same for all i or, equivalently, that M_{ti}/M_{tj} be the same for all t. If this condition holds, then by choosing P_t in the ratio of M_{ti} for any i, and then determining X_i from (3) for any t, a solution of (3) is obtained and, hence, a solution of (2) with $e = 1$.

If this condition does not hold, then let

(4) $$P_{rs} = \min_i M_{ri}/M_{si}$$

(5) $$X_{ij} = \min_t M_{ti}/M_{tj}.$$

Then let $\bar{e}$ be the largest e such that

(6) $$P_{rs} P_{st} \ldots P_{qr} \geqq ee \ldots e$$

and equivalently

(7) $$X_{ij} X_{jk} \ldots X_{hi} \geqq ee \ldots e.$$

Then also $\bar{e}$ is the largest e such that

(8) $$P_{rs}/e \geqq P_r/P_s.$$

Then (8) has a solution for P_t and, equivalently,

(9) $$X_{ij}/e \geqq X_i/X_j$$

has a solution for X_i. Let P_t be any solution of (8) with $e = \bar{e}$. Then, with $e = \bar{e}$ and $P_t = \bar{P}_t$, (2) has a solution $X_i = \bar{X}_i$, necessarily a solution of (9) with $e = \bar{e}$.

Thus the largest possible e has been found such that (2) holds for some P_t, X_i; and such P_t, X_i have been found. Then $\bar{P}_{rs} = \bar{P}_r/\bar{P}_s$ are a set of price indexes between pairs of countries, which are consistent in that they satisfy the circularity test

$$(10) \qquad\qquad \bar{P}_{rs}\bar{P}_{st}\bar{P}_{tr} = 1,$$

appropriate to a set of ratios, and which, with distance determined in the economic sense of cost efficiency, fit the constraints of the original data as closely as possible.

It should be noted that (1), with $P_{rs} = P_r/P_s$, implies

$$(11) \qquad\qquad M_{ri}e_{ri} = P_{rs}M_{se}e_{se}, \qquad e \leqq e_{ri} \leqq 1$$

for some e_{ti}. In other words, efficient parts $M_{ri}e_{ri}$ of the income M_{ri}, with efficiencies e_{ri} at least e, are determined to be of equivalent purchasing power by the price indexes P_{rs}. It could have been required to determine the largest $\bar{e}$ such that there exist $\bar{P}_{rs}$ and e_{ri} which satisfy (10) and (11), and this would have had the same result as the foregoing determination. Necessarily some $e_{ti} = 1$ and some $e_{ti} = \bar{e}$, and generally $w_{ti} = 1 - e_{ti}$ is an imputed inefficiency associated with income M_{ti} in country t.

3.7 *Rectification of Pair Comparisons*

For any price index formula P_{st} between two points in time, s and t, Fisher's "time reversal" test requires that $P_{ts}P_{st} = 1$, which requires in particular, what apparently is true for all the formulas discussed here, that $P_{tt} = 1$. Fisher defined the "time antithesis" to be $P_{st}^* = P_{ts}^{-1}$. Fisher "rectified" a formula by "crossing" it with its time antithesis so as to obtain an associated formula which satisfied the time reversal test. Then the time antithesis of the Laspeyres formula is the Paasche formula. By crossing these according to the geometric mean, Fisher's "ideal" index is obtained, which is therefore the rectification of the Laspeyres index, and similarly of the Paasche. It satisfies the time reversal test and for that reason he considered it ideal. Here a more general rectification procedure will be considered.

In fact, the important logic behind the time reversal test is that any index P_{rs} which is expressible as a ratio $P_{rs} = P_r/P_s$ must satisfy the test. Since a price index theoretically, at least here, arises as a ratio of price levels, meeting the reversal test is a significant requirement. But so just as well is the "circularity test," which he considered, but which none of the one or two hundred formulas he examined appeared to satisfy.

All familiar price index formulas satisfy what might be called the *identity test* $P_{tt} = 1$. The circularity test implies the equivalence of this to the reversal test, and its combination with either constitutes what should be called the *ratio test,* since it is the condition for the expression $P_{rs} = P_r/P_s$. The combination of the circularity and reversal tests is equivalent to the combination of the identity test with the *chain test*

$$(1) \qquad\qquad P_{rs}P_{st} = P_{rt}.$$

Also the chain test implies the equivalence of the identity and reversal tests and in combination with either is equivalent to the ratio test. But an algebraic formula cannot satisfy the ratio test unless it immediately presents a ratio, and it cannot do this if as in most standard formulas, the data for different periods are not entered as separate factors, which could cancel in multiplication.

Another approach to "rectifying" a set of P_{rs} as closely as possible with respect to the ratio test is to reconcile them as closely as possible with a set of ratios P_r/P_s. Thus, with any given P_{rs}, and any e, 3.7(6) is necessary and sufficient for (8) to have a solution for P_t. The largest value $\bar{e}$ of e for 3.7(8) can be determined, and then a solution $\bar{P}_t$ of 3.7(8) with $e = \bar{e}$ can be found. With $\bar{P}_{rs} = P_r/P_s$

$$(2) \qquad\qquad \bar{P}_{rs}/\bar{e} \leqq P_{rs} \leqq \bar{e}\bar{P}_{rs}$$

so that

$$(3) \qquad\qquad P_{rs} = \bar{P}_{rs}$$

if and only if $\bar{e} = 1$, and generally $\bar{P}_{rs}$ is the best approximation to P_{rs} which satisfies the reversal and circularity tests. Here again approximation distance is in the economic sense of cost inefficiency, which is appropriate since an economic error is an inefficiency.

A difficulty which arises with multinational price comparisons by means of one of the standard price index formulas based on price-quantity data is that the cirularity test is not satisfied; so a chain of comparisons is not consistent with the direct comparison, that is

(4) $$P_{ri}P_{ij} \ldots P_{ks} \neq P_{rs}.$$

One way of resolving this difficulty is to combine the directly determined P_{rs} to determine $\bar{P}_{rs}$ as above. The latter do satisfy the circularity test, or, since $\bar{P}_{rr} = 1$, equivalently the chain test, and approximate the P_{rs} as closely as possible, in the manner described. It should be noticed that this difficulty is automatically avoided if the method of sections 2.5 and 3.6 is used, since those determinations each ι ιve explicit or implicit reference to some particular utility function.

With just two periods, the ratio test reduces to the reversal test, so the process just considered can be seen as a generalization of Fisher's general rectification procedure. But now it will be seen more closely as a generalization.

The Fisher "ideal" index, arrived at as the rectification $\bar{P}_{01} = (P_{01}P_{10}{}^{-1})^{1/2}$ of the Laspeyres index P_{01}, by geometric crossing with its time antithesis $P_{10}{}^{-1}$, so as to obtain an index which satisfies the time reversal test, can also be arrived at as the best approximation, with efficiency distance, which satisfies time reversal. Thus consider

(5) $$\bar{P}_{01} = \bar{P}_{10}{}^{-1},$$

equivalently

(6) $$\bar{P}_{01} = \rho, \; \bar{P}_{10} = \rho^{-1},$$

such that

(7) $$P_{ij}/e \gtreqless \bar{P}_{ij},$$

equivalently

(8) $$\rho/e \gtreqless P_{01} \gtreqless e\rho,$$

(9) $$1/\rho e \gtreqless P_{10} \gtreqless e/\rho.$$

With P_{01}, P_{10} given, ρ is to be determined with e as large as possible. Equivalently

(10) $$1/e^2 \gtreqless P_{01}P_{10} \gtreqless e^2,$$

(11) $$\rho^2/e^2 \gtreqless P_{01}/P_{10} \gtreqless e^2\rho^2.$$

But with the largest e, and in fact any e, which satisfies (10), $\rho^2 = P_{01}/P_{10}$ automatically satisfies (11). The Fisher indexes $F_{01} = P_{01}/P_{10}$

and $F_{10} = F_{01}^{-1}$, among all numbers $\bar{P}_{01}$ and $\tilde{P}_{10}$ such that $\bar{P}_{10} = \bar{P}_{01}^{-1}$, are closest to P_{01}, P_{10} in that they satisfy (8) and (9) with e as large as possible.

Since P_{ij} could here be given by any formula, this argument, which deals with a special case of the previous analysis, is mainly a comment on Fisher's procedure of rectifying a formula by geometric crossing with its time antithesis or even with any other formula.

4.0 THEORY OF MARGINAL PRICE INDEXES

4.1 *Marginal Price Indexes*

Let R be a utility relation for which the associated utilities cost function can be represented by

$$(1) \qquad \rho(p, x) = \theta(p)\phi(x) + \mu(p).$$

By this property, R can be called a *linear cost utility*. With this classification, a homogeneous relation, which is characterized by the same utility property but with $\mu(p) = 0$, can be distinguished as a *homogeneous linear cost utility*. Thus here there is a particular generalization of homogeneity as applied to relations.

Since $\rho(p, x)$ is linearly homogeneous in p for all x, both $\theta(p)$, $\mu(p)$ in (1) must be linearly homogeneous, and $\phi(x)$ must be uniquely determined up to a linear transformation. Thus $\phi(x)$ is completely specified when its values are specified at two points which are not indifferent and then so are the other functions. A function associated with a linear cost relation in the same way that a linearly homogeneous function is associated with a homogeneous, or homogeneous linear, cost relation can be described as a *linear profile* function, for the reasons presented below. With this classification, a function which is linearly homogeneous appears as a *homogeneous linear profile* function.

From (1), for all p, x

$$(2) \qquad \theta(p)\phi(x) + \mu(p) \leqq px$$

and for all p, equality holds for some x, and R is quasi-concave if and only if for all x equality holds for some p. Whenever a utility relation is considered, it will be because it is compatible with given demands. But compatibility is preserved when the relation is replaced by its normalization obtained by taking the adjoint of its adjoint. That relation is automatically quasi-concave, its superior sets being the convex closures of those of the original. It appears from this that there is no essential loss of generality, so far as present questions are concerned, and a simplification in exposition, in assuming all utility relations dealt with to be quasi-concave. This is a fortunate circumstance for standard theory, which seems always to assume indifference contours to be concave. But it does not mean they really are. It is just that, in the limited language of economic choice, it is impossible to communicate that they are not.

A further simplicity which follows from strict quasi concavity is that expansion loci are paths, with a unique consumption corresponding to every level of income. Sometimes it is as well to assume this, again for simplicity of exposition, and also because an arbitrarily small modification can replace concavity by strict concavity, so there is no significant difference when error is allowed.

Because, for any p, $\rho(p, x)$ is a utility function which represents R, so is $\phi(x)$. The adjoint is

(3) $$\psi(u) = [1 - \mu(u)]/\theta(u),$$

and

(4) $$\psi(M^{-1}p) = [M - \mu(p)]/\theta(p),$$

so that

(5) $$\partial\psi(M^{-1}p)/\partial M = 1/\theta(p).$$

Thus $P = \theta(p)$ is the marginal price of utility $X = \psi(M^{-1}p)$ attained at elementary prices p with a level of expenditure M, and it is fixed when elementary prices are fixed.

The *profile*, for prices p, of a utility function $\phi(x)$ with adjoint $\psi(u)$, is $\psi(M^{-1}p)$. Here it appears that the profiles are linear. Such a property is preserved under linear transformations, but not more general ones. An equivalent characterization of linear cost utility relations is that they admit representation by a utility function with linear profiles. It is to be seen that still another equivalent characterization is that the expansion loci are linear.

To see this, assume, as would be permitted on grounds already stated, that $\phi(x)$ is quasi-concave. Then, by a general proposition, since its profiles also are concave, it is concave. Let y and z be two different demands at prices p which are compatible, that is yEp, zEp which is to say $\theta(p)\phi(y) + \mu(p) = py$; $\theta(p)\phi(z) + \mu(p) = pz$. Then, with $\beta + \gamma = 1$, it follows that

$$\theta(p)[\phi(y)\beta + \phi(z)\gamma] + \mu(p) = p(y\beta + z\gamma).$$

But then with $\beta, \gamma \geqq 0$, and $x = y\beta + z$, $\phi(x) \geqq \phi(y)\beta + \phi(z)\gamma$, since $\phi(x)$ is concave, and, as usual, $\theta(p)\phi(x) + \mu(p) \leqq px$. But this with the foregoing implies $\theta(p)\phi(x) + \mu(p) = px$, and shows that the demand of x at prices p is compatible, that is, xEp.

It has been shown that $y, z \; \varepsilon \; Ep \Rightarrow \langle y, z \rangle \subset Ep$, where $\langle y, z \rangle$ is the line segment joining y and z; that is, the expansion locus Ep is a convex set. But if it is a path, as it is if R is strictly quasi-concave, then it is a segment of a line. Since the line is in any case truncated within the commodity space, it cannot extend beyond a half-line. In fact, there may have to be a further interruption of a different nature, where the function becomes strictly quasi-convex, and where no demand is compatible, and this could leave at most a bounded segment. An intrinsic limitation of this kind is important in describing the range of incomes for which a comparison is valid.

It has been seen that if R is a quasi-concave utility order and (1) holds, then $\phi(x)$ has concave contours and profiles and hence is a concave function. Then it was deduced that the expansion sets Ep are convex, where xEp means $\rho(p, x) = 1$. Thus in particular, when the expansion sets are paths that cut every level of income (equivalently, every level of utility), in a single point, they must be straight lines to be convex.

Now a converse proposition will be shown. Suppose Ep are given as describing all levels of utility indicated by 0 and 1 and as convex. Then, between these levels R has the linear cost property (1).

For any u let $x_0(u)$, $x_1(u)$ denote any elements of the expansion set Eu in utility levels indicated by 0 and 1. Then, by hypothesis,

$$x_t(u) = x_0(u) + [x_1(u) - x_0(u)]t$$

where $0 \leqq t \leqq 1$, is also in Eu. Also, since $x_0(u)Rx_0(v)$ for all u, v, then

$$ux_0(u) = \min [ux : xRx_0(u)] \leqq ux_0(v).$$

Thus $ux_0(u) \leqq ux_0(v)$ and similarly, $ux_1(u) \leqq ux_1(v)$, for all u, v. It follows, multiplying these inequalities by $(t, 1 - t)$ and adding, that

$ux_t(u) \leqq ux_t(v)$ for all $0 \leqq t \leqq 1$. But $x_t(u) \; \varepsilon \; Eu$, for all u. It follows that, for all such t, $x_t(u)Rx_t(v)$ for all u and v. Thus, for all such t, $x_t(u)$ for all u describes an indifference surface. Hence, defining $\phi[x_t(u)] = t$, $\phi(x)$ is a utility function which represents R. Also, if $\phi(x) = t$, $yRx \cdot \iff \cdot ux \geqq ux_t(u)$ for all u. Hence

$$\rho(p, x) = \min \; [py : yRx] = \min \; [py : ux \geqq ux_t(u)] = px_t(p)$$
$$= px_0(p) + p[x_1(p) - x_0(p)]t = \theta(p)\phi(x) + \mu(p),$$

where

$$\theta(p) = p[x_1(p) - x_0(p)], \; \mu(0) = px_0(p),$$

as required.

The equilibrium relation E which holds between x, p in an R-compatible demand is given by

(6) $$xEp \equiv \theta(p)\phi(x) + \mu(p) = px.$$

Thus, with compatible demands (x_0, p_0) and (x_1, p_1) in a base and current period, or country, if

(7) $$\begin{aligned} M_0 &= p_0x_0, & M_1 &= p_1x_1 \\ m_0 &= \mu(p_0), & m_1 &= \mu(p_1) \\ P_0 &= \theta(p_0), & P_1 &= \theta(p_1) \\ X_0 &= \phi(x_0), & X_1 &= \phi(x_1) \end{aligned}$$

then

(8) $$P_0X_0 + m_0 = M_0, \quad P_1X_1 + m_1 = M_1.$$

But the m's and P's are determined by prices alone. Hence the condition $X_0 = X$ for *any* incomes M_0, M_1 to have the same purchasing power at prices p_0, p_1 is equivalent to

(9) $$M_1 - m_1 = P_{10}(M_0 - m_0)$$

where $P_{10} = P_1/P_0$ is the *marginal price index* between p_0 and p_1. Therefore, with any incomes M_0, M_1 constrained to purchasing power equivalence,

(10) $$\Delta M_1/\Delta M_0 = P_{10}.$$

This shows the definition of a marginal price index by its characteristic role as applied to income differentials which preserve equivalence, instead of to incomes themselves, about which nothing can be said without knowledge of the *original values* m_0, m_1. This contrasts with an ordinary price index P_{10} which gives

(11) $$M_1 = P_{10}M_0$$

as the relation between equivalent incomes, and hence the same relation between income differentials which preserve equivalence. Thus in the use of marginal price indexes there is a distinction between total incomes and income differentials which is effaced by ordinary price indexes.

It would seem that (9) is an appropriate relation for adjusting wages for price change as required by an escalator clause in a labor-management contract, to maintain economic equity, but (10) could be appropriate for adjustment of any other moneys which do not have the nature of base incomes, such as rents, allowances, and so forth.

4.2   *Method of Limits*

Continuing now, from 4.1(2),

(1) $$P_0 X_1 + m_0 \leq p_0 x_1$$
$$P_1 X_0 + m_1 \leq p_1 x_0$$

and from (8),

(2) $$P_0 X_0 + m_0 = p_0 x_0$$
$$P_1 X_1 + m_1 = p_1 x_1.$$

Now from (11) and (12),

(3) $$(p_1 x_1 - m_1)/(p_0 x_1 - m_0) \leq P_{10} \leq (p_1 x_0 - m_1)/(p_0 x_0 - m_0).$$

Thus, for any given pair of demands (x_0, p_0) and (x_1, p_1), if the hypothesis of their compatibility with R, for any values for m_0 and m_1, is accepted, then the bounds for P_{10} shown in (3) are determined. In the particular case with $m_0 = m_1 = 0$ these bounds coincide with the Paasche and Laspeyres price indexes. This circumstance can be amplified further later.

Now for any incomes M_0 and M_1, not necessarily $p_0 x_0$ and $p_1 x_1$, to be equivalent in purchasing power at respective prices p_0, p_1 it is necessary, by 4.1(9) and (3), that they be in the relation T_{01} depending on m_0, m_1 given by

(4) $\quad M_0 T_{01} M_1 \equiv (p_1 x_1 - m_1)/(p_0 x_1 - m_0) \leqq (M_1 - m_1)/(M_0 - m_0)$
$$\leqq (p_1 x_0 - m_1)/(p_0 x_0 - m_0).$$

Thus every M_0 corresponds to an interval of M_1 with upper and lower limits $(M_1)_u$, $(M_1)_l$ where

(5) $\qquad (M_1)_l - m_1 = [(p_1 x_1 - m_1)/(p_0 x_1 - m_0)] (M_0 - m_0)$
$$(M_1)_u - m_1 = [(p_1 x_0 - m_1)/(p_0 x_0 - m_0)] (M_0 - m_0)$$

which can define the *extreme equivalents* of M_0, and similarly with 0 and 1 interchanged. Then a particular value $\bar{M}_1$ between these limits is given by

(6) $\qquad (\bar{M}_1 - m_1)^2 = [(M_1)_l - m_1][(M_1)_u - m_1],$

which can define the *principal equivalent* of M_0. There may seem to be no reason for introducing this concept for a particular correspondent $\bar{M}_1$ of M_0. It is just a way of singling out a point in the interval $M_0 T_{01}$ of correspondents of M_0. However, M_0 is the principal correspondent of its principal correspondent: The one-to-one subcorrespondence $\bar{T}_{01}$ of the many-to-many correspondence T_{01} given by

(7) $\quad M_0 \bar{T}_{01} M_1 \equiv [(M_1 - m_1)/(M_0 - m_0)]^2$
$$= (p_1 x_1 - m_1)(p_1 x_0 - m_1)/(p_0 x_1 - m_0)(p_0 x_0 - m_0)$$

can define the *principal correspondence*. It holds between incomes M_0 and M_1 at prices p_0 and p_1 if and only if each is the principal correspondent of the other, in which case each is the principal correspondent of its principal correspondent. Note that if $m_0 = m_1 = 0$ then this is the correspondence associated with the Fisher price index.

The theory thus shows that the Laspeyres, Paasche, and Fisher indexes, understood in their role as price indexes, correspond to a special case, where the parameters m_0 and m_1 are zero.

A particular utility relation R which was presented earlier, has the property expressed by (1). With $\phi(x)$ fixed, by assigning values at two nonindifferent points, the other functions are fixed, and hence so are m_0 and m_1. For any M_0 there exists a unique M_1 such that

(8) $\qquad\qquad \psi(M_0^{-1} p_0) = \psi(M_1^{-1} p_1).$

It has been shown that this together with $x_0 E p_0$, $x_1 E p_1$ for any x_0, x_1 implies $M_0 T_{01} M_1$. Thus it would be exceptional that also $M_0 \bar{T}_{01} M_1$. But the particular utility relation R makes (8) specific and also m_0, m_1. Usually in practice there is nothing available but fragmentary demand data, even when, as here, there are only two reference periods or countries.

4.3   *Expansion Lines and Critical Points*

If at each of the prices p_0, p_1 just one demand is available, x_0, x_1, then only a rather loose analysis can be developed, as has just been done, where the parameters m_0, m_1 are unspecified. Even this analysis can be taken further, but not here. Instead it will be supposed that a second demand is available at each of the prices, say, y_0, y_1. By implication then, since compatible linear cost utility is to be considered, for which expansion loci are line segments, or possibly half-lines, what is being considered is a pair of segments $K_0 = \langle x_0, y_0 \rangle$, $K_1 = \langle x_1, y_1 \rangle$ of demands associated with prices p_0, p_1.

Let L_0, L_1 denote the carrier lines of K_0, K_1. These are the lines joining the extremities. It can be shown that, if

$$(1) \qquad \begin{vmatrix} p_0(x_0 - y_0) & p_0(x_1 - y_1) \\ p_1(x_0 - y_0) & p_1(x_1 - y_1) \end{vmatrix} \neq 0,$$

(and if this is not so then it can be made so, by distributing the data slightly, or at least within bounds of its conspicuous inaccuracy), then there exists a unique pair of *critical points* c_0, c_1 on L_0, L_1 such that $p_0 c_0 = p_1 c_1$, $p_1 c_0 = p_1 c_1$. These need not be on K_0, K_1 nor even in the commodity space. They are distinguished as being indifferent with respect to every compatible utility relation. Then a pair of half-lines L_0^*, L_1^* on L_0, L_1 with c_0, c_1 as vertexes are determined. The pair is selected according to the sign of the elements and the determinants of the foregoing nonsingular 2×2 matrix. Then the expansions (K_0, p_0), (K_1, p_1) are generally consistent, that is, compatible with any utility relation, regardless of properties, if and only if $K_0 \subset L_0^*$ or $K_1 \subset L_1^*$. Thus, should L_0^*, L_1^* happen not to lie in the commodity space at all then certainly the expansions are inconsistent. However, for *local linear cost consistency,* equivalently compatibility with a utility function which has linear expansion loci *in a convex neighborhood containing* K_0, K_1, it is necessary and sufficient that $K_0 \subset L_0^*$ and $K_1 \subset L_1^*$.

With c_0, c_1 as the pair of critical points on the carrier lines L_0, L_1, let

x_0, x_1 now be any other pair of points $p_0(x_0 - c_0) > 0$, $p_1(x_1 - c_1) > 0$. Then for consistency it is necessary that also $p_0(x_1 - c_1) > 0$, $p_1(x_0 - c_0) > 0$. Then the *critical determinant*

$$(2) \qquad \begin{vmatrix} p_0(x_0 - c_0) & p_0(x_1 - c_1) \\ p_1(x_0 - c_0) & p_1(x_1 - c_1) \end{vmatrix}$$

is nonzero by hypotheses (1). Then the *hyperbolic* and *elliptical* cases are distinguished by the sign, positive or negative, of (2). In the hyperbolic case, L_0^*, L_1^* correspond to $x_0 \ \varepsilon \ L_0$, $x_1 \ \varepsilon \ L_1$, where p_0x_0) p_0c_0, $p_1x_1 \geqq p_1c_1$. In this case, consistency of (K_0, p_0), (K_1, p_1) requires

$$(3) \qquad x_0 \ \varepsilon \ K_0 \Rightarrow p_0x_0 \geqq p_0c_0$$

$$x_1 \ \varepsilon \ K_1 \Rightarrow p_1x_1 \geqq p_1c_1$$

Inequalities are reversed for the elliptical case.

Let $F_0(M_0)$, $F_1(M_1)$ denote the points x_0, x_1 on L_0, L_1 with $p_0x_0 = M_0$, $p_1x_1 = M_1$.

With reference to the relation T_{01} given by 4.2(4), with the specification $m_0 = p_0c_0$, $m_1 = p_1c_1$ it can now be said that, at prices p_0, p_1, any incomes M_0, M_1 may be determined as of equivalent purchasing power with respect to some utility relation compatible with the expansions (K_0, p_0), (K_1, p_1), if and only if, first, these expansions are consistent; second, in the hyperbolic case,

$$(4) \qquad M_0 \geqq p_0c_0, \qquad F_0(M_0) \geqq 0$$

$$M_1 \geqq p_1c_1, \qquad F_1(M_1) \geqq 0,$$

and correspondingly in the elliptical case; and finally, $M_0T_{01}M_1$.

With the appropriate qualifications about the range of M_0, M_1 it appears thus that the relation T_{01} determines, for any M_0, the best possible bounds, that is, the limits of M_1 that can be established as equivalent with respect to some compatible utility relation.

Two peculiarities may be noted. No restriction at all has been made for the utility relation in the foregoing, but now two restrictions will be considered. The first is that the utility relation be of the linear cost type, at least in a convex neighborhood containing K_0, K_1. However, even if this restriction is imposed on the utility relation just described, the description remains valid. This is remarkable only because on the

face of the matter, it would seem that with this restriction the relation
T should be contracted to a proper subrelation.

The other restriction to be considered is a stronger one. It requires
the utility relation to be representable in a convex neighborhood containing K_0, K_1 by a general quadratic utility function. This implies
qualification under the first restriction, since quadratic representation implies linear expansion. Again on the face of the matter, quadratic consistency is a stronger condition than linear expansion consistency. In regard to any number of expansions, it is. But it is
surprising that for just a pair of expansions, it is equivalent. Then,
under this common consistency requirement, it is natural to ask what
is the subrelation, say $T_{01}{}^*$, of T_{01} corresponding to this further quadratic restriction. Certainly now it will be a proper subrelation, but
since, if there are any, there are infinite compatible quadratics, it
might be expected that $T_{01}{}^*$ would not be one-to-one, but that, for
every M_0, $M_0 T_{01}{}^*$ would be a subinterval of $M_0 T_{01}$, nonempty by consistency and with a variety of points because of the variety of compatible quadratics. However, it is established that $T_{01}{}^* = \bar{T}_{01}$, that is,
the quadratically determined correspondence $T_{01}{}^*$ coincides with the
principle correspondence given by 4.2(7), and moreover this is one-
to-one. Thus here there is a surprise opposite to the first. Introducing
the values of m_0, m_1, that formula becomes

(5) $M_0 \bar{T}_{01} M_1 \equiv [(M_1 - p_1 c_1)/(M_0 - p_0 c_0)]^2$

$$= p_1(x_1 - c_1) p_1(x_0 - c_0)/p_0(x_1 - c_1) p_0(x_0 - c_0).$$

It follows from the definition of the critical points c_0, c_1 on the carrier lines L_0, L_1 that c_0, c_1 in this formula could be replaced by any
point c on the *critical transversal* to L_0, L_1 obtained by joining the L's,
assuming L_0, L_1 are skew. But if L_0 and L_1 intersect in a point c, then
both c_0 and c_1 coincide with c, and no such transversal is defined. It
should be noted that if L_0, L_1 are skew, any compatible quadratic
is singular, that is, its matrix of second derivatives, which is constant,
is singular. In this case its expansion loci for p_0, p_1 do not lie in lines
but in linear manifolds at least as large as the joins of c with L_0, L_1.
For the expansion loci strictly to be lines, the quadratic must be regular, and in this case L_0 and L_1 must intersect.

If, in particular, the intersection is at the origin $c = 0$, then (5) becomes Fisher's formula. Then for consistency, the elliptical case is excluded entirely, since if $M_0 \leqq 0$ then $F_0(M_0) \geqq 0$ is impossible. Thus the consistency condition becomes simply $p_0 x_0 p_1 x_1 \geqq p_0 x_1 p_1 x_0$, corresponding to the remaining hyperbolic case. Since c_0 and c_1 appear as points where the gradient of any compatible quadratic must vanish, $c_0 = c_1 = 0$ corresponds to the case of a homogeneous quadratic. This reproduces the observation of Buescheguennce that the Fisher index is exact if a homogeneous utility function can be assumed to prevail. But, related to this, as a generalization, Wald has shown that if a pair of expansion lines are given, with associated prices, and it can be assumed that a general quadratic utility function prevails, then it is possible to determine a unique one-to-one correspondence between equivalent incomes at these prices. This is by his "new formula," which, because of Buescheguennce's proposition must be essentially a generalization of Fisher's formula. Consistency conditions were not treated and, hence, neither were the necessary restrictions on the range of those incomes for such comparison. But with the introduction of the concept of critical points certainly his formula must be identical with (13), which is transparently a generalization of Fisher. A generalization of Wald's formula appears in Afriat (1964).

This theory of marginal price indexes extends every feature of the theory of price indexes based on the traditional concept. Instead of a pair of demands (x_0, p_0), (x_1, p_1), which because of implicit homogeneity correspond in principle to a pair of linear expansions (x'_0, p_0), (x'_1, p_1), where x'_0, x'_1 are the rays through x_0, x_1, the data now consist of a general pair of linear expansions (K_0, p_0), (K_1, p_1), where K_0 and K_1 can arise from pairs of demands x_0, y_0 and x_1, y_1 not necessarily on the same ray. The Paasche-Laspeyres limits for a price index P_{10} become the limits given in (1) with $m_0 = p_0 c_0$, $m_1 = p_1 c_1$ for a marginal price index P_{10}. The index then has the role shown by 4.1(10), and m has the role shown by 4.1(9).

This theory of marginal price index construction, here restricted to data for two periods or countries, and dependent on consistency conditions, has a general extension for arbitrary data and with a relaxation of strict consistency to approximate consistency. But this development will be shown here only as it applies to the usual price indexes.

With all this, it still has to be claimed that marginal price indexes, as described here, are not yet general enough. They are not vulnerable to the objection made to price indexes, which was that the concept implies that the rich and poor have the same spending pattern. But they are vulnerable to the objection that the concept implies that rich and poor have the same *marginal pattern*. This is to say that an extra dollar given to a rich individual would be spent in identical fashion were it given to a poor one. This does not go so far as to say they enjoy all things in the same proportion and differ just in the scale corresponding to their different incomes, but it is a radical contradiction of reality nevertheless.

To escape this objection, a further method is possible, where the intervals of incomes to be compared can be dissected into consecutive corresponding subintervals, or steps, corresponding to different intervals of real income, where the foregoing scheme applies, but with different P_{10}, m_0, m_1 at each level. This corresponds to the concept of a utility relation determined by a finite set of indifference surfaces, each surface being the interface between consecutive intervals of real income. The interpolation between surfaces is by the unique linear cost utility relation they determine.

For arbitrary demand data, consistency of utility relations with such a form is not more restrictive than general consistency. Such a scheme for establishing equivalent real incomes, though it would not be put into operation by publication of a single number, as is the usual practice, would still have practical simplicity. It would establish corresponding income classes, and then different P_{10}, m_0, and m_1 for determining corresponding points in each pair of corresponding classes. Though a utility function conceptually underlies such information, there is no need to compute, let alone present, a particular one. In any case, such a scheme of information would present everything about such a utility function that would be relevant to the desired comparison.

The real-income classes correspond to any partition of the range. When there is just one class, the method is identical with the original marginal index method. Transition from one class to another can correspond to a significant shift of marginal pattern.

A more elaborate general analysis can apply to several periods or countries, and express approximation in terms of cost efficiencies. Any income in any period would have an imputed cost efficiency and an interval of corresponding incomes in every other period or country. Within each such interval of correspondents, a single point can be determined from the principal correspondence which is produced by the linear expansions across each real-income interval in the two periods or countries. This more elaborate method communicates information about underlying error and indeterminacy together with a one-to-one correspondence which represents a statistical resolution of both.

BIBLIOGRAPHY

Afriat, S. N. "Theory of Economic Index Numbers." Mimeographed. Cambridge, Engl., Department of Applied Economics, Cambridge University, May 1956.

———. "Preference Scales and Expenditure Systems." *Econometrica* 30 (1962): 305–323.

———. "A Formula for Ranging the Cost of Living." Abstract in R. L. Graves and P. Wolf, eds. *Recent Advances in Mathematical Programming: Proceedings of the Chicago Symposium, 1962.* New York, McGraw-Hill, 1962.

———. "The System of Inequalities $a_{rs} > X_r - X_s$." *Proceedings of the Cambridge Philosophical Society* 59 (1963): 125–133.

———. "An Identity Concerning the Relation Between the Paasche and Laspeyres Indices." *Metroeconomica* XV, I (1963): 38–46.

———. "On Bernoullian Utility for Goods and Money." *Metroeconomica* XV, I (1963), 38–46.

———. "The Construction of Utility Functions from Expenditure Data." *International Economic Review* 8, 1 (1967): 66–77.

———. "The Cost of Living Index." In M. Shubik, ed. *Studies in Mathematical Economics in Honor of Oskar Morgenstern.* Princeton, N.J., Princeton University Press, 1967, Chap. 23.

———. "The Construction of Cost Efficiencies and Approximate Utility Functions from Inconsistent Expenditure Data." Paper presented at the winter meeting of the Econometric Society, New York, 1969.

———. "The Method of Limits in the Theory of Index Numbers." *Metroeconomica* (1970).

Allen, R. G. D. "The Economic Theory of Index Numbers." *Economica,* New Series XVI, 63 (August 1949): 197–203.

Antonelli, G. B. *Sulla Teoria Matematica della Economia Pura* (1886). Reprinted in *Giornale degli Economisti* 10 (1951): 233–263.

Bowley, A. L. Review of *The Making of Index Numbers,* by Irving Fisher. *Economic Journal* 33 (1923) : 90–94.

———— "Notes on Index Numbers." *Economic Journal* (June 1928).

Buscheguennce. "Sur une classe des hypersurfaces. A propos de 'l'index idéal' de M. Irv. Fisher." *Recueil Mathematique* (Moscow) XXXII, 4 (1925).

Chase, Arnold E. "Concepts and Uses of Price Indices." Paper presented at the American Statistical Association meeting, August 1960.

Cournot, Augustine. *Researches into the Mathematical Principles of the Theory of Wealth* (1838). Translated by Nathaniel T. Bacon with an essay on Cournot and mathematical economics and a bibliography on mathematical economics by Irving Fisher (1924). Reprint: New York, Kelley, 1960.

De Finetti, Bruno. "Sulle stratificazioni convesse." *Ann. Mat. Pura Appt.* 4 (1949): 173–183.

Divisia, F. *Economique Rationelle.* Paris, 1928.

Dupuit, J. "De la mesure de l'utilité des travaux public" (1844). Reprinted in English translation as "On the Measurement of the Utility of Public Works," in *International Economic Papers,* No. 2. London, Macmillan, 1952.

Edgeworth, F. Y. "A Defense of Index Numbers." *Economic Journal* (1896): 132–142.

Fisher, Irving. *The Purchasing Power of Money.* New York, Macmillan, 1911.

————. *The Making of Index Numbers.* Boston, Houghton Mifflin, 1922.

————. "Professor Bowley on Index Numbers." *Economic Journal* 33 (1923): 246–251.

————. "A Statistical Method for Measuring Marginal Utility and Testing the Justice of a Progressive Income Tax." In *Economic Essays in Honor of John Bates Clark.* New York, 1927.

Fleetwood, William. *Chronicon Preciosum: or, an Account of English Money, The Price of Corn, and Other Commodities, for the last 600 Years—in a Letter to a Student in the University of Oxford.* London, 1707.

Foster, William T. Prefatory Note, to *The Making of Index Numbers* by Fisher (see above).

Frisch, Ragnar. "Annual Survey of General Economic Theory: The Problem of Index Numbers." *Econometrica* 4, 1 (1936): 1–39.

Georgescu-Roegen, N. "Choice and Revealed Preference." *Southern Economic Journal* 21 (1954): 119–130.

Gorman, W. M. "Separable Utility and Aggregation." *Econometrica* 27 (1959): 469–487.

————. "Additive Logarithmic Preferences: A Further Note." *Review of Economic Studies* 30 (1963): 56–62.

Haberler, Y. *Der Sinn der Indexzahlen.* Tubingen, 1924.

Hicks, J. R. *A Revision of Demand Theory.* Oxford, Clarendon Press, 1956.

Hotelling, H. "Demand Functions with Limited Budgets." *Econometrica* 3 (1935): 66–78.

Houthakker, H. S. "Revealed Preference and the Utility Function." *Economica,* N. S. 17 (1950): 159–174.

―――. "La forme des courbes d'Engel." *Cahiers du Seminarie d'Econometrie* 2 (1953): 59–66.

―――. "An International Comparison of Household Expenditure Patterns, Commemorating the Centenary of Engel's Law." *Econometrica* 25 (1957): 532–551.

―――. "Some Problems in the International Comparison of Consumption Patterns." In *L'évaluation et le rôle des besoins de consommation dans les divers régimes économiques.* Paris, Centre National de la Recherche Scientifique, 1963.

International Labour Office. *A Contribution to the Study of International Comparisons of Costs of Living.* Studies and Reports, Series N, 17. Geneva, 1932.

Keynes, J. M. *A Treatise on Money,* Vol. I, *The Pure Theory of Money.* New York, Harcourt, Brace, 1930.

Klein, L. R., and H. Rubin. "A Constant Utility Index of the Cost of Living." *Review of Economic Studies* 15 (1947): 84–87.

Konus, A. A. "The Problem of the True Index of the Cost of Living." *Economic Bulletin of the Institute of Economic Conjecture* (Moscow), 1924).

Lange, O. "The Determinateness of the Utility Function." *Review of Economic Studies* 1 (1934): 218–224.

Laspeyres, E. "Die Berechnung einer mittleran Waarenpreissteigerung." *Jahrbücher für nationaloekonomie und Statistik* (Jena) XVI, 1871: 296–314.

Lerner, A. P. "A Note on the Theory of Price Index Numbers." *Review of Economic Studies* (1935): 50–56.

Little, I. M. D. *A Critique of Welfare Economics.* New York, Oxford University Press, 1957.

Liviatan, Nissan, and Don Patinkin. "On the Economic Theory of Price Indices." *Economic Development and Cultural Change* IX (1961): 501–536.

Mathur, P. N. "Approximate Determination of Indifference Surfaces from Family Budget Data." *International Economic Review* 5 (1964): 294–303.

Midgett, B. D. *Index Numbers.* New York, Wiley, 1951.

Morgenstern, Oskar. *On the Accuracy of Economic Observations.* Princeton, N.J., Princeton University Press, 1963.

National Bureau of Economic Research. *Problems in the International Comparison of Economic Accounts.* Studies in Income and Wealth, Vol. 20. Princeton University Press for NBER, 1957.

Paasche, H. "Über die Priesentwickelung der letzten Jahre, nach den Hamburger Börsennotierungen." *Jahrbücher für Nationaloekonomie und Statistik* (Jena) XXIII (1874): 168–178.

Palgrave, R. H. I. "Currency and Standard of Value in England, France and

India, and the Rates of Exchange between These Countries." *Memorandum Laid Before the Royal Commission on Depression of Trade and Industry,* 1886, Third Report, Appendix B, pp. 213–390.

Pareto, V. "Économie Mathématique." *Encyclopedie des sciences mathématiques,* 1911. Reprinted in English translation as "Mathematical Economics," in *International Economic Papers,* No. 5. London, Macmillan, 1955.

Prais, S. J. "Non-Linear Estimates of the Engle Curves." *Review of Economic Studies* 20 (1952–53): 87–104.

Prais, S. J., and H. S. Houthakker. *The Analysis of Family Budgets.* Cambridge, Engl., Cambridge University Press, 1955.

Rajoaja, V. "A Study in the Theory of Demand Functions and Price Indexes." *Commentationes physico-mathematicae, Societas Scientiarum Fennica* (Helsinki) 21 (1958): 1–96.

Report of the President's Committee on the Cost of Living. Office of Economic Stabilization. Washington, D.C., 1945.

Report of the Price Statistics Review Committee. *Government Price Statistics, Hearings.* Subcommittee on Economic Statistics of the Joint Economic Committee. Part I, pp. 5–99. 87th Cong., 1st sess., January 1961.

Rose, Hugh. "Consistency of Preference: the Two-Commodity Case." *Review of Economic Studies* 25 (1958): 124–125.

Roy, R. "La distribution du revenu entre les divers biens." *Econometrica* 15 (1947): 205–225.

Ruggles, Richard. "Price Indices and International Price Comparisons." In *Ten Economic Studies in the Tradition of Irving Fisher.* New York, Wiley, 1967.

Samuelson, P. A. "Evaluation of Real National Income." *Oxford Economic Papers* N. S. 2, 1 (1950): 1–29.

———. "Structure of a Minimum Equilibrium System." In R. W. Pfouts, ed., *Essays in Economics and Econometrics.* Chapel Hill, University of North Carolina Press, 1960.

Schumpeter, Joseph A. *History of Economic Analysis.* New York, Oxford University Press, 1954.

Slutsky, E. E. "Sulla teoria del biancio del consumatore" *Giornale degli Economisti* (1915). Reprinted as "On the theory of the budget of the consumer," translated by O. Ragusa, in G. J. Stigler and K. E. Boulding, eds. *Readings in Price Theory.* Chicago, Irwin, 1952.

Staehle, Hans. "A General Method for the Comparison of the Price of Living." *Rev. Econ. Papers,* New Ser., 2, 1 (1950): 1–29.

Stone, Richard. "Linear Expenditure Systems and Demand Analysis; an Application to the Pattern of British Demand." *Economic Journal,* 64 (1954): 511–524.

Stone, Richard, assisted by D. A. Rowe, W. J. Corlett, R. Hurstfield, and M. Potter. *The Measurement of Consumers' Expenditure and Behavior in the*

United Kingdom, 1920–1938, Vol. I. Cambridge, Engl., Cambridge University Press, 1966.

Stone, Richard, and D. A. Rowe. *Ibid.,* Vol. II.

Theil, H. "The Information Approach to Demand Analysis." *Econometrica* 33 (1963): 67–87.

Ulmer, M. J. *The Economic Theory of Cost of Living Index Numbers.* New York, Columbia University Press, 1949.

Ville, J. "Sur les conditions d'existence d'une orphelimite totale et d'un indice du niveau des prix." *Annales de l'Université de Lyon* (1946). Reprinted in English translation as "The Existence Conditions of a Total Utility Function," in *Review of Economic Studies* 19 (1951–52): 128–132.

Viner, J. "The Utility Concept in Value Theory and Its Critics." *Journal of Political Economy* 33 (1925): 369–387, 638–659.

Volterra, V. "L'economia matematica." Review of *Manuale di Economia Politica,* by V. Pareto. *Giornale degli Economisti* 32 (1906): 296–301.

Wald, A. "A New Formula for the Index of the Cost of Living." *Econometrica* 7, 4 (1939): 319–335.

————. "The Approximate Determination of Indifference Surfaces by Means of Engel Curves." *Econometrica* 8 (1940): 144–175.

————. "On a Relation Between Changes in Demand and Price Changes." *Ibid.* 20 (1952): 304–305.

Walsh, C. M. *The Measurement of General Exchange-Value.* New York, Macmillan, 1901.

Wold, H. O. A. "A synthesis of pure demand analysis." *Skandinavisk Aktuarietidskrift* 26 (1943): 85–118, 221–263; *ibid.* 27 (1944): 69–120.

Wright, Georg Henrik von. *The Logic of Preference.* Edinburgh, Scotland, Edinburgh University Press, 1963.

COMMENT

CARLOS F. DÍÁZ-ALEJANDRO, Yale University

Afriat's main theses are set forth elegantly and forcefully. It makes no difference whether the distinctions be of time or place in the theory of index numbers (although he concentrates in his paper on time comparisons). Inherent in the price-level concept is the assumption that expansion paths are rays through the origin. The assumption of homogeneity, and the assumption that observed cost does not exceed minimum cost for value obtained, or "X-efficiency," are necessary if, in Fisher's terminology, we are to find a definite center of gravity of the shell fragments as they move in space.

Afriat is skeptical that we can meaningfully define "general purchasing power." Value, he tells us, is an attribute of a chooser, and his identity must be clear. Who is the chooser when we deal with public goods and "national wants"? Comparisons among countries whose wants are manifestly different highlight the problem, and Afriat doubts that comparisons of real national measures can be developed except where they refer directly to individuals. But even here, one can add, changes in taste by individuals threaten the basis for comparison. To take into account at least part of the plurality of purchasing power, he recommends the use of marginal price indexes.

The Afriat paper, rooted in utility theory, seems to say that the only purpose of index number construction is to measure *the* price level, general purchasing power, or welfare. Yet index numbers can be asked to perform other, often more modest, tasks. In those cases, index numbers may provide reasonably good answers, without much violence being done to the concept of what is being measured. Take, for example, the concept of productive capacity, used by Bergson in his paper included in this volume. But I suspect Afriat would point out that a clear definition of "general productive capacity" requires carefully spelled out assumptions, including explicit objective functions, which may not always be realistic.

A more modest task is to use index numbers to describe patterns of relative price structures in different countries, as a first step in analyzing the economic causes behind different patterns. For example, the relative prices of capital goods in Latin American countries and their changes through time can be described with such indexes. Unlike Fisher, we can say that the purpose of index numbers is not irrelevant to their construction. Indexes of relative prices in less developed countries (LDC's) can be a valuable tool in the analysis of development policies in those countries. They can reflect deviations from world market prices, due to commercial policies and other reasons, and indicate whether those deviations are becoming larger or smaller. One can test whether in fact the fastest-growing sectors in LDC's are those experiencing rising relative prices, thus yielding upward biases to national accounts measured at recent-year prices.

With a plentiful supply of computers, Afriat's plea for greater use of "marginal indexes" should be easy to respond to. Their greater use could cast light on patterns of income distribution, and on such matters as the impact of inflation on that distribution.

Because of its emphasis on very pure theory, the paper does not discuss several interesting issues to which more modest tools could be applied. One is Ruggles' redundancy problem: How many items should be gathered in the preparation of index numbers? Issues such as quality changes, new products, technical change, changes in taste, public goods and bads (for example, pollution), etc., are not explored in relation to index numbers.

We should be grateful to Afriat, however, for this useful and sophisticated reminder that one should be very careful when translating theory to empirical work, so as not to lose fidelity to the concept which one is supposed to be measuring.

MELVILLE J. ULMER, University of Maryland

Several points, central to the topic of this conference, are overlooked or in my judgment otherwise mistreated, in Afriat's paper. In the first place, he asserts that in principle the index number problem is the same whether the comparisons are over time or from place to place. This is a frequently repeated, and perhaps even an innocuous-sounding, statement, but I think that any resemblance it may have to the truth will tend to diminish rapidly the more we think about it. This is especially so, if "place-to-place" really refers to country-to-country comparisons, which I take to be the focus of attention here. Analytically as well as empirically, there is a distinct difference in the problems posed by temporal and locational real-income comparisons.

To clarify this difference, I should like to turn to the index number problem in its classic form, the one adhered to, in general, in Afriat's paper. The theory grew out of the problem of measuring a relative change in the cost of living from one period to the next in the same place, and ordinarily for people in a particular income class, such as urban workers. All the conditions of the problem, at least when the comparisons cover a short period of time, make it possible to adopt as reasonable assumptions: (a) constant tastes from one period to the

next, and (b) a common set of commodities. Indeed, the basic facts of
the problem do not seem to be seriously violated by proceeding, in
accordance with the technique of most analysts, to consider an individual representative of the income group, who is assumed to be enjoying a certain real-income level in the base period, say:

(1) $U_0 = U(q_{01}, q_{02}, \ldots, q_{0n})$

and a certain real-income level in the next period, say:

(2) $U_1 = U(q_{11}, q_{12}, \ldots, q_{1n})$

In these equations, the q's stand for the quantities of goods and
services consumed, the first subscript indicating the time period and
the second subscript indicating the commodity. The utility functions
in periods 0 and 1 are, of course, identical, because of the assumption
of constant tastes; but the particular levels of utility or preference
reached in the two periods, U_0 and U_1, may be different. Any differences in the two utility levels naturally would flow from the differences
in the q's, and these in turn would stem from two distinguishable
factors: (a) differences in relative prices between the two periods, and
(b) differences in money incomes.

Now in measuring price changes, if we use as weights the quantities
of period 0, we of course have the Laspeyres index, and if we use the
quantities of period 1, we have the Paasche index. It is true, as Afriat
remarks, and as I pointed out more than twenty years ago,[1] that these
two indexes do not provide the limits for the true index, or for anything else that is relevant. Indeed, strictly speaking, we may distinguish *two* true indexes. One would show the relative change in
costs from one period to the next needed to maintain the plane of
living actually enjoyed in period 0, and the other the corresponding
relative change in costs for maintaining the plane of living actually
experienced in period 1. In my own early study,[2] I showed how one
could estimate the probable difference between the Laspeyres and the
true index based on the given year's plane of living, and the difference

[1] Melville J. Ulmer, *The Economic Theory of Cost of Living Index Numbers*,
New York, Columbia University Press, 1949 (reprinted, New York, AMS Press,
1968), pp. 38–39.
[2] *Ibid.*, pp. 49–60.

between the Paasche index and the true index based on the other year's plane of living, that is, the differences:

(3) $$I_0 - I_L = d_0,$$

and

(4) $$I_1 - I_P = d_1,$$

where I_L is the Laspeyres index, I_P is the Paasche index, and I_0 and I_1 are the corresponding true index numbers.

The expected differences, d_0 and d_1, turned out to be very small, probably less than 1 per cent, and since the Laspeyres and Paasche indexes were themselves very close to each other in the extensive period covered by my experiment, we may conclude that the two true indexes, at least in year-to-year comparisons, were virtually identical.

Now the main reason for relating this ancient tale is to refresh your memory concerning the fact that comparisons of real income over time are, from a theoretical point of view at least, relatively straightforward. In deflation, we have excellent justification for using the Laspeyres index, or something like it. And if we had reason to believe that changes in living costs were significantly different for different income groups, a matter that worries Afriat, we could at some additional expense compute separate indexes for some of the different income classes, and weight them appropriately when deflating consumer expenditures or personal incomes.

On the other hand, country-to-country comparisons are of quite a different order, and in particular raise questions that lie distinctly outside the theoretical framework I have just described—a set of special and difficult questions, incidentally, that Afriat notably neglects in his paper. First of all, in the international setting, and unlike comparisons over time, we are comparing the prices faced by *different* sets of individuals. Second, the different sets of individuals ordinarily have demonstrably different tastes, and are conditioned by different customs and institutions, and nearly always, also, consume and produce significantly different sets of commodities.

One empirical symptom of these differences is the enormous disparity between the Laspeyres and Paasche indexes in intercountry comparisons. Even for a relatively homogeneous group of countries such as the Latin American nations, as Ruggles has shown, these differences are huge. Whereas Laspeyres and Paasche indexes, in temporal comparisons, remain within 1 per cent of one another, even when the base periods are as much as eighteen years apart,[3] and always show the same trend in prices, in one of the experiments conducted by Ruggles the differences in the geographic comparisons averaged about 50 per cent, were sometimes more than 100 per cent, and often showed entirely different price trends.[4] For example, using an Argentine basket of goods, Ruggles found that prices were 15 per cent higher in Brazil than they were in Argentina. Using a Brazilian basket of goods, he found that prices were 15 per cent lower in Brazil than in Argentina. And this, incidentally, was one of the more modest disparities disclosed by his study.

The fact is that in comparing prices or real incomes in two or more countries, we have no justification for using any of the simplifying assumptions that appear to be appropriate in temporal comparisons. We cannot refer to a common utility scale, or to a single, common utility function. We cannot properly assume a common set of commodities, since not only are many goods and services physically different among countries, but often similar physical characteristics mask important functional differences. For example, the bicycle is still an important means of transportation in Holland, while in the United States it is primarily a play toy or a sporting good.

Consequently, in practice, those who compare real incomes among countries ordinarily do so from the standpoint of production or productivity rather than of utility or welfare, which is the focal point of Afriat's analysis. It may in fact be hopeless to try to attach quantitative welfare implications to differences in per capita real consumption or per capita personal incomes among countries. If there is any hope for such efforts, I think it must clearly involve recognizing the distinctive problems involved, which in turn means breaking away from what I have termed the classic theoretical framework. Thus, confronting frankly the existence of different utility functions and different commodities would stimulate the search for some connecting link that

[3] *Ibid.*, p. 55.

[4] Richard Ruggles, "Price Indexes and International Price Comparisons," in *Ten Economic Studies in the Tradition of Irving Fisher*, New York, Wiley, 1967, p. 186.

could conceivably relate them. For example, we might try, deliberately, to formulate equivalent budgets in two or more countries for given, selected planes of living: in other words, market baskets that in the judgment of informed investigators are approximately equivalent in terms of welfare, given the different tastes, habits, and customs of the countries involved. Stated another way, a panel of intelligent observers, all of whom were well acquainted with two or more of the countries involved, would provide the link necessary for relating utility scales internationally; and in terms of this common international scale they would designate equivalent combinations of goods and services. Pricing these market baskets in the respective countries would make it possible to compare per capita consumption or real personal incomes in a way that would illuminate what we usually mean by "differences in levels of living."

For the whole GNP, including investment goods, government expenditures, and exports and imports, the approach just described would not apply at all. More theoretical work, I think, needs to be done on the possibility of attaching welfare implications to international GNP comparisons, and I do not see that Afriat's paper gets into this at all. Meanwhile, we are left with the alternative of relating aggregate productions among countries, using some international value standard for weighting the individual commodities or commodity groups, after the manner, perhaps, of the pioneering work of Gilbert and Kravis. But even in this more modest framework of comparing physical production, and never mind welfare, serious problems arise in international comparisons that far surpass in magnitude, complexity, and number those encountered in studies over time, as anyone who tried them knows.

For example, I think a good case can be made for viewing what are called technological external diseconomies as *negative* outputs. Over short periods of time, say in the United States, we have no significant fluctuations in these, and we perhaps lose very little, if anything, by neglecting them. But among countries, we often have great differences. Thus, by placing electric and telephone cables underground, Great Britain adds appreciably to the total net value actually produced by its electric power and telephone industries. By placing our cables above ground, we subtract—and this is the external diseconomy

—from our apparent net output. What may appear as a higher cost of a similar service in one country may actually represent more net service. Such problems along with the others discussed above, I think, represent the truly critical issues in index number theory as it relates to international comparisons. The fact that they received little or no attention in Afriat's paper raises a serious question about the usefulness of the framework he has adopted.

IRVING B. KRAVIS, University of Pennsylvania

The theories of interspatial and intertemporal price comparisons are, as Professor Afriat indicates, identical. All that the pure theory covers are comparisons of the money incomes required to make a single individual at a given point in time and space indifferent between two structures of relative prices.[1] The assumption that a given individual has constant tastes over time is an empirical one which is not strictly true (tastes for a given individual change during his life cycle) and certainly has no theoretical justification. Thus, if we rely on rigorous theory, we are not justified in talking about differences in cost-of-living levels either between two times or two places except from the standpoint of a single individual at one of the times or places. This means that we cannot compare welfare between either two times or two places without leaving the confines of the theoretical model.

There is nothing in this that makes it any less warranted, in principle, to inquire about the income that would be required to make John Jones indifferent between the Chinese price structure and the U.S. 1969 price structure with a $10,000 income than it is to ask how much Jones would need at the 1968 U.S. price structure to make him indifferent between that and his 1969 opportunities. The differences between intertemporal and international comparisons in practice lie not in that the one is covered by the pure theory while the other is

[1] See F. Fisher and K. Shell, "Taste and Quality Change in the Pure Theory of the True Cost-of-Living Index," in J. H. Wolfe, ed., *Value, Capital, and Growth; Papers in Honor of Sir John Hicks*, Edinburgh, Edinburgh University Press, 1968.

not but rather in the extent of the differences in the patterns of expenditure and in operational problems of price sampling.

What economic statisticians do in fact is to construct index numbers that measure differences in prices between two situations on the assumption that not only the tastes of each situation but the quantities of each good purchased would remain the same if the prices of the opposite situation prevailed.

Usually, though not always, the observed differences in price structure and in expenditure patterns will be larger for two situations separated in space than for two situations separated only in time. As a result, the expenditure required to purchase the basket of goods of either situation at the prices of the other will greatly exaggerate that which would be required to leave an individual in either one of the situations indifferent between the two price structures.

The other major difference arises out of sampling problems. It is, on the whole, easier to choose a sample of items for which to compare prices over time than between places. The reason is that the correlations between price movements over time for different products and product variants within one country are easier to identify than are the correlations between price differences between countries for different commodities and subcommodities.

REPLY by Afriat

The remarks of Diaz-Alejandro on essentials in my paper and also on an important absence are well taken. There are concepts and analytical techniques in it which are not close to the main interests of the conference and in any case cannot be treated briefly, so I must take up mostly the matter which is conspicuously absent, namely, the theory of production comparison. I will remark on some general questions about index numbers in responding to Ulmer's discussion.

In being asked to present a paper on comparison theory, there was a definite hint that I should attend to production. Unfortunately, I could think of nothing to say there that was essentially different from what might be said about consumption. Therefore, I took this to be an occasion for presenting a general position about index numbers, in the usual budget and utility framework.

In my approach to consumption analysis, which seems especially rewarding for index theory, there is analysis of a finite scheme of data by a finite method which does not involve special assumptions. This differs from the common method of associating the data with a special type of a function with parameters to be determined. The method applies just as well to production, especially joint production where production function technique is less workable. But this does not seem helpful for the production comparison question except possibly in the following fashion.

In an obvious sense, by turning everything around in my paper and making the appropriate verbal substitutions, the whole can be read as applying to production. All this depends on being able to entertain the concept of a capacity function, which determines the "capacity" necessary to produce a given output. This takes on the role of the utility function, upside down. The efficiency condition of minimum cost for utility gained becomes the condition of maximum profit for the capacity available. Everything goes parallel, only maxima and minima become minima and maxima and correspondingly all inequalities are reversed. The constructed ϕ's in my paper become capacity levels, and the reciprocals of the λ's multiplied by profits become marginal profitabilities of capacities. The approximation theory, which applies when the data reject the basic hypothesis and where exact efficiency is replaced by a certain level of efficiency, holds just as well with cost efficiency replaced by profit efficiency.

The outstanding question is whether or not the idea of a capacity function is acceptable. This is doubtful because productive capacity explicitly has many explicit dimensions which cannot be combined into one in a logical way. However, the question of productive capacity comparison seems to involve commitment to the idea that there is ultimately a single dimension which determines production possibilities. Therefore, if the question is to be pursued, it must be as if this were true. After hearing Mr. Usher's discussion of Mr. Bergson's paper, it seemed that this could be worth doing. My algebraical approach does in fact give a method for expressing several explicitly recognized capacities statistically as a single capacity. This is not presented in my paper and space cannot now be taken for it. The apparatus in my paper can be reinterpreted as for capacity comparison where no capacity variables are explicitly identified. The same dimension question inherently does not arise for utility. No doubt underneath utility there are many dimensions, but in the final act of valuation, as concerns choice under budgets, there is one that suffices.

Another question which could cause speculation is whether it is proper to think of the output of an economy as that which at the market prices gives maximum profit subject to the productive capacity limitation. This is especially true where there is decentralization. But some efficiency hypothesis must be made for an economic comparison, and this is clearly the only one which is available, in the particular framework of the question and the data. In an attempt to do something different, which I will come to later, welfare also is involved, and the efficiency hypothesis applies to welfare as limited by productive capacity. Market prices are less directly related to efficiency. Efficiency prices, which bear simultaneously on capacity and welfare, are defined in the hypothetical system, but are unknown. A further hypothesis is that market prices in the countries have only a tendency to be efficiency prices, and can be used, by taking their average, to estimate the efficiency prices. In other words, efficiency prices are taken to lie on the linear segment joining the market prices. This gives a method of capacity comparison in which the Paasche and Laspeyres indexes occur as limits, but in such a way that the puzzle about which should be greater or less, which presents itself in Usher's discussion, is entirely avoided.

Turning now to individual incomes rather than national ones, I note that Ulmer objected to an early remark in my paper, that the same elements are present in the question of real income comparison whether the reference be to different countries or different times.[1] Having in mind what I meant, which I believe is what is usually meant in this familiar observation, I still take it to be plainly true. This seems contrary to his suggestion that any resemblance it may have to the truth will tend to diminish rapidly, the more we think about it. It is likely therefore that what we are thinking about is

[1] The point of my remark was to suggest comparisons with a broader framework, where distinctions of time and place occur simultaneously.

different. Possibly it is that I am attending to the comparison question itself and he is attending to the further question of whether it is sensible to ask it. I have been unable to ask if he accepts this, in which case perhaps we could have some agreement, though I am unable to close either of our questions as firmly as he does.

To ask questions whether or not they are decidedly sensible is unavoidable, and is an old and no doubt worthy habit. I take it that the question of comparison of real incomes has some dilemmas about its significance, but my starting point has been that the question is in fact asked. I have taken a particular position about principles to be applied for answering it, given a specific scheme of data, and then been entirely concerned with the theory of computation which proceeds from that position. My limitation is that I have worked entirely within the framework of the question itself and the postulated scheme of the data. It could be that there is a different understanding of the question—possibly of greater relevance—which has been missed. It would be interesting to have a statement of it, preferably one which is entirely explicit. Such explicit statement calls for abstraction, and the only workable abstraction of which I am aware does not incorporate a distinction between comparisons which apply to different countries and different times.

Ulmer's remarks are stimulating as bringing basic questions into relief. My logical or methodological position must be different from his. Evidence of this is that, in my discussions, various formulas are derived in answer to formal questions which are posed about a scheme of data. Should two formulas, for different questions, turn out to be the same, they still have different theoretical contexts and correspondingly different meanings. The sometimes surprising experience that identical constructs appear in different contexts is common.

I have been unable to find any significance for the Paasche index outside the framework of the hypothesis that homogeneous utility prevails, together with efficiency. The data can reject that hypothesis, in other words fail in homogeneous consistency. The test turns out to be simply that the Paasche index not exceed the Laspeyres index. With that condition met, many homogeneous utility functions exist which are appropriate to the data under the efficiency hypothesis. To each corresponds a particular determination of the given cost index. The set of all such determinations describes an interval for which the Paasche formula determines the lower limit, and the Laspeyres formula the upper.

Should the homogeneity part of the hypothesis be dropped, a weaker test, for general consistency of the data, is appropriate. Then the range of determinations is wider, and the lower limit is given by a new formula, though the upper still by Laspeyres. In this more general context, the Paasche value ceases to be significant, and it need not even belong to the set of possible determinations. Here are propositions which are simple (though it is some work to prove them) and completely unambiguous. Whether or not they are useful for a particular application is another question entirely. That there is always the possibility of their routine application is undeniable. This is the same with linear regression analysis. It can always be done, whether or not it is worthwhile. I have in fact attempted to develop index number analysis as a form of routine statistical analysis, with various hypotheses concerning utility and efficiencies, and measures of significance, and a broader base for the data that can be used. Classical index formulas are recovered from more general formulas as corresponding to a case $k = 2$, and this general setting exposes their nature further. I believe that where index questions are asked, this kind of general method has scope for an answer, with the reservation that there is usually not one answer but a variety according to the hypothetical basis adopted.

This leads to a further question raised by Ulmer, one which rests on the manifest dissimilarities between countries and people. An answer, which is in my paper, is that in requesting an impartial general comparison, one is logically committed to viewing them statistically as basically similar, and to fashion a yardstick by ironing out their differences. It could be a yardstick of dubious value, but that reflects on the way the request is understood. I do agree with Ulmer that the intrinsic approach, that is, the approach based on demand data as reflecting utility, could be sterile where widely dissimilar countries are involved. More direct judgments from immediate experience have stronger bearing on the matter, as he suggests. Then statistical technique is needed for combining a variety of such judgments in a consistent way. This is what I have called extrinsic estimation, as distinct from direct utility and efficiency analysis of demand data, and my paper shows an effort in that direction. If there is a defense for the intrinsic method, it is that it is not involved in the hazard of direct judgments, but relies only on standard observations and the application to them of a statistical routine. With that it has a more scientific character. But its value for the intended use could be sacrificed in achieving this. No doubt it is better to be quite unscientific about an impossible question, and to be partly scientific about a question which is not altogether impossible—which is what the theory of extrinsic estimation attempts.

I must touch on one more item in Ulmer's discussion. He has not recognized the fault I found with the use of price indexes for establishing correspondence between equivalent individual real incomes. That fault cannot be mended by computing, as he suggests, different price indexes for different income classes. It could be mended by computing different marginal price indexes, together with one pair of correspondents in different income classes. If the income classes are arranged to correspond in real terms, as they would be in my method, then corresponding end points are such pairs of correspondents. My objection to conventional price indexes is that they have a theoretical meaning only in conjunction with the hypothesis that an individual will spend an increment of income on increments of goods in proportion to the totals he already has. That is, he will just move further along on the ray he is on. It is better to assume that the individual will move along a general straight line, not through the origin. This corresponds to the concept of a marginal index. If that is still not good enough, then the further scheme just described would be better. It allows for a shift in the direction of the line in making the transition from one real-income stratum to another, that is, piecewise linear approximation to expansion paths. It is clear, at least to me, that the concept of a marginal price index, which is a simple generalization of the concept which underlies the use of standard price indexes, is the proper practical instrument for establishing individual real-income comparisons, intertemporal or international, and by intrinsic or extrinsic estimation.

My general answer to Ulmer, or in agreement with him, is that the questions are not ended. Underneath index questions is a wider problem of developing statistical apparatus which can take better hold of that cardinal term of economic knowledge, the structure of wants. The classical approach is naive, but notice of its extraordinary persistence in economic thinking is hardly necessary to see it as basic. On its own, it corresponds to that stage of exercise in mechanics where there is nothing but point particles sliding on frictionless planes while held by light strings over inertialess pulleys, and so forth. Most likely it is necessary to have a thoroughly workable toy apparatus for such extravagant simplifications before there is the ground for supporting, and even operationally defining, further complexity. I have suffered the limitation of playing with that old toy, because I did not think it was working properly.

I have remarked on the absence of a treatment of production and productive capacity in my paper, and how something might have been done about it. Concerning welfare, if it is at all convincing, the story is identical, except that individuals become countries, consumption becomes production, and utility becomes welfare. However, following Bergson's paper and Usher's discussion of it, it occurred to me that something might be done which had a structure to it essentially different from that in pure consumption or pure production analysis. It is a theory of limits for the index of capacity comparison, where the upper limit is given by the maximum of the Paasche and Laspeyres indexes and the lower limit by the minimum. Thus, as is fortunate, it is inevitable that the formula for the upper limit is at least that for the lower; so they are consistent as upper and lower limits.

The basic efficiency hypothesis is welfare efficiency, or that production be such as to provide maximum welfare subject to capacity limitation. This, even with the homogeneity assumptions, is incapable of contradiction, given the data. This is in contrast to separate pure production or welfare analysis with prices having the usual efficiency role, expressing capacity-profit efficiency in one case and welfare-cost efficiency in the other. For the data to be consistent given the respective hypotheses, with the additional imposition of homogeneity, it is necessary that the Paasche be at least equal to the Laspeyres index in one hypothesis; and in the other, that it be at most equal. This comes from Usher's discussion. Thus usually one of the hypotheses of profit or cost efficiency must be rejected. There is an advantage in a theory of comparison which is not vulnerable to overthrow by rejection of its basic hypothesis, especially if the limits it provides are not worse than those from any other theory which holds up. This is the situation with welfare efficiency as against profit and cost efficiency. But to get the equivalent strength in regard to limits, the price data must enter, in the way already mentioned. Then finally, a theoretical interpretation of the equality of the Paasche and Laspeyres indexes can be shown. It appears as necessary and sufficient for the existence of universal homogeneous and convex technology and welfare in regard to which both countries can be presented with the three types of efficiency simultaneously, or more essentially, the two from which the third follows. The necessity is apparent again from Usher's discussion. All the hypotheses—about capacity, welfare, and various kinds of efficiencies—are of uncertain significance, and it is of no advantage to make any rigid commitments beyond those implicit in the comparison question itself. The best that can be attempted is a kind of analytical taxonomy, which gives a varied basis for interpretation of the data.

Bergson opened his paper with remarks, reaffirmed in subsequent discussion, which seemed a defense of his comparison work in the face of an unfriendly emphasis on exact concepts. It was argued that often many things have been done without a rigorous framework, but on intuitive grounds which might subsequently be proved sound. But perhaps just as well it might have been said that economics is rather different from other sciences, and the often ambiguous questions of economists are an original reality, and analysis had better give a tolerable account of them.

Uses of International
Price and Output Data

D. J. DALY

YORK UNIVERSITY

THIS paper was designed as a survey of some of the literature which has used quantitative data on international price and real income comparisons. Interest in this area grew out of a continuing study of the differences in real incomes, productivity, and the structure of relative prices between Canada and the United States. Some of the evidence on the Canada–United States differences and other recent empirical work on income differences for other countries was apparently very much at variance with the main assumptions of international trade theory. Some of the interpretations and evidence from the Canada–United States work appeared to be relevant for other countries as well.

Two sections will deal with the use of quantitative data on inter-country comparisons in estimating and testing some key propositions in economic growth and international trade. A number of valuable and comprehensive surveys in these areas had already been made during the 1960's, but this paper will introduce later evidence and incorporate new concepts in three areas: It will introduce the framework and evidence on real output per person employed, from some of the ten industrialized countries, that have been developed by E. F. Denison, Jean-Pierre Poullier, and Dorothy Walters. Secondly, the analysis and evidence from some of the work on effective tariff rates will be introduced to provide a rationale for some of the differences in production conditions in manufacturing between countries. Thirdly,

NOTE: This study has been improved by helpful comments on an earlier draft from E. F. Denison, H. G. Johnson, and Irving Kravis.

the recent theoretical formulations by Alchian and Hirshleifer on the role of length of run and total volume of production will be related to specialization in international trade. A number of these concepts and their empirical importance have been developed as part of the continuing study of the differences in real incomes, productivity, and the structure of relative prices between Canada and the United States, and some of these results to date will be drawn on.

INTERNATIONAL INCOME DIFFERENCES

One might have expected to find that the increased interest by economists in economic growth in the postwar period would provide a quantitative framework for studying income differences between countries. However, much of the work in the area of economic growth (with special emphasis on the supply side of the economy) has been formal and theoretical, rather than empirical. When it has been empirical, it has emphasized growth in a particular country, rather than making international comparisons of economic growth experience. The useful survey of economic growth by Hahn and Matthews excluded the quantitative aspects of economic growth and the relations between economic growth and international trade. They outline their scope as follows:

We restrict ourselves (except for occasional references) to the theoretical literature. . . . No discussion is presented of growth theory as applied to international trade. . . . The scope that has been chosen for the present survey reflects the increasingly formal character that has been manifested, for better or worse, in much of the literature in the period since Abramovitz's survey was written (1962).[1]

Colin Clark was an early pioneer in this area. Some of his ideas have had an important influence on subsequent work, such as his emphasis on the changing industrial composition of the labor force. He emphasized the long-term decline in agriculture and mining and the long-term increase in the importance of the service industries, and pointed out that similar differences appeared in the industrial structure of

[1] F. H. Hahn and R. C. O. Matthews, "The Theory of Economic Growth: A Survey," in *Surveys of Economic Theory*, New York, St. Martin's Press, 1965, Vol. II, pp. 1 and 2.

countries at various levels of economic development.[2] His comparisons of real national products in 1950 used information on relative prices for specific product groups, and the third edition incorporated the results of the first OEEC (Organization for European Economic Co-operation) study.[3] His work went on from the intercountry comparisons of levels to emphasize the role of industrial structure and changes in it. He also included international comparisons of capital-output ratios.

Simon Kuznets has also been productive in this, as in many other, areas of national income analysis. In a number of his studies of economic growth on a comparative basis he has included comparisons of international income differences. He has incorporated the results of the OEEC studies and the United Nations comparisons of calculated parity ratios.[4] The latter were based on the 1938 official exchange rates with some adjustments for subsequent price changes in the country concerned, relative to United States price changes. Other parts of his most comprehensive study also considered trends in industrial structure, distribution of product and income, international interdependence, and economic and social structure. One of the points he makes from the intercountry comparisons is the limited spread of modern economic growth.

One of the important contributions to the theory and estimation of economic growth was based on intercountry comparisons of value added in individual manufacturing industries.[5] Some of the assumptions made by Arrow, Chenery, Minhas, and Solow were that prices of product and material inputs do not vary systematically with the wage level, that overvaluation or undervaluation of exchange rates is not related to the wage level, and that the same technological alternatives are available to all countries.[6] The data for the intercountry compari-

---

[2] Colin Clark, *The Conditions of Economic Progress,* 3rd ed., London, Macmillan, 1957.

[3] *Ibid.,* pp. 18–74.

[4] Simon Kuznets, *Modern Economic Growth: Rate, Structure, and Spread,* New Haven, Yale University Press, 1966, pp. 359–399.

[5] K. J. Arrow et al. (H. B. Chenery, B. S. Minhas, and R. M. Solow), "Capital-Labor Substitution and Economic Efficiency," *Review of Economics and Statistics,* August 1961, pp. 225–250.

[6] *Ibid.,* pp. 227–228.

sons of value added by industry were made at official exchange rates or at free market rates where multiple exchange rates prevailed.[7] It should be noted that when careful comparisons of intercountry price levels are made, there are, typically, significant differences from the official exchange rates. There is also some evidence of a positive relationship between per capita real GNP and the difference between purchasing power and the official exchange rates.[8] Important though this study is in many respects, the quality of the underlying data on intercountry comparisons of real output by industry do not match the level of sophistication of the basic economic model on the substitution between labor and capital.

The most comprehensive study of economic growth using international comparisons of real income levels as a part of the analysis is the Brookings report, *Why Growth Rates Differ*.[9] In this study, the comparisons of levels of net national product in United States prices were used as an integral part of the investigation of changes since 1950 in net national product on both a total and per employed person basis. In studying the wide range of individual factors that contribute to economic growth, the report followed the method developed by Denison in his earlier volume on economic growth in the United States.[10] This distinguished between the contribution of the individual factor inputs (labor, capital, and land, with a number of breakdowns within each of those three basic factors), and output in relation to total factor inputs. More than twenty individual contributions to growth were estimated quantitatively for each country.

[7] *Ibid.*, p. 227.

[8] Bela Balassa, "The Purchasing-Power Parity Doctrine: A Reappraisal," *Journal of Political Economy*, 1964, pp. 584–596, Table 1 and Figure 1 and related text. It might be noted that Balassa emphasized the intercountry differences in prices and wages in the service industries, and the same relationship may not apply in manufacturing. This area was also discussed in the Grunwald-Salazar paper for this conference.

[9] Edward F. Denison, assisted by Jean-Pierre Poullier, *Why Growth Rates Differ—Postwar Experience in Nine Western Countries*, Washington, D.C., Brookings Institution, 1967. The same framework has been used for Canada–United States comparisons in Dorothy Walters, *Canadian Income Levels and Growth: An International Perspective*, Economic Council of Canada Staff Study No. 23, Ottawa, The Queen's Printer, 1968.

[10] Edward F. Denison, *The Sources of Economic Growth in the United States and the Alternatives Before Us*, New York, Committee for Economic Development, January 1962, Supplementary Paper No. 13.

In making the comparisons of net national product in real terms, Denison and Poullier updated the earlier pioneering OEEC studies for the nine countries covered.[11] In light of the marked changes in relative prices and relative quantities that emerged in the updating, the importance of more recent comprehensive studies of international comparisons of prices and purchasing power emerged.

It would take us away from the main theme of this paper to deal with the broader ramifications of this study.[12] In terms of the use of international comparisons of prices and real incomes as part of a broader study of economic growth over time, two parts of this study should be emphasized.

The first point to emphasize is that the role differences in the environment of the individual countries in 1950 are a significant factor in explaining subsequent differences in growth rates. For example, the individual European countries initially had levels of net national product per employed person well below the United States (whether measured in U.S. or European relative prices). The data and discussion of the individual sources of growth permit the key factors in postwar growth in the various countries to be identified. At the end of the 1940's, the individual European countries still had significant proportions of their labor force in the lower income sectors of agriculture and nonagricultural self-employment, and there was much more scope for growth from this source than in the United States, where this shift had already gone much further. Furthermore, the individual European countries had much lower levels of capital stock (including nonresidential construction, machinery and equipment, and inventories) than the United States, and a special adjustment was made for Germany, which still had an unbalanced capital stock in 1950. The structure of relative prices in Europe was also significantly different from that in the United States. Prices of machinery and equipment and consumer

[11] Milton Gilbert and Irving B. Kravis, *An International Comparison of National Products and the Purchasing Power of Currencies*, Paris, OEEC, 1954, and Milton Gilbert and Associates, *Comparative National Products and Price Levels: A Study of Western Europe and the United States*, Paris, OEEC, 1958.

[12] For fuller appraisals, see D. J. Daly, *"Why Growth Rates Differ*—A Summary and Appraisal," *International Review of Income and Wealth*, March, 1968, pp. 75–93; R. C. O. Matthews, "Why Growth Rates Differ," *Economic Journal*, June 1969, pp. 262–268; John Cornwall, "Postwar Growth in Western Europe: A Reevaluation," *Review of Economics and Statistics*, August 1968, pp. 361–368.

durables were relatively more expensive in the European countries than in the United States, and, with the rapid growth in the individual European countries, "income elasticities" provided an important source of the higher European growth. From 1950 to 1962, this contributed 0.46 to the growth rate for northwest Europe as a whole. The use of comparisons between the countries at a point in time was essential in identifying these special factors in growth from 1950 to 1962.

The second point to emphasize was that the comparisons between countries at a point in time were used as a basis for appraising some key elements in future growth prospects for the various countries. In summarizing the implications of the study, Denison stated

Comparisons with the post-war growth rates of European countries . . . do not provide grounds for dissatisfaction with the American growth record. The point needs stressing because the conditions that enabled Europe to obtain higher growth rates are not exhausted. Aside from short-term aberrations Europe should be able to report higher growth rates, at least in national income per person employed, for a long time. Americans should expect this and not be disturbed by it. Nothing in this analysis suggests that the conditions making for higher European growth would continue to operate if the European countries were to reach American levels of national income per person employed. . . . Any projection of future European growth must be critically affected by the investigator's judgment as to whether this productivity gap will be reduced in the future and, if so, how much and how fast.[13]

Denison provides information on the relative role of a variety of factors that account for differences in the level of net national product per person employed at a point in time and, also, data on changes over time in these factors. This information would be helpful in appraising medium-term growth prospects for the countries concerned.

More recently intercountry comparisons of level have been made as part of a study of growth over time, with emphasis on Japan and Soviet Russia.[14] This study puts rather more emphasis on differences in level than does Maddison's earlier investigation of comparative experience in Europe and North America. In that one, some of the

[13] *Why Growth Rates Differ*, pp. 340 and 344.
[14] Angus Maddison, *Economic Growth in Japan and the USSR*, London, Allen and Unwin, 1969.

main conclusions from the OEEC studies were summarized in about three pages,[15] but they were not knit into other parts of the book in any major way.

In summary, a number of studies of comparative growth have used intercountry comparisons of real output per capita or per person employed. This provides perspective on a much wider range of stages of economic development than would be obtained from the history of a single country. But such intercountry comparisons raise a wider range of issues concerning data, comparability of tastes, social and economic organization, and the extent to which theory can point up the key questions involved.[16] Some of these same issues are applicable to international trade theory.

TESTING INTERNATIONAL TRADE THEORY

The availability of data on the differences in real income and relative prices between a number of industrialized and developing countries permits some testing of the main competing and complementary theories of international trade. This section will concentrate on the "real" factors in international trade, such as differences in production conditions and factor quantities–factor prices on the interrelations between domestic production and the extent and composition of international trade.

It is clear that this is a large task. The amount of literature on the real and positive aspects of international trade has been tremendous, but the current state of this area of international trade theory has been well surveyed in the past.[17] However, much of the literature is theo-

[15] Angus Maddison, *Economic Growth in the West,* New York, Twentieth Century Fund, 1964, pp. 39–42.

[16] Irving Kravis, "The Scope of Economic Activity in International Income Comparisons," and Comments and Reply, in *Problems in the International Comparison of Economic Accounts,* Studies in Income and Wealth, Vol. 20, New York, National Bureau of Economic Research, 1957, pp. 349–400.

[17] The main surveys are Jacob Viner, *Studies in the Theory of International Trade,* New York, Harper & Row, 1937; Richard E. Caves, *Trade and Economic Structure: Models and Methods,* Cambridge, Harvard University Press, 1960; Gottfried Haberler, *A Survey of International Trade Theory,* Special Papers in International Economics No. 1, International Finance Section, Department of Economics, Princeton University, 1961; Jagdish Bhagwati, "Some Recent Trends in the Pure Theory of International Trade" in Roy Harrod and Douglas Hague, eds., *International Trade Theory in a Developing World,* London, Macmillan, 1963; Jagdish

retical in that it develops conclusions based on the logical development of certain explicitly stated assumptions. The extent of testing of
these conclusions against the real world has been much more limited,
however, and the implications of the available data for the theoretical
models have not always been made explicit. This section of the paper
will review the evidence on the two main theoretical views of the basis
of trade, namely, (1) the Ricardian emphasis on differing production
conditions in different countries; (2) the Heckscher-Ohlin-Samuelson
emphasis on differences in factor supplies and factor prices.

Linder's emphasis on demand conditions will be considered in the
next section, on Canada–United States comparisons. The groundwork
for these comparisons will be laid by supplementing and modifying the
two surveys of this area in the 1960's by Caves and Bhagwati [18] by
emphasizing the relative importance of labor costs in value added by
industry, by giving more attention to the data problems, and by incorporating results from some studies done since their surveys were
completed.

Differences in the Structure of Relative Prices

Almost all the pure theories of international trade emphasize that
trade takes place between countries because, in the absence of trade,
differences exist in relative prices between the countries concerned.
Trade tends to equalize prices of commodities, although the presence
of tariffs and transport costs can limit this. The major differences
among trade theorists emerge from differing emphases on the *reasons*
for the differences in relative prices. Before turning to the empirical
reasonableness of the several approaches to trade theory, some refer-

Bhagwati, "The Pure Theory of International Trade: A Survey," in *Surveys of
Economic Theory*, Vol. II; W. M. Corden, *Recent Developments in the Theory of
International Trade*, Special Papers in International Economics, No. 7, International
Finance Section, Department of Economics, Princeton University, 1965; and J. S.
Chipman, "A Survey of the Theory of International Trade," three parts in *Econo-
metrica*, 1965 and 1966.

Very useful volumes of readings containing a number of the major articles include
Howard S. Ellis and Lloyd A. Metzler, eds., *Readings in the Theory of International
Trade*, Homewood, Ill., Irwin, 1950; Richard E. Caves and H. G. Johnson, eds.,
Readings in International Economics, Homewood, Ill., Irwin, 1968; and Jagdish
Bhagwati, ed., *International Trade, Selected Readings*, Baltimore, Md., Penguin
Books, 1969.

[18] Caves, *Trade*, Chap. X, pp. 268–282, and Bhagwati, "Pure Theory," pp. 159–184.

ences to the evidence on the existence of differences in relative prices will be given.

Among developed countries, the most comprehensive surveys of statistical data on this point are still the two OEEC studies.[19] The first was based on a study of the United States, the United Kingdom, France, Germany, and Italy, primarily for 1950, but with occasional data for 1952 as well. The second study added four additional European countries (Norway, Denmark, Belgium, and the Netherlands) and provided 1955 estimates for the most important aggregates. The primary purpose of these studies was to prepare comparisons of national products and the major expenditure components in "real" terms. As part of the underlying methodology, data were prepared for the individual countries on both the prices and quantities of the individual items, and the data on prices were used as weights to prepare the more aggregative quantity comparisons.

In the first study some attention was given to the differences in relative prices in order to show their influence on the weighted aggregative quantities of the various products used. The product groups were subdivided into slightly more than fifty product classes, and there were significant differences in the purchasing power equivalents between the various pairs of countries. The differences in relative prices between the United States and the individual European countries were ranked from high to low, and grouped into approximate thirds. No allowance for differences in the quantitative importance of the items was made. These differences are shown in Table 1, together with the ratios of the highest to the lowest price relatives for the four individual European countries. It is apparent that the differences in the range of relative prices are very great. The highest price relative between Italy and the United States was about 20 times the lowest, while for the three other countries this ranged between 7 and 10 times! Some of these differences reflect the large relative price differences for services, as developed in the Comment by Balassa. The differences in price ratios for commodities

[19] Gilbert and Kravis, *An International Comparison;* and Gilbert and Associates, *Comparative National Products.* For references and discussion of later international price comparisons, see Wilfred Beckerman, *International Comparisons of Real Incomes,* Development Centre of the Organization for Economic Cooperation and Development, Paris, 1966.

TABLE 1

Selected Market Price Ratios, United States and
Four European Countries, 1950

	U.S.-U.K. (pounds to dollar)	U.S.-France (francs to dollar)	U.S.-Germany (DM to dollar)	U.S.-Italy (lire to dollar)
High	>0.270	>360	>4.20	>670
Low	<0.175	<210	<2.50	<330
Ratio of group boundaries	1.57	1.71	1.68	2.09
Ratio of highest to lowest price ratio	8	7	10	20

SOURCE: Milton Gilbert and Irving B. Kravis, *An International Comparison of National Products and the Purchasing Power of Currencies,* Paris, OEEC, 1954, Tables 21–24 and Figures 2–5 (pp. 53–56 and 58–59).

are less pronounced. Marked differences in the relative 1950 market prices of broad consumption categories also appear among the eight European countries.[20]

It is these differences in relative prices between countries at a point in time that contribute to the size of the quantitative differences in real incomes, depending upon which country's prices are used as weights. This raises the whole index number problem, which is quantitatively much more important in comparisons between countries than between different points of time within a particular country. The magnitude of the effect of these differences in relative price weights on real GNP per capita is shown in Table 2. Large differences associated with differences in weights appear quite generally in such international comparisons of real product where incomes differ, and this reappeared in the Bergson paper and the Grunwald-Salazar paper at this conference and was also raised by a number of discussants.

It should be noted that trade from the relatively low-cost supplier to other countries will occur only if the difference in the prices between the lower-cost country and the higher-cost country are equal to, or greater than, the costs of transportation and tariffs between the respec-

[20] Gilbert and Associates, *Comparative National Products,* Table 20, p. 62.

TABLE 2

Per Capita Gross National Product of the United States
and Eight European Countries Combined, 1955

United States	$2,310
Total of eight European countries	
(a) U.S. relative price weights	1,237
(b) European relative price weights	953
(c) Geometric average of (a) and (b)	1,086

SOURCE: Milton Gilbert and Associates, *Comparative National Products and Price Levels:
A Study of Western Europe and the United States,* Paris, OEEC, 1958, Table 1, p. 21.

tive countries, at prevailing rates of exchange between the countries.
Since the end of the Second World War, there has been a marked
reduction and elimination of quantitative controls, and the series of
general tariff reductions and the achievement of complete free trade
in industrial products within the Common Market and EFTA (European Free Trade Association) groups of countries have sharply reduced
the importance of tariffs and other restrictions on trade.[21] With the
increased freedom of trade and the narrowing in income differences,
one would expect to see a reduction in the extent of differences in relative prices since the OEEC studies of the early 1950's. It would be interesting to see this hypothesis tested in any renewed surveys of relative
prices and quantities for any of the countries studied before.

Labor Costs in Total Costs

Before one turns to the data on individual industries, some perspective on the importance of labor as a factor of production and an
element in total cost can be obtained by looking at labor's share of
national income. Different concepts can be used, but the material from
Why Growth Rates Differ can illustrate this for the main industrial
countries. From Table 3, it can be seen that labor income is almost
80 per cent of net national income in the United States, Canada, and

[21] For discussion of the continued importance of nontariff barriers to trade, see
Gordon Ohlin, "Trade in a Non-Laissez-Faire World," paper presented to the International Economic Association in Montreal, September 1968; and R. Y. Grey,
"Some Problems of Canadian Trade in a Non-Laissez-Faire World," paper presented to the Canadian Economics Association, June 1969.

TABLE 3

Distribution of Net National Income, 1960–62

(average of annual percentage)

	United States [a]	Canada	Northwest Europe [a]
Net national income	100.0	100.0	100.0
Labor income	79.9	78.1	76.5
Dwellings	4.2	4.8	2.4
Property income from abroad	0.7	−2.0	0.4
Other property income	15.2	19.1	20.7
Nonresidential land	2.5	2.9	3.5
Nonresidential structures and equipment	10.2	12.8	13.4
Inventories	2.5	3.4	3.8

[a] See Edward F. Denison, assisted by Jean-Pierre Poullier, *Why Growth Rates Differ — Postwar Experience in Nine Western Countries*, Washington, D.C., Brookings Institution, 1967, Table 4-1, p. 38; and Dorothy Walters, *Canadian Income Levels and Growth: An International Perspective*, Economic Council of Canada Staff Study No. 23, Ottawa, The Queen's Printer, 1968, p. 29.

northwest Europe.[22] A labor share this high can occur only if high proportions for labor income characterize a majority of the individual industries. Under these circumstances, an initial emphasis on wage and productivity differences in different countries, by industry, seems justified.

Ricardian Analysis

In terms of the initial theoretical formulation as a "logically true" proposition, this formulation dealt with two commodities and two countries, a single input (labor), and constant returns to scale. Differences in the relative labor productivities of different activities in the two countries then played a key role in the pattern of trade between the two countries.

[22] Two things about the concepts used by Denison should be noted. The distribution relates to *net* national income, after excluding an allowance for capital consumption at current replacement costs. The estimates also make an imputation for the distribution of income between labor and capital in the agricultural and other individual-enterprise sectors.

In moving from this simple and logically true analysis to an empirically refutable proposition, several additional hypotheses have been introduced explicitly or implicitly in the tests that could be or have been made. The basis of trade will eventually be in differences in relative prices of goods and services in the countries being studied. If labor costs are a large part of value added in the various industries, differences in relative wage rates or differences in relative labor productivities could play a role in the structure of trade. In testing the Ricardian tradition with contemporary data, it is clear that real problems are encountered even when data on real output per employed person are available by industry. Although this is the central thesis of the classical tradition, most economists would recognize the need to check the relative importance of the cost of other factors of production and their relative rates of return, and the relationship between total costs and export prices.

In the light of the relative importance of labor cost in net national income (or net value added), some further discussion of the role of differences in wage rates and differences in output in relation to labor inputs is desirable. However, the data on both these key areas are very limited, especially data on output per person employed in the *same* industry in different countries.

Data are available, however, for the United States and the United Kingdom by drawing on two pioneering studies of intercountry comparisons of productivity by industry.[23] Some data from these studies,

---

[23] L. Rostas, *Comparative Productivity in British and American Industry,* National Institute of Economic and Social Research, Occasional Papers, No. 13, Cambridge, England, 1948; and Deborah Paige and Gottfried Bombach, *A Comparison of National Output and Productivity in the United Kingdom and the United States,* Paris, OEEC, 1959. There was one important difference in the methods used in the two studies to estimate real output and productivity by industry. Rostas used measures of real output for key commodities (quantities of bricks, cement, rubber, tires, tobacco, coke, etc.) with no allowance for differences in intermediate inputs used. Paige and Bombach tried to obtain measures of value added by industry, which took account of differences in the quantities and prices of intermediate inputs and outputs by industry. Thus, they adopted the Geary method of estimating changes over time in the real value of output by industry and applied it to intercountry comparisons.

This difference in statistical procedure in estimating output by industry is analogous to the discussion of nominal and effective tariff rates by industry. The discussion of effective tariff rates in relation to productivity differences by industry will be discussed later in the context of Canada–United States comparisons.

Theory and Uses

TABLE 4

United States–United Kingdom Ratios of Output per Worker
and Wages, Selected Manufacturing Industries,
1937 and 1950

	United States–United Kingdom Ratios					
	Output per Worker		Average Wages		Wages per Unit of Output	
Industry	1937	1950	1937	1950	1937	1950
Pig iron	3.6	4.1	1.5	3.0	0.42	0.73
Motorcars	3.1	4.7	2.0	3.4	0.64	0.72
Machinery	2.7	2.4	1.9	3.6	0.70	1.50
Glass containers	2.4	2.7	2.0	3.2	0.83	1.18
Paper	2.2	3.4	2.0	3.6	0.91	1.06
Cigarettes	1.7	2.5	1.5	2.6	0.88	1.04
Leather footwear	1.4	1.7	1.5	2.9	1.07	1.71
Hosiery	1.8	1.9	1.9	3.3	1.06	1.74
Cotton spinning and weaving	1.5	2.5	1.7	3.3	1.13	1.32
Beer	2.0	3.0	2.6	4.0	1.30	1.33
Cement	1.1	1.2	1.7	2.7	1.54	2.25
Woolen and worsted	1.35	1.85	2.0	3.6	1.48	1.95
Men's and boys' outer clothing	1.25	1.7	2.3	3.6	1.84	2.12

SOURCE: Robert M. Stern, "British and American Productivity and Comparative Costs in International Trade," *Oxford Economic Papers*, October 1962, p. 284. The original data are from the Rostas and Paige-Bombach studies referred to in footnote 23.

on the relative levels of output per worker, average wages, and wages per unit of output by industry in the two countries, are shown in Table 4.

An important point illustrated in Table 4 is the very large differences from industry to industry in the output per worker ratios in the two countries in both 1937 and 1950. There are differences also in the ratios of wages by industry, but these are much smaller.[24]

[24] The correlation between relative wages and the relative output per worker by industry in the two countries is not significant. For 1937, the regression is negative, with a value of 0.15 but a standard error of 0.71. For 1950 it has a positive slope of 0.50, but a standard error of 0.73. In each case r^2 is close to zero.

In one of the other studies of intercountry differences in output per worker, this wide variation in productivity by industry was clearly apparent. Table 5 shows this for twelve industries for Canada, the United States, and the United Kingdom for 1935. The United States–Canada ratios range from 84 (for flour milling) to 260 (for coke), while the United Kingdom–Canada ratios range between 37 (biscuits) and 133 (coke). These contrasts are very large. Comparable data on relative wages have not been brought together for that period, but the differences would not be nearly as large as this.

The suggestion from the United States–United Kingdom data that some differences in relative wage rates for individual manufacturing industries exist for different countries is also reflected in a number of other studies, but these wage differences are not too large. Kravis com-

TABLE 5

Output per Wage-Earner Year, 1935

(Canada 1935 = 100)

	Canada	U.K.	U.S.
Soap	100	46	123
Leather footwear			
U.K. price weights	100	73	109
U.S. price weights	100	75	106
Canadian price weights	100	73	112
Rubber tires	100	82	154
Tobacco	100	90	132
Cement	100	123	100
Brewing	100	97	195
Biscuits	100	37	140
Flour milling	100	58	84
Bricks	100	108	130
Vegetable oils	100	90	189
Hosiery			
U.K. price weights	100	102	120
U.S. price weights	100	110	134
Canadian price weights	100	102	118
Coke	100	133	260

SOURCE: A. Maddison, "Productivity in Canada, the United Kingdom, and the United States," *Oxford Economic Papers* (New Series), October 1952, p. 237.

pared the ranking of average hourly earnings in twenty major manufacturing industries in Japan and the United States and found a coefficient of rank correlation of 0.82, which was significant at the 1 per cent level.[25] He suggests the probability that "for most industries, international differences in productivity are greater than international differences in wages." [26] Hal Lary brought together data on the average annual wage in thirteen industry groups for eleven countries. The ranking of industries from low to high wages was very similar in the seven developed countries (the United States, Canada, Sweden, Australia, the United Kingdom, Germany, and France). Among four developing countries (Mexico, Japan, Brazil and India) the ranking was somewhat less consistent.[27] Greater variation in the productivity ratios than in the rates of wages were also found in Canada–U.K. and Canada–U.S. data analyzed by Kreinin.[28]

The evidence thus far suggests that labor costs are a very significant share of net national income and that large differences in the relative levels of output per person employed in various industries in different countries exist. These output differences are much greater than the differences in earnings. Two further questions have been raised in earlier literature. One question is whether these differences in output per person employed are reflected in export prices and international trade; this literature will be reviewed here. The second question concerns the reasons for these differences in relative productivity levels; this question will be explored further in the next section on Canada–United States comparisons.

The major contribution in testing the Ricardian view on the differences in costs between countries was by G. D. A. MacDougall, using United States and United Kingdom data.[29] When relative output per worker was compared to relative exports, a high correlation coefficient

[25] Irving B. Kravis, " 'Availability' and Other Influences on the Commodity Composition of Trade," *Journal of Political Economy,* April 1956, p. 144.

[26] *Ibid.,* p. 145.

[27] Hal B. Lary, *Imports of Manufactures from Less Developed Countries,* New York, NBER, 1968, p. 68. He does not deal with the magnitudes of the differentials.

[28] Mordechai E. Kreinin, "The Theory of Comparative Cost—Further Empirical Evidence," *Economia Internazionale,* November 1969, pp. 2–14.

[29] G. D. A. MacDougall, "British and American Exports: A Study Suggested by the Theory of Comparative Costs," *Economic Journal,* December 1951, pp. 697–724, and September 1952, pp. 487–521.

was obtained and "a difference of 1% in relative price tends to be associated with a difference of 4–5% in relative quantity of exports." [30] This two-part article concentrated on the data for the interwar period.

Subsequently, this topic was re-examined for the same two countries for the postwar period. The earlier conclusions were largely reaffirmed, with some indications of some differential changes in output per person employed by industry over time between the two countries, and some allowance for changes in tariffs between the two countries. [31]

Most later studies have accepted the main implications of these studies on the empirical relevance and usefulness of the Ricardian emphasis on differences in relative productivity levels by industry, although some serious data problems are present. For example, it is difficult to match the employment data with the output data in volume terms. Thus, the 1937 data are not adjusted for purchases from other industries or employment in the supplying industries. The 1950 employment data again relate only to the specific industry, but in practice intermediate inputs are not always deducted.

Bhagwati raises a number of problems about these studies in his survey. He tested the relationship between labor productivity ratios and export price ratios and between unit labor cost ratios and export price ratios. In all cases the signs of the relationship were consistent with the Ricardian expectations, but the degrees of relationship were uniformly low (as measured by the r^2's) except for the arithmetic MacDougall sample for 1937. [32]

I would like to put forth an hypothesis in explanation of this result (as it seems to have been an important influence on Bhagwati's rather negative appraisal of the testing of the Ricardian theory). Rostas' 1937 data on productivity levels in the two countries were largely built up on actual physical measures of output in the individual industries, with no allowance for the use of purchased materials by those industries. This is conceptually a measure of the gross output of an industry

[30] *Ibid.*, December 1951, p. 712.

[31] Robert M. Stern, "British and American Productivity and Comparative Costs in International Trade," *Oxford Economic Papers*, October 1962, pp. 275–296; Donald MacDougall, Monica Dowley, Pauline Fox, and Senta Pugh, "British and American Productivity, Prices and Exports: An Addendum," *Oxford Economic Papers*, October 1962, pp. 297–304.

[32] Bhagwati, "Pure Theory," pp. 170–171.

measured in real terms. However, the 1950 data from Paige and Bombach tried to take account of the purchases of intermediate products
from other industries. This is conceptually a measure of the net value
added in an industry in real terms, and is equivalent to the use of the
Geary double deflation approach (designed to measure changes in real
output of individual industries over time) for intercountry comparisons. Because of the problems they encountered with this approach,
they sometimes ended up using output measures with no allowance for
differences in inputs from other industries.

The export price ratios used in all the studies are unit values (based
on trade statistics) of individual commodities. These are conceptually
closer to the measures of gross output (such as were developed by
Rostas for 1937) than to the measures of net value added (which were
derived by Paige and Bombach for 1950). If this interpretation is on
the right track, the close correlation between export price ratios and
labor productivity ratios for 1937 and the absence of a significant correlation in 1950 are not surprising. One would get a close correlation
between prices and *net* value added only if the commodity and industry definitions were the same *and* the relationships between output
and material purchases from other industries were the same between
the two countries. I would be very surprised if these conditions were
met.

There is indirect evidence *against* the assumption of similar relationships between value added and intermediate products by industry. The
recent discussion of tariffs and commercial policy has been enriched
by the literature on effective tariff rates, which is based on the importance of intermediate inputs as a factor in costs and differences in the
levels of tariff rates at various stages of processing. The theoretical
literature and empirical evidence suggest significant dispersions for
individual countries between nominal and effective rates for individual
industries.[33] A necessary (but not a sufficient) condition for a close

[33] W. M. Corden, "The Structure of a Tariff System and the Effective Protective
Rate," *Journal of Political Economy*, June 1966; Georgio Basevi, "The U.S. Tariff
Structure: Estimates of Effective Rates of Protection of U.S. Industries and Industrial
Labor," *Review of Economics and Statistics*, May 1966; Bela Balassa, "Tariff Pro-
tection in Industrial Countries: An Evaluation," *Journal of Political Economy*,
December 1965; and James R. Melvin and Bruce W. Wilkinson, *Effective Protection
in the Canadian Economy*, Economic Council of Canada, Special Study No. 9,
Ottawa, The Queen's Printer, 1968, and additional references cited therein. Denison

relationship between relative export prices and relative labor productivities on a net value added basis would be a close relationship between nominal and effective tariff rates. The evidence for a number of countries suggests that such a close relationship does not exist.

The preceding discussion of the productivity ratios for the United States and United Kingdom has concentrated on the numerator in the data. Problems are also encountered in the employment data by industry. In both the 1937 and 1950 comparisons the employment data relate to direct employment in the industry specified. The data are conceptually consistent with the measures of net output used in 1950, but not with the measures of gross output used for 1937, as they do not include employment in the material-supplying industries. The problems in obtaining measures of both output and employment that are conceptually comparable are thus very real.

This argument suggests that the absence of correlation between export price ratios and labor productivity ratios, which Bhagwati found, can reflect conceptual and statistical lack of comparability in the data rather than strong evidence against the Ricardian hypothesis. The other concern of Bhagwati, about the need for an explanation of the difference in the productivity ratios, will be considered in the discussion of the Canada–United States data.

Heckscher-Ohlin Analysis

Work along the Heckscher-Ohlin lines accepts the differing structure of relative prices in different countries, but emphasizes differing influences as underlying causal factors. Two key assumptions are the existence of similar production conditions in the several countries, and constant returns to scale. The differing relative use of the various factors of production in different industries, and differing relative supplies of factors in the various countries are regarded as crucial in explaining the differing structure of relative prices. International specialization would then emerge as a result of specialization by each of the various countries in those industries that involved more intensive

has pointed out that if the pattern of effective tariff rate structures were similar for the same industries in different countries, this would not be a sufficient condition for productivity differences between countries. The evidence on this point has not yet been explored.

use of the factors that were relatively more abundant (and thereby relatively less expensive) in that country.

The origin of this development in theory goes back to a Swedish essay by Heckscher in 1919 and Ohlin's book in 1935.[34] In subsequent development it was applied to the effects of tariffs on income distribution, factor price equalization, terms of trade, and many other topics.[35] Corden comments that "the dominating development in pure theory during the period under consideration has been the elaboration and filling-out of the Heckscher-Ohlin trade model."[36] However, much of this literature has been devoted to the development of a wide range of conclusions and implications from a number of initial assumptions. The degree of empirical testing of the main conclusions and the real-world relevance of these ideas have been much more limited.

It seems important to point out that both Samuelson and Ohlin have been acutely aware of the problems in applying the results of this framework of theory to the real world. Samuelson discussed this in his 1948 paper on factor price equalization.

There remains a third, and perhaps more fundamental, reason why factor prices need not be equalized: the Ohlin proportions-of-the-factors analysis of international trade has fundamental inadequacies and limitations.

The Ohlin analysis explains much; but there is much that it fails to explain; and if adhered to inflexibly, there is much that it can obscure. Its two central tenets are open to grave doubt: Is it reasonable and useful to set up the hypothesis that production functions are the same the world over? Is it possible to find reasonably homogeneous and commensurable factors of production in diverse parts of the world, so that relative proportions can be defined and compared?

Certainly no strong affirmative answers to these two questions can be given— as Ohlin himself has pointed out in a number of places. . . .

Space does not permit further elaboration on this important topic. We may conclude by saying that factor proportions explain only part of the facts of international economics. We must still set up hypotheses of differences in

---

[34] Eli Heckscher, "The Effect of Foreign Trade on the Distribution of Income," *Ekonomisk Tidskrift*, 1919, translated and printed in Ellis and Metzler, eds., *Readings*, pp. 272–300; and Bertil Ohlin, *Interregional and International Trade*, rev. ed., Cambridge, Mass., Harvard University Press, 1967.

[35] Fuller and fairly recent discussion is contained in the discussions by Caves, Haberler, Corden, Bhagwati, and Chipman referred to earlier.

[36] Corden, *Recent Developments*, p. 24.

international production and productivity, differences in effectiveness which are to be accepted as empirical facts even if not simply explainable.[37]

In the second edition of *Interregional and International Trade,* Ohlin expressed concern at the degree to which some elements of his initial work had been pushed by subsequent discussion. In Appendix II, "Reflections on Contemporary International Trade Theories," he discussed the factor proportions model and showed "the need for its extension to include the advantages of large-scale operations and different production functions." [38]

An understanding of this [i.e., using instead a model that permits different production functions in different countries] would constitute some protection against exaggerating the importance of the model in question. . . . It is because of these conditions and the importance of taxes, social costs, transport costs, etc., that I have found the intensive preoccupation with the factor proportions model after World War II—which started with Paul Samuelson's penetrating article "International Trade and the Equalization of Factor Prices" (*Economic Journal,* 1948)—to have a gradually declining "marginal utility" compared to the results that could be obtained with the same acumen, intelligence, and work if it were directed, e.g., toward a study of transportation costs and taxation in their relation to international trade.[39]

The number of efforts to test the empirical applicability of the Heckscher-Ohlin model has been much more limited than the number of theoretical studies. Several important empirical investigations have created considerable discussion. The remarks here will concentrate on comments made that are pertinent to the assumption that production functions in different countries are similar.

In a famous study, Leontief used the material from his input-output work on the American economy to study the capital and labor requirements in exports and imports. To explain the paradoxical results he obtained, he abandoned the assumption of similar production functions in different countries.

Let us, however, reject the simple but tenuous postulate of comparative technological parity and make the plausible alternative assumption that in

[37] P. A. Samuelson, "International Trade and Equalization of Factor Prices," *Economic Journal,* June 1948, pp. 181–183, reprinted in J. E. Stiglitz, ed., *The Collected Scientific Papers of P. A. Samuelson,* Cambridge, Mass., MIT Press, 1966, Vol. II, pp. 865–867.

[38] Ohlin, *Interregional and International Trade,* p. 311.

[39] *Ibid.,* p. 310. See also his comments on the papers by Bhagwati and Harry Johnson in Harrod and Hague, eds., *International Trade Theory,* pp. 398 and 420.

any combination with a given quantity of capital, one man-year of American labor is equivalent to, say, three man-years of foreign labor. . . .

Thus, without denying that capital can be substituted for labor, we must still look for some other reason in explaining the high productivity of labor in America as compared with the labor employed by similar industries abroad. Entrepreneurship and superior organization have often been mentioned in this connection. . . . To explain the comparative surplus of labor which our figures unmistakably reveal we must, however, also infer that entrepreneurship, superior organization, and favorable environment must have increased —in comparison with other countries—the productivity of American labor much more than they have raised the efficiency of American capital.[40]

In the article in which Arrow, Chenery, Minhas, and Solow introduced the constant elasticity of substitution production function, their data raised questions about the similarity of production conditions in different countries. In their conclusion they stated:

Although we began our empirical work on the naive hypothesis that observations within a given industry but for different countries at about the same time can be taken as coming from a common production function, we find subsequently that this hypothesis cannot be maintained. But we get reasonably good results when we replace it by the weaker, but still meaningful, assumption that international differences in efficiency are approximately neutral in their incidence on capital and labor. A closer analysis of international differences in efficiency leads us to suggest that this factor may have much to do with the pattern of comparative advantage in international trade.[41]

In a much larger study, Minhas considered also the rates of return to capital and labor in different industries in a number of countries, as well as differences in efficiency levels. A number of key conclusions are worth quoting here.

The realization of relatively low rates of return on industrial capital in the poor countries in spite of extremely low capital-labor ratios most likely is due to low levels of efficiency in the use of factors of production. These low levels of efficiency may result from a combination of a large number of factors like the lack of "third" factors, the presence of pronounced external effects,

[40] W. W. Leontief, "Domestic Production and Foreign Trade: The American Capital Position Re-examined," in Bhagwati, ed., *International Trade*, pp. 127 and 130.

[41] Arrow et al., "Capital-Labor Substitution," August 1961, p. 246.

or low rates of investment which inhibit the adoption of advanced technology, etc. One should not expect these factors to have a uniform impact on all the industries; their impact is quite varied. Nevertheless, in these differences in the levels of efficiency of factor use lies an important clue to many problems of economic development in underdeveloped areas. . . .

We have argued that the evidence on returns may be consistent with an aggregate production function, which is not strictly invariant across countries but admits differences in efficiency levels that are neutral in their impact on capital and labor returns.[42]

In conclusion, the empirical studies touched on here all raise serious questions about the appropriateness to real-world situations of the assumptions of similar production functions in different countries. This is in line with the studies on economic growth mentioned earlier. In the Denison and Poullier study, for example, of a difference of 41.0 percentage points in national income per person employed between northwest Europe and the United States, 29.7 percentage points reflected differences in output per unit of input, and only 11.3 percentage points, differences in factor inputs per employed person.[43] For this to be true for the economy as a whole, it must also be true in a majority of the individual industries. This point is developed further in the context of Canadian–U.S. comparisons in the next section.

The general conclusion from the summary of empirical work on international trade is that the overall evidence is uniformly inconsistent with the Heckscher-Ohlin hypothesis of similar production functions in different countries. It is ironic that the much earlier ideas of Ricardo continue to have a great deal of current applicability. Still missing in that tradition, however, is some interpretation of *why* production conditions in different countries are different for the same industries, and how this affects the structure of relative prices.

These questions will be explored further in the next section, on Canada–U.S. comparisons. The quantitative data and discussion explore some of the unresolved questions touched on in earlier pages that may have applicability beyond the North American continent from which they have been primarily derived.

[42] B. S. Minhas, *An International Comparison of Factor Costs and Factor Use,* Amsterdam, North-Holland, 1963, pp. 90 and 96.
[43] Denison, *Why Growth Rates Differ,* p. 332.

CANADA—UNITED STATES COMPARISONS

During the latter half of the 1960's, a series of studies has been completed that provides much more quantitative data on comparisons
between Canada and the United States. Much of this material has been
brought together into a conceptual framework that uses Denison's
work on United States and European growth for comparisons between
United States and Canada. Some studies incorporate differences in the
structure of tariff rates into estimates of effective tariff rates for Canada,
while other investigations have applied the work of Alchian and Hirshleifer on cost and supply at the level of the firm to the differences in
costs and productivity between Canada and the United States. In this
section, this material is brought together and cast into the framework
of a test of international trade theory for these two countries.

The Canadian tariff permits the firm to obtain higher prices for
manufactured products; productivity levels can, therefore, be lower
than in the United States, while profit levels stay about the same. Thus,
the productivity levels in Canada adjust to the tariff-influenced structure of relative prices. Recent work on costs at the level of the firm
provide a rationale for productivity differences between Canada and
the United States, even with common technological knowledge and
similar quantities of capital per worker. Further on, this material will
be related to the discussion of international trade theory.

Introduction

Canada is physically close to the United States. A very large proportion of the Canadian population is located within a hundred miles
of the United States border. There are many cultural similarities between the two countries apart from the important French-Canadian
part of Canada. American television, news, advertising, magazines, and
radio all provide many similarities in background, values, attitudes,
and products.

The ready flow of basic ideas on knowledge and technology, the flow
both ways across the border of technologists, teachers, and scholars, the
membership in and attendance at conferences of North American
professional associations promote awareness of new products and ideas

in Canada. This awareness is also facilitated by the high proportion of United States ownership and control of commodity-producing industries within Canada. The United States is the most important market for Canadian exports, and the most important source of Canadian imports. From the United States point of view, Canada is the largest market for exports and the most important source of imports, but it does not play the critically large role in total U.S. trade that the United States does in Canadian trade.

Differences in Tastes

Linder [44] has emphasized the role of differences in tastes as a factor in international trade between countries. However, differences in tastes do not seem to be an important factor in trade between Canada and the United States. Differences in the distribution of consumer expenditures in real terms between the two countries do exist, of course. For example, per capita expenditures on cars, consumer durables, and other manufactured products are lower in Canada than in the United States. However, these differences primarily reflect the lower levels of real income, and the relatively higher prices of manufactured products in Canada than in the United States. Basic differences in tastes do not seem to play an important role. Under these circumstances, the major attention will be given to differences in supply and production conditions between the two countries, with some perspective being provided initially for the economy as a whole.

Differences in Overall Inputs and Outputs

The work by Dorothy Walters provides some relevant basic information for the economy as a whole. [45] Since there is a significant difference

---

[44] S. Linder, *An Essay on Trade and Transformation*, New York, Wiley, 1961. However, it is not really clear what the effect of taste differences on relative prices would be. If the same items were being produced in both countries under similar production conditions and constant returns to scale, it is not clear that taste differences could affect relative prices at all. The inclusion of the Alchian-Hirshleifer emphasis on length of run as a factor in costs would facilitate the introduction of taste differences into a more complete interpretation. For a further discussion of the need for more clarification of the Linder hypothesis on the pattern of trade, see W. M. Corden, "Comment," in J. MacDougall et al., eds., *Studies in International Economics*, Amsterdam, North-Holland, 1970, pp. 52–54.

[45] Walters, *Canadian Income Levels*. For a fuller discussion of concepts, see Denison, *Why Growth Rates Differ*.

in the relative size of the two economies (the U.S. population and labor force being about ten times as large), the comparisons will be made on a per employed person basis. This also has the advantage of setting out the relative scope for differences in factor supplies on the one hand and productivity differences on the other for the two economies at the aggregate level.

For additional detail on the assumptions, methodology, and basic data, the reader should refer to the basic studies. At this stage, several key points in the statistical methods should be noted as a background for subsequent discussion. The comparisons are built on the official national accounts estimates for the two countries (with adjustments to go to net national income with depreciation valued at replacement cost). A crucial but difficult step in the calculations is to take account of price differences between the two countries. The results of the statistical work indicate that the levels of real income per person employed in Canada were about 15 to 20 per cent lower than in the United States, a difference that has varied within this general range throughout the current century. This difference in real income is about two percentage points less if United States price weights are used instead of Canadian ones.

The next key step in the process is to assess the degree to which this difference in real income per employed person might have reflected differences in the quantities of other productive factors used by the average employed person in the two countries. The basic methodology follows the approach developed in Denison's earlier book on the United States.[46] In a discussion of *Why Growth Rates Differ,* I have summarized these key steps:

Basic to his method in analyzing economic growth over time is the distinction between total inputs and output in relation to total factor input. The individual inputs follow the classical distinction between labor, capital and land, and time series are developed for each of the individual inputs. The measure of labor input takes account of changes in the age and sex composition of the labor force and hours worked. It also takes account of changes in the quality of the labor force in so far as it is influenced by the levels of formal education of those in the labor force. The measures of capital input are based on the stock of capital in the form of housing and inventories in

[46] Denison, *Sources of Economic Growth.*

addition to non-residential structures and equipment. The input of land is based on measures of non-residential site land, agricultural land and the rental portion of mineral land. When an over-all measure of these three major inputs (with subcategories for each of the major inputs) is to be prepared, some system of weights to combine them into a comprehensive index of inputs is necessary. For this, Denison uses the distribution of national income. This involves some assumptions about the relationships between the contribution of inputs to output and the related distribution of income, and the effects of substitution between factors. Denison uses differences in income as weights for the individual age, sex and education categories in building up the major input measures.[47]

In using this framework for comparisons of differences in levels of real national income per person employed, a comparison of the levels of total factor input per person employed and total output per person emloyed gives a measure of differences in output per unit of input. Denison explores these differences, including such factors as differences in the allocation of resources, economies of scale, and any differences in pressure of demand or irregularities in farm output. These results are summarized in Table 6.

Table 7 shows the contribution of each factor to the difference in national income per person employed in the two countries. It indicates that Canada has a level of factor inputs per employed person almost the same as that of the United States, but a level of output in relation to inputs that is appreciably lower.

How do these data throw light on the earlier Ricardo and Heckscher-Ohlin discussion? The quantitative size of the differences in output per unit of input suggests important differences in production relations between the two countries—a result for the economy as a whole much more in line with Ricardo than Heckscher-Ohlin assumptions about production relations in different countries. The differences in the availability of agricultural land and mineral resources per person employed between Canada and the United States point up the continued importance of natural resources in Canada.[48] For this sector,

[47] D. J. Daly, *"Why Growth Rates Differ*—A Summary and Appraisal," *International Review of Income and Wealth,* March 1968, pp. 76–77.

[48] The amount of agricultural land per person employed in Canada is almost double that in the United States, while the value of mineral resources (as measured by output) is about 70 per cent larger. However, when the weight for these two categories is only about one-fourth of the land income share, and less than 1 per

Theory and Uses

TABLE 6

Importance of Factors Affecting National Income Level, Canada Compared with the United States, 1960

(United States = 100)

	Canada
Net national income per person employed	81.7
Input per person employed	98.9
Labor quality	100.1
Hours worked [a]	103.8
Age-sex composition [a]	102.2
Education [a]	94.3
Capital	90.5
Dwellings	94.5
Foreign investments	−241.2
Nonresidential structures and equipment	107.3
Inventories	107.8
Land	124.0
Output per unit of input	82.6

SOURCE: Walters, *Canadian Income Levels*, p. 109 (see Table 3, footnote *a*, above). Subsequent revisions in the Canadian national accounts would reduce these differences slightly, and also some of those in Table 7.
[a] After adjustment for zero-quality difference in "no productivity difference" sectors.

the Heckscher-Ohlin emphasis on resource availability continues to be important in the Canada–U.S. comparison.

Some orders of magnitude of the differences in productivity from one industry to another in comparisons between the United States and Canada can be seen in Table 8. The variations in productivity are very large, much larger than the differences in wage rates. The degree of relationship between wage rates and output per worker is not significant.[49]

cent of national income, its measured contribution can only be small in relation to the total income difference.

[49] r^2 is 0.035, and the standard error of the slope is 0.35, compared to 0.47 for the regression coefficient.

The data is subject to all the statistical problems mentioned previously in the

TABLE 7

U.S. Contribution to Differences Between Canadian and
U.S. National Income per Person Employed, 1960
(differences are in percentage points in U.S.
prices; net national income is on
base U.S. = 100)

	Canada
Net national income per person employed	81.7
U.S. contribution to difference	18.3
Breakdown of contribution	
Factor input per person employed	0.7
Labor	–
Hours worked	−2.8
Age-sex composition	−1.6
Education	4.4
Capital	1.3
Housing	0.2
Foreign investments	2.0
Nonresidential structures and equipment	−0.7
Inventories	−0.2
Land	−0.6
Output per unit of input	17.6
Resource allocation	
Agricultural inputs	1.5
Nonfarm self-employment	−0.6
Economies of scale	
National market	4.6
Local markets	0.6
Shift work	NA
Difference in pressure of demand	1.4
Difference in agricultural output	0.0
Residual productivity	10.1

SOURCE: Walters, *Canadian Income Levels,* p. 170 (see Table 3, footnote *a*, above).

TABLE 8

United States–Canada Ratios of Output
per Worker and Wage Ratio, 1947

	U.S.–Canada Ratios		
	Output per Worker	Wage Rate	Wage per Unit of Output
Cotton textiles	0.33	1.27	3.85
Fertilizers	0.72	0.90	1.25
Cement	0.76	1.11	1.46
Lime	0.80	1.10	1.38
Primary aluminum	0.94	1.40	1.49
Flour	0.96	1.35	1.41
Macaroni	0.97	1.44	1.48
Pulp and paper	0.98	1.00	1.02
Meatpacking	1.06	1.38	1.30
Leather footwear	1.12	1.02	0.91
Bread and biscuits	1.25	1.58	1.26
Automobiles and parts	1.33	1.24	0.93
Primary iron and steel	1.35	1.10	0.82
Bricks	1.40	1.17	0.84
Hosiery	1.45	1.16	0.80
Petroleum refining	1.52	1.65	1.09
Rubber tires	1.52	1.42	0.93
Brewing	1.69	0.64	0.38
Tobacco products	1.74	1.56	0.90
Coke	1.88	1.37	0.73
Chewing gum	1.99	1.67	0.84

SOURCE: Output per worker index ratio from J. H. Young, "Some Aspects of Canadian Economic Development," Ph.D. dissertation, Cambridge University, England, 1955, p. 61. Wage rate ratio from Mordechai E. Kreinin, "The Theory of Comparative Cost—Further Empirical Evidence," *Economia Internazionale,* November 1969, p. 10.

One interesting result from Dorothy Walters' work is that the capital stock of equipment per person employed in manufacturing is about the same in Canada as in the United States and the construction stock was

United States–United Kingdom comparison. Some later unpublished work by Craig West of the staff of the Economic Council of Canada would give quite different results for the same industries covered earlier by Young.

even higher in Canada on the same basis. This is a striking result, bearing in mind the significant differences in factor prices in the two countries. Some evidence on such prices is given in Table 9.

How is it that about the same quantity of machinery and equipment per person employed was used in both countries, whereas prices of machinery in Canada at that time were about one-fourth higher and hourly earnings about one-fifth lower? One possibility is that there are differences in the degree of capital intensity that only appear at a finer level of industrial detail, with certain resource-processing industries using more capital in Canada, while other areas of secondary manufacturing use less. Another possibility is that the costs of developing special machinery for Canada that would take account of lower wages there would be more expensive for the small Canadian market than would producing or importing the United States designs, which had been developed for a different pattern of factor prices. This latter view is relevant to an explanation for the use of United States–and European-designed machinery in manufacturing in some of the developing countries of Asia, Africa, and South America.

Thus far, the evidence for the economy as a whole is much more in line with the Ricardian view, which emphasizes differences in production relations, than with the Heckscher-Ohlin emphasis on differences in factor supplies and factor prices. The next section will look at the pattern of relative prices and relative productivities in Canada and

TABLE 9

Comparative Material and Factor Prices,
Canada and the United States, 1965

(United States = 100)

Average hourly earnings in manufacturing	81
Machinery and equipment prices	125.6
Long-term corporate bond prices	123.2
Selected materials prices	120

SOURCE: D. J. Daly, B. A. Keys, and E. J. Spence, *Scale and Specialization in Canadian Manufacturing*, Economic Council of Canada Staff Study No. 21, Ottawa, The Queen's Printer, 1968, p. 29.

the United States, with more emphasis on the commodity-producing industries.

Differences in Relative Prices and Productivity

The structure of Canadian merchandise trade has traditionally been based on the export of a relatively limited number of natural resource products, and the import of a wide range of manufactured products, industrial materials, and components, and a variety of tropical fruits, spices, etc. During this century exports have included metals, lumber and forest products, petroleum, and grain.[50] During the latter part of the 1960's the range of exports has widened to include a markedly greater number of manufactured products, which have increased to about 30 per cent of total exports. The United States dominates the country composition of Canadian trade, with exports to the United States now amounting to about 60 per cent of total exports, and the share of imports from the United States amounting to 70 per cent of total imports.

Because of the high proportion of Canadian trade with the United States, the geographic proximity of the two countries, and the relatively easy transportation connections, there is inevitably a close tie-in between the prices of individual items in Canada and the comparable product in the United States. However, the structure of relative prices in the two countries is far from identical. The presence of tariffs in the two countries and of transportation and other costs contribute to important price differences beween them.[51] These price differences permit and encourage different responses by producers and consumers.

The presence of tariffs in both the United States and Canada has an important influence on the price differences for individual commodities. For products in which Canada is an exporter, the upper limit on those prices would be the price in the United States *less the United States tariff* (together with any allowance for transport costs from the

[50] David W. Slater, "Changes in the Structure of Canada's International Trade," *Canadian Journal of Economics and Political Science,* February 1955, pp. 1–19; and B. W. Wilkinson, *Canada's International Trade: An Analysis of Recent Trends and Patterns,* Montreal, Private Planning Association of Canada, 1968, especially Chaps. 2 and 3.

[51] W. P. Travis, *The Theory of Trade and Protection,* Cambridge, Harvard University Press, 1964, develops the general analysis of how tariffs influence the applicability of international trade theory to contemporary economies.

Canadian producer to the United States market).[52] However, for products in which Canada is an importer (or where imports *could* develop even though domestic production was currently important), the upper limit on domestic prices in Canada would be the price in the United States *plus the Canadian tariff* (together with any allowance for transport and other costs to the Canadian market).[53] Thus, the presence of tariffs in the two countries affects the structure of relative prices within Canada—with prices of industrial materials for export being relatively lower, and the prices of manufactured products being relatively higher, than in the absence of tariffs.[54]

Given the effect of tariffs on the structure of relative prices in the two countries, the idea of the effective tariff rate should be introduced. A brief statement can illustrate the idea.

The basic argument of the effective protection concept is that nominal tariff rates give an inaccurate indication of the extent to which the tariff structure protects the value added in a given industry. A nominal tariff on the final output of the industry permits the producer to raise the price at which he sells his product domestically while still remaining competitive with imports. But if there are tariffs on his inputs of material and components as well, these tariffs in turn raise the cost of the inputs to him regardless of whether he imports them or buys them domestically. If he buys domestically, the supplier of them can charge up to the foreign price plus the tariff on imports. The net effect of the nominal tariff structure on the price the producer can charge for his output domestically relative to the prices he must pay for his intermediate inputs—hence the effect upon his value added—is called the "effective protection" that [the] producer enjoys.[55]

[52] To simplify the exposition in the text, no reference to the exchange rate between the Canadian and United States dollar has been introduced. A reference to the exchange rate could be made in relation to price differences between the two countries on both the export and import side, but it would not affect the overall point being developed in the text.

[53] For a development of these points, see H. C. Eastman and S. Stykolt, *The Tariff and Competition in Canada,* Toronto, Macmillan, 1967, pp. 22–25.

[54] Tariffs can also affect relative prices in the United States, but in light of the lesser importance of international trade in relation to the domestic economy, the quantitative effect is not expected to be as great as in Canada. This is in line with the smaller relative effect of tariffs on the U.S. economy found by the Wonnacotts.

[55] James R. Melvin and Bruce W. Wilkinson, *Effective Protection in the Canadian Economy,* Economic Council of Canada, Special Study No. 9, Ottawa, The Queen's Printer, 1968, p. 4. For further discussion see Corden "Structure of a Tariff System," pp. 221–237; Balassa, "Tariff Protection," pp. 573–594; Basevi, "The U.S. Tariff Structure," and additional references in the bibliography of the Melvin-Wilkinson study.

Three features of the Canadian economy make the effective tariff notion particularly relevant. One is the extent of imports of a wide range of industrial materials, machinery, and equipment into Canada, especially from the United States. A second aspect is the widespread practice of setting prices of manufactured products within Canada on the basis of the duty-paid value of the comparable item if it were to be imported.[56] This is one of the assumptions now commonly made in the literature on effective tariffs.[57] A third feature is the typically higher tariff rate on the more highly processed stages of manufacture compared to the primary and intermediate stages. This feature is found in the tariff structure of most industrialized countries.

Two important conclusions emerge from the calculation of effective tariff rates for Canada. One is that the effective rates are substantially higher than the nominal rates. Another is that there is a significantly larger dispersion around the average tariff rate for effective rates than nominal rates. Both of these points emerge in Table 10.

How does this discussion of tariffs and effective tariff rates affect the differences in prices of manufactured products in Canada and the United States? The differences in tariff rates and the tendency for prices of export items to be close to world prices introduces important differences in the price structure from what would prevail in the absence of tariffs. A high tariff rate permits a Canadian producer to produce in Canada at prices above the U.S. domestic price. For other reasons, he can hire labor at wages well below the U.S. level. The output per worker can be well below the level in the same industry in the United States, even with the same amount of capital and other inputs. When the effective tariff results are introduced, the net difference in price between the intermediate input price and the finished goods price becomes even greater. There is also a wider deviation from one

[56] A number of interviews were made by the Economic Council of Canada on this point in preparing material for the Third Annual Review. However, it is also apparent that a number of Canadian manufacturers did not initially increase their prices, at the time of the devaluation of the Canadian dollar in 1962, to the full extent of the devaluation.

[57] The Melvin-Wilkinson study for Canada assumes "that domestic producers all price at world price plus the tariff: hence pre-tariff price is assumed to be the observed post-tariff price less the tariff" (p. 9). They discuss the reasonableness of this assumption for Canada on pages 49–50.

TABLE 10

Weighted Means, Standard Deviations, and Rank Correlation
Coefficients for Nominal and Effective Tariffs
for 133 Canadian Industries, 1963

	Weighted Mean	Standard Deviation	Rank Correlation with Nominal Rates
Nominal rates	13.1	8.0	
Effective rates			
Calculation 1	21.0	19.4	.86
Calculation 2	24.4	20.5	.83

SOURCE: James R. Melvin and Bruce W. Wilkinson, *Effective Protection in the Canadian Economy,* Economic Council of Canada Special Study No. 9, Ottawa, The Queen's Printer, 1968, p. 29. The two alternative calculations of effective rates are based on different assumed rates for intermediate inputs where insufficient detail is provided in the Census of Manufactures.

product to the other in the levels of effective tariff rates than in nominal rates.

The general argument developed here would regard the differences in the productivity ratios in manufacturing between the two countries as a response to the pattern of effective tariff rates in Canada. In products with a high effective tariff rate, the gap in productivity between the two countries can be very wide and still permit Canadian production of the items. The protected Canadian producer is not driven out of business by foreign competition. However, profits are not especially high, nor is output as efficient as it might be. On the other hand, on items with a low effective tariff rate, or where Canadian producers were exporting to the United States market, the productivity gap would have to be much less. These productivity differences could persist as long as the structure of tariff rates in the two countries remained unchanged, even though there was full knowledge of the basic technology used in the United States, and Canadian workers had capital facilities comparable to those being used in the United States.

In light of the emphasis on the effects of tariffs on the Canadian price structure and levels of productivity, it might be noted that a recent estimate of the costs of tariffs would put them at about 10.5 per cent of Canadian GNP in 1958.[58] This is considerably higher than the range of estimates usually made for other countries. Most estimates of the costs of the tariff are based on the effects of tariffs in the country concerned on prices to consumers. This procedure was followed in an earlier study of the Canadian tariff by J. H. Young.[59] The Wonnacotts' study extended this estimate in two directions. They included an estimate of the U.S. tariff on Canadian GNP and also included the effect of tariffs on production as well as consumption. Many of the estimates of the effects of tariffs in other countries assume constant returns to scale and similar production conditions in the countries concerned. This assumption rules out many of the factors that have been found to be critical for Canada.[60]

A more explicit discussion of how the tariff can contribute to persistent productivity differentials seems desirable, as the literature on international trade has given insufficient attention to this area. In a broad review of international trade theory, Corden states, "Some of the considerations that have not been emphasized in the models [of customs unions] are also those which have been neglected in ordinary tariff theory—economies of scale, the effects of free trade or protection on efficiency, and the effects of growth." [61] A key element in the differences in costs per unit of output in manufactured products between the two countries is the typical short production runs in Canada. Recent developments in the theory of production and costs of the firm throw new light on this important area.

Alchian and Hirshleifer have developed the rationale of how the

[58] Ronald J. Wonnacott and Paul Wonnacott, *Free Trade Between the United States and Canada: The Potential Economic Effects,* Cambridge, Harvard University Press, 1967.

[59] J. H. Young, *Canadian Commercial Policy,* Ottawa, The Queen's Printer, 1967; and J. H. Young, "Some Aspects of Canadian Economic Development," Ph.D. dissertation, Cambridge University, England, 1955.

[60] D. J. Daly, B. A. Keys, and E. J. Spence, *Scale and Specialization in Canadian Manufacturing,* Economic Council of Canada, Staff Study No. 21, Ottawa, The Queen's Printer, 1968; H. E. English, *Industrial Structure in Canada's International Competitive Position,* Montreal, Private Planning Association, 1964; H. C. Eastman and S. Stykolt, *The Tariff and Competition in Canada,* Toronto, Macmillan, 1967; John Dales, *The Protective Tariff in Canada's Development,* Toronto, University of Toronto Press, 1967.

[61] Corden, *Recent Developments,* p. 55.

volume of accumulated past output affects the level of costs per unit in the current period. A central point is that marginal cost *increases* with the rate of output per unit of time, but *declines* with a higher volume of output. This basic distinction is illustrated with examples from costs for book printing, airframes, telegraph companies, electric power, airlines, hotels, quantity discounts and size of shipments.[62] There is considerable evidence that the tariff in Canada permits short runs of a wide range of manufactured products, with a resultant higher price and lower level of productivity in Canada than in the comparable industry in the United States. The existence of the tariff and the relatively easy entry into manufacturing production in Canada has led to the establishment of a larger number of firms and plants in Canada than in the United States, with each plant producing a wider range of products than a U.S. plant of the same size.

Implications for International Trade Theory

The key point in this brief review of the evidence on Canada–United States differences in prices and productivity raises serious questions about the applicability of the Heckscher-Ohlin theory to Canada–United States trade. Crucial to the latter formulation was the assumption of constant returns to scale and of similar production conditions in the countries concerned. The assumptions usually also exclude transport costs and tariffs. Much of the international trade literature of recent years has been devoted to a spelling out of the logical implications of the assumptions under a variety of conditions. In almost all of the tests of that theory, questions about the applicability of the assumptions of similarity of production conditions or production relations have come up. The data for Canada suggest to me that the assumptions which emphasize differences in the productivity ratios (or production relations) between countries have more applicability than the assumption of similar production conditions. Furthermore,

[62] A. Alchian, "Costs and Outputs," in M. Abramovitz and others, *The Allocation of Economic Resources: Essays in Honor of B. F. Haley,* Stanford, Stanford University Press, 1959; Jack Hirshleifer, "The Firm's Cost Function: A Successful Reconstruction?" *Journal of Business,* July 1962, pp. 235–255. For additional references to the related literature on learning by doing and progress cost functions, see Daly, Keys, and Spence, *Scale and Specialization in Canadian Manufacturing,* pp. 41–47.

the extent of differences in production conditions is probably even more important in most other intercountry comparisons than in the Canada–United States comparisons. The discussion has introduced the Alchian-Hirshleifer emphasis on length of run explicitly into international trade, and built on the theory of effective tariff rates. Although some discussions of customs unions, economic integration, and income differences have recognized the role of length of run, I have not been able to find any explicit references to the Alchian-Hirshleifer articles in discussions of international trade.

However, there are two aspects of the Heckscher-Ohlin line of approach that are relevant to the Canadian–United States discussion. One is the relative supply of industrial raw materials in Canada, which has been mentioned before, to which the availability and price of particular factors of production are still relevant and appropriate. However, even for Canada this is an increasingly small part of the total economy. Another pertinent feature is the Stolper-Samuelson theorem on the effects of tariffs on the distribution of income. This grew out of the discussion of the Australian tariff, in which labor was regarded as the relatively scarce factor, whose share was increased by the existence of the tariff.[63] In Canada, there is considerable evidence that trained management is the scarce factor, reflecting a lower level of education in the Canadian labor force compared to the United States, and the larger number of plants and firms encouraged by the tariff.[64] Insofar as this is true, the costs of the tariff fall on the Canadian consumer and industrial worker. However, there is a degree of income redistribution associated with the tariff that gives a relatively higher rate of return to management in Canadian manufacturing than would prevail under free trade. However, with the limited supply of trained people, the tariff has probably permitted a lower level of management to persist behind the tariff than under free trade conditions. Some pragmatic integration of the Ricardian emphasis on the one hand

[63] W. F. Stolper and Paul A. Samuelson, "Protection and Real Wages," *Review of Economics and Statistics*, 1941, pp. 58–73, reprinted in Ellis and Metzler, eds., *Readings*, and in Bhagwati, ed., *International Trade*; and Jagdish Bhagwati, "Protection, Real Wages and Real Incomes," *Economic Journal*, 1959, pp. 733–744, reprinted in Bhagwati, ed., *International Trade*.

[64] D. J. Daly, "The Changing Environment for Management in Canada," paper presented to the Canadian Association of the Schools of Business at York University, June 1969.

with the Heckscher-Ohlin-Stolper-Samuelson ideas on the other may be necessary as part of a complete and balanced story.

COMMENT

BELA BALASSA, The Johns Hopkins University and the
International Bank for Reconstruction and Development

Professor Daly's purpose has been to survey recent work on international price and cost comparisons. In so doing, he has also ventured into the discussion of particular issues in international trade theory. Needless to say, a survey of this sort can hardly be carried out in depth in the confines of a single article. This fact in part explains certain deficiencies of the paper, such as the cursory treatment of several topics, the omission of a few important contributions, and the reliance on obiter dicta at various points of the argument. In the following, I will consider some of the issues raised by Daly.

ECONOMIC GROWTH AND INTERNATIONAL COMPARISONS OF PRICE AND REAL INCOME

Among empirical studies on international comparisons of income levels and economic growth, Daly cites contributions by Colin Clark and Simon Kuznets, the Arrow-Chenery-Minhas-Solow paper on the CES production function, and Denison's *Why Growth Rates Differ*. A surprising omission is Chenery's attempt to derive patterns of industrial growth by the use of regression analysis of cross-sectional data of a large number of countries. This has been continued and extended by the United Nations and again by Chenery and Taylor.[1] The latter study has also utilized time series data as well as a combination of time series and cross-sectional observations.

There is further need to distinguish between problems of measurement and the sources of economic growth. As regards the first, Daly notes the fundamental similarity of intertemporal and interspatial

[1] Hollis B. Chenery, "Patterns of Industrial Growth," *American Economic Review*, September 1960, pp. 624–54; U.N. Department of Economic and Social Affairs, *A Study of Industrial Growth*, New York, 1967; and Hollis B. Chenery and Lance Taylor, "Development Patterns: Among Countries and Over Time," *Review of Economics and Statistics*, November 1968, pp. 391–416.

comparisons. An additional consideration is the choice between using the country's own prices or those of other countries in measuring the rate of economic growth in a particular country. While at first sight "borrowing" the prices of other countries for the calculations may seem to make little economic sense, the usefulness of such calculations becomes apparent for countries where prices are greatly distorted by the application of protective measures.

For simplicity's sake, let us first take the case of the proverbial small country of international trade theory that can affect neither the prices of its exports nor of its imports. Infant industry considerations apart, welfare maximization would require the country to specialize in conformity with price relations on the world market that express the choices open to it. Rates of economic growth, then, should be properly evaluated at world market prices. In turn, in the case of countries that can affect their terms of trade, the evaluation should take place at the world market prices that would obtain in a free trade situation.

Estimation at world market prices results in substantial reductions in measured growth rates in the case of countries where the highly protected manufacturing sector has been growing more rapidly than the rest of the economy, since in such countries domestic prices overstate the contribution of manufacturing to national income. This was the case, for example, in Hungary where the adjusted growth rate was 3.5 per cent in 1960–65 as compared to an unadjusted rate of 4.5 per cent. Among developing countries, unadjusted and adjusted growth rates were 2.6 and 2.2 per cent for Argentina in the period 1953–63 and 3.8 and 3.3 per cent for Pakistan in the period 1950–67.[2]

The second problem is to explain intercountry differences in growth rates, measured in an appropriate fashion. Here we have several studies predating Denison, including comparisons of the sources of economic growth in the Soviet Union and in Western industrial countries that involved estimating increases in total factor productivity.[3] More re-

[2] Bela Balassa, "Growth Strategies in Semi-Industrial Countries," *Quarterly Journal of Economics*, February 1970, p. 44; and Bela Balassa and Associates, *The Structure of Protection in Developing Countries*, Baltimore, Johns Hopkins University Press, 1970, Chap. 2. In the latter volume some of the qualifications of the estimates are also discussed.

[3] Cf. e.g., A. Bergson, "National Income" in *Economic Trends in the Soviet Union*, A. Bergson and S. Kuznets, eds., Cambridge, Mass., Harvard University

cently, in comparing the growth performance of selected eastern and western European countries, estimates of total factor productivity have been adjusted for economies of scale and improvements in the quality of labor and capital.[4]

TESTING INTERNATIONAL TRADE THEORY

Turning to writings "on the real and positive aspects of international trade," Daly claims that "much of the literature is theoretical . . . [and] the extent of testing of these conclusions against the real world has been much more limited . . ." (see Testing International Trade Theory). He further asserts that ". . . all the pure theories of international trade emphasize that trade takes place between countries because . . . differences exist in relative prices between the countries concerned. . . . The major differences among trade theorists emerge from differing emphases on the *reasons* for the differences in relative prices" (*loc. cit.;* emphasis Daly's).

In making these statements, Daly ignores a substantial body of the literature on international trade that has assumed importance over the last decade. The origins of these developments can be traced back to an article by Irving Kravis, who put forward the view that "availability" is an important determinant of international exchange. Availability, in turn, is conditioned by a country's natural resource endowment, its level of technological sophistication, and the importance of product differentiation in modern industry.[5]

Kravis's contribution has been followed by theoretical and empirical work on the product-cycle hypothesis by Vernon and his collaborators, by studies on the effects of research and development expenditures on

Press, 1963, pp. 1–37; Evsey D. Domar et al., "Economic Growth and Productivity in the United States, Canada, United Kingdom, Germany and Japan in the Postwar Period," *Review of Economics and Statistics,* February 1964, pp. 33–40; and Bela Balassa, "The Dynamic Efficiency of the Soviet Economy," *American Economic Review, Papers and Proceedings,* May 1964, pp. 490–505.

[4] Bela Balassa and Trent Bertrand, "Growth Performance of Eastern European Economies and Comparable Western European Countries," *American Economic Review, Papers and Proceedings,* May 1970, pp. 314–20.

[5] Irving B. Kravis, " 'Availability' and Other Influences on the Commodity Composition of Trade," *Journal of Political Economy,* April 1956, pp. 143–55. The article is cited in a different context in Daly's study (footnote 25), but no reference is made to Kravis's discussion of the role of nonprice factors in determining international specialization, which is the central issue in the article.

international specialization, and by investigations of the interrelationships of foreign investment and trade.[6] The hallmark of this literature, ably summarized by Harry Johnson,[7] is indeed its emphasis on the nonprice factors affecting trade flows as well as an intertwining of theoretical and empirical research.

DIFFERENCES IN THE STRUCTURE OF RELATIVE PRICES

Next, Daly turns to the problem of differences in relative prices among countries that affect international comparisons of real incomes. He submits that such differences are "quantitatively much more important in comparisons between countries than between different points of time within a particular country" (Differences in the Structure of Relative Prices). This conjecture may apply in some situations, but not in others; indeed no a priori statement can be made as to the possible magnitude of these differences. Thus, while relative prices may differ little between adjacent countries with similar living standards and a large volume of trade among them, in countries undergoing structural transformation relative prices may change to a considerable extent in two or three decades. In this connection, reference can be made to the so-called Gerschenkron effect which pertains to the over- (under-) estimation of growth rates in such countries by the use of the Laspeyres (Paasche) formula.

Daly further considers relative prices of consumption categories in major industrial countries in 1950, and suggests that the large differences shown in these ratios are explained by the substantial barriers to trade existing at the time. In presenting the data, however, he lumps together goods and services, although the latter do not enter international trade, and service prices are not equalized even under free trade. Rather, the relative prices of services are a function of

6 On these points, see Raymond Vernon, "International Investment and International Trade in the Product Cycle," *Quarterly Journal of Economics,* May 1966, pp. 190–207; G. L. Hufbauer, *Synthetic Materials and the Theory of International Trade,* Cambridge, Mass., Harvard University Press, 1966; D. B. Keesing, "The Impact of Research and Development on United States Trade," *Journal of Political Economy,* February 1967, pp. 38–48; and W. Gruber, D. Mehta, and R. Vernon, "The R & D Factor in International Trade and International Investment of United States Industries," *ibid.,* February 1967, pp. 20–37.

7 H. G. Johnson, *Comparative Cost and Commercial Policy Theory in a Developing World Economy,* Stockholm, Alqvist and Wiksell, 1968.

differences in per capita incomes which in turn reflect intercountry differences in productivity.[8] Indeed, in the classification scheme used in Daly's Table 1 most services have low prices in European countries relative to the United States.[9] And if we consider the somewhat broader consumption categories for which data are given in absolute terms, the exclusion of services reduces the ratio of the highest and the lowest price relatives between the United States and the United Kingdom from 4.5 to 3.1; between the United States and France, from 5.8 to 4.3; between the United States and Germany, from 6.2 to 5.5; and between the United States and Italy, from 11.3 to 3.7.[10] As expected, the exclusion of services makes the greatest difference in U.S.-Italian comparisons, where income and productivity differences are the largest.

TESTING RICARDO

Daly next turns to Professor Bhagwati's criticism of the conclusions I earlier derived from an empirical testing of the Ricardian explanation of international specialization.[11] Since Bhagwati is the other appointed critic of Daly's paper, I will refrain from discussing Daly's objections to his argument. I will use the occasion, however, to put forward my own objections to it.

Bhagwati takes issue with the method originally used by Mac-Dougall [12] which involved testing the Ricardian theory in regard to U.S. and U.K. exports by relating ratios of export sales of various commodity categories in third markets to ratios of labor productivities

[8] Bela Balassa, "The Purchasing-Power Parity Doctrine: A Reappraisal," *Journal of Political Economy,* December 1964, pp. 584–96.

[9] Milton Gilbert and Irving B. Kravis, *An International Comparison of National Products and the Purchasing Power of Currencies,* Paris, OEEC, 1954, Tables 21–24, pp. 53–56.

[10] Milton Gilbert and Associates, *Comparative National Products and Price Levels: A Study of Western Europe and the United States,* Paris, OEEC, 1958, Table 27, p. 80. I have excluded from the calculations alcoholic beverages and tobacco on which the incidence of excise taxes varies greatly from country to country.

[11] Bela Balassa, "An Empirical Demonstration of Classical Comparative Cost Theory," *Review of Economics and Statistics,* August 1963, pp. 231–38.

[12] G. D. A. MacDougall, "British and American Exports: A Study Suggested by the Theory of Comparative Costs," *Economic Journal,* December 1951, pp. 697–724 and September 1952, pp. 487–521. See also Robert B. Stern, "British and American Productivity and Comparative Costs in International Trade," *Oxford Economic Papers,* October 1962, pp. 275–96.

in these same categories. It will be recalled that my calculations showed a high correlation between productivity ratios and export ratios and that this result has been interpreted as evidence for the validity of Ricardo's hypothesis.

Bhagwati suggests that this interpretation would be valid only if there was also a high correlation between productivity ratios and price ratios, since it is via prices that productivity is related to exports, if at all.[13] He finds that "regressions of export price ratios on labour productivity ratios are almost entirely hopeless"[14] and submits that "these results . . . cast sufficient doubt on the usefulness of the Ricardian approach (as generally understood). Contrary, therefore, to the general impression (based on the MacDougall, Balassa, and Stern results) there is as yet no evidence in favour of the Ricardian hypotheses."[15]

The conclusions suggested by Bhagwati do not stand up to scrutiny, however, as his approach rests on the incorrect identification of prices and unit values. In the article, Bhagwati speaks of export prices throughout, although the available data are unit values rather than prices. Now, since with two or three exceptions the commodity categories used in the investigation are heterogeneous, ratios of unit values do not appropriately represent price ratios.

At the same time, in the case of heterogeneous commodity categories, the observed correlation between productivity ratios and export ratios can be explained if we consider that higher productivity levels, calculated in value terms, can be translated into lower prices *or* higher quality. While both of these tend to improve a country's export performance, the former would lead to lower and the latter to higher unit values.[16] Correspondingly, if the effects of productivity on prices

[13] Jagdish Bhagwati, "The Pure Theory of International Trade," *Economic Journal,* March 1964, pp. 9–11.

[14] *Ibid.,* p. 15.

[15] *Ibid.,* p. 16.

[16] Also, Bhagwati does not find "plausible" the possibility that "labour productivities approximate the *pre-trade* prices but that trade leads to boosted profits in the export industries . . ." (p. 10n), in which case productivity ratios could be related to export ratios without being correlated with price ratios. Clearly, we need empirical data to test this proposition, but the finding that productivity ratios are better correlated with export ratios than are rates of unit costs may be interpreted as partial evidence for the above proposition (cf. Balassa, "An Empirical Demonstration," p. 237).

and quality are randomly distributed, we cannot expect a high correlation between ratios of productivity and unit values; consequently, a low correlation between the two variables in no way affects the validity of testing the Ricardian hypothesis by relating productivity and export ratios.

I come now to Bhagwati's contention that we cannot expect to find a close relationship between productivity ratios and export ratios, since substitution elasticities differ among commodities.[17] The answer simply is that the proof of the pudding is in the eating: such differences do not appear to be substantial enough to have materially affected the results. In other words, a high correlation is observed despite possible interindustry differences in substitution elasticities.

But how are we to explain the observed interindustry differences in productivity ratios that appear to be correlated with export ratios? Bhagwati claims that "the reliance of the prediction on labour productivity unaccompanied by any explanation of why the labour productivity is what it is . . . restricts the utility of the prediction." [18] The answer to this question was given in my article, where I stated that the Ricardian hypothesis "presupposes the existence of intercountry differences in production functions"; [19] productivity differences, then, are taken as a proxy for differences in production functions.

One last point should be noted. According to Bhagwati, "the results would surely be more in conformity with the spirit of the Ricardian approach if the *indirect* labour productivities were also computed" [20] in addition to direct productivities. This statement is open to criticism. While Ricardo dealt with the case of commodities that use only primary factors (or a single factor), an extension of his argument to commodities utilizing intermediate inputs would lead to the conclusion that, as long as intermediate inputs are traded, labor productivity incorporated in their manufacture is irrelevant for comparative advantage and international specialization.[21]

[17] "Pure Theory," p. 11.
[18] *Ibid.*, p. 17.
[19] Balassa, "An Empirical Demonstration," p. 231.
[20] "Pure Theory," p. 14.
[21] On this point, cf. Bela Balassa, Stephen Guisinger, and Daniel Schydlowsky, "The Effective Rates of Protection and the Question of Labor Protection in the United States: A Comment," *Journal of Political Economy*, September-October 1970.

HECKSCHER-OHLIN ANALYSIS

Daly further suggests "the overall evidence is uniformly inconsistent with the Heckscher-Ohlin hypothesis of similar production functions in different countries" (Heckscher-Ohlin Analysis). I have no quarrel with this proposition; no international economist would. It seems to me, however, that some of the evidence presented by Daly is not quite to the point.

In reference to Leontief's well-known study on U.S. trade patterns, Daly contends that "to explain the paradoxical results he obtained, [Leontief] abandoned the assumption of similar production functions in different countries" (Heckscher-Ohlin Analysis). This interpretation is hardly correct. As Daly himself notes, Leontief has raised the possibility that "one man-year of American labor is equivalent to, say, three man-years of foreign labor." [22] Such an assumption does not involve differences in production functions; we have only to express American and foreign labor in equivalent units.

It may be added that the empirical testing of the Heckscher-Ohlin hypothesis would still be quite easy if we accepted the contention of the originators of the CES production function that "the evidence on returns may be consistent with an aggregate production function, which is not strictly invariant among countries but admits differences in efficiency levels that are neutral in their impact on capital and labor returns." [23] Finally, economies of scale and "learning by doing" are not inconsistent with the hypothesis of identical production functions among countries. Such considerations can be introduced by making costs depend on relative factor prices, the level of output (economies of scale) and cumulated output (learning by doing).

Daly puts considerable emphasis on learning by doing. He claims to have introduced new concepts in his paper, among other things, by

[22] W. W. Leontief, "Domestic Production and Foreign Trade: The American Capital Position Re-examined," *Economia Internazionale*, February 1954, pp. 9–45, reprinted in Richard E. Caves and H. G. Johnson, eds., *Readings in International Economics*, Homewood, Ill., Irwin, 1968, pp. 503–527.

[23] B. S. Minhas, *An International Comparison of Factor Costs and Factor Use*, Amsterdam, North-Holland, 1963, p. 96. The efficiency term has been estimated in U.S.-Peruvian comparisons in Christopher Clague, "An International Comparison of Industrial Efficiency: Peru and the United States," *Review of Economics and Statistics*, November 1967, pp. 487–93.

relating the recent theoretical formulations by Alchian and Hirschleifer on the length of the production run to specialization in international trade (p. 86). He also suggests that differences in the length of the production run largely explain differences in U.S. and Canadian productivity levels (Differences in Relative Prices and Productivity).

The importance of learning by doing for international specialization has been known for some time. In U.S.-Canadian relationships, the point was made fifteen years ago by J. H. Young.[24] The problem is discussed in considerable detail in some of my own writings where a number of relevant papers are also cited.[25] Furthermore, Arrow's path-breaking contribution to the theoretical implications of learning-by-doing has spawned a number of articles on the subject.[26] Nevertheless, further empirical research would be necessary in order to judge the relative importance of the length of the production run in explaining productivity differentials between the United States and Canada or between any other pair of countries.

All in all, the survey on "Uses of International Price and Output Data" leaves this reader rather unsatisfied. In extending his attention to international trade theory Daly has used a broad palette, with the result that few topics have been adequately discussed. A more judicious choice of topics and material would have brought greater returns.

JAGDISH N. BHAGWATI

Daly's paper is a worthwhile survey of a number of topics which have one common denominator: They all involve the use of interna-

[24] Cf. his "Some Aspects of Canadian Economic Development," Ph.D. dissertation, Cambridge University, England, 1955; and his "Comparative Economic Development and the United States," *American Economic Review, Papers and Proceedings,* May 1955, pp. 80–97.

[25] See Bela Balassa, *The Theory of Economic Integration,* Homewood, Ill., Irwin, 1961, Chap. 6; and Balassa, *Trade Liberalization among Industrial Countries: Objectives and Alternatives,* New York, McGraw-Hill, 1967, Chap. 5.

[26] Cf., e.g., K. J. Arrow, "The Economic Implications of Learning by Doing," *Review of Economic Studies,* 1962, pp. 154–74; E. Sheshinski, "Optimal Accumulation with Learning by Doing," section 6 in Karl Shell, ed., *Essays on the Theory of Optimal Economic Growth,* Cambridge, Mass., MIT Press, 1967; S. Clemhout and H. Y. Wan, "Learning-by-Doing and Infant Industry Protection," *Review of Economic Studies,* January 1970, pp. 33–56.

tional data on prices, outputs, incomes, etc. This inevitably makes my task as a discussant very difficult, however, as I will have to select a few topics for detailed comment, while neglecting the rest. Following the theory of comparative advantage, I shall concentrate on the areas where my competence is greatest.

A

Let me begin with the important question of measuring growth rates, on which Balassa touched. He has already shown how the measured growth rates may differ, depending on whether goods are evaluated at domestic or foreign prices. The problem here, however, is not entirely one of measurement but also of concept. Why do we wish to use foreign prices at all? If we correctly answer that question, we should also know *which* foreign prices to use, and what the limitations of such calculations would be. Clearly, the use of international prices in evaluating income and its growth has been advocated, for some years now, by a number of theorists of international trade and also of cost-benefit analysis (e.g., Little, Scott, Scitovsky, Usher, among others), entirely because international prices are taken to represent "true opportunity costs." However, all the usual qualifications to which the theory of international prices as true opportunity costs is subject must apply as well to any methods of income evaluation based upon it. These qualifications arise particularly because a country may have a less than infinitely elastic demand for its exports or supply of its imports; and the choice of technology (including the pattern of trade) may have also to be determined in the context of *growth-theoretic* second-best considerations (such as that the savings of the economy may be a function of market-imputed incomes, and intertemporal utility maximization for any stated time horizon may then require that the pattern of trade be other than that dictated by current international prices). Note further that, even if we were to apply the *static* efficiency theory and use international prices as true opportunity costs, assuming unrealistically that the country has no monopoly power in trade (and hence introducing errors in our calculations on that account), we would have to worry about two difficult problems:

1. We would have to take international prices *not* in terms of U.S. prices for Argentine calculations, as indicated in Balassa's example in

his discussion, but rather in terms of the c.i.f. values of imports (from the cheapest source) and f.o.b. values of exports (to the highest-priced destination) for the country in question, for it is *these* prices that would represent the true opportunity costs and *not* the domestic prices of goods abroad; and these prices may well be difficult to come by with accuracy.

2. Further, in a world with transport costs, we do not have one unique vector of international prices. In principle, there are f.o.b. prices and c.i.f. prices on every good, and there are a number of goods which are not traded and whose prices, at any equilibrium solution, lie between their c.i.f. and f.o.b. values. Hence, we would have to be able to classify each good we wished to evaluate at its "true" international price as an exportable, or an importable, or a nontraded good, and this could not be done until we knew the optimal equilibrium exchange rate and the overall solution to the general equilibrium model. Only if we knew that would we be able in principle to categorize each good correctly.

Once these problems are fully understood, it should be possible to avoid the haste shown by several estimators, who drew adverse quantitative inferences about the economic performance of a country only because a crude estimate of growth rates measured in the prices of some foreign country (such as the United States) turned out to be lower than the growth rate measured in domestic prices. It also becomes obvious then that a *range* of estimates of incomes and growth rates at international prices, instead of a single estimate, must be provided, using a sensitivity analysis approach, to emphasize that the calculations require heroic conceptual and measurement assumptions.

B

The next point I wish to make relates to the Ricardian theory of comparative advantage and to tests of it. I am grateful that Daly has deemed it useful to refer to my review of these tests (undertaken by MacDougall, Stern, and Balassa) and to offer to explain why my negative review of these tests, and of the predictive ability of Ricardian theory interpreted as a labor productivity theory, may not be warranted. Professor Balassa has also touched upon this question, offering yet another, and more sweeping, rejection of my negative findings. I am, unhappily, afraid that Daly's doubts and Balassa's firm rejection are both ill-taken and that there is cause to reject the MacDougall-Stern-Balassa findings until further empirical evidence is found along lines which I suggested in my review.

Before I do that, let me first say that I still think the correct way to look at Ricardian theory in a multifactor world is, as Minhas and I have indicated earlier, to think of the trade pattern as reflecting international differences among production functions of a Hicks-neutral variety. In fact, the Arrow-Chenery-Minhas-Solow (ACMS) findings support the view that this might be the case in the real world.

However, the approach to Ricardian theory in the literature on the empirical patterns of trade has been to seek correlations of one kind or another between labor productivity ratios and the pattern of trade (frequently export performance of two exporters in third markets). In the first place, I find this approach totally arbitrary. Why take labor productivity and not capital productivity, for example, if one factor has to be chosen? In fact, as Hal Lary has emphasized in his recent work, skilled labor's returns could be taken out of the wage data and treated as returns to human capital; and most land rents could be treated again as returns to capital inputs into "natural" land; so we could end up thinking that capital is the most important factor, rather than labor. In either case, the choice of the single factor in terms of which productivity is to be defined would be quite arbitrary; hence the basic unattractiveness of any empirical investigation which proceeds to show simple correlations between productivity in this sense and export performance. But let us grant that the correlation is established empirically; what does it really mean?

In answering this question, I said that the most it could mean was that higher labor productivity meant lower prices and greater competitiveness and hence superior export performance. Therefore, I proceeded to use the data from the MacDougall-Balassa-Stern literature to see if any correlation between labor productivity and prices could be established. I naturally had to take unit values, which alone were available for this purpose, and I cited a number of qualifications in this regard. It was surprising to find that the relationship between labor productivity and price was extremely poor; hence I argued that we had to withhold judgment on whether the Ricardian theory "explained" the pattern of trade, even if we were willing to buy this "arbitrary-factor-productivity" approach. And I called for more systematic empirical analysis, using better and more appropriate data, to see if labor productivity or labor costs correlated well with prices.

Balassa does *not* offer this exercise; nevertheless, we are asked to accept his correlation between export performance and labor productivity. He reasons that higher labor productivity may result not merely in lower prices but also in better quality. True; and this too was a question I raised in discussing the meaningfulness of the MacDougall-Balassa type of work on comparative export performance on a cross-sectional basis among different industries when the product differentiation among the two trading countries' different industries may vary widely. The answer to Balassa is straightforward: If the tendency to take higher productivity in better quality rather than lower price is evenly distributed and therefore is similar among different industries, then there is no bias from this complication. He produces no theoretical argument to suggest that there should be a bias on this account; hence his belated defense of the failure to investigate whether labor productivity differences had anything to do with the ability to compete via price advantage (in the widest sense) is not persuasive. If he is still interested in convincing us that labor productivity differences significantly determine the pattern of trade, he has to show first that they are correlated significantly with competitive price advantage (in the widest sense). If the birth rate in China has a high correlation with the death rate in India, I am afraid that I would still refuse to accept a Chinese-birth-rate "theory" of the Indian death rate, unless it was shown to me that it made theoretical *and* statistical sense outside of the correlation itself! That this analogy is far from being inappropriate is readily understood when it is realized that (among other deficiencies noted in my earlier review) there is really little reason from a theoretical point of view to expect such a correlation between the Balassa measure of labor productivity and export performance: The labor productivity measured for these exercises is *direct* labor productivity whereas export performance must depend on gross output competitiveness which must clearly reflect direct *and* indirect cost considerations. Hence, at best, we should expect the correlation to hold, in theory, between export performance and direct plus indirect labor productivity underlying the exports in question. This takes me directly into Daly's critique.

He asks whether we should not correlate prices with the value-added productivity of labor rather than with its gross output productivity. He thinks that where the former concept was used, my relationship between prices and labor productivity was not too weak. Since I used the 1950 data from Paige and Bombach which apparently applied the net value-added concept in defining labor productivity, and I used the Rostas data for 1937 for gross output productivity, my results were presumably weaker for 1950. However, I find this suggestion difficult to accept. It seems to me that the correct approach has to be the estimation of direct and indirect labor productivity to see whether this "true" labor productivity really accounts for the price of the gross output. Until we have done this, we cannot really develop any basis for thinking that the labor productivity approach is meaningful even in the limited sense of establishing a plausible correlation between competitiveness and labor productivity in industries. I might finally add that Kravis has expressed strong doubt to me concerning whether the Paige-Bombach data are truly on a net value-added basis: if they, too, are substantially on a gross output basis, then Daly's explanation of the findings of my tests is also statistically weak.

C

Let me finally touch on the question of the empirical relevance of the Heckscher-Ohlin theory. Without a doubt, Daly is quite right in thinking that we ought to change this theory in the generalized Ricardian direction, by allowing for international differences in production functions. The ACMS work, quite aside from the Denison-type work on Canada which he refers to, would support this view. Indeed, there is a fair amount of trade-theoretic work which explores precisely the question of trade among countries which are in a Ricardo-Heckscher-Ohlin world.

At the same time, it is worth noting that the early disillusion with the utility of the Heckscher-Ohlin approach, which stemmed from the paradoxical findings of Leontief for the U.S. pattern of trade, has steadily been eroded. Work has proceeded quite intensively along two different lines: The early pioneering and brilliant work of Minhas, which seemed to establish the empirical reality of factor-intensity reversals, has generated a massive empirical literature which reverses these findings, thus underlining the empirical realism of the Heckscher-Ohlin assumption that factor intensities are nonreversible; and work on human capital has tended to support the view that adjusting the paradoxical trade pattern findings by separating out returns to human capital may sometimes work in the direction of re-establishing the empirical relevance of the Heckscher-Ohlin theory.

REPLY by DALY

My two discussants were selected on the basis of their previous writing and experience in the field of international trade and economic development, particularly as my paper raised a number of questions on the applicability to the real world of some of the major emphases in trade theory of recent years. One of those attending jokingly commented that I couldn't be accused of selecting them on the basis of sympathy to the themes of my paper!

A few sentences of restatement of my aims might be in order. As many of the papers planned for the conference were quite specific and deliberately narrow in focus, a more comprehensive paper to put parts of the field in a broader context seemed desirable. Some of my own recent work has been on comparisons between Canada and the United States, using the conceptual framework developed by Denison. This involved quantitative data on comparisons of real income per employed person in the two countries and a quantitative distribution of the main sources of income differences. On the basis of the research work completed thus far, two points emerged that were emphasized in the paper for this conference. One was that there were very significant differences in output in relation to total factor input in the two countries. A second was that the particularly large differences in secondary manufacturing could be explained by the emphasis on length of run developed by Alchian and Hirshleifer. An initial study of a fairly large body of literature on international trade and intercountry comparisons suggested that these points had *not* been discussed fully in the literature. Furthermore, these points were applicable to a much wider range of countries than just Canada and the United States.

Let me restate what seems to be the response to these points by Bhagwati and Balassa.

1. The empirical relevance of Heckscher-Ohlin: The main theme of the discussion in the paper is that the evidence suggests there are significant differences in production conditions between countries, even after allowing for measurable differences in factor inputs (including adjustments for quality of labor as measured by educational differences, differences in capital, and natural resource differences as they are reflected in rent). Balassa has no quarrel with this proposition, and his earlier work has consistently put more emphasis on the Ricardian stream of theory. Bhagwati states: "Professor Daly is undoubtedly right in thinking that we ought to change this theory in the generalized Ricardian direction, by allowing for international differences in production functions." I regard this and the tone in his concluding paragraphs as reflecting an important shift away from his emphasis on the Heckscher-Ohlin theory in his 1964 *Economic Journal* article. In that survey he did not, in my opinion, test the Heckscher-Ohlin theory as carefully and critically as the Ricardian one. It is to be hoped that future theoretical and applied work in international trade will include even more systematically and explicitly the significant differences in production conditions that most recent empirical work has been emphasizing.

2. Alchian-Hirshleifer in relation to international trade: One of the points emphasized in my paper is that length of run should be explicitly considered as a variable in production conditions, and that this is frequently empirically relevant for international trade. I am disappointed that Bhagwati did not deal with this point at all. Balassa accepts the empirical importance of this point, and has touched on it in several of his own studies. In discussing the theoretical underpinnings of specialization in *Theory of Economic Integration* and *Economic Development and Integration* he refers to Allyn Young's 1928 article and Stigler's 1951 article.[1] In his *Trade Liberalization Among*

---

[1] B. Balassa, *Theory of Economic Integration*, Homewood, Ill., Irwin, 1961, pp. 156–159; and *Economic Development and Integration*, Mexico, Centro de Estudios Monetarios Latinoamericanos, 1965, pp. 149–153.

Industrial Countries he expresses concern about the limited attention to dynamic effects of trade liberalization associated with economies of scale and improvement in production methods from intensified competition:

These sources of gain have received relatively little attention in the trade literature, and static considerations also predominate in the traditional theory of customs unions. Economies of scale have apparently been regarded as an unimportant complication for customs union theory, and little consideration has been given to the impact of increased competition on the methods of production.[2]

I have been unable to find any explicit reference to the Alchian-Hirshleifer articles (which give the most complete and systematic discussions of this in the literature of production and cost theory of the firm) in Balassa's large contribution to the international trade literature, and he apparently doesn't consider it important enough to refer to it. Neither discussant has referred to any previous literature applying the Alchian-Hirshleifer concepts to international trade.

Although both Balassa and I would emphasize the importance of differences in production conditions in manufacturing between countries, we would put quite a difference in emphasis on the empirical importance of the product cycle hypothesis on the one hand and product diversity and length of run on the other. It is to be hoped that future theoretical and applied work in international trade will explicitly include a discussion of product diversity and length of run as factors in domestic production and in international trade in manufactured products.

Scale and Specialization in Canadian Manufacturing contains empirical evidence on the length of the production run in explaining productivity differentials between Canada and the United States in ten manufacturing industries, and other studies emphasizing the same points have also been published before and since. Differences in the length of production run have been more important than other factors such as differences in education, capital, plant size, or knowledge of production techniques. In the light of the importance of differences

[2] B. Balassa, *Trade Liberalization Among Industrial Countries: Objectives and Alternatives*, New York, McGraw-Hill, 1967, p. 95. Pages 95–101 cover some features of market size, economies of scale, and standardized products.

in the length of production run in explaining productivity, it would be useful to study these factors in other countries as well.

3. Testing Ricardo: In commenting on this topic, my two discussants have had an opportunity to return to an area on which they have expressed differing views before. All three of us would agree that we do not have enough data at the industry level on productivity differences, price differences, and international trade for different countries, to test fully the Ricardian assumptions in relation to domestic production and trade, even for the United States and the United Kingdom where the published data are better than for any other pair of countries that I know of. Both discussants have tended to restate their earlier positions, without much consideration of later and relevant data on the United States and the United Kingdom. On the basis of the data we do have, it seems to me that the evidence provides relatively more support for significant differences in production conditions for the two economies as a whole, and for significant differences at the individual industry level within manufacturing. The United Kingdom also has less physical and human capital per employed person than the United States, but the differences in inputs are less important than the differences in output in relation to overall inputs. When the data by industry are limited and costly, we cannot afford to ignore the implications of the evidence for the total economy.

Bhagwati would dismiss comparisons of labor productivity ratios as totally arbitrary. He wonders why labor productivity and not capital productivity is selected. My response would be that labor is such a very important factor, as measured by shares of national income, that it *should* be emphasized. Data on this point are included in my paper, in Table 3, and Bhagwati apparently overlooked this and the related discussion in making his comments. The importance of such additional factors as physical capital, education, and land rents on overall productivity differences can also be studied. Tables 6 and 7 in my paper show such data for Canada and the United States. Similar data for the United Kingdom and six other countries in northwestern Europe are also available. The key importance of differences in output per unit of input, and the relative unimportance of differences in other factor inputs per employed person, suggest that the primary emphasis on labor productivity is much less arbitrary than an emphasis on physical and/or human capital, on the basis of the evidence for about ten developed countries.

4. Prices and quantity indexes: My paper dealt briefly with the effects of using domestic or foreign prices in intercountry comparisons of prices and real product. The large differences in comparisons of level at a point in time were emphasized. Both Bhagwati and Balassa went on to discuss a different, but related, point on the use of domestic and foreign prices for analyzing differences in growth rates over time.

My comment that the differences in relative prices between countries at a point in time were typically larger than changes in relative prices over time within a particular country was an empirical generalization and not an a priori statement. The importance of this point was made at the conference in the Bergson and Grunwald-Salazar papers, and in the discussion of Afriat's paper. A number of studies of the effects of Paasche and Laspeyres formulas in measuring price and volume changes over time in industrialized countries indicate negligible differences in the alternative measures of price and volume changes, even over extended periods.

Both discussants have added to the conference and the volume by the range of their comments and their additional references to the literature. Both of them commented from the point of view of specialists in international trade and economic development, and commented on certain topics in detail. However, most of those attending the conference were more familiar with national income concepts and data than international trade, and the purpose of the paper was to build some bridges between these two fields. The discussion confirmed my earlier thinking that some bridges needed to be built and indicated the part of the landscape where they might do the most good. However, more complete foundations and surfacing seem necessary before the professionals will be willing to go back and forth with any assurance and enthusiasm.

Current International Comparisons

The Comparative National Income
of the USSR and the United States

ABRAM BERGSON

HARVARD UNIVERSITY

INTRODUCTION

HOW Soviet and U.S. real national income compare is a question of much interest in the West. The question began to be considered primarily in the appraisal of Soviet military potential, and continues to be of concern for this reason, though no longer as much so as at the height of the Cold War. In a more academic context, comparison of the outputs of the two countries has long been a means of putting the Societ economy in perspective and so facilitating understanding of its functioning. Such a comparison may also serve as a point of departure for normative appraisal of the Soviet performance.

This essay presents some further calculations on this matter. I draw heavily on, indeed have done little more than synthesize the results of, research done by others. It may have been possible, however, to improve on comparative data now available on national income in the two countries.

Theory teaches that comparisons of real national income in different countries, like such comparisons within a single country at different times, may have to proceed somewhat differently depending on which of two analytic purposes is in mind: appraisal of comparative "production potential" or appraisal of comparative "welfare." I take as a

NOTE: Simon Kuznets kindly read a preliminary draft, and I have profited from his comments on it.

As so often in the past, I am much indebted to Mary Towle for impeccable typing.

This study and the Reply, below, were done with the aid of a grant from the National Science Foundation (Contract G-1525).

desideratum here the appraisal of comparative production potential. To what extent such an abstract desideratum can be achieved is another matter, but the inquiry is usefully organized nevertheless with it in mind.

Because of the dating of the basic data, I calculate national income for both countries initially for 1955. Comparative magnitudes that are derived for that year, however, may be extrapolated to more recent years by use of published indexes of the change over time in physical volume.

While national income purportedly represents the sum of "final" goods and services produced by a community, it almost inevitably omits diverse activities which contribute to final output, and includes others which at least in part might properly be considered intermediate rather than final. This is a familiar theme, and need not be elaborated here, but it should be observed that in 1955 the USSR was still much behind the United States in terms of degree of industrialization, though of course not nearly as far behind as in 1928, on the eve of the five-year plans. Thus, in 1955, over two-fifths of the Soviet labor force was still employed in agriculture. For the United States, the corresponding figure was 8.4 per cent.[1]

As generally understood, the degree to which national income omits final activities, or includes intermediate ones, depends on the degree of industrialization. On balance, output of a less industrialized country tends to be understated relative to that in a more industrialized one.

That should be so here, but the two countries considered also differ in their social systems. Curiously this probably has tended to limit rather than compound the understatement of output in the USSR relative to the United States. Thus, one of the most important omissions from national income is home processing. Because of the notably extensive employment of women in the USSR, however, the volume of home processing there must be less than normal for a country of a comparable degree of industrialization.[2] Because of the

---

[1] See the references cited below.

[2] In the USSR in 1960 women accounted for more than half of all civilian employees, and for some 47 per cent of all civilian employees outside agriculture. In the United States in the same year women accounted for 29 per cent of all civilian

wholesale socialization in the Soviet Union, many independent activities of a kind that might tend to escape reporting, and hence inclusion in national income, have also been drastically curtailed, if not wholly eliminated, there.

THE CALCULATIONS

Comparative data have been compiled on Soviet and U.S. national income by final use, and also in a highly summary way on Soviet and U.S. national income by industry of origin. The former data are the more basic here, however, and for the present I focus on them. Following the path blazed long ago by Gilbert and Kravis,[3] I have tried to compile measures in terms of the prices of both countries. That is, I take as a point of departure data for each country on its national income by final use in terms of its own prices, and in each case derive corresponding figures in terms of the prices of the other country.

In Tables 1 and 2 are shown the data on national income by use with which I began, and the corresponding figures derived in terms of prices of the other country. As indicated, in measuring national income I focus particularly on gross national product.

In the tables, the final use categories are to be construed as the designations would ordinarily imply, but it should be observed that for the United States the figures on defense cover practically all of the relevant outlays. For the USSR, however, the corresponding data refer essentially to the so-named category in the government budget. The precise scope of this category is still controversial, but there are clearly significant omissions. One omission is the support of quasi-military internal security forces. In Tables 1 and 2, this is included, along with internal security generally, under government administration. Much defense-related research may fall under communal services rather than defense, while atomic weapon development and stockpiling may at least in part be omitted from defense and find its way instead into

employees. See Abram Bergson, "Comparative Productivity and Efficiency in the USSR" (hereafter, Bergson, *Productivity*), in Alexander Eckstein, ed., *Comparisons of Economic Systems,* Berkeley, Calif., 1971.

[3] Milton Gilbert and Irving B. Kravis, *An International Comparison of National Products and the Purchasing Power of Currencies,* Paris, Organization for European Economic Cooperation, 1954.

TABLE 1

Gross National Product by Final Use, USSR and United States, 1955

	In Prevailing Rubles			In Adjusted Rubles			In Dollars		
	USSR (bil.)	U.S. (bil.)	USSR ÷ U.S. (per cent)	USSR (bil.)	U.S. (bil.)	USSR ÷ U.S. (per cent)	USSR (bil.)	U.S. (bil.)	USSR ÷ U.S. (per cent)
Household consumption	659.2	3,267.4	20.2	473.5	2,376.8	19.9	64.4	239.28	26.9
Communal services, incl. health care and ed.	102.5	198.1	51.7	93.2	160.9	57.9	34.7	29.86	116.2
Consumption, all	761.7	3,465.5	22.0	566.7	2,537.7	22.3	99.1	269.14	36.8
Govt. admin.	29.5	42.8	68.9	27.4	36.4	75.3	8.8	8.29	106.2
Defense	105.4	212.1	49.7	99.5	205.9	48.3	29.9	38.06	78.6
Gross invest.	246.6	628.7	39.2	238.1	605.6	39.3	43.0	84.07	51.1
Nonconsumption, all	381.5	883.6	43.2	365.0	847.9	43.0	81.7	130.42	62.6
GNP	1,143.2	4,349.1	26.3	931.7	3,385.6	27.5	180.8	399.56	45.2
Excl. selected final services [a]	1,016.3	4,273.8	23.8	809.7	3,312.7	24.4	124.0	364.0	34.1

[a] GNP less labor outlays for communal services and government administration, and military pay and subsistence under defense.

TABLE 2

Gross National Product per Capita by Final Use, USSR and United States, 1955 [a]

	In Prevailing Rubles			In Adjusted Rubles			In Dollars		
	USSR	U.S.	USSR ÷ U.S. (per cent)	USSR	U.S.	USSR ÷ U.S. (per cent)	USSR	U.S.	USSR ÷ U.S. (per cent)
Household consumption	3,359.8	19,766.5	17.0	2,413.3	14,378.7	16.8	328.2	1,447.5	22.7
Communal services, incl. health care and ed.	522.4	1,198.4	43.6	475.0	973.4	48.8	176.9	180.6	98.0
Consumption, all	3,882.2	20,964.9	18.5	2,888.3	15,352.1	18.8	505.1	1,628.1	31.0
Govt. admin.	150.4	258.9	58.1	139.7	220.2	63.4	44.9	50.2	89.4
Defense	537.2	1,283.1	41.9	507.1	1,245.6	40.7	152.4	230.2	66.2
Gross invest.	1,256.9	3,803.3	33.0	1,213.6	3,663.6	33.1	219.2	508.6	43.1
Nonconsumption, all	1,944.5	5,345.3	36.4	1,860.4	5,129.4	36.3	416.5	789.0	52.8
GNP	5,826.7	26,310.3	22.1	4,748.7	20,481.5	23.2	921.5	2,417.2	38.1

[a] USSR population, 196.2 million; United States, 165.3 million. Differences between indicated totals and sums of items are due to rounding.

gross investment. Under communal services, health care and education for the United States include private as well as public outlays. The private outlays are accordingly excluded from household consumption. For the USSR, reference is only to public outlays, but these are nearly comprehensive in that country.

These are perhaps the more interesting incongruities affecting our final use categories, but there are others. The reader with special interests, therefore, may wish to refer to the principal sources on which I have drawn for data on national income by use in national prices: for the USSR, RAND studies by me and by others associated with me; and for the United States, publications of the U.S. Department of Commerce. These studies are cited in appendixes A and B. These are the first two of a set of three mimeographed appendixes that are available on request.[4] I also explain there some revisions and rearrangements of published data that seemed in order for present purposes.

When output is calculated in ruble values I have compiled data in terms not only of prevailing but adjusted prices. The latter are essentially prevailing ruble prices after deduction of the famous turnover tax and the addition of subsidies. I have explored at length in previous studies the problem posed for the valuation of Soviet national income by the proverbial limitations of prevailing ruble prices.[5] Suffice it to say that in approaching the problem I take as a point of departure the factor cost standard of valuation that theory teaches is appropriate, where production potential is the object of interest. The calculation in adjusted prices is to be viewed in that light. In fact, even adjusted rubles are rather remote from the factor cost standard of theory, but they still seem preferable to prevailing rubles if production potential is of concern, and are by no means lacking in merit, I think, as a practical expedient.

Where output is calculated in dollar values, I have considered only

4 Of my RAND studies, the chief is *The Real National Income of Soviet Russia Since 1928* (hereafter, *Real SNIP*), Cambridge, Mass., 1961. The main Commerce Department publication used is *The National Income and Product Tables of the United States, 1929–1965* (hereafter, *National Income–1966*), Washington, D.C., 1966.

5 See *Real SNIP*, Chap. 3; Bergson, *Productivity*.

prevailing prices. A further computation in terms of dollar factor cost would have been to the good, but the results probably would not be very different from those where valuation is in prevailing prices.[6] Even dollar factor cost, of course, is not the same thing as the factor-cost of national income valuation theory. It no doubt does not diverge as much from the latter ideal, however, as do adjusted rubles.

For Soviet national income, I draw on earlier studies primarily for data in prevailing rubles, but corresponding data in adjusted rubles have also been compiled previously. I do little more here than revise these figures to make them conform to the data used on national income in terms of prevailing rubles. Moreover, once U.S. national income is calculated in terms of prevailing rubles, corresponding data in terms of adjusted rubles may be derived by applying to the prevailing ruble values of outlays in different use categories appropriate coefficients obtained from the calculations of Soviet national income in prevailing and adjusted rubles. I explain in appendixes A and B the calculation of national income in adjusted rubles from data in prevailing rubles for both the USSR and the United States.

As an element in national income in prevailing prices, farm income in kind is valued throughout at average realized farm prices. Thus, for each country farm income in kind is valued initially in terms of average realized farm prices in the country in question and then in terms of average realized farm prices for the other country. In the calculations in adjusted rubles, average realized farm prices are adjusted for taxes and subsidies along with prices generally.

Outlays in prevailing prices of one country are translated into outlays in prevailing prices of the other primarily by deflation, that is, by application of ruble-dollar price ratios for different groups of goods that were compiled from corresponding ratios for different commodities. In the case of outlays on commodities I rely chiefly on ruble-dollar price ratios that are either taken from or calculated from data

[6] See Abram Bergson and Hans Meymann, Jr., *Soviet National Income and Product, 1940–1948*, New York, 1954, p. 103, n. 18; Morris Bornstein, "A Comparison of Soviet and United States National Product," in Joint Economic Committee (hereafter, JEC), *Comparisons of the United States and Soviet Economies*, Part II, 86th Cong., 1st Sess., 1959, p. 380.

in unclassified reports of the U.S. Central Intelligence Agency,[7] and in a study by Abraham S. Becker for the RAND Corporation.[8]

In these studies, ruble-dollar parities have been compiled from ruble price quotations obtained mainly from Soviet price handbooks and observers' reports and corresponding U.S. price data compiled by the U.S. Bureau of Labor Statistics. U.S. price data were also obtained from the Sears, Roebuck catalogue and by special inquiry. For construction, reference was made to Soviet cost estimates used in revaluation of capital assets and to U.S. reported contract prices.

In translating farm income in kind, I refer to data on both physical structure and average realized farm prices. Average realized farm prices for the USSR are Nancy Nimitz's as given in a RAND study and for the United States are those reported in government publications.

In the foregoing ways I also obtain parities for translation of commodity components of outlays for final services, such as health care, education, and government administration. Corresponding expenditures for labor services are converted by reference to data from diverse sources on employment and average earnings in the two countries. Outlays for services of military personnel, including military subsistence, are translated in the same way as expenditures for labor in outlays for health care, education, government administration and the like.

As is proper, I try throughout to use price ratios with Soviet weights to deflate ruble outlays and ratios with U.S. weights to deflate dollar outlays. Details on sources and methods used in translating outlays from one currency to the other may be found in appendixes A and B.

---

[7] "A Comparison of Consumption in the USSR and US," ER 64-1, January 1964, and "A Comparison of Consumption in the USSR and US (Supplement)," ER 64-1-s, January 1964 (hereafter, *Consumption);* "1955 Ruble-Dollar Price Ratios for Intermediate Products and Services in the USSR and US," June 1960 (hereafter, *Intermediate Products*); and "1955 Ruble-Dollar Ratios for Construction in the USSR and the US," ER 64-26, August 1964 (hereafter, *Construction*). I have satisfied myself that these reports are scholarly studies, and have utilized them as such. As will appear, at important points the results would not have been greatly affected if reference had been made instead to alternative sources that are sometimes available.

[8] "Prices of Producers' Durables in the United States and the USSR in 1955" (hereafter, Becker, *Prices*), RAND RM-2432, Santa Monica, Calif., August 15, 1959.

APPRAISAL

Calculations of the sort that have been described are almost inevitably crude. Those made here are no exception to that rule. Appraisal of their reliability, however, may be facilitated if I now examine summarily the more important sources of error, and consider whether a bias is likely in one direction or the other. Of particular interest here is the translation of outlays from one currency to another. I focus especially, therefore, on the ruble-dollar price ratios for different groups of goods used in the translation. Where one currency is translated into the other by use of physical volume indexes rather than by deflation, reference is to the implied rather than explicit parities. It should be borne in mind that where the error in such parities takes the form of an overvaluation of the ruble, Soviet outlays in dollars are overstated and U.S. outlays in rubles are understated. Undervaluation of the ruble has a reverse effect.

Price Quotations

In each country the price of any commodity considered in the compilation of parities ideally should represent the average unit value at which the commodity is delivered to its final use. In fact, the price quotations considered in compiling the parities used here are often otherwise. Among other things, ruble retail prices often refer to Moscow while dollar retail prices are often taken from a Sears, Roebuck catalogue. Use of Moscow retail prices, however, probably does not lead to any very consequential error.[9] As for the Sears, Roebuck prices, these were used for many nonfood items. In calculations of the kind described here, such a use of Sears, Roebuck prices is often made, but the validity of this procedure still remains to be tested systematically.[10]

[9] Such prices are used without correction primarily in the case of foods. According to data assembled by Janet Chapman, however, Moscow prices for twelve major foods averaged 101 per cent of corresponding all-USSR average prices in 1936. Also Moscow and all-USSR average prices have moved closely together since that date. See Janet Chapman, *Real Wages in Soviet Russia Since 1928,* Cambridge, Mass., 1963.

[10] In response to an inquiry regarding the representativeness of Sears prices, Dr. Arthur M. Ross, then commissioner of the U.S. Bureau of Labor Statistics, commented as follows in a letter of January 30, 1967: "Unfortunately, it is not possible to make a positive statement in this regard, nor have we made any definitive

Except for alcoholic beverages, the dollar retail prices considered omit state and local sales taxes. The resulting undervaluation of the ruble for all household consumption might be on the order of 1 or 2 per cent.[11]

For producers' durables, the values to be deflated in both countries are inclusive of freight charges. That is customary in national income calculations, and also proper, at least where the concern is to appraise production potential.[12] Ruble-dollar price ratios are compiled, however, from f.o.b. shipper prices. Moreover, transportation and distribution charges probably account for a larger share of delivered prices in the United States than in the USSR. Hence, here too, the ruble is undervalued, and perhaps appreciably. Thus, for gross investment as a whole the adjusted ruble may be undervalued by as much as 5 per cent, where Soviet weights are applied, and 3 per cent where U.S. weights are applied. A similar undervaluation occurs in the defense ruble, where the parity for producers' durables is taken as a surrogate for that for munitions.[13] A further error of uncertain nature is introduced

study of the subject. Sears' prices for various items are set according to various marketing strategies, availability of resources, and a variety of other competitive factors. As a result, prices for some items may be higher than average; others may be lower. Sears' catalog prices are used on a limited basis in the Consumer Price Index, particularly for the small cities (under 50,000 population) where mail-order buying is still important. On the basis of our own observations, we would conclude that Sears' prices are generally somewhat lower than are prices for nationally advertised brands having comparable descriptions, but are about the same as private brands offered by other stores.

"If the foregoing has not really answered your question, I would hasten to add that we in the Bureau of Labor Statistics, as well as researchers in the academic world and in private industry, have extensively used prices from the Sears' catalog as a general indicator of retail price levels for many commodities, particularly in making international comparisons."

[11] For household retail nonfood purchases, I use a Soviet-weighted parity of 17.4 rubles to the dollar and a U.S.-weighted parity of 18.4 rubles to the dollar. Adjusted for state and local sales taxes omitted from dollar prices, these parities might have fallen to, say, 16.8 and 17.7 rubles to the dollar, respectively. The omitted state and local sales taxes, I believe, are those of a general sort, as distinct from excises on tobacco and gasoline. On the possible magnitudes involved, see *National Income–1966*, pp. 54–55. With indicated reductions in ruble-dollar parities for household retail nonfood purchases, the corresponding adjusted ruble-dollar parities for household consumption would fall by 0.6 and 1.7 per cent. The parities for household nonfood purchases also figure somewhat in my calculations at other points.

[12] See Bergson, *Productivity*.

[13] On the possible importance, for the parity for producers' durables, of the omission of transportation and distribution charges, see Becker, *Prices*, pp. 16–17.

wherever U.S. price quotations were obtained only from selected manufacturers.

As indicated, parities for construction are compiled from Soviet cost elements rather than final prices. Since such estimates are based on established input norms, which are often exceeded, the ruble must be appreciably overvalued at this point.[14] Although average construction prices could not be compiled for either country, an attempt was made to pair projects that were "similarly" located in the two countries.

Comparability of Commodities

In compiling ruble and dollar price quotations for different commodities, studies on which I draw have sought to assure that relevant economic features of commodities paired in the two countries are comparable. This desideratum too, however, was often difficult to realize. Resulting errors in the calculations must vary in different cases, but we must consider that the production of defective or otherwise substandard goods, while a feature in any modern economy, is by all accounts notably pervasive in the USSR. For example, among products examined in the first half of 1962 by inspectors of the Ministry of Trade of the Russian Soviet Federated Soviet Republic, 32.7 per cent of clothing articles, 25 per cent of knitwear, and 32.6 per cent of leather shoes were rejected or reclassified to a lower quality category. Among clothing and knitwear articles inspected by the Ministry of Trade of the Ukraine during 1963, 20 to 25 per cent were condemned as defective.[15] In all these cases it is consumers' goods that are in question, but production of substandard qualities is often reported for producers' goods as well.

How does this affect comparability? So far as substandard goods are in fact rejected or reclassified to a lower quality category, their production need not affect comparability at all, but it would be surprising if such goods were not often sold simply as standard goods. This might be so in any case, but is more likely in the USSR where both consum-

[14] *Construction*, pp. 9–10; A. I. Kats, *Proizvoditel'nost' truda v SSSR i glavnykh kapitalisticheskikh stranakh*, Moscow, 1964, p. 56.

[15] Abram Bergson, *The Economics of Soviet Planning*, New Haven, Conn., 1964, p. 295.

ers' and producers' goods have been chronically disposed of in a seller's market.[16] By implication, goods in the USSR that are nominally comparable to those in the United States must often be inferior in fact. At this point, therefore, the ruble-dollar price ratios should tend to overvalue the ruble. The overvaluation, I believe, could be consequential.

I have referred primarily to commodities, but what has been said should also apply essentially to construction. Thus, here as elsewhere an attempt was made to pair quotations for comparable projects, but at least in the case of housing the end products of Soviet construction work have been notoriously deficient in quality. This could be only partly taken account of in pairing quotations. Hence, here too the ruble should be overvalued.

Comparability of Services

While the parities used for construction, including housing, probably overvalue the ruble, differences in quality are allowed for in the derivation of a parity for housing services. The allowance is arbitrary, but the direction of any resultant error is conjectural.

On the other hand, for a variety of other final services, the calculations expressly or by implication take comparative wages as an appropriate parity for deflation of outlays for labor. Hence, labor inputs are taken to be of the same quality in the two countries. This is, of course, a conventional kind of assumption in national income accounting, but needless to say it may be materially in error. The calculations in question here are a case in point, for the ruble, very possibly, is often overvalued in respect of the labor component of final services. That seems likely when we consider, for example, that the average level of education of labor employed in final services must usually be less in the USSR than in the United States. Also, relatively more women are often employed in such services in the USSR than in the United States, and one perhaps need not be an antifeminist to feel that quality is sometimes inferior on that account as well.[17]

16 There are many signs, though, that at least for consumers' goods this is no longer as true as it was in earlier years.

17 In 1960, according to computations of a Denison type, one Soviet worker was comparable on the average to 0.97 of a high school graduate. The corresponding figure for the U.S. worker was 1.17. See Bergson, *Productivity*. Soviet labor must

TABLE 3

Labor Outlays in Selected Final Services,
USSR and United States, 1955 [a]

| | Ratio: Outlays to GNP (per cent) | |
	USSR	U.S.
Output valued in:		
Prevailing rubles	11.1	1.7
Adjusted rubles	13.2	2.2
Dollars	31.4	8.9

[a] The services included are health care, education, government administration, and defense (military personnel only).

At any rate, as was to be expected, the parities used to translate outlays for final labor services are far more favorable to the ruble than are those used to translate expenditures for commodities. Hence, relative to total output Soviet outlays for final labor services became quite large in dollars and U.S. outlays for such services notably small in rubles (Table 3). An overvaluation of the ruble at this point, therefore, could be important. Partly for this reason, in Table 1, I have compiled comparative data on GNP exclusive, as well as inclusive, of final labor services. Among the use categories considered, final labor services are especially important in communal services. The comparative results obtained for such outlays must be read accordingly.

It remains to refer to one other source of incomparability, that resulting from the treatment of retail trade services. In each country prices of goods purchased at retail include trade markups. When commodities are paired in the two countries, however, the character-

tend to be of relatively higher quality in final services than in other sectors, but it should often be inferior to that in the United States. See, for example, *Consumption,* p. 38.

For the services considered an additional source of bias favorable to the USSR is the use of inputs as a surrogate for output, and together with this the omission of any allowance for capital inputs. But this is a deficiency in the initial computation of national income in national prices, rather than in the deflation.

istics of the commodities alone are considered. Hence, no allowance is made for differences in the quality of trade services through which the commodities are supplied. As even the casual observer soon becomes aware, quality of trade services does differ in the two countries. Partly because of the relatively limited facilities available, partly because of the difference in trade technology, and partly because of the chronic shortages of goods in relation to demand, trade services in the USSR must be, by any standard, markedly inferior to those in the United States per unit of goods sold.[18] Here, too, therefore, the ruble must be overvalued.

Representativeness

Ruble-dollar price ratios for different groups of commodities (as distinct from labor services) were compiled from more or less extensive samples of price relatives. While care was taken to try to assure that the samples were representative, that was often difficult, for the price relatives for different kinds of commodities sometimes varied widely. Resulting sampling errors could be correspondingly large. The dispersion is especially great in the case of producers' durables. The sample considered for these goods comprises over five hundred items representing more than half of U.S. purchases of producers' durables, but the parities derived could still err. For construction but twenty-five pairs of projects could be considered, but curiously the resultant price ratios do not vary very widely.

As for the direction of error, that is conjectural, but the samples tend almost inevitably to be more representative of varieties of goods produced in the USSR than of those produced in the United States. Thus, higher-quality commodities produced in the United States often had to be omitted because they had no counterpart in the USSR. Such omissions do not affect the representativeness of parities compiled with Soviet weights, but they do affect the representativeness of those compiled wih U.S. weights. Very possibly here too there is a tendency toward overvaluation of the ruble. Commodities not produced in the USSR properly should be represented in the U.S. weighted parity, and ideally at ruble prices corresponding to costs of producing very limited supplies in the USSR. For goods that are of high quality in the United

[18] Marshall I. Goldman, *Soviet Marketing*, New York, 1963.

States, presumably the ruble prices in question would be especially high. Hence, ruble-dollar parities would tend to shift against the ruble with the inclusion of such goods.[19]

Substitutions

Ruble-dollar price ratios compiled for one category of outlays almost inevitably had often to be used in deflation of another. How the results are affected is uncertain, but it should be observed that the most important example is the ratio for producers' durables. As indicated, that was also used to deflate munitions procurement.

Appraisal Concluded

In sum, the parities used are subject to error at many points. The direction of error is not always clear, and insofar as it is it is sometimes adverse and sometimes favorable to the ruble. Errors of the latter sort, however, seem decidedly the more important (Table 4). By implication, whether the calculations are in rubles or in dollars, Soviet output probably is overstated relative to that of the United States.

In appraising the calculations, I have focused on the parities applied. The comparative data on national income in national prices from which I start also have their limitations, and so too does the translation of such data into adjusted rubles, whether for the USSR or the United States. Moreover, the adjusted rubles in any event leave something to be desired analytically. This is also true of U.S. dollar prices, though not to the same degree.[20]

All this, however, is fairly familiar, and what must be of concern now is whether such further deficiencies might offset or compound the relative overstatement of Soviet output already noted. This could be the subject of an essay in itself, and I can refer to only one aspect, but it is an outstanding one: the possibility often suggested that Soviet

---

[19] The deficiency in parities at this point, it should be observed, is independent of that due to incomparabilities resulting from matching U.S. products with substandard Soviet products.

[20] So far as our comparative data in national prices are in error, the presumption must be that the fault lies more with the data in rubles than with those in dollars. On the reliability of ruble data such as are employed here, see *Real SNIP*. I also discuss at length in that study the nature and limitations of further data such as are compiled here in adjusted rubles.

TABLE 4

Biases in Ruble-Dollar Price Ratios Applied
or Implied in Deflation

Source of Bias	Probable Direction, Whether Undervaluation ("−"), or Overvaluation ("+") of Ruble
Defective price quotations	
Omission of state and local sales taxes from U.S. retail prices, use of f.o.b. shippers' prices for producers' durables	−
Use of Soviet cost estimates for construction	+
Mismatching of inferior quality goods	+
Noncomparability of labor services	+
Noncomparability of retail trade services	+
Underrepresentation of high-quality goods	+ [a]

[a] For ratios with United States, weights only.

real national income suffers relative to that of the United States because of the undervaluation of farm labor services, and so of farm output, so far as it reflects that undervaluation.

How to value farm labor services is a matter on which students of national income do not always agree, but it is usually assumed, I think, that such services are accounted for ideally at a "real" wage corresponding to that of industrial labor of the same skill, and at a money wage corresponding to differential rural living costs. The principle perhaps is not as compelling as has been supposed,[21] and is also

[21] Insofar as rural living costs are below those in the city, application of the principle must in itself tend to distort real national income comparisons, and in a manner adverse to a country such as the USSR, where the agricultural labor force is relatively large. At least such distortion occurs where, as here, the ultimate concern is with production potential. The principle becomes more defensible, however, if national income data are compiled not for their own sake but for use in the calculation of productivity. Farm labor services must then be valued as an input, though at a relative money wage which also reflects the lower cost of rural living. With such valuation, the distorting effect of differential living costs on measures of comparative output is offset. See Bergson, *Productivity*.

not easy to apply. But it should be observed that in money terms the typical farm worker in 1955 earned in the USSR some 5,244 rubles per man-year, or 55 per cent of the average industrial wage; and in the United States, some $1,762 per man-year, or 40 per cent of the average industrial wage.[22] Differentials in real earnings between farm and industry in the two countries presumably are less than those in money earnings indicated by these data. Also, especially in the USSR, skill levels in the country must be markedly below those in the city.

But farm labor services may even so be undervalued. While the undervaluation may occur in both countries, it necessarily would operate to the disadvantage of the USSR. These further data suggest, however, that the distortion cannot be serious:

	GNP: USSR ÷ U.S. (per cent)	
	With Adjusted Ruble Valuations	With U.S. Dollar Valuations
As initially computed (Table 1)	27.6	45.2
With farm value added in each country increased to 1.5 times initial level	29.5	46.0

An increase in the average prices, net of materials cost, at which farm output is valued to as much as 1.5 times the initial level apparently would increase Soviet national income relative to that of the United States, but only to a limited extent.[23]

OTHER COMPUTATIONS

Relative levels of prices and output in the USSR and the United States have been the subject of a number of previous studies both by Western scholars and Soviet agencies or individuals. I propose, where possible, to compare summarily the data presented here with the re-

---

[22] *Ibid.*

[23] The recalculation in effect increases farm factor charges generally by 50 per cent. In terms of adjusted rubles, farm factor charges consist almost exclusively of wages, so the recalculation results in a more or less corresponding increase in labor charges alone. In terms of dollar prices, farm factor charges include sizable nonlabor charges; so the implied increase in labor charges alone is appreciably greater than 50 per cent. The recalculation uses the estimates of GNP by industrial origin presented below (National Income by Industrial Origin).

TABLE 5

Average Ruble-Dollar Price Ratios, Consumers' Goods
and Services, Kaplan-Wainstein and Bergson

	Bergson, 1955 [a]		Kaplan-Wainstein, 1954 [b]	
	Soviet Weighted	U.S. Weighted	Soviet Weighted	U.S. Weighted
Household purchases of commodities [c]				
Food [c]	11.2	17.5	12.9	14.6
	(11.7) [d]	(17.7) [d]		
Nonfood	17.4	18.4	11.5	20.6
	(14.7) [d]	(18.2) [d]		
Housing	1.32	1.32	2.5	2.5
Housing; services	3.2	5.1	4.4	5.4

[a] Taken from or calculated from data in CIA, *Consumption* (footnote 7, above). See appendixes A and B.

[b] Norman Kaplan and Eleanor S. Wainstein, "A Comparison of Soviet and American Retail Prices in 1950," *Journal of Political Economy,* December 1956, pp. 475, 486; "A Note on Ruble-Dollar Comparisons," *ibid.,* December 1957, p. 543. For housing Kaplan-Wainstein parity for 1950, 2.9, extrapolated to 1954 by reference to implicit deflator for housing in *National Income–1966* (see footnote 4, above), pp. 162–163. The official Soviet rental rate used in computing the 1950 parity still applies in 1954.

[c] For the USSR, the Bergson parities refer to household purchases in state and co-operative shops only. The corresponding Kaplan-Wainstein parities refer to prices in these shops, though purchases in collective farm markets are apparently considered in determining commodity weights.

[d] For figures in parentheses, alcoholic beverages have been shifted from foods to nonfoods.

sults of the more interesting alternative computations that have been made by others. While laborious, this comparison may contribute further to the appraisal of calculations in a still relatively hazardous field.

Kaplan-Wainstein

In Table 5 are shown a number of ruble-dollar price ratios for consumers' goods and services that have been compiled by Norman M. Kaplan and Eleanor S. Wainstein, together with corresponding parities used in this study. As explained, the latter were taken from or derived from data in a CIA report, *Consumption* (see footnote 7, above).

Soviet and U.S. prices changed only slightly from 1954 to 1955, so although the Kaplan-Wainstein parities refer to 1954, this should have very little effect on their comparability with the 1955 parities that I use. For household purchases of commodities, I show the parities used here and parenthetically, the corresponding parities with alcoholic beverages classified with nonfoods rather than foods. The parenthetic data are to be compared with those of Kaplan and Wainstein, who likewise classify alcoholic beverages with nonfoods rather than foods.

Even so, the Kaplan-Wainstein parities sometimes differ markedly from those used here. The sources of such differences are difficult to summarize, but I should explain that, thorough as the Kaplan-Wainstein study is, I have felt it in order to rely instead on data in or derived from *Consumption*, chiefly because the latter is a later study resting on a larger sample of commodities (48 foods and 76 nonfoods, versus 37 foods and 57 nonfoods covered by Kaplan and Wainstein); because the weights used, as is desirable here, relate to 1955, while those used by Kaplan and Wainstein relate to 1954 for the USSR and 1950 for the United States; and because the Kaplan-Wainstein ruble-dollar ratios for 1954 were extrapolated somewhat crudely from corresponding ratios for 1950.

Although parities for housing services differ widely, in both cases reference is to the official Soviet rental rate, on the one hand, and U.S. Bureau of Labor Statistics rental data on the other. For this reason it is difficult to choose between the two computations.[24] The reasons for my use here of the parities from *Consumption* for services other than housing are much the same as those for using the corresponding parities for commodities.[25]

[24] The parity used here, however, is based, in the case of the U.S. rental rate, on an extrapolation backward from 1959, and this may be more reliable than the Kaplan-Wainstein one, which involves a corresponding extrapolation forward from 1950. The calculations also differ insofar as that relied on here deducts and the Kaplan-Wainstein one includes kitchen space in computing the average U.S. rental per square meter. If the kitchen space were included here, our ruble-dollar rental parity would rise from 1.32 to 1.52. The calculations also differ regarding, among other things, the discount for inferior Soviet quality. With the Kaplan-Wainstein discount, our rental parity would rise further to 1.72.

[25] Reference for the USSR is to services other than trade union and other dues, which are deflated separately.

While the ruble-dollar price ratios applied in this study sometimes differ much from those of Kaplan and Wainstein, it is reassuring that the divergencies are not systematic. Thus, if I had deflated instead by the Kaplan-Wainstein parities, total outlays in the categories in question would be little affected:

	Household Purchases of Goods and Services [26]	
	USSR	United States
1. As originally calculated (billions of dollars)	51.8	3,221.4
2. Recomputed with Kaplan-Wainstein parities (billions of dollars)	50.1	3,275.1
3. Ratio, (2) ÷ (1) (per cent)	96.7	101.7

Bornstein

The average ruble-dollar price ratios implied for consumption (including communal services) in the present study, on the one hand, and in the calculation of comparative Soviet and U.S. national income by Morris Bornstein, on the other, are perhaps misleadingly close (Table 6). In any event, it should be observed that in deflating household consumption Bornstein uses the Kaplan-Wainstein parities. These, to repeat, sometimes differ widely from the parities used here. Also, Bornstein values farm income in kind at urban retail prices. While an allowance is made for distribution costs, this is quite small relative to the spread between retail and realized farm prices, at least in the USSR where retail prices include large turnover taxes. Hence, foodstuffs constitute a larger share of household consumption for Bornstein than in my computations, where farm income in kind is valued at average realized farm prices. Parities for consumption generally, especially that based on Soviet weights, are necessarily affected.[27]

[26] For the USSR, household purchases of goods in state and cooperative shops only.

[27] For Bornstein, Soviet consumption of farm income in kind amounts to 145.0 billion rubles. The corresponding figure obtained in this study is 80.4 billion rubles. In allowing for distribution costs, Bornstein deducts but 12 per cent from Soviet state and cooperative and 9 per cent from collective farm market prices. The corresponding deduction made from U.S. retail prices is not indicated, but if it is at all comparable to those used for Soviet retail prices it would be much smaller than the gap between retail and average realized farm prices in the United States: 59 per cent in 1955. See U.S. Department of Agriculture, *Agricultural Statistics, 1956,* Washington, D.C., 1957, p. 458. On Bornstein's calculations on consumption of farm

TABLE 6

Average Explicit or Implied Ruble-Dollar Price Ratios, 1955,
Bornstein and Bergson

	Bergson		Bornstein [a]	
	With Soviet Weights	With U.S. Weights	With Soviet Weights	With U.S. Weights
Consumption, incl. communal services	7.7	12.9	8	15
Govt. admin.				
Wages	2.7	2.3	2	2
Nonwages	11.1	15.4	2	2
All	3.4	5.2	2	2
Defense	3.5	5.6	4	5
Gross investment				
Producers' durables	4.1	6.4	4	6
Construction	7.0	7.1	6	8
Other	6.3	13.0	5	7
All	5.7	7.5	5	7
GNP	6.3	10.9	6.1	12.1

[a] Bornstein, in JEC, *Comparisons* (see footnote 6, above), Part II, pp. 385–386.

For government administration, Bornstein deflates throughout by a single parity relating to comparative money wage levels in the two countries. I differ from him here chiefly insofar as I have deflated separately (as is more correct) the nonwage component of this outlay category.[28] As the near agreement on parities for defense suggests, Bornstein and I are more or less in accord on major components, though here too there are interesting differences. Thus, Bornstein deflates military subsistence by a parity relating to commodity prices. I treat such subsistence as a part of military earnings, and translate it

income in kind, see Morris Bornstein et al., "Soviet National Accounts for 1955" (processed), 1961, pp. 103ff.

[28] The divergence between Bornstein and me for wages alone occurs primarily because for the USSR, I include here militarized internal security forces that Bornstein classifies with defense.

TABLE 7

Comparative Data on GNP of USSR and United States, 1955, Bornstein and Bergson

	USSR (billions)	U.S. (billions)	USSR ÷ U.S. (per cent)
In Prevailing Rubles			
Bornstein	1,285.8	4,802.1	26.8
Bergson	1,143.2	4,349.1	26.3
In U.S. Dollars			
Bornstein	212.4	397.5	53.4
Bergson	180.8	399.56	45.2

along with military pay by reference to a parity for wages of military labor services.[29]

In deflating gross investment, Bornstein admittedly often proceeds rather arbitrarily. I may have been able to improve on his calculations at this point, but as it turns out, our parities for major components of gross investment differ little.

While Bornstein and I are frequently more or less in accord on average ruble-dollar price ratios for major categories, we differ widely in our comparative data on gross national product (Table 7). For the United States, the divergence results mainly from the fact that our parities do differ, especially for consumption, by far the chief outlay. For the USSR, differences in parities also matter, but the divergence in our measures of GNP occurs chiefly because, as already noted, Bornstein values farm income in kind at approximately retail prices. Valuation here at average realized farm prices is in conformity with the conventional procedure, and is also, I believe, theoretically more appropriate where production potential is appraised. The implied omission of home processing from farm income in kind, however, is a limitation.[30] Bornstein also includes in the Soviet GNP admittedly

[29] I refer to military subsistence as a component of defense. The Bornstein procedure is proper, and is followed here for military subsistence as a component of household consumption.

[30] On the difference between Bornstein and me regarding the ruble value of farm income in kind, see footnote 27, above. Bornstein does not supply a breakdown of

highly conjectural estimates of "concealed" defense expenditures. The explicit budgetary figure that I rely on instead is no doubt an underestimate, but some extrabudgetary defense expenditures find their way into other outlay categories, and so are still represented in GNP as calculated. Our calculations also differ to some extent at other points.

Despite all divergencies, Bornstein and I hardly differ on the relation of Soviet and U.S. output in rubles. We differ markedly, however, on the corresponding magnitude obtained from dollar valuations (Table 7).

Kats

Diverse ruble-dollar price ratios for different categories of goods are found in various Soviet sources. I shall consider here only a few Soviet-weighted ones given or implied in a calculation of Soviet "final social product" by final use in dollar prices by A. I. Kats. "Final social product" is a relatively novel concept in Soviet national income accounting, and as Kats makes clear,[31] also a controversial one, but essentially it is nothing other than "national income" as usually understood in the USSR, but before the deduction of depreciation on "productive capital." Final social product thus corresponds broadly to "gross national product" as usually understood in the West, but diverges from the latter in a famous way so far as final social product fails to include a variety of personal and other final services.

The scope of different use categories considered is also sometimes strange to Western eyes. In juxtaposing Kats's parities with mine (Table 8), therefore, I focus on only the final social product as a whole, and two major uses which could also be delineated in essentials in my calculations.[32] In addition to the comparisons in the table, two further

Soviet household consumption in dollars but presumably his estimate of Soviet farm income in kind in dollars markedly exceeds mine of $5.8 billion.

[31] *Op. cit.,* Chap. 1.

[32] The scope of the two use categories will be sufficiently clear if I explain that for comparison with "fund of personal and social consumption," I aggregate these outlays in my calculations: (i) "Household consumption," excluding housing, and diverse other services, principally of a personal sort; (ii) "communal services," outlays for commodities only; (iii) "government administration, outlays for commodities only; and (iv) depreciation on housing and other "nonproductive" capital, including that in education, health care, and government administration. As indicated, the second use category considered is itself an aggregate of a number delineated in Kats (Table 8). For comparison with this I aggregate these use categories in my

TABLE 8

Average Explicit or Implied Ruble-Dollar Price Ratios
(Soviet Weights), Kats and Bergson

Category in Soviet Data	Kats[a] 1959	Bergson 1955
"Fund of personal and social consumption"	9.0	12.7
"Growth of consumption capital" ; "Replacement and accumulation of productive fixed capital" ; "Growth of stock and other outlays"	4.7	5.6
"Final social product"	6.9	9.0

[a] A. I. Kats, *Proizvoditel'nost' truda v SSSR i glavnykh kapitalisticheskikh stranakh*, Moscow, 1964, pp. 51ff. Kats's parities are multiplied by 10 to put them in terms of the pre-1961 Soviet monetary unit considered in this essay.

ones may be made. As he explains, Kats uses a parity of 6.4 rubles to the dollar for housing construction, and one of 3.7 rubles to the dollar for other construction. In my calculations, the parity for housing is 6.6 rubles to the dollar, and for construction generally 7.0 rubles to the dollar.

Kats's parities and mine evidently diverge markedly, his being consistently more favorable to the ruble than mine. My parities relate to 1955 and his to 1959. Dollar prices rose moderately from 1955 to 1959, the GNP deflator having risen by 11.8 per cent by the end of the interval. During the same period, ruble prices apparently were relatively stable.[33] By implication, a part of the difference in parities must be due to the difference in dates considered. For the rest, Kats

calculations: (i) "Gross investment," less depreciation on housing and other nonproductive capital; (ii) "defense," other than military pay and subsistence. Note that as a form of consumption (as distinct from a form of income) military subsistence is already included in my household consumption. In rearranging my accounts in the foregoing ways, I draw on data in appendixes A and B and in the sources cited there.

[33] According to official data, wholesale prices of industrial goods, inclusive of the turnover tax in 1960, were the same as in 1955. Retail prices in 1959 in government and co-operative shops were 1.4 per cent above those of 1955, while those in the collective farm market were below the earlier level. Average money wages, however, rose by 10.5 per cent over the interval in question. See *National Income—1966*, pp. 158–59; Tsentral'noe statisticheskoe upravlenie (hereafter, TSU), *Narodnoe khoziaistvo SSSR v 1960 godu*, Moscow, 1961, pp. 717, 737; TSU, *Narodnoe khoziaistvo SSSR v 1965 g.*, Moscow, 1966, pp. 167, 567.

explains that his parities are compiled largely from data of the Ministry of Trade and have their limitations. For example, the sample of commodities considered is "not always sufficiently broad," and parities within commodity "groups" are often averaged arithmetically without weights, while no account is taken of the high prices prevailing in collective farm markets in the USSR. From the meager information supplied on the underlying calculations, however, it is difficult to judge their reliability. The difference in our results must be viewed in this light.

NATIONAL INCOME BY INDUSTRIAL ORIGIN

The comparative data on national income by industrial origin are set forth in Table 9. As before, I refer particularly to gross national product. The contribution of a sector to that output consists, therefore, of its "value added," as usually understood, though reference here, of course, is to additional value gross of depreciation.[34]

Data on gross national product in different valuations are those already derived in the calculations of output by final use. This is also true of the figures on the value added of selected final services, since, except for housing, such value added consists only of wages, and data on wages paid in the services in question have already been compiled in the calculations on output by final use.[35] For housing, it seemed best to refer to final outlays, as also derived previously, rather than to try to disentangle value added from materials inputs in these outlays.

In Table 9, nonfarm value added was calculated as a residual.[36] Hence, in computing national income by industrial origin it remained only to determine the value added of agriculture. Essentially, such value added is obtained as the excess of net farm output (i.e., farm output net of production expenses in kind) over other material inputs

[34] As Professor Kuznets has made clear to me, at least for the United States, the sectoral data sometimes more nearly represent "gross domestic product originating" than "value added," insofar as the principal sectoral contributions are net not only of materials but of productive services obtained outside the sector.

[35] See appendix tables 1 and 6. In Table 9, I consider for "defense" the earnings, including subsistence, of military personnel only, wages paid civilians under "defense" in the United States being assumed to be more correctly classified as nonfarm income.

[36] Here and elsewhere reference is to the nonfarm sector, exclusive of selected final services.

TABLE 9

Gross National Product by Industrial Origin, USSR and United States, 1955

	In Prevailing Rubles			In Adjusted Rubles			In Dollar Prices		
	USSR (bil.)	U.S. (bil.)	USSR ÷ U.S. (per cent)	USSR (bil.)	U.S. (bil.)	USSR ÷ U.S. (per cent)	USSR (bil.)	U.S. (bil.)	USSR ÷ U.S. (per cent)
Farm	185.3	280.1	66.2	212.6	321.8	66.1	13.8	18.59	74.2
Nonfarm (excl. selected final services)	822.6	3,949.2	20.8	588.8	2,946.8	20.0	103.8	311.69	33.3
Selected final services									
Health care, ed., govt. admin., defense	126.9	75.3	168.5	122.0	72.9	167.4	56.8	35.54	159.8
Housing[a]	8.4	44.5	18.9	8.3	44.1	18.8	6.4	33.74	19.0
All	135.3	119.8	112.9	130.3	117.0	111.4	63.2	69.28	91.2
GNP	1,143.2	4,349.1	26.3	931.7	3,385.6	27.5	180.8	399.56	45.2

[a] Gross outlays, before deduction of materials inputs.

to agriculture. Net farm output and material inputs to agriculture, other than production expenses in kind, are determined for each country initially in terms of its own currency, and then translated into the other's currency by application of suitably weighted ruble-dollar parities. Here and in the further translation made from prevailing to adjusted rubles, I rely on sources and methods such as were used in the compilation of comparative data on output by final use. Details are in Appendix C.

These calculations are often crude, and any error at this point necessarily affects as well the calculation of nonfarm output as a residual. The resultant error in nonfarm output would not be at all proportionate, however, for the nonfarm sector is by far the larger one in both countries (Table 9). Since the figures on selected final services that have been used are also inexact, the data compiled on national income by industrial origin must, in general, be considered to be relatively tentative, but they still have the merit that they permit further comparison of the computations of this essay with previous work by others. Thus, the data compiled on relative output of the two countries in the farm and nonfarm sectors may be juxtaposed with similar measures compiled by others. While illuminating the reliability of my calculations, the juxtaposition may also provide a useful perspective on previous findings on relative output by sector. Even among Western studies, these have sometimes diverged widely. As a result, comparative sector output has been a notably controversial theme.

Farm Output

The comparative data compiled here on value added of agriculture in the USSR and the United States appear to be the first of their sort, but computations have been made previously of the relative levels of farm output in the two countries, where output is more or less gross of material inputs. The results of three such computations are shown in Table 10, together with my measures of value added. I also show corresponding measures compiled here on "net farm output," representing total output less production expenses in kind, and "net farm output, adjusted," or net farm output after the further deduction of purchased farm inputs.

Of the three computations by others, two—one by the U.S. Depart-

TABLE 10

Comparative Farm Output, USSR and United States, Alternative Computations

	Ratio: USSR to U.S. (per cent)	
	With Ruble Valuation	With Dollar Valuation
Bergson:		
Net output, 1955	55.2	63.1
Net output, adjusted, 1955	60.1	70.1
Value added, 1955	66.1	74.2
U.S. Dept. of Ag.: "Production," 1958 [a]		62.5
		(53.5) [b]
Pryor-Staller: "Production," 1955 [c]		52.9
Zlomanov-Kotkovskii: "Gross output" (Soviet concept), 1959 [d]	69.7	81.8
	(63.4) [b]	(74.4) [b]

[a] U.S. Department of Agriculture, *The World Agricultural Situation, 1961*, Washington, D.C.

[b] Data in parentheses obtained by extrapolation to 1955. For the USSR, see Douglas B. Diamond, "Trends in Output, Inputs and Factor Productivity in Soviet Agriculture," in JEC, *New Directions in the Soviet Economy* (hereafter, *New Directions*), Part II-B, 89th Cong., 2nd Sess., 1966, p. 346. For the United States, see *National Income–1966*, pp. 28–29.

[c] Frederic L. Pryor and George J. Staller, "The Dollar Value of the Gross National Product in Eastern Europe, 1955," *Economics of Planning*, 1966, no. 1, p. 7.

[d] L. P. Zlomanov and I. I. Kotkovskii, "Sopostavlenie ob'emov sel'skokhoziaistvennogo proizvodstva SSSR i SSHA," *Sorevnovanie dvukh sistem*, Moscow, 1965, p. 323.

ment of Agriculture, the other by Frederic L. Pryor and George J. Staller—are in dollar prices. Both indicate a level of Soviet output relative to that of the United States distinctly less than is shown by any of my measures in dollar prices. Note that in the case of the Agricultural Department computation Soviet output is already relatively low for 1958, the year studied, but becomes still lower if the calculated output ratio for that year is extrapolated to 1955, the year I consider. The third computation, by two Soviet writers, L. P. Zlomanov and I. I. Kotkovskii, values output in both rubles and dollars. Extrapolated to 1955 from 1959, the year they consider, their measures approximate mine for net output adjusted, but are more favorable to the USSR than mine for net output without adjustment.

Such varying results tend to underline the margin of error in all computations alike, and perhaps mine not least, but, partly because of the limited detail at hand on the calculations made previously, interpretation of their divergences from my measures is not easy. The reader will wish to know, however, that for the Agricultural Department and for Pryor and Staller "production" apparently corresponds broadly with net output adjusted, as construed in this essay. Their calculations, however, do sometimes differ in scope from mine for that category. For example, in the case of Pryor and Staller, even production expenses in kind are deducted only for grain, potatoes, and milk.[37] Index numbers of farm output were compiled by Pryor and Staller by aggregation of quantities of different products, rather than by deflation, as was done here, and that apparently was also the procedure of the Agricultural Department. The dollar prices of the Agricultural Department are those in world markets (i.e., wholesale or export prices in major exporting countries) and these must often differ markedly from the dollar average realized farm prices that are considered in this essay. The "wholesale" dollar prices used by Pryor and Staller must also diverge from the latter. Because of sharp differences in production structure in the USSR and the United States,[38] such divergencies in price weights could be important.

Zlomanov and Kotkovskii focus on "gross production" as understood in the USSR, i.e., even production expenses in kind are not deducted. Among the different categories of output I consider, therefore, gross production is most comparable to net output, but is still "grosser" than the latter. Farm output is calculated by aggregation of quantities

[37] See Frederic L. Pryor and George J. Staller, "The Dollar Value of the Gross National Product in Eastern Europe, 1955," *Economics of Planning*, 1966, no. 1, pp. 6–7, 20. As for the Agricultural Department data, in a letter of August 1, 1960, the late Lazar Volin informed me that these ". . . attempt to represent roughly net agricultural production. Included are gross crop production, minus feed, seed and waste; the gross output of livestock products without allowance for animals produced and added (net) to the national herd minus milk fed to animals (for some countries), and minus an allowance for livestock products produced with imported feed in Western and Eastern Europe. No deduction was made for inputs from the non-agricultural sector, such as chemicals, machinery, fuel and other materials."

[38] See appendix tables 8 and 10.

of different products, though the nature of the ruble and dollar prices considered is unexplained.[39] Soviet official statistics on the output of different farm products are believed often to be inflated.[40] If only because of the use of such data, the Zlomanov-Kotkovskii calculation is apt to be unduly favorable to the USSR.

Industrial Output

Divergencies are also evident between my measures of nonfarm output in the USSR and the United States, and similar data compiled previously (Table 11). The latter data in all cases relate, however, to "industry." This is in the Soviet sense, and thus includes not only manufacturing, but mining and utilities. But even so "industry" still falls short of the nonfarm sector as understood here, which also includes construction, transportation, and trade. This difference in scope presumably affects the comparative results of my calculations and the previous ones, though just how is not very clear.

We may also compare explicit or implied ruble-dollar price ratios (Table 12) in all but one of the earlier computations with mine. The difference in scope may not be as important here as in the comparison of physical volume. In any event, parities are of prior interest in this inquiry, since no data even in national currencies have been compiled here on industry as such.

My calculations, however, continue to diverge from the others. For parities as for physical volume, the difference in scope must be a factor, though its import is still difficult to judge. For the rest, the limitations of my calculations may again be relevant, but the previous calculations, as their authors usually make clear, are also subject to error. Thus, all rest on one or another or both of two dubious, though understandable, assumptions: (i) the value added per unit of output of different products in either currency is the same in the two countries; and (ii) value added per unit of output is proportional to the price of the product. The calculations are also obviously often crude at other points, and

[39] The "comparable" ruble prices used in Soviet calculations of Soviet farm output over time, however, turn out to be of a complex sort. See Roger E. Neetz, "Inside the Agricultural Index of the USSR," in JEC, *New Directions in the Soviet Economy*, Part II-B, 89th Cong., 2nd Sess., 1966, pp. 486ff.

[40] See Douglas B. Diamond, "Trends in Output, Inputs and Factor Productivity," in *ibid.*, pp. 96ff.

TABLE 11

Comparative Nonfarm and Industrial Output, USSR and
United States, Alternative Computations

	Ratio: USSR to U.S. (per cent)	
	With Ruble Valuation	With Dollar Valuation
Bergson: Value added, nonfarm, 1955	20.0	33.3
Nutter: Value added, industry, 1955 [a]	19.7	23.4
Campbell-Tarn: Value added, industry, USSR, 1955, U.S., 1963 [b]	29.5	34.5
	(38.0) [c]	(44.4) [c]
Thornton: Value added, industry, 1960 [d]	36.6	58.0
	(26.7) [e]	(42.3) [e]
Revenko: "Production," industry, 1960 [f]		58
		(40) [e]

[a] G. Warren Nutter, *Growth of Industrial Production in the Soviet Union*, Princeton University Press for NBER, 1962, pp. 237–342.

[b] Alexander Tarn, "A Comparison of Dollar and Ruble Values of the Industrial Output of the United States and USSR," *Soviet Studies*, April 1968, pp. 484–86.

[c] Figures in parentheses obtained by extrapolation of U.S. data to 1955. For U.S. industrial output, see *Federal Reserve Bulletin*, January 1968, p. A-56.

[d] Judith Thornton, "Estimation of Value Added and Average Returns to Capital in Soviet Industry from Cross Section Data," *Journal of Political Economy*, December 1965, p. 631.

[e] Figures in parentheses obtained by extrapolation to 1955. For U.S. industrial production, see note c. For that of the USSR, see R. V. Greenslade and Phyllis Wallace, "Industrial Production in the USSR," in JEC, *Dimensions of Soviet Economic Power*, 87th Cong., 2nd Sess., 1962, p. 120. For Soviet industrial production for Revenko, however, see *Narkhoz–1964*, p. 124.

[f] A. F. Revenko, *Sopostavlenie pokazatelei promyshlennogo proizvodstva SSSR i SSHA*, Moscow, 1966, p. 48.

it may not be amiss to feel that the difference between my parities and the others originates partly in these circumstances. In Tarn's computation (representing a revision and elaboration of earlier ones made in collaboration with Robert W. Campbell), the difference in date must also be a factor. This may be true too for the computation of Thornton. It is not clear, however, to what extent, if at all, parities for 1955 from which she begins (actually compiled from much the same in-

TABLE 12

Explicit or Implied Ruble-Dollar Price Ratios, Soviet and U.S.
Nonfarm and Industrial Value Added

	Rubles per Dollar	
	With U.S. Weights	With Soviet Weights
Bergson: Value added, nonfarm, 1955	12.7	7.9
with rubles adjusted	9.5	5.7
With rubles net of turnover tax		
Nutter: Value added, industry, 1955 [a]	8.7	7.3
Tarn-Campbell: Value added, industry, USSR,		
1959, U.S., 1963 [b]	4.6	3.9
Thornton: Value added, industry, 1960 [c]	7.4	4.7

NOTE: Complete citations are given in footnotes to Table 11, above.

[a] *Growth of Industrial Production*, p. 380.

[b] *Soviet Studies*, April 1968, pp. 484–85. Parity with Soviet weights implied in alternative computations of Soviet value added of 1955 in rubles of 1959 and dollars of 1963. Parity with U.S. weights implied in alternative computations of U.S. value added of 1963 in rubles of 1959 and dollars of 1963. Post-January, 1961, rubles converted here to pre-January, 1961, rubles at the rate of ten of the latter to one of the former.

[c] *Journal of Political Economy*, December 1965, p. 631. Post-January 1961 converted here to pre-January 1961 rubles as in footnote *b*.

formation on ruble-dollar relations as I use) are adjusted to relate to 1960. That is the year on which she focuses.[41]

[41] To be somewhat more specific regarding the different calculations, Nutter's deflators (see Table 11, footnote a, above) are explicit rather than implied, and are derived by aggregating average parities for "intermediate products and consumer non-durables," on the one hand, and "machinery and equipment" on the other. Those for "intermediate products and consumers' durables" are calculated from value added data in national currencies and output relatives, and thus rest on assumption (i). Assumption (ii) is introduced because some of the parities considered for machinery and equipment relate to prices rather than value added per unit.

Thornton (Table 11, footnote d, above) describes her computations only summarily. Essentially value added in each of three sectors, "light industry," "food-processing," and "all other industry" is deflated by parities relating to product prices. While the parities are adjusted for turnover taxes, the calculation evidently still involves assumption (ii). Tarn (Table 11, footnote b, above) proceeds rather by the alternative method of aggregating output relatives with value added weights, though for machinery and equipment this output relative is determined by deflation. His calculation thus rests on assumption (i).

While the foregoing methodological features must be consequential, one wonders

The Soviet writer A. F. Revenko describes the methods and procedures used in deriving his index of Soviet industrial output relative to that of the United States, but supplies hardly any details of the actual computations. Essentially the concern is to measure "gross ouput by the factory method," as understood in the USSR. This requires adjustment of American production data to allow for differences between the United States and the USSR in plant specialization. That must often be difficult to do. Comparative data are compiled primarily by the aggregation of physical quantities in identical prices. Recourse is also had, however, to deflation in order to include output of "incomparable" products and the like.

Gross National Product

In the study already cited, Pryor and Staller compile comparative data on Soviet and U.S. output not only for agriculture but for other sectors. For industry they rely on the calculations of Tarn and Campbell that were considered above, but by aggregating sectoral data they find that in 1955 the Soviet gross national product was 44 per cent of that of the United States. That is with output valued primarily in dollar prices, but with "services" assumed to be less productive in the USSR than in the United States. With services taken to be equally productive in the two countries, the corresponding figure is 50 per cent.[42] With such a treatment of services, I find that in 1955 in dollar prices the Soviet gross national product was 45 per cent of the United States. These comparative results must be read, of course, in the light

whether more detailed aspects may not sometimes be at least comparably so. Suffice it to mention the use by Nutter of a U.S.-weighted parity for machinery and equipment that is taken from Becker, *Prices,* without adjustment for the difference between July 1 and average 1955 prices (one of the infrequent general revisions of Soviet wholesale industrial prices occurred on July 1, 1955) and for the omission of metalworking machine tools; his crude extrapolation of that parity to obtain a corresponding one with Soviet weights; the use by Tarn of ruble-dollar ratios, which were clearly often determined rather arbitrarily in the CIA study drawn on, as parities for different types of machinery and equipment; and Thornton's apparent use as parities for "all other industry" of ruble-dollar ratios for producers' durables that Bornstein adapted, 1 believe, in part more or less arbitrarily from Becker, *Prices.*

Dollar and ruble price trends from 1955 to later years if anything should have been somewhat favorable to the ruble. See *National Income–1966,* pp. 160–61, and above (footnote 23).

[42] *Economics of Planning,* 1966, no. 1, pp. 2, 15.

of divergencies noted between my calculations and those of Pryor and Staller for agriculture and between my calculations for the nonfarm sector and those of Tarn and Campbell for industry.

CONCLUSIONS

My calculations, although inexact, may shed further light on the comparative volume and structure of output in the USSR and the United States. In 1955, at the end of the fifth Five Year Plan, the USSR still lagged far behind the United States in total output. Thus, Soviet GNP is found to be but 28 per cent of that of the United States if valued in rubles [43] and 45 per cent of that of the United States if valued in dollars (Table 1).

Relations of different uses and sources of output in the two countries are very broadly similar to that for the GNP itself, but there are often incongruities. To refer to only a few of outstanding interest, reflecting the special nature of the growth process in the USSR, particularly the famous "Soviet model," and related defense policies, that country compares much more favorably with the United States in nonconsumption than in consumption. Thus, Soviet nonconsumption is 43 per cent of American nonconsumption in rubles and 63 per cent in dollars. Soviet consumption, however, is but 22 per cent of American consumption in rubles and 37 per cent in dollars (Table 1).

As late as 1955, however, application of the Soviet model had only very partially compensated for the "later start" by the USSR. The result, as not always understood, was that the USSR still compared much more favorably with the United States in farm than in nonfarm output. In agriculture, the Soviet Union produced 66 per cent as much as the United States in rubles and 74 per cent as much as the United States in dollars. In the nonfarm sector, however, the USSR was but 20 per cent as productive as the United States in rubles and 33 per cent as productive in dollars (Table 9).

Because of the larger population in the USSR, comparisons in per capita terms are necessarily less favorable to that country than those of an absolute sort. Suffice it to say that the Soviet GNP per capita is 23 per cent of that of the United States in rubles and 38 per cent in

[43] Here and later, ruble data cited are of the adjusted variety.

dollars. The corresponding figures for per capita consumption are but 19 and 31 per cent. In per capita nonconsumption, however, the USSR is 36 per cent of the United States in rubles and 53 per cent in dollars (Table 2).

As the cited findings illustrate, we encounter at almost every point in striking degree the familiar phenomenon of index number relativity. Measures in terms of alternative valuations diverge markedly. This is perhaps not very surprising in view of the still relatively limited advance of industrialization in the USSR compared with the United States. The index number relativity is hardly more pronounced than that observed in a comparison of Italian per capita output with that of the United States (below, Table 15). According to a number of indicators, the USSR and Italy should have been at a broadly similar stage of industrialization in the years considered.[44] Moreover, as for Italy, so for the USSR, the calculation in foreign national prices is less favorable to the foreign country than is that in dollars. That is, of course, in conformity with the pattern for Western countries generally that Gilbert and Kravis observed long ago.[45] It is also the pattern that is theoretically to be expected.[46] Its appearance here, therefore, is surely to the good.

Index number relativity reflects differences in price and output structure, and conformity of the relativity observed here to the normal pattern is to the good at least in part because that is further reassurance on the matter alluded to at the outset: the usability of ruble prices for national income measurement. From the same standpoint, though, it should be observed that, as revealed in data compiled for this study, the Soviet price structure differs not only from that of the United States but also from that of Italy, a country which, to repeat, seems to be at a similar economic stage as the USSR. The differences are sometimes striking (Table 13). Perhaps most notable are the low prices of producers' durables relative to foodstuffs in the USSR, compared with not only Italy but even the United States. Expectations of many proponents to the contrary notwithstanding, socialism, as found in the USSR, has clearly meant cheap machines rather than cheap food.

[44] See Bergson, *Productivity*.
[45] See footnote 3, above, and Table 13, footnote a, below.
[46] See Bergson, *Productivity*.

TABLE 13

Explicit or Implied Ruble-Dollar Price Ratios, 1955, and
Lira-Dollar Price Ratios, 1950 [a]
(ratio for GNP = 100)

	Prevailing Rubles per $1		Adjusted Rubles per $1		Lira per $1	
	With Soviet Quantity Weights	With U.S. Quantity Weights	With Soviet Quantity Weights	With U.S. Quantity Weights	With Italian Quantity Weights	With U.S. Quantity Weights
GNP	100	100	100	100	100	100
Consumption						
All	122	118	110	111	102	102
Food [b]	197	160			122	88
Housing	21	12	25	16	36	21
Health care and ed.	48	61	52	64		
Health care	44	71			96	55
Education	49	46			56	40
Govt. admin.						
All	54	48	60	52	41	64
Wages	43	21	52	27	35	20
Other	168	141	160	139	202	154
Defense						
All	56	51	63	64	72	91
Military personnel	38	22	42	26	37	21
Other	81	61	96	76	136	125
Gross investment						
All	90	69	106	85	139	103
Producers' durables	65	59			247	159
Construction	111	65			90	56

[a] For ruble-dollar ratios; see appendixes A and B; lira-dollar ratios, Milton Gilbert and Associates, *Comparative National Products and Price Levels*, Paris, OEEC, 1958.
[b] For ruble-dollar ratios, includes alcoholic beverages.

Here and elsewhere, however, peculiarities in the Soviet price structure have to be read in the light of the distinctive nature of the "Soviet model" generally. From that standpoint, the peculiarities must often connote a correspondence of ruble prices to "scarcity values" rather than the reverse, and necessarily it is conformity of a country's prices to its own scarcity values that counts for national income measurement. But, while implications of the present study for the ruble price structure are properly underlined, I cannot reopen the large issue concerning the limitations of ruble prices for national income valuation, and so will say no more about that question.

In this essay, I took as an ultimate desideratum the compilation of data on national income that might illuminate comparative pɪ duction potential. However the ruble-dollar price ratios are read, the national income measures compiled are certainly remote from the sort ideally prescribed by theory for that purpose. As still is not always grasped, though, on an analytic plane divergent index numbers such as have been observed imply a related divergence in capacity to produce different output mixes. Thus, relative to that of the United States, Soviet output is, to repeat, smaller in rubles than in dollars. Theoretically, the implication is that Soviet productive capacity compares more favorably with that of the United States regarding its own output mix than regarding the American one. With all the limitations of our measures, that is certainly a plausible result.[47]

I have referred to three Soviet calculations of comparative output in the USSR and the United States, one of agricultural output in rubles and dollars, another of national income in dollars, and a third of industrial output in dollars. It should be observed that in the case of the second and third, the authors expressly choose to value output in dollars rather than rubles. That is done avowedly for diverse reasons, principally the relatively low value attached to "means of production" compared with "means of consumption" when computations are in rubles. As a result, with a ruble valuation, the calculated volume of Soviet relative to American output is "artificially" reduced.[48] According to the calculations of this essay, with the dollar valuation stressed in the USSR, Soviet output is raised relative to that of the United States. Indeed, though the contrary is sometimes asserted in the

[47] It must be assumed that "production possibilities," or more correctly the "feasibility locus," is concave or at least not very convex to the origin. See Richard H. Moorsteen, "On Measuring Productive Potential and Relative Efficiency," *Quarterly Journal of Economics,* August 1961; *Real SNIP,* Chap. 3; Bergson, *Productivity.*

[48] Kats, *op. cit.,* pp. 49–51; A. F. Revenko, *Sopostavlenie pokazatelei proizvodstva SSSR i SSHA,* Moscow, 1966, pp. 49–51.

TABLE 14

Gross National Product, Selected Final Uses, and Sectoral
Contributions, USSR and United States, Comparative
Volume, 1955 and 1965 [a]

(United States = 100)

	1955		1965	
	With Ruble Valuation	With Dollar Valuation	With Ruble Valuation	With Dollar Valuation
GNP	27.5	45.2	35.0	57.5
Consumption	22.5	36.8	24.4	40.3
Nonconsumption	43.0	62.6	72.7	98.1
Value added, farm	66.1	74.2	71.9	76.5
Value added, nonfarm	20.0	33.3	29.3	51.6
GNP per capita	23.2	38.1	29.5	48.5
Consumption per capita	18.8	31.0	20.6	34.0
Nonconsumption per capita	36.3	52.8	61.4	82.8

[a] Data for 1955 in Tables 1, 2, and 9, extrapolated to 1965 on following basis:

GNP: For 1965, as per cent of 1955, taken to be 178.4 for USSR and 140.3 for the United States, as indicated by data in Stanley H. Cohn, "Comparative Growth Record of the Soviet Economy," in John Hardt et al., "Recent Soviet Performance: Selected Aspects," Research Analysis Corporation, August 1968, p. 18; *National Income–1966*, pp. 4–5.

Consumption: For 1965, as per cent of 1955, taken to be 160.2 for USSR, as indicated by David W. Bronson and Barbara S. Severin, "Recent Trends in Consumption and Disposable Money Income in the USSR," in JEC, *New Directions*, Part II-B, p. 521. The corresponding index for the United States is taken to be 146.3, as indicated by the following data in billions of 1958 dollars:

	1955	*1965*
Personal consumption expenditures	274.2	396.2
Government purchases of goods and services, less public construction, for "health and hospitals," "sanitation," "veterans benefits and services: hospitals and medical care"; "education"	15.5	27.6
All	289.7	423.8

For personal consumption expenditures, see *National Income–1966*, pp. 48–49. Government purchases of goods and services for indicated items in current dollars from *ibid.,* pp. 62–69, 80–81. I deflate by the implicit GNP deflator for state and local expenditures, as given in *ibid.,* pp. 158–59.

Nonconsumption: Calculated as a residual.

Value added, farm: For USSR, net farm output, adjusted, less nonfarm material inputs to agriculture, the 1965 amounts of which are taken to be 135.7 and 190 per cent

Notes to Table 14 (concluded)

respectively of the corresponding 1955 totals (appendix Table 7). See Douglas B. Diamond, "Trends in Output, Inputs and Factor Productivity in Soviet Agriculture," in JEC, *New Directions*, Part II-B, p. 348. For the United States, the difference between net farm output and "intermediate products other than rents," the 1965 amounts of which are taken as 121.8 and 133.3 per cent respectively of the corresponding 1955 totals (appendix Table 9). See *National Income–1966*, pp. 28–29.

Value added, nonfarm: Calculated as a residual after allowance for farm value added and the following data on selected final services in 1965 in 1955 prices (billions):

	USSR		United States	
	In Adjusted Rubles	In Dollars	In Adjusted Rubles	In Dollars
Health care, ed., govt. admin., wages	123.2	59.3	74.7	37.4
Defense: military pay and subsistence	21.3	9.7	19.3	8.8
Housing, gross outlays	14.5	11.2	71.4	54.7
All	159.0	80.2	165.4	100.9

For the USSR, I extrapolate from 1955 data in appendix Table 1, by reference to employment data in Murray Feshbach, "Manpower in the USSR," in JEC, *New Directions*, Part III, pp. 746, 770–73, and *Real SNIP*, p. 364; and data on housing space in Oleg Hoeffding and Nancy Nimitz, "Soviet National Income and Product, 1949–55," RAND RM-2101, Santa Monica, Calif., April 6, 1959, pp. 100–103; *Real SNIP*, pp. 315–316; and Abraham S. Becker, *Soviet National Income, 1958–1964*, Berkeley, Calif., 1969, pp. 335ff. For the United States, I extrapolate from 1955 data in appendix Table 6 by reference to employment data in *National Income–1966*, pp. 110–11, and data on housing outlays in 1958 prices in *ibid.*, pp. 48–49.

GNP, consumption and nonconsumption per capita: For 1955 population, see Table 2. Population 1965, for USSR, 230.6 million; for the United States, 194.6 million.

USSR, the increase is marked.[49] Granting the limitations of ruble prices, however, that result far from being "artificial" is, as indicated, the expected one.

I have focused in this essay on 1955, a year for which available data are favorable to calculations such as mine. It may be hoped that with further research similar calculations will become possible for more recent dates. Meantime, we are able to extrapolate some of the major findings by using available related measures of changes in physical volume over time in the two countries.

If the results (Table 14) are at all near the mark, we may conclude that over the decade 1955–65 the USSR has gained on the United States in every sphere, but very unevenly. Hence, structural differences

[49] V. Starovskii, "Sopostavlenie ekonomicheskikh pokazatelei SSSR i SSHA," *Voprosy ekonomiki*, 1960, no. 4, p. 107.

that prevailed initially are sometimes ameliorated, as where the Soviet relative standing in respect of nonfarm output gains on that in respect of farm output. But they are sometimes compounded; for example, the Soviet relative standing in consumption, if anything, suffers in comparison with that in nonconsumption. As reported, Soviet consumption has risen sharply since the mid-fifties, but so too has U.S. consumption. As it turns out, the USSR still surpasses the United States much more in the growth of nonconsumption than of consumption. Interestingly, in total volume of nonconsumption, the USSR actually matches the United States in 1960, with valuation in dollars, though it still lags with valuation in rubles.

I have focused on comparisons of the USSR with the United States, but other countries too have been compared with the United States, and the USSR may be thus contrasted, if only indirectly, with them as well. Thus, in terms of per capita GNP the USSR apparently was more or less on a par with Italy in 1955 and still remained so in 1965

TABLE 15

Comparative GNP per Capita, by Final Use,
Italy and United States, 1955 and 1965 [a]

(United States = 100)

	1955		1965	
	With Foreign National Valuation	With U.S. Dollar Valuation	With Foreign National Valuation	With U.S. Dollar Valuation
Per capita:				
GNP	24	35	32	46
Consumption	24	34	30	42
Nonconsumption	23	36	36	56

[a] For 1955, see Milton Gilbert and Associates, *Comparative National Products and Price Levels,* Paris, OEEC, 1958, pp. 36, 86. Magnitudes in this source for 1955 extrapolated to 1965 by reference to calculations for the United States explained in notes to Table 14, and to data in Organization for Economic Cooperation and Development, *General Statistics,* January 1965, p. 77, and *Economic Survey of Europe in 1966,* New York, 1967, Chap. 1, p. 2.

(Tables 14 and 15). In contrast to the extreme disproportion between consumption and nonconsumption in the USSR, however, the two sorts of outlays enjoy practically the same balance in Italy as in the United States in 1955. By 1965, Italy stood higher relative to the United States in nonconsumption than in consumption, but the disproportion is still hardly comparable to that in the USSR. The USSR thus has only been able to match Italy in overall growth while enjoying much less of its fruits in the form of consumption than has that country. The partial reason must be that nonconsumption includes not only growth-inducing investment but defense outlays, and that the latter have been relatively larger in the USSR than in Italy. Familiar doubts about the efficacy of the famous Soviet growth model, however, seem here compounded, but this must be the subject of another inquiry and cannot be pursued now.

COMMENT
Rush V. Greenslade, Central Intelligence Agency

First, I wish to comment briefly on the data and procedures used in Bergson's comparisons of the United States and the USSR and then at greater length on the economic significance of the comparisons.

Bergson's compilation of the existing data is complete. I do not believe there is any way to improve the coverage of the comparisons substantially unless the Russians publish more. Soviet economic data, as most economists are aware, are fragmentary, poorly defined, misleading, and on occasion simply untrustworthy. We are all indebted to Bergson for having carried out the voluminous job of data checking and testing and evaluating which was required in the construction of these comparisons.

THE DATA

The comparability and representativeness of the product and price sample leave much to be desired, as Bergson fully explains in his paper. He points out that the quality of Soviet goods is frequently below nominal standards because of a pervasive seller's market, and hence are inferior to supposedly comparable U.S. goods. This low and variable quality of goods is worth emphasizing because of its direct bearing on the bias in the comparison. In addition, it points up the problem of interpretation arising from the absence of market-determined prices in the USSR, which I will discuss below.

As regards representativeness the sample is limited to those prices which the Russians have published. This leaves out not only the prices of goods that the United States produces but the USSR does not, but also those prices the Russians want to leave out. In the field of producers' equipment, it also leaves out the nonserial production of machines, the so-called one-time orders. There is good reason to believe that the ruble-dollar ratios for serially produced goods are lower than for custom-made goods or one-time orders. Furthermore, one-time orders, according to recent Russian reports, include many serially produced goods modified only in trivial ways, and hence significantly overpriced. I assume the incentive to mislabel and overprice machinery operated in 1955 as well as in recent years. Then as now, enterprise performance was measured and judged by an index of value of output. The selective bias in the sample of machinery and equipment helps to explain why the ruble-dollar ratio for investment equipment, and military equipment, is so low.

The problem of diversity is one that is not explicitly discussed by Bergson. The mix of products, both intermediate and final, is decided in the USSR by enterprises and planners who are overwhelmingly concerned with cost and physical quantities of production. The influence of customers, excepting probably the armed forces, who are also concerned with the utility of the products, is minimal. One important aspect of mix is the diversity or variety of goods.

This problem is not simply the usual problem that poorer countries have less diversity than richer countries. The Soviet menu of consumers' goods and services is a short one, far shorter than its putative per capita income would justify—as visitors to both the USSR and Europe (East or West) testify. In poor countries where markets operate, at least we can say that consumers have that diversity relative to quantity that they are willing to pay for. In the USSR we know that quantities are emphasized at the expense of variety not only because of administrative necessity—the things left out are things the administrative system finds hard to produce—but also because extension of variety is always likely to reduce economies of scale somewhat.

This discussion of diversity refers to the effect of the reduced shopping list on measurement. Because of it the dollar value of Soviet product is overstated and the ruble price of U.S. product is understated. This question must be separated from the questions of whether the Soviet system could increase variety at final or intermediate levels and whether by so doing it would raise or lower efficiency. The degree to which an increase in the variety of final goods, as ordered by Gosplan, would increase consumer utility and, hence, offset the reduction in quantity depends on the system's success in choosing the right varieties. Likewise, the degree to which an increase in the variety of intermediate goods at the expense of quantity would increase or decrease the quantity of final goods depends on the efficiency of the system in choosing and producing the right varieties. Speculation as to the effect of such changes has no bearing on the measurement issue. The measurement issue is that the variety of final goods is restricted in the Soviet economy to a far greater extent than in market economies of comparable per capita incomes and this dimension of performance is not reflected in the comparison of the United States and the USSR.

THE PROCEDURES

In dealing with miserly data doled out by a noneconomizing system, the investigator must adopt many compromises. Bergson's procedures are as good as various possible alternatives, as far as the plausibility of the results are concerned. However, a few statements about alternatives may help to reveal the difficulties and uncertainties in such a comparison.

The first problem is measuring farm income in kind. The issue is between measuring this kind of income at farm gate prices (average realized prices of farm commodities) or at retail prices less transportation and distribution value added. In the ruble measure of Soviet national income the question is whether one includes in the price of commodities consumed in kind some value for imputed rent; the average realized prices do not, but the retail prices would, since they include the famous Soviet turnover tax. In the dollar valuation of Soviet income in kind the question is how much home processing to impute to peasants and how to value it. As Bergson himself suggests, his use of farm gate prices probably underestimates the degree of processing in the peasant consumption in kind. In any event, I agree with Bergson that the use of ruble-dollar ratios for retail prices probably overstates the dollar value of Russian peasant consumption by underestimating the distribution and transportation shares of food prices in the United States.

Another problem is the question of illegal activities for private gain. There is, according to rumor as well as the Soviet press, a great deal of private service, of private processing of state materials, and also of simple sale for private gain of stolen state goods. Bergson, wisely perhaps, chose not to try to account for these activities of unknown magnitude. Nevertheless, consumption, I suspect, is significantly understated by the omission of these activities.

EVALUATION OF THE COMPARISONS

I subscribe to Bergson's summary appraisal that biases in the ruble-dollar parities are mostly favorable to the ruble, that is, the ruble is overvalued. Possibly, however, the understatement of farm income in kind and the omission of some private activities may partially offset the overvaluation in dollar prices. This is not intended as a comment on direction of bias as much as it is on degree of uncertainty.

SIGNIFICANCE OF THE COMPARISONS

Bergson's objective is a comparison of the production potential of the two economies as opposed to a comparison of welfare. The comparison in dollars can be thought of as the relative capacity of the two countries to produce the Soviet mix of output. The assumption is that the United States could shift resources at initial relative prices to produce an output mix proportional to the Soviet mix. The comparison in rubles assumes a shift of the Soviet economy to the U.S. mix. This interpretation clearly depends heavily on market-determined prices, and market processes for transferring resources between uses. The near absence of market-determined prices and market processes in the USSR casts a great deal of doubt on the usefulness and validity of the interpretation. It is likely that the United States had the potential in 1955 to shift reasonably well to the Soviet mix, except for natural resource constraints, such as oil deposits. But these constraints can normally be overcome by foreign trade. Presumably, this would be true of any larger and technologically more advanced country in comparison with a smaller one, and the smaller and poorer country would have less of an ability to shift its output mix, for example, the United States against Switzerland. However, by considering the alternatives provided by foreign trade, the problems of changing patterns of use could be thought of as soluble even by a smaller economy.

The Soviet economy, in contrast, is quite different institutionally. Not only is it far inside its technical production possibilities function, but its processes for and efficiency in transferring resources contrasts with those of market economies. Its inability to take full advantage of foreign trade exemplifies an inherent difficulty in allocating resources to their highest value uses. The problem is not in actually moving labor or redirecting capital assets. Indeed, in 1955 the USSR was carrying out a massive movement of labor and capital to plough up the New Lands of Kazakhstan and West Siberia for wheat growing. However, the movement of resources is carried out by administrative direction and not by market forces, and the output results are frequently disappointing. The resources are deployed not only for the end uses desired by the leaders but in the industry branches specified by them. This is to say that the entrepreneurship is performed through sweeping policies decided by a relatively few high-level leaders, and there is no automatic trial and error process to clean up the wreckage in their track. The New Lands program was a success but Khrushchev's later attempt to build a large, modern, chemical industry quickly was not. Similarly, his plan for catching up with the United States in meat production fell far short and was a massive waste of badly needed grain. Examples could be multiplied to indicate that the leaders frequently err and that, at best, they perceive only a few of the possible opportunities. These institutional rigidities suggest a relatively low efficiency in transferring resources.

There are two kinds of empirical evidence directly relating to the mobility of resources in the USSR. Recent studies have shown that the elasticity of substitution of capital for labor in the USSR is very low—in the neighborhood of 0.2 or 0.3 against 0.5 in the United States. Secondly, the time for completion of new investment projects, by which most redirection of resources is accomplished, is much longer than in Western market economies. These difficulties in transferring resources bear on the significance of the comparison of the USSR and the United States in ruble prices. I would think that the USSR would have great difficulty in shifting toward the U.S. mix.

In order to shift to the U.S. mix the USSR must not only expand quantities of some categories of goods and reduce others but it must also radically expand the variety of models, styles, etc., to reach, let us say, even the Italian level of diversity, let alone the U.S. one. Secondly, the expansion of many goods requires complementary services. For example, the Russians are currently attempting an expansion of passenger automobile production, from 300,000–400,000 a year to a million a year, with the help of the Fiat Company of Italy. I anticipate they will succeed in two or three years, perhaps. However, it will be much more difficult to achieve corresponding quantities of highways, maintenance and repair service facilities, and spare parts. Seemingly, chronic difficulties in providing retail, personal, and repair services have hampered Soviet programs for housing, consumer durables, and consumption in general for decades.

The Soviet economy is in a state of widespread disequilibrium in the micro-allocation of resources. Indeed, one of the most important uses of the comparison of the United States and the USSR is to support that statement, as Bergson has shown.[1] In addition, however, no forces seem to be working toward reduction of disequilibrium. This implies either that the Soviet feasibility locus [2] is more convex than that of a market economy or that its probable shape is much more uncertain. The uncertainty is compounded by the observation that the slope of the relative price plane along which shifting of output mix is assumed to occur surely cannot be assumed to be tangent to the feasibility locus. The prices that are available are state- or enterprise-determined, and not market prices equating supply and demand.

My intent is not to dwell on the inefficiency of the Soviet economy, but to point out the consequences of its institutional arrangements for

[1] See A. Bergson, *Economics of Soviet Planning*, New Haven, Yale University Press, 1964.

[2] This phrase, as used by Bergson, expresses the thought that the USSR's output is far inside its technical production possibilities curve.

the problems of measurement. The ruble measure of relative size almost surely overstates the relative ability of the Soviet economy to produce the U.S. mix of output, significantly more, I suggest, than the lira measure of comparative size of the United States and Italy, which Bergson presents, overstates the ability of the Italian economy.

A final problem is that production potential cannot be separated from welfare or utility. Production must produce utilities or it is not production. A major weakness of the Soviet economic system is its relative inability to produce what customers want or need. The problem for an international comparison is not only the relation of Soviet preference functions to Western or U.S. preference functions, but the extent to which the USSR is producing in detail according to any utility function, even one that might be said to express planners' preferences. This is in part the quality problem which Bergson recognizes, and which may result in a large overstatement of USSR production, particularly of services. But, in addition, it is a problem of the mix of production.

Consider the low price of producers' equipment relative to consumer goods in the USSR as compared with the United States or Italy, as cited by Bergson.[3] If this were a meaningful comparison, one would expect the USSR to be exporting machinery and equipment in substantial quantities. But on the contrary, the USSR in 1955 did not export nearly as much machinery and equipment as it imported in trade with the West, and still does not. Indeed, currently it is a large net importer of machinery and equipment from Italy. The inability to export those types of machines which seem to be relatively cheap is the result of lack of durability, lack of repair services and spare parts, and unresponsiveness to individual consumers' needs for special tailoring or modification of equipment. The export market places a radically different valuation on these goods than the internal pricing system.

In this sense, the comparison of the United States and the USSR in dollar prices overstates the utility of the Soviet mix. Or to reverse the statement, the dollar comparison understates the ability of the United States to produce a mix equivalent to the Soviet mix in utility. The dollar value of the Soviet output is obtained by pricing goods and

[3] See Table 13.

services at dollar prices of physically comparable U.S. goods (of venerable vintage in some cases) or, in their absence, at cost. Many of these goods would cost more to produce in the United States than better and more up-to-date substitutes. In the case of innumerable types of machinery, it would cost more to produce the Soviet design in the United States than a superior U.S. design. According to the dollar comparisons the USSR has been producing more farm equipment than the United States since at least 1955, and cumulatively, over the whole period of fifteen years probably more than twice as much. Yet it is hardly disputable that the United States currently gets a great deal more agricultural work done per year by machines than the USSR.[4] It is clear that the United States could have generated a stock of farm equipment capable of carrying out the volume of machine processes actually achieved in the USSR over the last fifteen years with a much smaller annual expenditure on equipment and spare parts. The U.S. machinery would be of a different design and mix, more productive, more durable, easier to repair, more efficiently used, etc. It need not be mentioned that the corresponding U.S. requirement for labor to produce the Soviet output would still have been drastically smaller than in the USSR.

The import of these arguments (granting my allegations of fact) for the meaning of the comparison of a central administered bureaucratic production system with a market system is something like this. Production potential in a market environment implies a potential contingent only on a change in demand. The ability of the productive organizations to carry out the shift is not essentially questioned. However, the ability of the Soviet economy to shift investment goods or defense equipment and research and development to production in the style and diversity of U.S. consumer goods, i.e., to the production of meat, of vegetables and fruit, of single-family dwelling units, etc., at estab-

---

[4] The cumulative value of farm equipment in the USSR for 1955–68 inclusive in 1955 rubles is 15,500 million rubles. This excludes spare parts (see *Narodnoe khoziaistvo SSSR* for various years). Converted at Bergson's dollar-ruble ratio of 2.63, the value in 1955 dollars is $41 billion. U.S. production of agricultural equipment in *current* prices for 1955–68 is about $23.5 billion. (See Bureau of the Census, *Annual Survey of Manufactures*, for 1955–66; 1967 and 1968 extrapolated by the Federal Reserve Board index of farm equipment.) This statistic includes spare parts. Deflated to 1955 dollars, the U.S. total would be less than half the USSR total. Both U.S. and USSR data exclude tractors.

lished prices is questionable under present management institutions. The meaning of the comparisons is uncertain in the sense that the interpretation of the comparative ability to produce alternative mixes is contingent on some unspecifiable kind and degree of managerial reorganization in the USSR. Perhaps the meaning of these comparisons should be construed very literally. The dollar value of Soviet GNP is what it would cost to produce the Soviet mix in the United States (but not what the U.S. market would be willing to pay for it). The ruble valuation of the U.S. product is the cost of producing under Soviet conditions a product the composition of which is restricted to goods produced in the USSR.

ZOLTAN KENESSEY, United Nations Statistical Office

INTRODUCTION

The introduction to Bergson's paper—stating that the comparison of the real national incomes of the Soviet Union and of the United States in the West "began to be considered primarily in the appraisal of Soviet military potential"—reminds one of the beginnings of national income (and wealth) estimations and comparisons approximately three hundred years ago.

In fact the emergence of the first national income concepts (and more generally that of the science of statistics in the form of political arithmetic) is closely interwoven with rather similar needs for international comparisons at that time. Sir William Petty, when he constructed the first national income estimates in 1665 and 1676 for England, at the same time tried to compare the income and resources of England with those of France and the Netherlands. Not unlike researchers three centuries later (sitting in Cambridge, Massachusetts, or in Moscow) he was not entirely able to repeat, for the other two countries in which he became interested, the more detailed estimates he had prepared for his own country. So for France and the Nether-

NOTE: Responsibility for the views expressed here is entirely mine. Neither the United Nations, with which I am currently affiliated, nor the Hungarian Central Statistical Office, where I formerly served, are in any way accountable for the opinions expressed here by me.

lands his evaluation was based on population figures and on his estimates of productivity in various occupational groups in the two countries. On the basis of his findings, he derived ten "Principal Conclusions," three of which were: [1]

That France cannot, by reason of Natural and Perpetual Impediments, be more powerful at Sea, than the English or Hollanders

That the People, and Territories of the King of England, are Naturally near as considerable, for Wealth, and Strength, as those of France

That the King of England's Subjects, have the Stock competent, and convenient to drive the Trade of the whole Commercial World.

In history books it is also mentioned that because of their delicate nature and to avoid diplomatic complications with France, the calculations of Petty were published with the permission of the king only after Petty's death, in 1690 and 1691.[2]

The second set of national income estimates for England, prepared by Gregory King first for the year 1688 and then for 1695, were also accompanied by numerical estimates for France and Holland. King estimated the national income of all three countries in pounds sterling, but again (and quite naturally) his estimates for England were much more detailed than those for the other two countries.

This detour into the times of Petty and King may remind us about the seldom mentioned impact of war and military rivalries on our science. Most people are aware of the important impact of such rivalries on the development of surgery or nuclear physics. However, in the field of economics and statistics not only the general public, but quite a few professionals are unaware of some important influences of a similar nature.[3] It would not serve much purpose to lament about this state of affairs (apparently quite unchanged over the last three centuries) but still it is hard to rejoice unreservedly about some otherwise

[1] William Petty, *Economic Writings*, ed. C. H. Hull, Cambridge, Engl., 1899, vol. 1, pp. 247–48.

[2] Naturally this fact ought to be of only historical interest in our enlightened times, when the kings of England and the czars of Russia have long ceased to rule over what is today the United States of America and the Union of Soviet Socialist Republics.

[3] For example, the larger-scale application of national accounting (and indeed the organization of the Central Statistical Office in the United Kingdom) is not too widely recognized in its relationship to the war efforts of Britain during the crucial years of the early 1940's.

impressive gains made in economics and statistics on such a basis. Economists and statisticians probably do not share the feelings of grave responsibility expressed by many nuclear scientists for the results of their professional activities. Despite the material differences between nuclear physics and economics and statistics, in the light of the apparent historical trends, complacency is probably not the best attitude for our profession either.

It should be noted that Bergson is placed in the good company of Sir William Petty and Gregory King, the truly great forebears of our science, because his work follows the same traditon and because he has had to face the same kinds of unique problems during his investigations. It is hoped that since he has been placed in that company, and the respect due him for his great efforts has been expressed, he will not feel aggrieved if one turns now to dwell on various aspects of these unique problems.

CONCERNING THE OVERALL RESULTS OF THE COMPARISON

Probably a natural first reaction to the very interesting investigation produced by Bergson is to look at its overall numerical results, i.e., to the relationships estimated for the national income of the USSR vis-à-vis the United States. According to Table 14 of his study, the 1965 GNP of the USSR valued in rubles is estimated as 35 per cent of that of the United States, and in dollars as 57.5 per cent of the GNP of the United States. One way to look at these figures is to compare them with estimates of a similar nature published in the Soviet Union.[4] As it is shown below in terms of dollar valuation a tentative attempt can be made at such a comparison with the use of the data published in the latest issue of the Soviet statistical yearbook.

According to the latest official estimates of the Central Statistical Administration of the USSR the national income of the Soviet Union in 1968 was 243.1 billion rubles.[5] At the official exchange rate the dollar equivalent of this sum is given as $270.1 billion.[6]

[4] L. I. Nesterov and Y. N. Ivanov (both from the Statistical Office of the United Nations) made available quite a few new Soviet publications in the area of USSR-U.S. comparisons for the preparation of the present comments, for which sincere thanks is expressed here.

[5] *Narodnoe khoziaistvo SSSR v 1968 godu,* USSR Central Statistical Administration, Moscow, 1969, p. 569.

[6] *Ibid.,* p. 146.

In that same table the dollar value of the Soviet national income is also given with a correction for the differences between the price levels of the USSR and the United States. From the context of the table it can be inferred that the national income of the USSR—which is estimated to be $326.4 billion [7]—is given at U.S. prices. In order to achieve conceptual comparability the national income of the United States is given by the yearbook according to the methodology applied by the Central Statistical Administration. The estimate for the U.S. national income in 1968 is $513.2 billion.[8]

Thus using the methodology applied by the Central Statistical Administration, and dollar rather than ruble valuation, the national income of the USSR in 1968 was 62.8 per cent of that of the United States in the same year.

It is somewhat interesting to compare this with the extrapolation of results from other sources, using the statistical indexes of the growth of the national income of the Soviet Union and the United States as published in the same issue of the yearbook.

As mentioned above, in the present study by Bergson, the 1965 GNP (not national income, which was compared above) of the USSR valued in dollars is given as 57.5 per cent of the U.S. value. (See Bergson's Table 14.) In the Soviet statistical yearbook (page 144) the 1968 level of the USSR's national income is 26 per cent higher and that of the United States is 15 per cent higher than in 1965.

Using for extrapolation these figures (which relate to the growth of the national income as opposed to that of the GNP) in combination with the 1965 percentage established by Bergson for the USSR compared to the United States (in dollar values and adhering to the GNP concept) yields 63 per cent for the USSR for 1968—a remarkably close figure to that published on the base of the Soviet national accounting methodology with the adoption of U.S. prices for the valuation of the Soviet national income.

While the data included in the yearbook do not extend to comparisons in ruble valuations for the two countries involved, it can be noted that in the above-mentioned estimate for 1968, 243.1 billion

[7] *Loc. cit.*
[8] *Loc. cit.*

rubles are equated with $326.4 billion, implying the equivalence (in the given context) of 134 U.S. cents with 100 kopecks.

Admittedly the extrapolation of the Bergson results for 1965 to 1968 with other indicators (i.e., with those related to GNP rather than to the national income in the materials product system sense) would produce results only somewhat different. Even in terms of a GNP-oriented comparison it would appear permissible, for a crude extrapolation for the short period involved, to disregard whatever distortions arise because of the assumption that the service sector grew at the same rate as that observed for the other GNP components.

At any rate the rather marked closeness of the two dollar-valuation estimates can be interpreted either from a more formal and critical or from a rather broad standpoint.

The relative closeness of the results obtained by researchers on either side of the Atlantic is gratifying to me. Apparently this is a broad view of the problem, based on the assumption that even within a single country the national income and product estimates performed by the agencies having access to a very wide range of data are subject to variations and/or errors. It is conceivable that two competent and independent teams of statisticians within a single country, having access to the same basic data and following the same broad accounting principles, could come out with somewhat different results for the GNP (or national income) of their country in any given year. International comparisons are even more subject to limitations, especially if they are performed in a noncollaborative manner, as here. Consequently, while the formal accuracy of one or the other of the two estimates may be questioned, the closeness of the two numerical results should be interpreted as a very reassuring fact about the order of magnitude of the levels of the two countries.

Adherents of a more formal standpoint (whom I do not wish to join) would probably base their dislike of the quoted results on the following logic: The Soviet estimate adheres to an MPS (materials product system) concept for both countries. The Bergson study is based on a GNP-related concept. The differences in the share of services within all economic activities in the United States and the USSR are quite marked. Consequently, either the Soviet estimate or that of

Bergson must be off the mark. (A real skeptic among them would probably add: It is possible that both of them are.)

It is not my task to defend either Professor Bergson or the Soviet estimators against any of these "rigorous" critics. In the final analysis, in fact, only a very thorough study of all the details of the two estimates (amounting to a repetition of the calculations, which I certainly cannot do) could justify definitively the broad standpoint advocated in the present notes. However one—admittedly not decisive—argument against the formal attitude may deserve mention.

The adoption of the logic cited above and a strict argument in favor of either of the two results may lead to strange assumptions, such as the following: Bergson is perhaps *overstating* and/or the Soviet Statistical Yearbook is perhaps *understating* the dollar value of the Soviet GNP (or Soviet national income) since a priori the relationship between the two countries should show a higher percentage for the Soviet Union on an MPS basis than on a GNP basis.

If the results of the two estimates are as close as in this case, someone stressing the sole reliability of the result of the Bergson estimate may find that he has to agree to a higher MPS ratio in favor of the Soviet Union than that published in the USSR. Again, someone accepting absolute validity for the Soviet estimate may agree that, a priori, a GNP ratio between the two countries ought to be smaller than that estimated for the USSR vis-à-vis the United States on the MPS basis.

According to such reasoning, an accompanying and consistent U.N. national accounts system estimate for the published Soviet calculations may lead to a "lower" result for Soviet GNP than that produced by Bergson (hence the assumption of the implicit *"overstatement"* by Bergson in favor of the Soviet Union). On the other hand an accompanying and consistent MPS estimate for the Bergson study may produce a "higher" result for Soviet national income than that produced by the Soviet statisticians (hence the assumption of the implicit *"understatement"* in the Soviet Statistical Yearbook).

To avoid any misunderstanding I wish to underline that I do not share the reasoning outlined above or the implicit assumptions mentioned. In fact I firmly believe that in the given context the broader point of view on the subject—as opposed to a formalistic approach with possibly strange implications—is both more appropriate and more constructive.

It is interesting to note that recent estimates developed by the United Nations Economic Commission for Europe (based largely on the short-cut method of F. Jánossy and published in the *Economic Survey of Europe in 1969*) are rather closely in the middle range of the two limits produced by Bergson for the USSR-U.S. comparison. (Some remarks on the ECE work are contained in the appendix to this comment.)

METHODOLOGICAL PROBLEMS

In commenting on a few methodological problems, it is desirable to state the significance of the objective of Professor Bergson's paper as the study of the "comparative 'production potential' " [9] rather than the investigation of the quite important but more elusive welfare concept.

If one thinks of the various possible uses of the results of real product comparisons (as mentioned below) it is clear that the choice made by Bergson in this respect is not only the more practical one but also the one which suits the majority of the final purposes listed here for the use of international comparison results: [10]

Assessments of welfare levels (standard of living, real incomes, etc., compared in different countries)

Studies of economic efficiency

Comparisons of economic and military power

Agreements concerning cost-sharing between nations (in the budgets of international organizations, common defense arrangements, etc.)

Formulation of foreign aid policies (taking into account the capabilities of the donors and the needs, the level of economic development, etc., of the recipients)

Economic policy or planning (the comparative data serving as information or even as a set of development targets)

[9] See first paragraph of his paper, above.

[10] See "Plans for International Product and Purchasing Power Comparison" (mimeo), U.N. Statistical Office and University of Pennsylvania International Comparison Unit, August 1968, p. 5.

Analysis of foreign markets (the purchasing power of markets abroad, price competitiveness of different countries, etc.)

Integration processes (judging the possibilities and impact of specialization, cooperation, common markets, the movements of the factors of production, etc.)

Construction and verification of economic theories (models of growth, etc.)

Statistical purposes (to obtain weights for regional or world indexes etc.)

One would think however that if the basic data permit it, a more explicit decomposition of the underlying factors leading to the differences observed in the comparison of the "productive potential" of the two countries studied would be of great interest.

Admittedly no way can be found for any "complete separation" of the influence of prices on quantity comparisons or vice versa. Still if the necessary basic information is available the performance and the showing of the more detailed results for such comparisons in the following form [11] is of some help:

Quantity comparison with the price weights of the base country:

$$\Sigma Q_1 P_0 / \Sigma Q_0 P_0$$

Quantity comparison with the price weights of the other country:

$$\Sigma Q_1 P_1 / \Sigma Q_0 P_1$$

Price comparison with the quantity weights of the base country:

$$\Sigma P_1 Q_0 / \Sigma P_0 Q_0$$

Price comparison with the quantity weights of the other country:

$$\Sigma P_1 Q_1 / \Sigma P_0 Q_1$$

Especially for the analysis of production potential a somewhat more direct investigation of the influence of the quantity and price measures (and weights) on the results obtained can be of great interest. For

[11] Milton Gilbert and Irving B. Kravis, *An International Comparison of National Products and the Purchasing Power of Currencies,* Paris, Organization for European Economic Cooperation, 1954, p. 63.

example the interpretation (in the context mentioned above) of the statement of Bergson that it was his aim "to use price ratios with Soviet weights to deflate ruble outlays and ratios with U.S. weights to deflate dollar outlays" [12] presents some difficulty for the reader. Generally, it appears appropriate to underline here that for studies of this nature the significance of the "quantity approach" is somewhat greater than that of the "price approach." [13]

The methodological problems related to the price observations are also quite complex.[14] On the one hand it would be quite unfair to dwell upon the nature and possible deficiencies of the basic price information available to Bergson for his study. His control over any deficiencies of this sort was obviously limited. Still the uneasiness one feels about some problems of the basic data is hard to eliminate. Obviously, this is no comment on the quality of the very detailed investigation done by Bergson. However, even the most excellent compilation and evaluation of basic data (in this case, price observations) may not eliminate such uneasiness in the reader, especially as to the problems of matching identical or comparable products for pricing.

Clearly there is no need to idealize price data collection by any government statistical organization. If one reads the report of the Stigler Committee [15] or other relevant materials, the situation in this respect would not appear ideal in many ways. Still the same documents also give a much better feeling for the complex efforts undertaken to improve price data collection. It appears enough to refer to the study of sampling problems for the U.S. Bureau of Labor Statistics Consumer Price Index [16] as opposed to the much more unexplored question of the representativeness of Sears, Roebuck prices.[17] The

[12] See last paragraph of The Calculations, in his paper.

[13] Especially because of the problems related to the system of relative prices in the USSR, extensively investigated in Bergson's *The Real National Income of Soviet Russia since 1928*, Cambridge, Mass., Harvard University Press, 1961.

[14] Because of the relative lack of emphasis on quantity observations in the paper it would not appear useful to dwell here on problems related to the quantity approach.

[15] Report of Price Statistics Review Committee, *The Price Statistics of the Federal Government*, New York, NBER, 1961.

[16] *The Consumer Price Index: History and Techniques*, BLS Bull. 1517, 1966.

[17] One should not be too much surprised if the estimators of the dollar values of the USSR national income in the Central Statistical Administration in Moscow also had a Sears, Roebuck catalogue on their shelves.

sample of prices used for the USSR in the study quite possibly has its limitations as well.

Under the given conditions there is apparently no remedy for these problems. Noncollaborative comparisons—as it can be demonstrated from Petty and King to Bergson and the Soviet yearbook—by their nature have these kinds of limitations. The only possibility of overcoming this obstacle lies in the bilateral, cooperative approach to such studies advocated below.

CONCLUSIONS

On the preceding pages due respect was paid to Professor Bergson for undertaking this very complex and very demanding study. Taking into account all the difficulties such studies have to face, his investigation is certainly quite impressive. The closeness of the overall ratio obtained for the USSR vis-à-vis the United States in dollar values is also very interesting.

Naturally there remain numerous methodological, political, numerical, and other points on which disagreement could be aired. But in view of the overall significance of such studies, and in order to stimulate the thinking about the possibilities for overcoming the inherent limitations of all investigations conducted in a noncollaborative manner, the more constructive approach of discussing the questions of collaborative comparisons is attempted.

The road to bilateral cooperative arrangements for studies aimed at USSR-U.S. comparisons is obviously not an easy one. The results of such comparisons are obviously not only of an academic interest.

Fully recognizing all the difficulties involved in the arrangement of a cooperative study it still does not appear superfluous to list some of the comparative advantage of the cooperative approach over even the best organized and most ingenious unilateral work in this area.

Apparently, only with the cooperation of the national statistical services of these two great countries would it be possible to base the comparisons on the most reliable primary data for quantities, prices, and expenditures. Anyone familiar with the intricacies of national accounts estimates must admit that without access to the great variety of data available within the statistical services and in other governmental and nongovernmental organizations, the reliability of estimates must suffer considerably.

In the case of quantity and price data, the direct help and involvement of national statistical services, at least in two important aspects, it is quite indispensable. On the one hand, without such assistance it is extremely difficult to assess the representativeness of the items included in the sample in relation to the vast total population of goods to be compared. It is quite possible that the quantity or price information somehow available to private research is not unreliable per se. However, another matter is whether the information available is well enough chosen for inferences to be drawn from it with respect to the total population of goods. The best possible sampling frame is certainly available only to national statistical services.

Another important aspect of the involvement of the statistical services (and through them of other national authorities) in the procurement of price and quantity data is related to the possibilities of achieving a much higher degree of comparability (and/or quality adjustments) for the products and services studied. Anyone with experience in this area can testify about the formidable difficulties encountered here—even when such help is made available. Without such help the task is really overwhelming.

It should also be mentioned that in choosing the most effective general methodology it is advantageous to have the cooperation of the national statistical services. While quite a few methodological procedures may look impeccable in theory, only with the cooperation of the two sides involved in such an undertaking is it possible to judge their effectiveness within the statistical-economic context of the two economies being compared. This is not to say that success is secured only with complete unanimity as to the best methodology for a comparison. Nevertheless, the discussion of the methods—even if complete agreement cannot be reached—may be of enormous help in selecting the best path for the solution of the innumerable problems which have to be faced.

Other remarks on the advantages of a cooperative approach could be made. However, this is hardly needed since most of the arguments are rather self-evident. It can be safely assumed that the vast majority of researchers would agree to such an assessment. Probably the more experienced they are in "unilateral" work in this area—like Bergson—the more they could say about the possible advantages of a cooperative approach.

The real difficulty, they would say, is not in their doubts about the advantages of the cooperative approach but in its feasibility. Naturally, on this crucial point they may be right. On the other hand, perhaps not enough has been done to explore the possibilities in this area.

Possibly, direct cooperation for such a study may be too difficult to organize. Perhaps the exploration of proper arrangements for indirect cooperation, possibly with the help of an international organization, would yield somewhat better results.

At least one remark should be made about the latter approach. An international organization could, with the help of the national statistical services, certainly go further than private researchers—and still work on its own responsibility, i.e., without necessarily implying responsibility by the countries for the results so achieved.

At the same time an international organization could prove to be a place where ideas concerning the optimal ways to achieve comparability could be best exchanged and where the interpretation of the results could be safeguarded against unilateral or extreme views or against propagandistic use.

It is hoped that the widespread efforts for such comparisons by many researchers in the two largest producers of the present-day world economy will not remain unrewarded in the future. There can be little doubt that even a measure of cooperation in this field would materially improve the depth of such investigations.

One could argue that much of the above is not directly related to the impressive work of Bergson in this area. It is contended, however, that his stimulating paper should encourage everyone interested in research in this field to explore every possibility for improvement in this important realm of economic studies which had its beginnings in efforts of men like Sir William Petty and Gregory King.

APPENDIX

The significance of extensive direct cooperation of the national statistical services of the countries studied in international comparisons does not decrease even if such work is carried out by international organizations (which usually have better contacts with their member countries and whose multinational staff has better access to sources of data and a rather wide knowledge on methodological differences, etc.).

The comparisons recently performed by the U.N. Economic Commission for Europe can be mentioned in this respect. For the *Economic Survey of Europe in 1969* a rather detailed study was prepared with the aid of certain short-cut methods, based on physical or "nonmonetary" indicators of output and/or consumption, using regression techniques. The approach adopted for the study largely followed the method as developed earlier in Hungary by F. Jánossy.[18] This work is a quite interesting and certainly worthwhile attempt at finding a less expensive type of method than that followed by those who delve into the difficulties of making detailed price and quantity comparisons. Nevertheless, the interpretation and acceptance of the results is not without difficulties.

According to the calculations, the 1965 per capita gross domestic product of the USSR was about 40.5 per cent of that of the United States.[19] These estimates fit comfortably within the two limits given by Bergson for the per capita GNP relationship of the two countries in the same year (29.5 per cent in ruble values and 48.5 per cent in dollar values).[20] Naturally the same can be said about total GDP (about 48 per cent on the base of the ECE calculations), which is also neatly within the range of the estimates given by Bergson—35 per cent and 57.5 per cent.[21]

Considering the different methodology applied by Bergson and the ECE, the closeness of the results is quite remarkable. One is tempted to conclude (as in the case of the comparison of the Bergson figures with those of the Soviet Statistical Yearbook in dollar values) that broadly speaking the results confirm each other.

While this may be the best conclusion to be drawn, a few problems nevertheless remain. Although the overall results of these three estimates are rather close to each other, in certain respects the discrepancies are quite pronounced. In the case of Bergson's estimates compared

---

[18] F. Jánossy: *A gazdasági fejlettség mérhetösége és uj mérési módszere,* Budapest, Közgazdasági Kiadó, 1963.
[19] See table at end of this appendix.
[20] See Bergson's Table 14.
[21] *Ibid.*

to those in the Soviet yearbook, for example, the comparisons of the output originating in industry and agriculture are rather different. Compared with the ECE estimates for consumption (USSR per capita total consumption is given as about 32 per cent of the United States in 1965) the two limits given by Bergson are 20.6 and 34 per cent (in ruble and dollar values) and the assumed differences in the scope of consumption would not appear to explain completely the closeness of the ECE estimate to the higher (dollar-valuation) figure given by Bergson.

Other problems could be mentioned as well. On a priori grounds it would appear doubtful whether the figures computed by the ECE for Hungary and the USSR are good approximations for the comparison of these two countries (for 1965 the per capita GDP is given as $1,015 for Hungary and $1,053 for the USSR). Most Western estimates assume a somewhat larger difference in favor of the USSR as do the calculations performed within the Council for Mutual Economic Assistance (the latter being based on a different concept). On the other hand Bulgaria fares somewhat "worse," according to the ECE study in per capita GDP (compared to the USSR) than according to the CMEA comparisons (performed on an MPS basis).

Considering the great interest, and much better analytical possibilities, in the more detailed results of such comparisons, the closeness of the overall estimates does not seem to give sufficient assurance about the divergencies seen in certain aspects.

One interesting feature of the ECE study is the publication of the standard errors of the estimates. In the case of the USSR the "confidence limits" at a 5 per cent significance level (as a percentage of the average estimate) are given as ±24 per cent. For the United States the same limits are ±10 per cent and for Hungary, ±15 per cent. This attempt at judging the reliability of the figures published is certainly most welcome. Nevertheless, if one takes them seriously, the differences observed by the ECE for the Hungary-USSR comparison cannot be taken as having material significance.

All in all the foregoing remarks mean to illuminate only one point, namely, that the work performed by international organizations is likely to have a marked advantage over unilateral efforts only in those cases where (and to the extent that) the direct and extensive cooperation of the countries studied can be obtained.

Per Capita Gross Domestic Product, 1965

	At Official 1965 Exchange Rate	ECE Physical Indicators; Estimates in "Average" Prices	Standard Error of Estimate (dollars) [a]	Confidence Limits at 5 Per Cent Significance Level (as per cent of average estimates) [a]
Austria	$1,273	$1,459	$ 57	±8
Belgium-Luxembourg	1,782	1,886	74	±8
Denmark	2,132	1,820	76	±9
Finland	1,750	1,585	87	±11
France	1,922	1,616	58	±8
Greece	677	758	63	±18
Ireland	943	1,239	66	±11
Italy	1,021	1,190	50	±9
Netherlands	1,537	1,796	64	±7
Norway	1,910	1,668	58	±7
Portugal	405	733	57	±16
Spain	680	939	55	±12
Sweden	2,536	2,171	86	±8
Switzerland	2,274	1,863	105	±12
Turkey	284	333	25	±16
United Kingdom	1,802	1,929	73	±8
West Germany	1,913	1,854	64	±7
Japan	868	1,293	92	±15
Canada	2,500	2,218	90	±9
United States	3,553	2,597	126	±10
Australia	2,057	1,889	71	±8
New Zealand	1,999	1,850	107	±12
Bulgaria	–	877	87	±21
Czechoslovakia	–	1,427	110	±16
East Germany	–	1,437	92	±13
Hungary	–	1,015	73	±15
Poland	–	989	93	±20
Romania	–	697	63	±19
Soviet Union	–	1,053	121	±24
Yugoslavia	–	692	55	±17

SOURCE: U.N. Economic Commission for Europe, *Economic Survey of Europe in 1969*, Part I, Chap. 4, App. Table V.

[a] Based on the assumption of randomness of the sample; see text.

DAN USHER, Queen's University

National income is a summary statistic, one number to describe the size of a complete economy or to compare the sizes of two economies. Bergson presents the number and explains how he got it, what sources of data were used, and how the data were combined. There is, however, a sense in which the number is not fully explained. Users of income comparisons—politicians, economists, and interested laymen—would find the summary statistic more informative if they were told precisely what it is that is being summarized. When one reads that Russian household consumption per head is between 17 per cent and 22 per cent of American household consumption per head, one finds oneself asking "What do the Russians eat?" and "How are they housed?" and "How extensive are their medical services?" One would like to know precisely what goods and services Americans have that the Russians do not. The information might be presented in a long table comparing American and Russian incomes quantity by quantity and price by price in as much detail as the data allow, with footnotes specifying assumptions made in identifying Russian and American quantities and in choosing prices. Perhaps one can get this information from the primary sources Bergson cites, but the amount of detective work required would be considerable, for the construction of the Russian accounts seems to be a vast joint effort of many scholars continually cribbing from one another and developing layer upon layer of estimates. It would be helpful if Bergson could cut through all this and take us back to prices and quantities per head.

In introducing the study, Bergson says that income comparisons may have two objectives: "appraisal of comparative 'production potential' or appraisal of comparative 'welfare.' I take as a desideratum here the appraisal of comparative production potential." This objective leads Bergson to compare ratios of income at adjusted rubles (suitable for production comparison) as well as at prevailing rubles (suitable for welfare comparison). I would like to make a few remarks on relations between welfare and production comparisons and on the extent to which they may be distinguished. I will not discuss complications that arise from the existence of international trade, nor will I discuss the comparison of income classified by industry. I shall concentrate on comparison of final goods and services in closed economies.

In Table 2 of Bergson's paper, we see that the ratio of Russian to American income is 38.1 per cent at American prices, 22.1 per cent at prevailing rubles, and 23.2 per cent at adjusted rubles. Let us think of America as the base year and of Russia as the current year so that the first of these numbers is the Laspeyres index and the latter two are variants of the Paasche index. To say that one intends an income comparison to reflect "welfare" or "production potential" is to say that one has certain questions in mind which one hopes to answer by means of the data. Two questions might reasonably be asked about production.[1] First, what fraction of the American output could Russia produce if Russia chose a basket of goods and services in the same proportions as goods and services in the American basket? Second, what fraction or multiple of the Russian output could America produce if America chose a basket of goods and services in the same proportions as goods and services in the Russian basket? I shall refer to the answer to the first question as the true production comparison at the American mix of goods and services, and to the answer to the second question as the true production comparison at the Russian mix of goods and services. The two true ratios of Russian production potential to American production potential will be designated T_{PA} and T_{PR}.

Similarly, there are two welfare questions: First, what multiple of the typical Russian income would one need in Russia to be as well off as the typical American? Second, what multiple of the typical American income would one need in America to be as well off as the typical Russian? I shall refer to the answer to the first question as the comparison by American standards and to the answer to the second question as the comparison by Russian standards. The two ratios of income answering these questions will be designated T_{WA} and T_{WR}.

Relations among the true welfare comparisons, the true comparisons of production potential, and the observed Paasche and Laspeyres indexes are illustrated in Figure 1. Russia has a comparative advantage

[1] See A. Bergson, *The Real Income of Soviet Russia since 1928*, Cambridge, Harvard University Press, 1961, Part 1; and R. Moorstein, "On Measuring Productive Potential and Relative Efficiency," *Quarterly Journal of Economics*, 1961, pp. 451–67.

FIGURE 1a

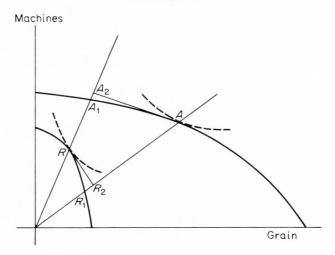

FIGURE 1b

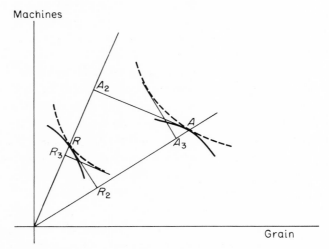

NOTE: In Figure 1a, $T_{PA} = R_1/A$; $T_{PR} = R/A_1$; $P = R_2/A$; $L = R/A_2$. In Figure 1b, $T_{WA} = R_3/A_2$; $T_{WR} = R_2/A_3$. For fuller explanation of figures, see text.

in machines and America has a comparative advantage in grain, but as the curves are drawn America can produce more grain and more machines than Russia at any mix of output. The American output is designated A and the Russian output is designated R. The heavy curved lines through A and R are American and Russian production possibility curves, and the curved dashed lines are indifference curves. Tastes are the same in both countries in the sense that the countries have one set of indifference curves in common. The relative prices of grain in America and Russia are slopes of the "budget constraints" AA_2 and RR_2.

As illustrated in Figure 1a, the Paasche and Laspeyres indexes of output are $P = R_2/A$ and $L = R/A_2$, and the true productivity indexes are $T_{PA} = R_1/A$ and $T_{PR} = R/A_1$. Figure 1b is the same as Figure 1a wherever the points are labeled identically. The point A_3 is a projection onto the line from A to the origin of the tangent to the American indifference curve at Russian prices. Thus R_2/A_3 is the ratio of Russian income to the income in rubles needed to make a Russian as well off as an American. The true welfare comparisons at American standards and at Russian standards are: $T_{WA} = R_3/A_2$ and $T_{WR} = R_2/A_3$. From Figure 1 it may be seen that two sets of inequalities must always hold: $T_{PA} < P < T_{WR}$ and $T_{WA} < L < T_{PR}$. These inequalities are true as long as the indifference curves are convex, the production possibility curves are concave, and the indifference curves are tangent to production possibility curves at the chosen mix of output.

The reason for developing these inequalities here is to deal with the question of whether and under what circumstances the Paasche and Laspeyres indexes are upper and lower limits to the true indexes we are searching for. It follows directly from the inequalities that when the Paasche index exceeds the Laspeyres index the two indexes may bracket the two true indexes of production potential but cannot under any circumstances bracket the welfare indexes. Similarly, when the Laspeyres index exceeds the Paasche index, the two indexes may (and probably do) bracket the two true welfare indexes, but the true indexes of production potential lie outside the range of the Paasche and Laspeyres indexes.

Bergson's data furnish an example of the latter case. Since the Laspeyres index (38.1 per cent) exceeds the Paasche index (22.1 per cent), it follows that $T_{PA} < P < L < T_{PR}$. (The middle inequality is an empirical fact; the other two inequalities are a logical consequence of the concavity of production possibility curves.) In a sense, the observable indexes of comparative real income are the wrong limits to the numbers Bergson is searching for. Should the Americans try to produce a basket of goods and services in proportion to the Russian basket, they could produce something less than 2.3 times the Russian income (2.3 = 1/0.38). But nothing in the statistics indicates how much less. There is no lower limit at all, and for all we know the true figure might be less than 1. Similarly the Russians, if they tried to produce a mix of outputs proportional to the American mix, would produce something less than 22 per cent of the American output, but again there is no lower limit. That, unfortunately, is all that can be inferred from the data.

Difficulties arising from the absence of outer limits in comparisons of production potential are compounded by problems encountered in choosing commodities to be compared. The diagrams have been drawn as though the division of output into a finite number of commodities were God-given. In fact, we choose the commodities, and the result of the comparison is influenced by our choice. Suppose that Russia and America grow different varieties of wheat. Before a comparison of income can begin, someone must draw equivalences between Russian and American wheat by weight, by calorie content, by protein content, by world prices, or whatever. And prior to this decision someone must decide that Russian and American wheat are one and the same commodity for the purpose of income comparison. For the sake of the argument, suppose that differences of soil and climate in Russia and America are so great that Russian wheat will not grow in America and American wheat will not grow in Russia. I think we would still classify Russian and American wheat as the same commodity but our reason for doing so would be that they are nearly perfect substitutes *in use* despite the fact that there is no substitution between them *in production*. In these circumstances our ideal of an income comparison reflecting pure "production potential" becomes completely unattainable. Either we must say that America simply cannot produce the Russian mix of goods and vice versa, or we must deal in comparisons where considerations of welfare have been brought to bear in organizing statistics at a lower level. Bergson has chosen the latter course, and I think it is the right one, but in interpreting his data as measures of production potential we must recognize that either he or someone else who prepared the primary data has had to introduce considerations of utility, welfare, and taste to work the primary data into a form amenable to income comparison.

The issue of the existence of upper and lower limits to the true ratios of welfare and production potential may be clarified by reinterpreting the relation between the Paasche and Laspeyres indexes, and by considering three simple cases of the situation described in Figure 1. It is a fact that

$$L > P \leftrightarrow \Sigma_i v_i p_i q_i < 1$$

and

$$L < P \leftrightarrow \Sigma_i v_i p_i q_i > 1$$

where v_i is the value of the output of the ith commodity in the base year, p_i is the change in the price of the ith commodity between the base year and the current year as a multiple of the average change in prices, and q_i is the change in the quantity between the base year and the current year as a multiple of the average change in quantities. Thus to say the $L > P$ is to say that the p_i and q_i tend to be negatively correlated or that the economy is moving along demand curves between the base year and the current year. To say that $P > L$ is to say that the p_i and q_i are positively correlated and that the economy is moving along supply curves between the base year and the current year.

The three paradigm cases are the "taste case" illustrated in Figure 2a, the "technology case" illustrated in Figure 2b, and the "tax case" illustrated in Figure 2c. The top half of each figure is a simplification of Figure 1, and the bottom half conveys the same information as the top half in the language of demand and supply curves.

In the taste case, indifference curves are homothetic, that is to say, every indifference curve is a scaled up or scaled down version of every other curve, price ratios depend only on proportions of grain and machines consumed, and all income elasticities equal 1. In interpreting Figure 2a, one might imagine either that the Russians and Americans

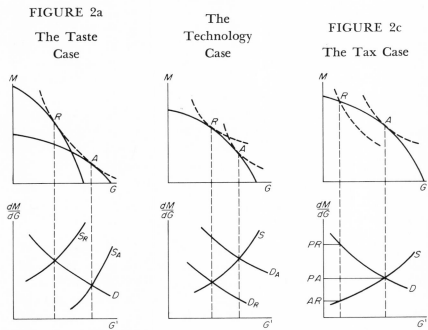

FIGURE 2a

The Taste Case

FIGURE 2b

The Technology Case

FIGURE 2c

The Tax Case

M = number of machines.

G = tons of grain.

G' = output of grain as a percentage of the output at A divided by output of machines as a percentage of the output at A.

PA = relative price of grain and machines in the United States.

PR = relative price of grain and machines in prevailing rules.

AR = relative price of grain and machines in adjusted rubles.

NOTE: In Figure 2a, indifference curves are homothetic. In Figure 2b, production possibility curves are homothetic. In Figure 2c, both sets of curves are homothetic and $L > P$ at prevailing rubles, $P > L$ at adjusted rubles.

are equally well off or that the American indifference curves are scaled up or down so that the American curve containing the point A coincides with the Russian curve containing the point R. The demand curve for grain in the bottom half of the figure is the locus of the relative quantity of grain and the relative price of grain as traced out along any indifference curve. Similarly, the height of each supply curve is the derivative of the corresponding production possibility curve. Between A and R the supply curve shifts, causing a movement along a common demand curve; price and quantity are negatively correlated and

$$T_{PA} < P < T_{WR} = T_{WA} < L < T_{PR}$$

The true welfare indexes are equal and are bounded by P and L, but the indexes of production potential lie outside these limits.

In the technology case, the production possibility curves are homothetic, and the indifference curves are not. One of the production possibility curves is scaled up so that the two production possibility curves coincide. Indifference curves differ because tastes differ or as a consequence of income effects. Here the demand curves shift between A and R and the supply curve is constant; consequently,

$$T_{WA} < L < T_{PR} = T_{PA} < P < T_{WA}$$

In this case, the true productivity indexes are bracketed by P and L, but the welfare indexes lie outside these limits.

In the tax case, production possibility curves and indifference curves are both homothetic, and American and Russian relative prices differ because the countries have different systems of taxation. For convenience, suppose that the American tax structure is ideal and that the Russian tax structure is not. A Russian excise tax on grain creates a spread between the demand price of grain (the slope of the indifference curve at R) and the supply price of grain (the slope of the production possibility curve at R). The demand price is what Bergson calls price in prevailing rubles, and the supply price is what Bergson calls price in adjusted rubles. As there are two prices at R, a movement from A to R may be thought of as being along a demand curve when prices are in prevailing rubles or along a supply curve when prices are in adjusted rubles. Consequently, $P < T_{WR} = T_{WA} < L$ when prices are measured in prevailing rubles, and, $L < T_{PA} = T_{PR} < P_{(AR)}$ when prices are measured in adjusted rubles. This is a statistician's ideal, with two sets of Paasche and Laspeyres indexes, one set bounding true welfare indexes and the other set bounding true production indexes.

Bergson's data look more like the taste case than the technology case because the Laspeyres index is greater than the Paasche index even at adjusted rubles.[2] There is a tendency toward the tax case, for

[2] These results are consistent with a large body of evidence that the structure of taste is more stable than the structure of technology in international comparisons

the Paasche index, while always less than the Laspeyres index, is some-what greater at adjusted rubles than at prevailing rubles—23.2 per cent as against 22.1 per cent in Bergson's Table 2.

The influence of taxes may be greater than these data suggest. First, it is almost impossible to account for all sources of divergence between demand prices and supply prices in both countries. Bergson's conver-sion of prevailing rubles into adjusted rubles accounts for some sources in Russia and none at all in the United States. A full and complete conversion of prices to adjusted rubles and adjusted dollars might substantially reduce the spread between the Laspeyres and Paasche indexes. Second, the spread between the two indexes might have been widened by the way services were evaluated. It is my impression that for some items such as education and defense, where direct measures of output are hard to come by, Bergson assumed that the marginal products of Russian and American workers were the same. I cannot very well criticize Bergson for doing so because I have made the same assumption in less justifiable circumstances, and because he frequently had no alternative. Nevertheless, this assumption may overstate Russian output. The Russians, who appear to be less efficient than the Ameri-cans in making goods, may also be less efficient in rendering services. If so, quantities are overstated and prices are understated accordingly because prices are imputed by dividing quantity into value. This may account for some of the very low Russian prices in Bergson's Table 13, especially wages in public administration and defense.

REPLY by Bergson

I can comment on only a few of the many interesting questions that the discussants of my paper raise. To refer first to Dan Usher: Hicks and Samuelson showed long ago how index numbers of real national

and in comparisons over time. In studies of economic growth, this is called the Gerschentron effect. See E. Ames and J. Carlson, "Production Index Bias as a Measure of Economic Development," *Oxford Economic Papers,* March 1968; P. Jonas and H. Sardy, "The Gerschentron Effect: A Re-examination, *Review of Economics and Statistics,* February 1970; and Y. Toda, "On International Com-parison of Consumption: Studies in Index Number Theory and Measurement," Ph.D. dissertation, Harvard University, 1969.

income might serve as observations on changes in production capacity, as represented by the production possibility schedule. Essentially, if such schedules are, as usually assumed, concave from below, one may infer from $\Sigma p_1 x_2 \geqq \Sigma p_1 x_1$ that the basket of goods produced in 2 is beyond the capacity of 1. Hence, production possibilities in 2 are greater than in 1 in the vicinity of the observed point in 2. Similarly, if $\Sigma p_2 x_1 \geqq \Sigma p_2 x_2$ the basket of goods produced in 1 is beyond the capacity of 2, and production possibilities in 1 are greater than in 2 in the vicinity of the observed point in 1.

Note that, as so often in index number theory, inferences are only of an ordinal sort. Production capacity is said to be greater in one situation than in another, and that is all. Moreover, as Hicks and Samuelson made clear, even these inferences, strictly speaking, presuppose valuations of an ideal kind: Relative prices correspond to marginal rates of transformation. In the article that I cited, however, Moorsteen showed that with such valuations real national income data may also be construed as representing comparative magnitudes of production capacity. Thus, data in the prices of 2 measure the ratio of capacities to produce 1's composite, and data in the prices of 1 measure the ratio of capacities to produce 2's composite. The measures are precisely accurate if production possibility schedules are linear. Otherwise, they are more or less approximate, depending on the degree of concavity or convexity of the schedules.

In my essay, I refer also to a previous study of mine (*Real SNIP*), which may have contributed further to this analysis. Thus, data in prices of either 1 or 2 are observations on relative capacities to produce either mix. Under certain conditions, however, data in prices of 1 are, as Moorsteen assumed, more accurate than data in prices of 2 as observations on relative capacities to produce 2's composite. Similarly, data in prices of 2 are more accurate than data in prices of 1 as observations on relative capacities to produce 1. The conditions are: (i) Production possibility schedules are, as with Hicks and Samuelson, concave from below, or at least not very convex; and (ii) the Gerschenkron effect holds, that is, data in prices of 2 are more favorable to 1 than data in prices of 1, and conversely.

To all this, Professor Usher has now added a further proposition. To conform with his notation, let us designate by T_1 and T_2 the true measures of changes in production capacity in respect of 1's composite, on the one hand, and 2's composite, on the other. Also, L is the index of real national income measured in 1's prices, and P is the index of real national income in 2's prices. Then, if $L > P$ and production possibility schedules are concave from below,

$$(1) \qquad\qquad T_1 < P < L < T_2$$

In effect, the two true measures fall outside the two index numbers. If $P > L$, the two index numbers may bracket the two true measures, but, as I indicated, the case where $L > P$ is the one favorable to Moorsteen's argument. And, to come to my essay, with the United States as 1 and the USSR as 2, $L > P$ in my calculations. Usher therefore properly stresses that case. What, however, follows?

Usher apparently considers (1) as practically fatal to calculations such as I present, at least where the concern is to measure production capacity. Rather than bracketing the true measures, the usual index numbers leave them unrestricted. Differences in production capacity, therefore, remain quite indeterminate. That surely is too pessimistic a conclusion. After all, if $L > P$, we may still infer that $L < T_2$ and $T_1 < P$ whenever production possibility schedules are concave from below. Those would seem to be interesting implications.

More important, Usher apparently sees index numbers of real national income as serving only to delimit the true measure of production capacity. Moorsteen, to repeat, showed that such index numbers may also be viewed as approximations to true measures. That is not at all the same thing. At least, an index number may be an upper or lower bound for a true measure, and yet be considered a poor approximation to it. Alternatively, we may be uncertain whether a true measure lies above or below an index number, and still feel it to be closely approximated by that number. The degree of approximation of an index number to a true measure does indeed depend on the curvature of the production possibility schedules. That is not known with any certainty, but it is open to inquiry, and meantime it does seem illuminating to view index numbers, as Moorsteen does, as not only delimiting but approximating relative production capacity.

Indeed, should we view them, as Usher does, only in the former way, the situation would be if anything worse than what he portrays. Even if $P > L$, as he is aware, the two index numbers may still not bracket the true measures. If production possibility schedules are concave from below, it may be inferred as before that $L < T_2$ and $T_1 < P$, but we may or may not have $T_2 < P$ and $T_1 > L$. And purely a priori, we cannot be sure that schedules are concave to begin with.

To repeat, however, $L > P$ in my essay. That is also a usual case, for the Gerschenkron effect has been encountered again and again in real national income calculations. Implications of the data for production capacity when $L > P$, therefore, are of particular interest.

While Usher refers to Moorsteen's article, he does not consider my elaboration of it in *Real SNIP*. It may be worth noting, therefore, that for the case where $L > P$ and production possibility schedules are concave, (1) is already more or less implied in my analysis there. Usher, however, has made the matter explicit. That is to the good, but the consequences do not seem nearly as serious as he supposes.

I have followed Usher thus far in assuming that, as with Hicks and Samuelson, prices are such as to yield ideal valuations. In the real world, that is hardly so, and the ruble prices of the USSR are no exception to that rule. In my essay, I try to deal with the resultant problem by translating into "adjusted rubles" index numbers compiled initially in terms of prevailing ruble prices. The adjusted ruble standard is an expedient whose rationale and limitations I have discussed at length in previous studies. I am no more able here than I was in my essay to explore that theme again.

It should be observed, though, that Moorsteen's interpretation of real national income may, if anything, gain in interest relative to Usher's because of the divergencies of ruble prices from scarcity value. By all accounts, these divergencies go hand in hand in the USSR with a marked shortfall from production possibilities. That is as might be expected, and one need not ponder long to be aware also that in such circumstances real national income data can serve at best as observations, not on production possibilities, but on some kind of "feasibility locus" reflecting the prevailing inefficiency. The nature of that locus and the manner in which it may be observed are among the matters that I have sought to explore elsewhere.[1] For fairly obvious reasons,

---

[1] See especially, Bergson, *Productivity*.

though, uncertainties about whether one or another true measure lies above or below one or another index number seem only to be compounded in this case. It is reassuring, therefore, that national income data even so may be at least broadly indicative of production capacity as represented by the feasibility locus.

Prevailing dollar prices also have their limitations. These did not seem serious enough to warrant the sort of revaluation made for data in prevailing ruble prices. There probably is the more reason at this point, however, to stress the Moorsteen interpretation of real national income data compared with Usher's.

If national income data are so difficult to construe theoretically, why trouble to apply the theoretic analysis at all? At the risk of underlining the obvious, perhaps I should explain that, esoteric as the theory is, it still seems to facilitate organization of the inquiry and interpretation of the results. Not to be underestimated either, I think is the value of the discipline imposed on practitioners in limiting subjective judgments in an area where opportunities for such judgments are proverbially large; and at the same time in helping assure a desirable uniformity in conventions in different investigations. All this presupposes, however, an understanding that production capacity is apt to be elusive empirically, and that what can be achieved at most is not a precise and definitive measurement, but a contribution to informed appraisal. Usher apparently would have us seek only the ideal. It would be a sad day for economics if such a counsel of perfection were ever widely heeded.

Usher explores theoretically the use of real national income data to measure not only production capacity but welfare. In my essay I focused exclusively on production capacity, and so will not try to react to Usher's discussion of welfare. Perhaps I should explain, however, that I stressed production capacity chiefly because difficulties in compiling appropriate data for that application only seem compounded where the concern is with welfare and where, accordingly, relative prices are supposed to correspond to marginal rates of substitution. Most importantly, such a desideratum is especially difficult to approach in the USSR in the comparative valuation of consumers' and capital goods. That is so whether welfare is envisaged (as it usually is) in terms of consumers' preferences, or (as is often suggested it should be) in terms of planners' preferences. The reasons for the difficulty are of a familiar kind, and need not be labored.

In replying to the discussants of his own essay, Afriat too has inquired further into the pure theory of production capacity measurement. While the inquiry apparently was stimulated by the exchange between Usher and me, I must leave comment on it to another occasion. Afriat, however, ascribes to me an aversion to exact concepts. If he had troubled to acquaint himself with my previous efforts, in writings cited in my essay, to formulate an appropriate conceptual framework for production capacity measurements, I doubt that he could have labored under such a misapprehension. Perhaps my reply to Usher will also indicate how far Afriat is from the mark. In properly seeking theoretic rigor, however, we must be careful not to succumb to a stultifying empirical perfectionism. With all their limitations, national income data have something interesting to tell us about production capacity, if we will only listen.

There is little basis to try either to add to or subtract from Greenslade's interesting comments. He seems to assume, though, that in compiling price data for the USSR we are limited to quotations which the Soviet government sees fit to release. In fact, the sample of commodities for which comparative ruble and dollar price quotations can be assembled leaves much to be desired, but at least for consumers' goods it is compiled not only from Soviet official releases but to a considerable extent from foreign observers' reports.

Greenslade is certainly right that Soviet planning has tended to sacrifice variety for volume of output, and no doubt the sacrifice has often been inordinate. For many goods, even the reduced costs realized under the protracted serial production that the limitation on variety made possible must have exceeded their worth to users. That must have been so for producers' as well as consumers' goods. Since the goods in question are apt to be produced in relatively large quantities in the USSR, I agree that there may be further cause here of overstatement of Soviet output relative to the United States where the concern is to appraise welfare. Where the concern is to measure production capacity, it is not easy to see why the inordinate stress on volume should cause bias one way or the other.[2]

Theoretic treatments of production capacity measurement usually abstract from international trade. As Greenslade points out, however, such trade affords the opportunity to any country to carry out commodity transformations that may be costly to realize through domestic resource transfers. Indeed, given trade, transformations are always possible along a linear schedule, at least if the country in question does not trade on so large a scale as to affect world prices. With transformations along a linear schedule, however, circumstances are ideally favorable for interpretation of national income data in the Moorsteen manner. One is tempted to see in trade, therefore, a way of circumventing difficulties of production capacity measurement such as have been discussed. What is then measured, though, is in effect "purchasing power" in world markets. That is of interest, but for clarity it should be considered that it is not the same thing as production capacity, as usually understood, and that too is of interest.[3]

Greenslade is troubled by the problem posed for the compilation and interpretation of comparative national income data for the USSR and the United States by the pervasive replacement in the former country of market processes by centralist planning and by the associated inefficiency. I am too; but, as indicated, I have tried to deal with these issues elsewhere and cannot reopen them in any serious way here.

On such a problematic question as the comparative national income of the USSR and the United States, I am naturally gratified to learn of the close agreement between my results and those of the ECE study

[2] Even for welfare appraisal, only the calculations in rubles should be affected, and, for obvious reasons, a bias there seems, if anything, more likely in the calculations in adjusted rubles, which correspond to Soviet factor cost, than in those in prevailing rubles, which often diverge from such costs in the direction of user values.

Note that so far as quantity has been stressed inordinately over quality in the case of producers' goods, Soviet output currently must be below the level that could have been achieved if previously the mix of producers' goods had been a more economical one. Greenslade rightly points out, though, that this does not bear at all on the question of whether current Soviet output, as calculated, is overstated or not.

[3] Note also that the linear "purchasing power frontier" has a slope corresponding to world prices, and that among the vectors culminating on the frontier the one corresponding to actual output represents not total output, but the output of tradable goods alone.

to which Kenessey refers. In his thoughtful discussion, Kenessey also compares my results with data published by the Soviet Central Statistical Administration (TSU). The comparison is made difficult by the differences in methodology, especially the exclusion of diverse final services from the TSU data for "net material product," and their inclusion in my figures on the gross national product. Does not the use of the Soviet national income concept and the resultant exclusion of services tend to favor the USSR in a comparison with the United States?

That is certainly a plausible theory, and, while Kenessey himself expressly disavows it, I am grateful to him for referring to it, for there is thus an opportunity for me to underline an interesting aspect of my calculations: Paradoxically, the facts on the comparative volume of services in the USSR and the United States are otherwise than is suggested.

The final services omitted from net material product are broadly of the sort that I refer to in my essay as "selected final services." As appears from my Table 1, Soviet GNP suffers rather than benefits, relative to that of the United States, when such services are omitted. That is the result whether the valuation is in rubles or in dollars, but especially in the latter case. What is the explanation? Among the services in question are defense pay and subsistence. Perhaps chiefly on that account, the volume of services relative to goods in the USSR is larger than might be supposed in comparison with the corresponding relation in the United States (see my Table 3). Moreover, as indicated in my essay, the parities used to translate service outlays from rubles to dollars and from dollars to rubles are highly favorable to the ruble.

The comparison between my data and those of TSU must be read in that light. As Kenessey points out, my results are nominally close to those of TSU. On the indicated theory, therefore, one would have to conclude that, allowing for the difference in concepts, either I am somewhat overstating or the TSU is somewhat understating Soviet national income relative to that of the United States. In fact, so far as there is nominal agreement between TSU and me, the implication is, I think, the reverse: Allowing for the difference in concepts, either I am somewhat understating or TSU is somewhat overstating Soviet national income relative to that of the United States.

In comparing the two calculations, however, it should be considered that they differ in other respects besides the treatment of services. As implied, I refer to output gross and TSU to output net of depreciation. Very likely there are other methodological divergencies as well. Only meager information is available on the TSU calculation, but, if we may judge at all from the calculations of the Soviet economist A. I. Kats (see my Table 8 and related portions of my essay), my measures probably also differ from Soviet measures such as those of TSU in basic data and more specific procedures.

Kenessey urges the possible value of cooperation between Soviet and U.S. economists as a means of improving on calculations such as mine. Anyone seriously interested in the advance of real knowledge concerning the two economies can only endorse his suggestion. Let us hope that the time is not far off when it can be implemented.

The Role of the Price Structure

Economic Integration,

Rates of Exchange, and

Value Comparisons in Latin America

JOSEPH GRUNWALD

AND

JORGE SALAZAR-CARRILLO

DEVELOPMENT economics has accelerated the interest in comparative economic studies. Such studies often require the translation of values from one national currency to another. The main objective of this paper is to outline a set of techniques which can be used for the comparison of costs, income, expenditures, and other value data among a group of countries.

The need for comparative studies is especially important among countries which are embarking on a process of economic integration. This paper refers to studies which focus on the eleven countries which make up the Latin American Free Trade Association (LAFTA): Argentina, Bolivia, Brazil, Chile, Colombia, Ecuador, Mexico, Paraguay, Peru, Uruguay, and Venezuela.

Section I indicates the nature of the Latin American integration movement. Section II describes briefly a cooperative research program

NOTE: Joseph Grunwald and Jorge Salazar-Carrillo are senior fellows at The Brookings Institution. The former, coordinator of the ECIEL program described below, is mainly responsible for sections I–III of this essay and the latter for sections IV–VI. The late Stanley Braithwaite, of the Economic Commission for Latin America, Irving Kravis, and Richard Ruggles made important contributions to the international price comparison study in which Brookings is currently collaborating with Latin American research institutes. During the early stages of the project they gave valuable advice on the methodology at a special meeting convened in Buenos Aires, and thereafter were always available for consultations. The views expressed in this paper are those of the authors and do not purport to represent the views of the staff, officers, or trustees of The Brookings Institution.

of comparative studies (known by its Spanish acronym, "ECIEL") related to the economic development and integration of the LAFTA countries and examines the experience of the first ECIEL study. The importance of exchange rates in this study and the problems of converting costs from one currency to another are analyzed in section III.

The remaining sections deal with the current international price comparison study of the ECIEL program. Some of the methodological questions that arise in value comparisons are analyzed in sections IV and V. The procedures followed in the study are discussed in section V, and preliminary results are presented in section VI.

I. THE LATIN AMERICAN INTEGRATION MOVEMENT

The first successful steps toward economic integration were taken at the end of the 1950's. These resulted in the formation of the Central American Common Market (CACM) in 1960 and the Latin American Free Trade Association (LAFTA) in 1961. The move has progressed farthest in Central America, where five small republics comprising CACM have successfully removed almost all tariff barriers to trade among themselves. LAFTA, which now encompasses Mexico and all of South America except the Guianas, has encountered far greater difficulties. Within LAFTA a subregional arrangement, the Andean group of the five Western countries in South America, came into being in 1969 and holds out greater promise for progress in integration, at least in the short run, than LAFTA as a whole.

A special coordinating commission for Latin America (CECLA) was created on an *ad hoc* basis in Alta Gracia, Argentina, in 1964 to work out a common Latin American position vis-à-vis the United Nations Conference on Trade and Development (UNCTAD), whose first meeting took place in Geneva later that year. CECLA has continued to meet on occasion to deal with questions on international trade and development in relation to UNCTAD in particular and the outside world in general. In the spring of 1969 it took upon itself the difficult job of coordinating Latin American attitudes on economic issues vis-à-vis the United States. This effort resulted in the "Consensus of Viña del Mar" which was presented to President Nixon in June of 1969.

CECLA is a first attempt to reach a Latin American consensus on international economic matters, but its bargaining power with the rest of the world cannot be significant if it is not backed up by a common market arrangement or permanent regional institutions.

LAFTA

The Montevideo Treaty, which brought LAFTA into existence, established a rather complicated trade-negotiation system aimed at the gradual elimination within twelve years—or by mid-1973—of customs duties and any other restrictions on substantially all reciprocal trade. Each party to the treaty was committed to granting annually to other LAFTA members reductions in duties and charges equivalent to 8 per cent of the weighted average applicable to countries outside the agreement; a free trade zone would thus be achieved by the end of the period. Every three years these concessions, open in the meantime to withdrawal through renegotiation, were to be consolidated into a common schedule of products on which all customs duties and other charges on intrazonal trade would be eliminated before mid-1973. This common schedule was to constitute, in terms of the aggregate value of trade among the member countries, 25 per cent of such trade by mid-1964, 50 per cent by mid-1967, 75 per cent by mid-1970, and "substantially all of such trade" at the end of the period.

An impressive number of escape clauses was made available to member countries with respect to trade in agricultural products and in cases of intrazonal trade disequilibriums and seriously unfavorable overall balance-of-payments situations. The treaty offered special provisions for the less developed countries within the region: nonreciprocal trade concessions, special nondiscriminatory measures aimed at protecting their industries, and collective arrangements for financial and technical assistance.

Commitments outside of trade liberalization were put in extremely vague language. They envisaged the reconciliation of overall import and export policies vis-à-vis the rest of the world and the coordination of the treatment of capital and services coming from outside the area. They also pledged progressively closer coordination of industrialization policies.

During the first eight years of LAFTA, a maze of about 11,000 concessions on individual trade items was negotiated in successive annual meetings of the Conference of Contracting Parties. Partly as a result of these concessions and partly because the emergence of LAFTA led to the discovery of many trade opportunities, trade among the members expanded more rapidly than their world exports. The intra-regional share of total trade rose from 6 per cent in 1961 to over 12 per cent in 1968.

The Montevideo Treaty was only the beginning of a long process of political and economic adjustment among a group of countries that, in spite of a common historical tradition and considerable cultural affinities, had followed very different economic paths. Inter-Latin American economic relations have never played a major role in the development of the large and middle-sized republics, which were characterized by autarkic industrialization and a growing dependence on the developed outside world. The Montevideo Treaty, therefore, represented a compromise—at the level of the lowest common denominator—among many conflicting political and economic forces. It tried to accommodate the three leading industrial countries (Argentina, Brazil, and Mexico), as well as the others with their varying degrees of bargaining power. Finally, it had to consider the interests and attitudes of international organizations and of countries outside the region.

The unequal development levels of LAFTA countries proved to be one of the important stumbling blocks in the way of more rapid economic integration. The least-developed countries (Bolivia, Ecuador, and Paraguay) received some preferential treatment, consisting mainly of unilateral trade concessions on the part of the rest of the group. But they have been unable to improve their positions within the area, and their trade deficit with the zone has persisted.

As a result of the nationalist outlook of Latin American governments and the pressures from domestic and foreign interests, little progress has been made on intracountry and intraregional industrial specialization, whether in private or state-controlled activities. In the area of private industry, 16 complementarity agreements had been signed and ratified by the end of 1970, the first few mainly on the initiative of foreign enterprises operating in various countries at the same time. These agreements provided for eliminating customs duties and other restrictions, not only on final-use products but also on components and necessary raw materials, and they permit better horizontal and vertical integration of productive units, most of them belonging to a small number of foreign-owned corporations. The contribution of these agreements to the expansion of intrazonal trade and the growth of the involved industries has so far been negligible.

While the Central American Common Market has continued to progress, the integration movement within LAFTA has slowed down significantly since the mid-1960's. Several attempts were made to inject dynamism into LAFTA, such as a high-level report by four leading Latin American statesmen, prepared at the request of Chile's President Frei in 1965.[1] The most important effort derived from the rising interest of the United States in Latin American economic integration which resulted in the "summit" meeting of President Lyndon Johnson with the heads of state of nearly all Latin American countries in Punta del Este in 1967. The Action Program which emerged from this meeting and was primarily designed to lead to a regional common market by 1985 has remained a document without implementation. Neither the large Latin American countries nor the United States followed through with active support.

The slowdown in the integration movement within LAFTA was formally recognized in the "Protocol of Caracas," which was signed by all "contracting parties" at their ninth conference in December 1969. The protocol postpones for an additional seven years, from December 31, 1973, to December 31, 1980, the full operation of the free trade area. Furthermore the minimum annual 8 per cent reduction in tariffs was reduced to 2.9 per cent in future negotiations, and the system of the common schedule mentioned earlier was suspended until 1974. At the same time the protocol instructed LAFTA's Standing Executive Committee to complete studies, before the end of 1973, which would result in the design of new procedures for the common schedule and the creation of "conditions favorable to the establishment of a Latin American common market."

Andean Integration

Besides the small Central American Common Market, the most encouraging sign of progress in Latin American economic integration

[1] See Raul Prebisch, Felipe Herrera, Carlos Sanz de Santa Maria, and Jose Antonio Mayobre, "Proposals for the Creation of the Latin American Common Market," *Journal of Common Market Studies,* September 1966.

is the signing of the Subregional Andean Integration Agreement by Bolivia, Colombia, Chile, Ecuador, and Peru in May 1969. Venezuela, which participated in the lengthy negotiations leading to the treaty, did not sign but has the option of joining later. The Andean group was created within the LAFTA context, and the treaty was approved by the full LAFTA membership. In addition, the Andean group established the Andean Development Corporation of which Venezuela is also a member.

The Andean treaty provides for the automatic and irrevocable reduction of tariff and nontariff barriers so that there would be substantially free intra-Andean trade by the end of 1980. By that date, a common external tariff, to be established gradually, is also to go into full effect. Moreover the treaty provides for the elaboration of sectoral development programs, special treatment of Bolivia and Ecuador as less developed nations within the group, and coordination of economic policies. A complementarity agreement in the petrochemical industry is already in effect within the Andean group. The Andean Development Corporation is designed to promote and help finance regional investments.

Including Venezuela, the Andean group represents about one-fourth of Latin America in important aspects (gross national product, population, and area), and if successful, may well provide the needed stimulus for effective integration not only of the subregion, but also eventually of all of LAFTA and, indeed, of Latin America as a whole.

II. THE FIRST ECIEL STUDY

One of the gaps in the regional integration movement was the lack of serious and specific studies. In 1963 several major Latin American economic research institutions joined forces under the coordination of staff members of The Brookings Institution for the purpose of undertaking studies in a common research program related to the region's economic integration. While the program's major objective is to prepare professionally competent studies which will yield useful results, an important by-product is to strengthen the economics profession in Latin America through this cooperative effort and to aid in the development of the participating institutions.

There are now nineteen institutes collaborating in the eleven countries which constitute the Latin American Free Trade Association. The focus of the research program, known as ECIEL (Estudios Conjuntos sobre la Integración Económica Latinoamericana) has been the preparation of comparative studies of Latin American countries.

The basic coordination of the program is effected mainly through periodic seminars. These meetings are attended by the principal researchers concerned with the project in each participating institution and a number of observers from nonparticipating institutions who are specifically invited. The purpose of the seminars is to work out the methodology and procedures, to present and examine each institute's progress report, to analyze the experience in the field, and to resolve research and coordination problems to facilitate international comparative analyses. The seminars are scheduled at about six-month intervals, and at each meeting the steps for the next stage of the project are planned as carefully as possible. In the interseminar periods, the coordinator keeps in close touch with all the institutes, and gives, wherever necessary, methodological, technical, and administrative support.

Several studies have been undertaken by ECIEL, and the first of these, now completed, deals with the integration of specific industries in LAFTA.[2]

The generally vague conception among Latin American economies of the losses and gains involved in lowering trade barriers for manufactured products led the participating institutes to study the absolute advantage of LAFTA members in selected industries. The specific aim of this research was to indicate minimum cost locations and size of plants in selected industries within a potential regional common market in 1975 and to estimate the benefits to be derived from the regional integration of these industries.

Six product groups were selected for the study but not all of them are strategic for economic integration: some member countries that have little possibility of competing in important industries may have an absolute advantage in producing other types of products. In order to include institutes from as many countries as possible in the preparation of cost studies, some less important products (from an integration

[2] The discussion which follows is based on ECIEL, *Industrialization in a Latin American Common Market,* ed. Martin Carnoy, Washington, D.C., Brookings Institution, forthcoming.

point of view) were included in the project. The selected products are (a) nitrogenous fertilizers—ammonia, ammonium nitrate, ammonium sulphate, and urea; (b) methanol and formaldehyde; (c) kraft paper, kraft pulp, and newsprint; (d) agricultural tractors; (e) universal parallel lathes; and (f) milk products—powdered milk and cheese.

Methodology

The work was divided into four stages: (a) estimation for each LAFTA member of the demand for the given product in 1975; (b) estimation of costs of production of the selected products in various countries; (c) estimation of the costs of transportation of the selected products between points of production and points of consumption, and, where there was more than one stage of production involved, between points of production of primary-stage products and points of production of secondary-stage products (also, estimation of transport costs between United States production points and LAFTA consumption points in order to compare importation with area production); (d) combination of the previous three estimates to find the optimum location of plant(s) in LAFTA for each product or product group. This optimum minimizes the total cost to the area of meeting the projected 1975 demand.

The basic unifying analytical tool which incorporates the demand projections, cost analyses, transportation cost assumptions, and exchange rate assumptions is a modified linear programing model which was used to calculate the optimum production locations to satisfy projected 1975 demands for every product studied in all countries of the Latin American Free Trade Association, assuming all customs tariffs are eliminated for goods produced within the region. Essentially what the model does is to find the cheapest way of supplying the projected demand from within the area, balancing the economies of scale possible, as production at any one point increases, against the increasing transport costs of serving ever more distant markets.

Using this model it was also possible to calculate both the costs of producing the selected commodities at locations other than the optimum production sites, and the costs for each particular country of buying from different locations. The first kind of analysis estimates how much it would cost the common market region to deviate from one or more minimum-cost locations (the optimum may include more than one production point). The second represents a welfare analysis in which an attempt is made to measure the benefits or costs to the consumers in each country of buying the particular product from different locations. The estimates were made by comparing costs to national consumers for the alternatives of (a) producing the products studied nationally instead of buying from the regional optimum location, and (b) importing from the United States instead of buying from the regional optimum.

Limitations

The difficulties in this project are quite apparent, especially since no precedents for such studies exist either for the European Economic Community or any other area. First of all, information is limited. Basic data may simply not exist or if they do, they may be deficient and unreliable. Then there are the problems inherent in making projections. The impossibility of foreseeing all sorts of changes and indirect effects poses a particular problem in developing countries. Production processes and technology will not remain the same, relative prices will differ, and other factors will be modified in directions which are difficult to predict.

Furthermore, the study has the limitation of dealing with only a few specific industries rather than with the economy as a whole, thus constituting a "partial equilibrium" analysis. Ideally, all industries and segments of the economy should be considered within the framework of a "general equilibrium" analysis, in order to measure both the direct and indirect impacts of economic integration. The partial equilibrium approach used really estimates which countries, given a certain set of assumptions, are likely to have absolute advantages in producing a specified product. If the country which would produce it under the partial equilibrium estimates of minimum-cost location would have still greater advantages in producing other goods, it might not be the optimum site in which to locate production of the goods under study.

The implication is that the results do not give locations that can be properly called "optimum" but rather "minimum cost." Obtaining the optimum requires a general equilibrium which considers all the interrelations in an economy, including limitations on total resources available in each area and in the region as a whole. To do this in a comprehensive fashion is not yet feasible because of computational problems, not to speak of the impossibility of getting all the necessary data. Present economic techniques do permit undertaking a highly aggregative type of analysis in some developed countries, but such global studies say almost nothing about specific products or industries, and would therefore not have served the purposes of the study, even leaving aside the probability that in developing countries this kind of aggregative analysis might abstract from reality more than the partial equilibrium analysis employed.

Conclusions

Whatever the shortcomings of data and theory may have been, several important conclusions may be drawn from this project apart from the specific determination of the minimum-cost locations and welfare gains and costs from the integration of certain industries. For integration policy in particular, there are three main general conclusions:

a. While there may be only one economic minimum-cost set of production points for an industry in a regional common market, in each of the industries studied there are at least several other possible combinations which would not seriously violate economic precepts of efficiency. As defined here the economic optimum is that pattern of location of a particular industry where the costs of production and transportation to the regional markets are at a minimum. Consequently, the meaning of the foregoing conclusion is that there are alternative locations where costs are not much higher than at the optimum. On the other hand, there always are many other possible production patterns whose deviations from the optimum would be very expensive. The existence of several relatively efficient locations has significant implications for policy formulation because it permits a sufficient leeway for making politically acceptable decisions without incurring excessive economic costs.

b. A related but distinct conclusion is that there are many countries in Latin America which would benefit directly from economic union and that not all industrialization due to integration would concentrate in those countries which already have a large industrial plant.

The fear that, because of the unequal development levels existing in the region, industrial investment will tend to be polarized in a few of the larger and richer countries, has restrained Latin American governments and businessmen from moving boldly toward a common market. The results of this study suggest that, at least in the case of the industries examined, this fear is not well founded. This appraisal is reinforced by the inference of the first conclusion which indicates that in some cases weaker countries could be included in regional investment programs without a serious misallocation of resources.

c. The results also show that Latin American production for a regional market at the optimum (minimum-cost) or near-optimum locations would be competitive with imports from developed countries in most of the industries studied. The notion that Latin American manufacturing could never compete with goods from the United States and other highly industrialized countries has also been a deterrent in the regional integration movement. The study suggests that whenever output levels are large enough to take advantage of the benefits of large-scale production (economies of scale), as they would be in the case of many commodities in a Latin American common market, and transportation costs are significant, then Latin American production costs would permit competition with imports from developed countries even without tariff protection.

III. THE INDIFFERENCE RATE OF EXCHANGE

The chief problem in bringing together the cost estimates prepared by the individual institutes for a particular product was the difficulty of comparing value data in different monetary units. Thus an important criticism of any study of this kind is that its results depend on the rates of exchange in the countries studied. The prevailing rates may not be the "correct" ones to use because of under- or overvaluation of the currency and other biases.

The costs of production were estimated for each producing country in terms of local currency. Imported inputs were specified in dollars (or other foreign currencies) and for some purposes were converted to the national monetary unit at the rate of exchange of an indicated date. To compare production costs of a given product among various locations, some specified rates of exchange must be used to convert the national currencies involved. Thus the rate of exchange between two countries is a crucial variable in determining the optimal location of production.

The Concept

As a first approximation to a sensitivity analysis, the "free" rate was used in addition to the official rate where it was suspected that the official exchange rates were highly overvalued. The free rate used was the "grey market" rate prevailing for tourist and other nontrade transactions. Thus the probable equilibrium rate under existing trade policies would lie between the official and free rates. Since the study deals only with six industry groups, it was clearly impossible to determine either equilibrium or parity exchange rates from the results of the analysis.

In order to go beyond the limited analysis of using two rates of exchange, a second approximation was made to estimate the sensitivity of the minimum-cost production pattern for each product to variations in exchange rates at each major location of production in the region. A new concept of "indifference rates of exchange" was introduced, defined as that rate between the currencies of B and C at which the importing country A in the region is indifferent between buying good X from country B or country C. Thus if X costs 4 pesos or 10 cruzeiros in A, importers in A are indifferent to buying from B in pesos or C in cruzeiros as long as the exchange rate in A is 2.5 Cr/peso. If the two currencies have an exchange rate of 2.0 Cr/peso in A, A's importers will buy X from B; if the exchange rate is 3.0 Cr/peso, they will buy X from C.[3] In other words, the indifference rate is that rate between two

---

[3] The exchange rates refer to the relationship between the currencies of countries B and C in country A. A simple example will clarify this. The three cases mentioned in the text can be illustrated as follows (The currency in country A is the "escudo," in country B, the "peso," and in country C, the "cruzeiro"):

	Rates of Exchange		Ratio of Cruzeiro to Peso
(1) 1 escudo = 4	pesos = 10	cruzeiros	2.5
(2) 1 escudo = 4	pesos = 8	cruzeiros	2
(3) 1 escudo = 4	pesos = 12	cruzeiros	3

If product X costs 4 pesos or 10 cruzeiros A will be indifferent between buying in B or C only in case (1), because in either place it would have to spend one escudo. In case (2) X would cost more than one escudo when bought from C but again only one escudo when bought in B. A will buy from C in case (3) because the cost is less than one escudo while it is one escudo when bought in B.

currencies which reduces the advantage of a given location over a competitor to zero; these "indifference rates" are intended to indicate the switchover points in competitive position (based on average costs in decreasing cost industries and marginal costs in increasing cost industries).

Bias

The indifference method contains some biases in estimating the switchover points. The more important source of bias might be that part of the cost of the products studied, particularly transport and imported capital cost, is originally in U.S. dollars or other foreign currency and is converted to the national currency at given exchange rates.

The indifference rates of exchange were calculated on the basis of the following expression:

$$R_{ij} = c_i(1 + a_iX_i)/c_j(1 + a_jX_j)$$

where R_{ij} is the indifference rate between country i and j, c is the domestic production cost in national currency in country i or j, a is the ratio of transport and imported capital cost in foreign currency to production cost, and X_i and X_j are the exchange rates used to convert foreign costs to the national currencies in countries i and j respectively. It is clear that the more unrepresentative of the equilibrium rates of exchange the X's are, the greater the possible bias in the calculated indifference rates of exchange could be. If the aX's are small in both countries, the bias will be insignificant. Even if the X's are very distorted, the bias may be small when, say, the currencies of both countries are overvalued by a similar degree. Only in the extreme and probably rare case in which a_i is very different from a_j, and the distortion in X_i very different from the distortion in X_j, can the bias be substantial.[4]

Results

Despite the biases in the indifference rate method, the estimates of the indifference rates show approximately how sensitive the minimum-

[4] In the ECIEL industrialization study it was estimated that the maximum bias was about 20 per cent (see ECIEL, *Industrialization,* Chap. II).

cost-location estimates are to the choice of exchange rate used. Some countries cannot compete in any product studied when their official and free rates of exchange are used in the calculations, while other countries are consistently low-cost producers at their prevailing official and free exchange rates. In some cases, a small change in exchange rates changes the minimum-cost location; in other cases, the minimum-cost location is quite insensitive to such rate changes. In industries where only small differences in costs of production exist between countries, the sensitivity is greater than in industries where the advantage of one country over others is large.

In Table 1 an example is drawn from the ECIEL industrialization study to illustrate the meaning of the indifference rates of exchange. The table indicates the estimated 1975 cost of universal parallel lathes of a certain standard in six Latin American countries when purchased from each one of the producing countries, Argentina, Brazil, and Chile. The estimates were made under the "low" assumption of

TABLE 1

Delivered U.S. Dollar Cost of Universal Parallel Lathes in
Six Latin American Countries, Produced in Argentina,
Brazil, and Chile, and Implicit Indifference
Exchange Rates Projected to 1975

Country of Consumption	Country of Production			Indifference Exchange Rates		
	Argentina	Brazil	Chile	P/E	Cr/E	Cr/P
Argentina	$2,962	$3,986	$2,775	33.2	634	19.0
Brazil	3,042	3,929	2,860	32.8	603	18.3
Chile	3,014	4,042	2,726	33.8	651	19.0
Colombia	3,270	4,264	3,006	33.8	625	18.5
Mexico	3,315	4,297	3,050	33.8	620	18.5
Paraguay	2,897	3,997	2,806	32.8	625	19.0

NOTE: Exchange rate per U.S. dollar used for conversion to dollar costs: Argentina, 155 pesos (P); Brazil, 2,200 cruzeiros (Cr); Chile, 5 escudos (E). Ratio of exchange rates: P/E = 31.0, Cr/E = 420.0, Cr/P = 14.2.

SOURCE: ECIEL, *Industrialization in a Common Market*, ed., Martin Carnoy, Washington, D.C., Brookings Institution, forthcoming, Chap. VII, Table 4.

transportation costs, and production costs were converted at the "free" (brokers') rates of exchange prevailing in 1963. (For the purposes of this table only one production point in each of the producing countries was considered.) The table also shows the implicit indifference rates of exchange. For example, the indifference rate of exchange between Argentina and Chile was calculated by converting the dollar costs in columns (1) and (3) back into the respective national currencies and dividing (1) by (3) [or, simplified, (1) ÷ (3) × 31; 31 is the ratio of the Argentine rate to the dollar (155) to the Chilean rate to the dollar (5)].

The table indicates that at the free rate of exchange Chile would be competitive with Argentina and Brazil in all six countries in the production of lathes: The indifference rates are above the free exchange rates of 31 pesos and 420 cruzeiros to the escudo. But the indifference rate of exchange with Argentina in each case is less than 10 per cent above the ratio of the free rates of the two countries. Thus Chile would not be competitive with Argentina in any of the countries at the official rate of 3.5 escudos to the dollar, even if the Argentine rate were set at the official one of 140 pesos to the dollar (the indifference rates would be below the official exchange rates of 40 pesos to the escudo). At the official rate (3.5 escudos to the dollar or 629 cruzeiros to the escudo) Chile could still, but barely, compete with Brazil in four of the six countries. Argentine lathes cost less than their Brazilian counterparts in all countries at the free rate of exchange as well as at the official Argentine rate of 140 pesos to the dollar (or 15.7 cruzeiros to the peso).

While indifference rates of exchange must not be confused with equilibrium rates of exchange, because they refer only to rates between two countries for a given product in the purchasing countries, they are indicative of the sensitivity of minimum-cost points to exchange rates. For the purposes of sensitivity analysis the use of two exchange rates, the official and free ones, could be considered a first approximation; the use of indifference rates, a second approximation.

It was in the effort to approximate more closely a "true" set of rates of exchange that the ECIEL group embarked upon the project of international price comparisons which will be examined below. In the attempt to arrive at a set of exchange rates which would permit a better comparison of values than the use of either the official or free rates of exchange, the price comparison study constitutes a further approximation. This study is not geared to the comparisons of industrial costs as dealt with in the first ECIEL project, but the study is expected to go a long way toward making possible reasonable comparisons of values among Latin American countries and between them and several third countries.

IV. INTERCOUNTRY VALUE COMPARISONS—SOME ALTERNATIVES

If comparisons of value figures in different currency units are to enlighten rather than confuse, it is necessary to have a set of rates equating these values in real terms. For example, if labor income is to be compared between two countries, it is necessary to equate the values in a way that would permit the comparisons to be carried out in terms of goods and services actually consumed in each country. In undertaking such value comparisons, several methods have been used. It would be useful to review them and ponder briefly about their appropriateness.

Official, Free, and Equilibrium Exchange Rates

The use of official exchange rates to convert value data from different countries into a common currency unit presents a host of problems. First, in many countries it is impossible to determine the official exchange rate because a number of rates exist for different foreign trade transactions. It can be argued that a weighted average of these rates is an appropriate estimate of the official exchange rate, but such a computation would require detailed information on foreign transactions. In many cases such data are difficult to obtain.

Second, even if an average could be computed or the official exchange rate determined, it would be found that for most countries these rates would either be undervalued or overvalued. This means that the internal prices of goods are either too low or too high in comparison with their international prices. In countries where the rate of increase in prices is significant and exchange rates are fixed, currencies tend to become overvalued. This is especially true if adjustments to these rates are infrequent and usually take place after they are overdue. In contrast, countries with stable prices and fixed exchange rates will tend to have undervalued currencies. Overvaluation of the exchange rate is also implicit whenever exchange controls are in effect and other restraints to foreign trade are severe.

Where the exchange rate is over- or undervalued, its use in value comparisons introduces distortions. If an overvalued exchange rate is used, the data will be inflated when converted into a common currency. The opposite will be the case if the exchange rate is undervalued. Given that overvaluation is typical in Latin America, the use of official rates in value comparisons is inappropriate. These complications and distortions affecting official exchange rates also prevail in other developing nations, and affect many of the developed countries as well. Thus, the problem is a general one.

In some cases, it is possible to estimate adjusted exchange rates based on par values during a particular period in which free trade was prevalent, with an adjustment tied to the movement of national price indexes. In making national income and gross product comparisons the United Nations, in its yearbooks on national accounts statistics, has converted the data of particular countries by using this method. These adjustments are clumsy, and chances of error are high in the selection of the initial period and in the time series adjustment.

This method is a specific application of the purchasing power parity doctrine put forth by Gustav Cassell.[5] As some writers have pointed out recently, there are several versions of this doctrine. The adjusted exchange rate approach is based on what Balassa has called the "relative" purchasing power parity doctrine.[6] Any relative purchasing power par calculation is affected by the difficulties noted above with regard to adjusted exchange rates. Even if the initial par values are not over- and undervalued, the movement of wholesale or consumer price indexes in the countries involved generally does not run parallel to changes in their equilibrium exchange rates.[7]

[5] See Gustav Cassell, "Abnormal Deviations in International Exchanges," *Economic Journal*, September 1918; Cassell, *The World's Monetary Problems*, London, 1921; and other works by the same author.

[6] Bela Balassa, "The Purchasing-Power Parity Doctrine: A Reappraisal," *Journal of Political Economy*, December 1964, p. 591.

[7] See Leland Yeager, "A Rehabilitation of Purchasing-Power Parity," *Journal of Political Economy*, December 1958; Gottfried Haberler, *A Survey of International Trade Theory*, Special Papers in International Economics 1, Princeton, 1961, pp. 45–51; Balassa, "Parity."

In countries where foreign exchange markets are government controlled, "free" rate quotations rather than official ones could be used.[8] Free rates probably reflect more accurately than adjusted ones the degree of over- or undervaluation of the official rate, since they are somehow determined by the market. But free rates are still poor approximations of equilibrium exchange rates. Generally, free rates are determined in parallel markets and are greatly influenced by particular types of transactions (capital movements, tourism, special imports, etc.). Thus, the degree of under- or overvaluation involved in the use of these rates would still be uncertain. Therefore, it seems that available exchange rates or those that could be easily derived from published data cannot be used in a straightforward manner for value comparisons.

The degree of under- or overvaluation should be judged only relative to a certain set of conditions. These concepts have been used in connection with the traditional concept of an equilibrium rate of exchange.[9] This is the exchange rate that would obtain within a framework of unrestricted trade, full employment of labor, and the absence of short-term capital movements. Recently, a new concept of equilibrium rates has been suggested: those rates that would equilibrate international payments within the existing structure of monetary, fiscal, and trade policies.[10] The latter definition will be termed the "actual" equilibrium rate of exchange, and the former one will be called the "free trade" equilibrium rate of exchange. According to Balassa and Schydlowsky, the prevailing exchange rate is frequently a good estimate of the "actual" equilibrium rate of exchange under existing policy conditions. However, this would not be the case if temporary capital movements are taking place or foreign exchange reserves are changing involuntarily.

The "actual" equilibrium rate can be expected to differ significantly

[8] In developing countries free rates are usually determined in the "black," "street," or so-called grey markets, which involve only certain kinds of transactions, primarily tourism and capital movements.

[9] See Ragnar Nurkse, "Conditions of International Monetary Equilibrium," *Essays in International Finance*, No. 4, Spring 1945 (International Finance Section, Princeton University).

[10] See Bela Balassa and Daniel M. Schydlowsky, "Effective Tariff, Domestic Cost of Foreign Exchange, and the Equilibrium Exchange Rate," *Journal of Political Economy*, May-June 1968, pp. 356–58.

from the equilibrium rate of exchange that would hold under free trade conditions. If restrictive trade policies influence value figures to a degree that varies from country to country, any deviation from free trade values would bias international comparisons. For example, take two countries similar in every respect and with the same rate of exchange with respect to the dollar. In one country there are no trade restrictions, while the other has a 10 per cent ad valorem general tariff which is required to balance its international payments. The tariff would inflate value figures in the latter country, and the use of the identical rates would bias the comparisons.

Only the equilibrium exchange rates under free trade conditions reflect the "true" internal and external purchasing power of the currencies involved and would seem to be appropriate for value comparison. Among the rates that could be obtained without much difficulty, free rates of exchange appear to be the best approximation of "free trade" equilibrium rates.[11] Given the complexities involved in calculating equilibrium exchange rates, it would be useful to explore in greater detail the circumstances under which free rates could be considered acceptable approximations to equilibrium ones.

In developed economies free rates and official rates usually coincide.[12] Given that exchange rates are generally officially determined and upheld by government intervention in the foreign exchange markets, they may coexist with nontransitory disequilibriums in the balance of payments, concealing a divergence even from the "actual" equilibrium rate of exchange, let alone from free trade equilibrium. Recent cases in point have been the experience with the U.S. dollar, the German mark, and the Japanese yen.

In a limited number of developed countries, either the degree of government intervention in the foreign exchange market is small or rates are permitted to fluctuate freely. Under these circumstances prevailing rates can be considered good approximations of the equilibrium rate of exchange under the existing set of trade and other policies. But

[11] In fact, adjusted exchange rates based on the "relative" purchasing power parity doctrine may be further away from equilibrium exchange rates than official rates, as will be shown in section VI.

[12] In certain developing countries official rates can also be considered equivalent to free rates. This is the case with certain convertible or "strong" currencies like the Mexican peso and the Venezuelan bolivar.

still the disparity in relation to free trade equilibrium is probably large. In developing economies, where free rates are determined in marginal markets and in which the level and variety of trade restrictions is considerable, the divergence is much larger.

But there would also be objections to the use of even "free trade" equilibrium exchange rates in value comparisons, assuming they could be properly estimated. The fact is that equilibrium rates, like the other exchange rates discussed above, equilibrate all international flows and not just those on traded goods and services. An equilibrium rate is based not only on intercountry price relatives (free of the effects of trade restrictions not including transportation costs) of tradable goods and their trade volumes, but also on other current and capital account transactions. A country with a substantial amount of capital inflows, for example, would have a higher-valued currency than if its exchange rate were determined only on the basis of trade flows. The opposite would be the case if large profit remittances flowed out of the country. This in effect disconnects the internal from the external level and structure of prices. As a result the equilibrium rate is not a good measure of the internal purchasing power of the currencies.

Moreover, not all goods and services in the economy enter into the determination of the equilibrium rates. Only tradable goods do. The currency of a country in which services are particularly cheap will have a higher relative purchasing power if all goods and services are considered rather than just tradables. It appears then that the usefulness of "free trade" equilibrium rates for value comparisons is limited because such rates are basically pertinent only to foreign transactions.

Implicit Rates

Other solutions to the value comparison problem have been based on the relationship of certain types of prices in different countries at a given date.[13] This is the case of what Balassa calls the "absolute" version of the purchasing power parity doctrine. Traditionally the calculation of purchasing power parities has been based on prices taken from the consumer or wholesale price indexes.[14] However, if a currency

[13] For example, the relationship of Argentine to Chilean prices for the same set of commodities, expressed in their respective local currencies in a given year.
[14] See Balassa, "Parity," and the other references cited in footnotes.

converter generally applicable to value figures is needed, it should be based on prices from all the different sectors of the economy. One way of doing this would be to cover the different sectors of gross domestic product or gross national product. The calculation of "absolute" purchasing power parity rates based on the concept of gross product deflators should provide parity rates that are more representative and widely applicable than those based on consumer or wholesale price indexes.[15]

In order to distinguish among the different purchasing power concepts used in the literature and mentioned in this study, the "absolute" purchasing power parity rates calculated on the basis of gross domestic product or gross national product deflators will be referred to in this paper as "implicit rates."

While gross product deflators are better than purchasing power parity rates based on consumer and wholesale price indexes, there are other problems. Gross product deflators are not available in many developing countries. Moreover, they are aggregated indexes and risky to use in international work because of the difficulty in comparing the quality of the goods and services among different countries.[16] With new developments in the field of index number computation [17] and with the increasing usefulness of value comparisons, it seems worthwhile to calculate implicit rates on the basis of price information specifically collected for such purposes.

If purchasing power parity rates are calculated covering the different sector components of the economies involved and are based on special price collections, they would appear to be the most adequate solution to the problem of value comparisons. They are not limited to particular sets of commodities and are not directly influenced by in-

[15] For criticisms of the use of cost-of-living or consumer price indexes and wholesale price indexes in the calculation of purchasing power parities see the Balassa articles cited above, and Haberler, *Trade Theory*, pp. 49–50.

[16] One of the main criticisms of both the "absolute" and "relative" versions of the purchasing power doctrine deals with the detailed statistical problems involved in the calculation of parity rates (see Yeager, "A Rehabilitation").

[17] Considerable redundancy has been found among the baskets of goods used in the calculation of price indexes. Thus, subsets of these lists have been found to replicate with a high degree of accuracy the results of larger lists. Richard and Nancy Ruggles have been working on these aspects at Yale University (see Richard Ruggles, "Price Indices and International Price Comparisons," in *Ten Economic Studies in the Tradition of Irving Fisher,* New York, 1967, pp. 180–81).

visible items in the balance of payments. On the other hand they are based on the internal purchasing power of the currencies involved, thus constituting an appropriate basis for international valuation.

These rates can be calculated from the production side or from the expenditure side of the gross product accounts. Both of them are valid, each being specially suited to particular kinds of comparisons. The production side presents problems which are very difficult to handle, although the data that could be generated would be very useful. Much more experience exists with the expenditure side, and the problems of data gathering are simpler.

It is important to point out, however, that when cost or price comparisons are undertaken primarily for the purpose of analyzing trade possibilities, equilibrium rates of exchange rather than implicit rates are appropriate. In this case the question asked is not, for example, if the wage levels in one country really represent a higher standard of living in real terms than in another, but rather whether labor costs are low enough in one of the countries for specialization in labor-intensive goods.

V. THE CALCULATION OF IMPLICIT EXCHANGE RATES

In its project on international price comparisons the ECIEL joint research program,[18] which is based on comparative studies, focuses on the analysis of implicit rates in the LAFTA countries.[19] Prices were specially collected for this purpose in each country to constitute a Latin American basket of goods and services classified according to the categories and subcategories of the gross domestic product. Because of the difficulties involved in calculations based on the product side, the study followed the expenditure-side approach.

The basis for accurate value comparisons across countries lies in "normalizing" the influence of prices in the value figures. This requires

[18] See Appendix C for a list of the ECIEL institutes participating in the international price study.

[19] The ECIEL study builds upon the pioneering study in Latin America by the U.N. Economic Commission for Latin America (ECLA), "A Measurement of Price Levels and the Purchasing Power of Currencies in Latin America, 1960–62," mimeo, Santiago, Chile, 1963. However, the methodology of both the ECLA study and the present study follow in important respects the pathbreaking work of Milton Gilbert and Irving Kravis, *An International Comparison of National Products and the Purchasing Power of Currencies,* Paris, 1954.

their proper deflation. An overall implicit rate is not appropriate for this purpose. For each type of value comparison there is a particular set of prices to be considered. Therefore the volume of information to be collected in the study was designed to make possible the calculation of implicit rates or equivalences at low levels of aggregation, not only for sectors, such as capital formation, government consumption, etc., but also for subsectors, such as food, services, meat, tropical fruit, etc. Such detail makes possible a larger number of value comparisons.

Methodology

The national accounting concept chosen for the study was the gross domestic product. Its breakdown by expenditure category is shown in Appendix A. This concept was preferred to gross national product because the latter is less amenable to international comparisons, in that the item "net factor incomes received from or paid abroad" varies substantially from country to country. Furthermore, the gross domestic product estimates are in greater use in Latin America.

The Selection of Prices. A set of goods was selected to represent each of the expenditure categories in Appendix A. These were chosen according to procedures described below. Final purchasers' (market) prices were collected for these commodities and services in the countries included in the comparison, keeping the characteristics of the outlets and transactors as homogeneous as possible across countries.

Implicit rates could alternatively be calculated on the basis of factor costs. Given the number of goods included in the study and the amount of information required in the calculation of their factor costs, this would constitute an undertaking far beyond the resources of the ECIEL program. On the other hand, implicit rates calculated from factor costs differ from those calculated at market prices only if the structure of taxes, subsidies, tariffs, etc., among the countries involved is dissimilar. In this study it is assumed that the implicit rates calculated on the basis of market prices would not differ significantly from the rates calculated at factor costs. To test this assumption, a detailed study on the impact of government controls on market prices will be attempted as a by-product of the research described here.

The prices obtained are for May 1968. For seasonal goods, prices refer either to the month of heaviest sales or to the month of lowest prices, adjusted by the price change to correspond to May 1968. Goods affected by abnormalities in supply or demand during May 1968 were priced when "normalcy" was restored, with the prices adjusted to May 1968.

After some experimentation it was found that the relation of prices to size of container, volume, etc., was approximately linear in most cases, and the relationship did not appear to change much from country to country. Thus, each country was mainly priced on the basis of the uniform units of measurement specified in the price inquiry. Whenever such units were atypical, the most common size was selected in the country in question and the price adjusted on the basis of a linear extrapolation.

These and other similar factors divide the market for each product into several compartments. An agricultural product at the peak of production is different from an agricultural product traded during the off-season; a commodity bought from the small grocery store cannot be considered the same as an identical commodity bought from a large supermarket; a transaction involving one orange is not the same as a transaction involving two dozen oranges. In order to determine these differences several alternatives have been priced in some cases; in others, a specific alternative was priced on a uniform basis in all countries.

Prices were collected in either the capital or the most important city in each of the LAFTA countries. It is expected that the implicit rates calculated from these prices would not differ significantly from those calculated from national price averages. (This assumption will be tested in the future. If rejected, the prices collected will be adjusted to correspond to national averages.)

The goods selected for pricing were common to all participating countries. Experimentation with the existing data (price indexes, family budget studies, national accounts data, apparent consumption estimates, etc.) suggests that the products included in the common list of goods are quite representative of the expenditure patterns of each of the countries involved. This is not to deny that there are important goods that appear only in a particular nation.[20] However, it was always

[20] The experience of the ECLA study indicated that these goods would not present significant problems (see ECLA, "Measurement," pp. 65–67).

possible to find a similar good whose price behavior resembled that of the unique good and which could be found in the other countries. In such cases the weights corresponding to the unique goods were allocated to these similar items. On the other hand, whenever a good included in the common list was missing in two or three countries, the prices of substitute goods were included. If no appropriate substitutes for the product in question could be found, a price was imputed from the prices of similar products.[21] If none of these alternatives was suitable, the good was dropped from the common list. The prices are expressed in terms of the respective national currency units of each country.

Indeterminacy of the Results. It is well known that the weighting schemes used affect the calculation of the implicit rates. In fact, in determining the implicit rates between two countries, two legitimate answers are generated by alternatively using one country's weights and then the other country's weights. The true implicit rate would generally lie between these two rates,[22] and several formulas have been suggested to estimate it. These formulations result in a single rate basically as a result of crossing either the two rates or the weights of the countries *ab initio.* This study will calculate implicit rates for each pair of countries in the binary fashion described above, and it will also attempt to determine an unequivocal set of implicit rates that could be used for value comparisons within the LAFTA region.

For the latter purpose it is necessary to have a common list of goods and an average set of weights for the region as a whole. An alternative is to estimate the implicit rates from the whole set of binary rates, as Kloek and Theil have suggested.[23] The preliminary results presented below are based on a uniform list of goods and on an average (or crossed) set of weights for all Latin American countries.

Several index number formulas can be used to combine and weight the prices of the different products and countries, producing an average price relationship. This average price ratio constitutes the implicit

21 This procedure is equivalent to attributing the weights of those goods that are missing to similar goods for which prices exist.

22 On this point see International Labour Office, *International Comparisons of Wages,* Geneva, 1956, pp. 34–37.

23 T. Kloek and H. Theil, "International Comparison of Prices and Quantities Consumed," *Econometrica,* July 1965.

rate for the countries involved. The varied index number formulations that will be computed and compared in this study are reviewed in Appendix B.

The Expenditure Weights Used. As pointed out above expenditure weights are used in this survey. Not only are these more stable across time and countries, but they constitute a better measure of the importance of each product. Moreover, with the basic exception of food, quantity data are very hard to obtain.

The starting point for the weights is the national accounting framework of the different countries. Data on the expenditure categories of GNP are being collected for every country involved, but a more detailed breakdown of these categories is needed in most cases. A common set of definitions and a uniform classification were determined following in the main the U.N. system of national accounts (SNA). They diverge from the SNA because (a) the national account practices that are most common in Latin America had to be followed; (b) the classification had to be made more flexible for specific research objectives; and (c) the nature of government consumption had to be redefined to exclude the value of those goods and services that most evidently have counterparts in private consumption (basically expenditures on education and health).

Whenever the ECIEL classification differed from the SNA, the following criteria were used in determining the way in which GDP categories and subcategories would be further disaggregated:

a. The importance of the items, subdivisions, and subcategories in the LAFTA countries, as indicated by price index weights, family budget studies, apparent consumption data, etc.

b. The similarity in market behavior of items and groups of items.[24] Goods with similar market behavior were grouped together as much as possible, so as to minimize price dispersion within subcategories and other subdivisions. This also facilitates the replacement of certain

---

[24] Goods with similar demand and supply characteristics which are affected by changes in demand and supply conditions in more or less the same manner are defined as having the same market behavior. For example, all meats have a relatively high income elasticity, but there would be significant differences between pork and beef. On the other hand bread and cereals do not have a high income elasticity. However, there are differences between wheat and bakery products.

goods not found in particular countries by other products in the same grouping.

c. The division of the categories (in terms of subcategories and sub-divisions) into parts of approximately equal importance. This is quite helpful in making the results of the calculations within each category, subcategory, or subdivision not dependent on just a small number of crucial groupings. No grouping within a particular subdivision should be of so little importance as to be irrelevant or so large as to be crucial.

The data required to implement such an ambitious attempt at sub-classification are obtained from several sources. Unpublished estimates available at the national accounting offices in the participating coun-tries are used to supplement published data. In the private consump-tion sector, the results of a series of family budget studies undertaken by the ECIEL program are being used to provide detailed weights at the item level. These item weights are then combined to derive weights at higher levels of aggregation. For capital formation the additional data needed in breaking down the categories come from estimates of apparent consumption in value terms. Special data are also being gathered to provide for more detailed subcategories on construction expenditures. Government expenditure figures and government bud-gets are being used to provide a finer breakdown of the national ac-counts estimates of government consumption.

Expenditure data would initially refer to 1967, as generally there is a three-year lag in their publication in Latin America. Although it can be assumed that there would be no radical change in relative terms in the expenditure data between 1967 and 1968, the year of the price col-lection, it is planned to use 1968 data if they can be obtained in time for publication.

The Construction of a Representative Basket of Goods and Services for LAFTA Countries. In 1960–62, the Economic Commission for Latin America (ECLA) undertook a study which constitutes the forerunner to the one described here. Although significant changes were intro-duced in the methodology of the present study, it was considered important to ensure the comparability of both surveys as much as pos-sible, not only to permit a direct comparison of the results, but also (a) to test the use of price indexes in the extrapolation of implicit rates, given that ECLA has updated its survey in this fashion; and (b) to permit a sounder selection, through regression methods, of a subset of goods that could be priced regularly in Latin America, for the purpose of calculating on a periodic basis the implicit rates among these countries.

Thus in the construction of a representative basket for LAFTA countries, the ECLA experience and the ECLA lists were the starting point. Also considered were the post allowances lists compiled by the United Nations, the U.S. State Department, and the German Foreign Office. Yet, the real determining elements in the construction of the ECIEL basket were the expenditure patterns of each of the countries involved. This required a careful review of the information contained in price indexes, family budget studies, national accounts data, and other pertinent sources.

Certain guidelines were followed in the selection of the items. The number of items selected in each subdivision was made dependent on the expenditure in the particular subdivision relative to total expenditure in the countries involved. The heterogeneity of the subdivision was also a determining factor. Ceteris paribus, a heterogeneous subcategory requires larger representation than a homogeneous one. Unique goods were avoided as much as possible (things like *tortillas* in Mexico, *hallacas* in Venezuela, *sopa paraguaya* in Paraguay), but the basic ingredients used in the manufacture of these goods (for example, corn) were included if the unique goods were important. Goods which could not be specified in a simple and straightforward manner were also avoided. Thus a tentative basket was constructed.

Each country checked the specifications of the goods included in this tentative basket against the goods used in their own price indexes and specifications. The weights of the goods whose specifications in the tentative basket and in the consumer price index of each country were considered to be close were added up country by country. These weights were found to represent over 75 per cent of the total consumer price index weights in almost every one of the countries included. Moreover, the price movement of the goods with close specifications seemed to simulate quite well the movement of the consumer price indexes in the different countries over recent years. Submitted to this sort of checking procedures, the tentative basket was changed several times until a final satisfactory listing was reached. The final list of goods was then put through pilot tests in several countries to determine its practical applicability.

It has been previously noted that in the calculation of sets of rates for value conversion it is important that the prices used refer as much as possible to goods of the same quality in the different countries. A standard of quality must be provided. Although specifications are quite helpful, they are not sufficient. It is necessary to supplement them by the selection of a country to serve as a point of reference for quality comparisons. For private consumption, Chile was selected as the base. This meant that a close survey of Chilean qualities was made, and comparable qualities (brands, models, types, varieties, etc.) were selected in the other countries. Brazil was selected as the base country for investment goods.

The Price Collection. Although the ECIEL seminars serve to determine the procedures to be followed and to ensure their understanding on the part of the participants, a visiting committee of members of the participating institutes, Brookings, and ECLA traveled to each country just prior to the price collection. Its principal mission was to help train interviewers, to ensure quality comparability, and to conduct a final check on methodology and procedures. The committee carried out the quality surveys in Chile and Brazil and developed a set of common practices. The institutes tested the questionnaires, worked on the application of the sample design (choosing the neighborhoods, selecting the outlets, etc.), and trained the interviewers and supervisors.

The committee checked all these aspects in the field. In particular, its members visited the stores, together with the supervisors and interviewers, to determine the brands, models, varieties, types, etc., that had to be priced in each country, thus ascertaining comparability with particular qualities in the base countries. They also made sure that the stores and neighborhoods selected were comparable. The prices collected correspond to those paid by the middle-income levels in these countries. These levels were defined as the six middle deciles in the distribution of families by income in each country.

The Processing of the Data. Special consistency sheets were designed at Brookings to facilitate a preliminary checking of the surveys in the field. Thereafter, the basic information was recorded on special coding sheets. These coding forms, together with copies of the questionnaires and consistency sheets, were sent to Brookings toward the end of 1968. At Brookings the data were thoroughly verified. First, the questionnaires were reviewed together with the consistency and coding sheets. After some preliminary corrections, adjustments, and editing, the data were punched on cards and run through a series of tests of extreme values. Listings of these cards were examined in great detail and checked against price index information from the different countries and against extrapolated prices from the ECLA survey. As a result of this battery of tests further verification on quality classification, extreme prices, units of measurement, and other matters was requested from the field. The cards were then given a final editing in accordance with the response from the field and were recorded on tapes (unedited records were also kept). A final checking was undertaken based on an examination of unweighted intercountry price relatives for all the qualities and products included in the survey.

After editing, a price file was created, consisting of two tapes. One tape contained the prices listed consecutively. The other registered these prices according to their characteristics or attributes. This second tape included all the lists that could be formed by classifying prices according to attributes. For example, all prices gathered in big supermarkets were in one list; all prices from Chile, in another list, etc.

This setup permits an easy access to the data file and facilitates tabulations across several attributes. For example, the intersection of the Chile, large supermarkets, and good-quality lists defines an intersecting list of good-quality prices for large supermarkets in Chile. The intersection of the Colombia, large supermarkets, and good-quality lists determines a similar intersecting list. From these two intersecting lists, implicit rates or equivalences on the basis of good-quality products priced in large supermarkets in Chile and Colombia can be computed. In similar fashion different types of comparisons can be worked out by combining the different lists in various ways.

The expenditure data, following the breakdown indicated in Appendix A, are being put together at Brookings from information sent from the field. The checking to which these data are submitted is not as strict as that given to the prices, because the latter are directly generated in this study while expenditures are based on existing data.[25]

VI. SOME PRELIMINARY RESULTS

The implicit rates presented in this section cover only private consumption. Results on the other sectors of GDP are not yet available. Implicit rates for private consumption can be considered as reasonable approximations to those corresponding to all GDP sectors.[26]

Expenditure data from the ECIEL consumer surveys, which are needed for a breakdown of private consumption expenditures, are not yet available. Therefore, average Latin American expenditure weights derived from 1960 ECLA data are used in this paper.[27]

A matrix of implicit exchange rates, calculated within the limitations noted above, is presented in Table 2. The countries appearing as denominators are the base countries. Each row is the set of implicit rates when that particular row country is used as a base. For example, the implicit rate of the Argentinian peso with respect to the Brazilian currency would be 90.05 pesos per new cruzeiro; the implicit rate of the Chilean escudo would be 2.39 escudos to one new cruzeiro, and so on.

All rates presented in this paper have been calculated by using the

[25] Exceptions are the data originating in the ECIEL private consumption expenditure surveys, which are thoroughly checked at Brookings. These studies also cover the LAFTA countries.

[26] Private consumption expenditures average close to 75 per cent of total expenditure in Latin American countries. The findings of ECLA indicate that implicit rates based on private consumption are relatively close to those calculated from total GDP (see ECLA, "Measurement," p. 190).

[27] Richard Ruggles kindly supplied these expenditure weights calculated on the basis of ECLA price and quantity information. The ECLA data cover all of Latin America, not only the LAFTA countries. But it is expected that LAFTA weights would not differ significantly from Latin American weights. Most of the materials from the 1960–62 ECLA survey used in this study refer to 1960, the year in which most of the data were collected. The 1962 ECLA data are based primarily on extrapolation.

Although the most recent expenditure surveys in the countries involved could have been used, it was felt that expenditure weights did not vary greatly between 1960 and the date of the most recent survey, which, in the majority of the countries, is already several years old. Furthermore, it has been shown that as long as the same set of weights applies to the different countries, even significant changes in expenditure weighting systems do not make much difference in the results (see Ruggles, "Comparison," pp. 187–91). It is planned to use the expenditure weights derived from the ECIEL consumption study in the final publication of this project.

TABLE 2

Matrix of Implicit Rates on the Basis of Private
Consumption Expenditures, May 1968 [a]

Denomi-nator	Numerator										
	Argen-tina	Bo-livia	Bra-zil	Chile	Colom-bia	Ecua-dor	Mex-ico	Para-guay	Peru	Uru-guay	Vene-zuela
Argen-tina	1.00	0.04	0.01	0.03	0.05	0.05	0.04	0.36	0.13	0.57	0.01
Bolivia	23.18	1.00	0.26	0.62	1.12	1.25	1.03	8.33	3.08	13.30	0.45
Brazil	90.05	3.86	1.00	2.39	4.32	4.84	3.97	32.15	11.93	51.58	1.73
Chile	37.29	1.61	0.42	1.00	1.81	2.03	1.66	13.50	4.97	21.55	0.72
Colom-bia	20.64	0.89	0.23	0.55	1.00	1.12	0.92	7.46	2.75	11.94	0.40
Ecuador	18.48	0.80	0.21	0.49	0.89	1.00	0.82	6.66	2.46	10.66	0.36
Mexico	22.58	0.97	0.25	0.60	1.09	1.22	1.00	8.08	3.00	12.95	0.44
Para-guay	2.79	0.12	0.03	0.07	0.13	0.15	0.12	1.00	0.37	1.60	0.05
Peru	7.55	0.32	0.08	0.20	0.36	0.41	0.33	2.70	1.00	4.32	0.15
Uru-guay	1.75	0.08	0.02	0.05	0.08	0.09	0.08	0.63	0.23	1.00	0.03
Vene-zuela	51.68	2.23	0.58	1.39	2.51	2.81	2.29	18.73	6.87	29.97	1.00

[a] The weights used are 1960 expenditure weights derived by Richard Ruggles from unpublished ECLA data. They are Latin American averages.

Walsh geometric index formulation (Appendix B, formula 6). Thus the weights are the same irrespective of the country used as the base. Since this formula is circular or transitive, the results are invariant to changes in the base country.

Comparison of Implicit and Exchange Rates

In section IV it was argued that while exchange rates cannot be used for value conversion, implicit rates can be. Also the proposition advanced by Gustav Cassell, referring to the closeness of these two kinds of rates, was rejected by implication. The question then arises as to what sort of relationship could be expected between exchange rates and implicit rates.

Bela Balassa attempts to answer such a question. For this purpose he specifies a two-country, three-good model with one of the goods not traded. The model is also based on the assumptions of labor as a limiting factor, constant input coefficients and costs, small productivity differences in the production of the nontraded good, and equalization of the prices of traded goods. In his model "the currency of the country with the higher productivity levels will appear to be overvalued in terms of purchasing-power parity." [28] In the next sentence Balassa writes: "If per capita incomes are taken as representative of levels of productivity, the ratio of purchasing-power parity to the exchange rate will thus be an increasing function of income levels." [29]

The Relationship of Implicit Rates and Official Exchange Rates. It would be useful to look at the relationship between exchange rates and implicit rates as a first step in testing Balassa's proposition, which was derived from data for developed countries, within the Latin American context. Let us then compare the official exchange rates of the LAFTA countries with the implicit rates arising from the ECLA study of 1960–62. The latter have been updated by extrapolation through the use of national price indexes.

The ECLA implicit rates adjusted to May 1968 appear in Table 3. In the same table, the official exchange rates corresponding to May 1968 are also shown. Both sets of rates are expressed in terms of the U.S. dollar. The ECLA rates are based only on private consumption expenditures. Glancing at the figures in Table 3, it appears that the implicit rates for Latin American currencies are lower than the official exchange rates. In the terminology of Balassa's article, these currencies were undervalued in terms of the implicit rates in May 1968.[30]

[28] Balassa, "Parity," pp. 585, 586.
[29] Here the term "purchasing-power parity" as used by Balassa pertains to the "absolute" version of the doctrine and can be considered equivalent to implicit rates.
[30] The use of the concepts of over- and undervaluation in this context may create misunderstandings. They derive from the often unstated assumption in articles written in this area of international trade that implicit rates resulting from a comparison of prices across countries actually indicate the extent of over- and undervaluation, because they are approximations to the equilibrium exchange rate. Actually the concepts of over- and undervaluation are relative ones and have been applied in accordance with different standards. For example, these concepts can be tied to the balance of payments situation, the "actual" equilibrium exchange rate, or the "free trade" equilibrium exchange rate.

In this section the concepts of over- and undervaluation shall be used relative to the implicit rate in order easily to link the results presented with Balassa's framework and terminology. Clearly, no policy recommendations should be drawn from the use of such terms in this article. (For a recent specific instance in which "absolute" purchasing power parities have been used to recommend devaluation or appreciation see H. Houthakker, "Exchange Rate Adjustment," in Joint Economic Committee, *Factors Affecting the U.S. Balance of Payments,* 88th Cong., 2nd sess., December 1964.)

Role of the Price Structure

TABLE 3

Comparison of Official Exchange Rates and ECLA
Adjusted Implicit Rates, May 1968 [a]

(in national currencies per dollar)

	Official Exchange Rates	ECLA Rates
Argentina	350.00	231.34
Bolivia	11.88	8.29
Brazil	3.22	2.44
Chile	6.66	4.30
Colombia	16.30	8.74
Ecuador	18.18	11.97
Mexico	12.50	7.19
Paraguay	126.00	78.56
Peru	38.70	26.80
Uruguay	250.00	126.61
Venezuela	4.50	3.63

[a] ECLA rates are implicit rates for 1960–62 brought up to date by the use of national price indexes. They are based on private consumption expenditures only.

In order to make the comparison with the ECIEL results, it is necessary to link the set of implicit rates (presented in Table 2) to the dollar by estimating the implicit rate of a particular LAFTA country relative to the U.S. dollar. The lower the estimated rate beween the currency of the selected LAFTA country and the U.S. dollar, the lower will be the implicit rates between the other LAFTA countries and the United States, and vice versa.

Because this estimated implicit rate between the selected LAFTA country and the United States is a rough estimate, it is wise to work with a range of values rather than a single one. Assume that the lower bound of this range is the adjusted implicit rate between the selected country and the United States as calculated by ECLA (Table 3). Take the official exchange rate as the upper bound on the assumption that the implicit rate could not be higher, because if it were it would suggest that the currency is not undervalued but overvalued with respect to the U.S. dollar. As the implicit rates obtained for the other LAFTA countries are dependent on this range, it would be useful to select as a pivot the LAFTA country whose implicit and official exchange rates in relation to the U.S. dollar differed least in May 1968.

Venezuela meets this condition, as can be seen from Table 3, and was selected as the link between the United States and the rest of LAFTA. Two sets of implicit rates between the LAFTA currencies and the dollar were calculated for May 1968. One set was based on the official rate of 4.50 bolivars to the dollar; the other used the adjusted ECLA rate of 3.63 bolivars to the dollar as the link. It is expected that the true implicit rate between Venezuela and the United States will be somewhere within this range or very close to its lower limit. The two sets of implicit rates are given in Table 4.

If the results in Table 4 are compared with the official exchange rates shown in Table 3, the apparent conclusion that all LAFTA countries had undervalued exchange rates on May 1968 is corroborated. This result holds even under the upper-bound assumption for the

TABLE 4

Implicit Rates per U.S. Dollar for LAFTA Countries
as Calculated from ECIEL Rates Under
Different Assumptions, May 1968 [a]

(in national currencies per dollar)

	Assumed Implicit Rate	
	4.50 Bolivars per Dollar	3.63 Bolivars per Dollar
Argentina	232.55	187.59
Bolivia	10.03	8.09
Brazil	2.60	2.10
Chile	6.25	5.04
Colombia	11.28	9.10
Ecuador	12.65	10.21
Mexico	10.32	8.33
Paraguay	84.29	67.99
Peru	30.93	24.95
Uruguay	134.85	108.78

[a] Implicit rates calculated on the basis of private consumption expenditures only. Venezuela is not included.

bolivar-dollar implicit rate. The implicit rate would have to be much higher for these results to be generally reversed. Thus, in relating Latin American countries to the United States, the results presented in this paper agree with the propositions derived from Balassa's model.

The Effects of Economic Development. These findings are not surprising, granted the level of economic development of the Latin American countries compared with the United States. The calculation of implicit rates involves a price comparison, not only of tradable goods, but also of purely domestic goods which do not normally enter into international trade. As Harrod indicated in the 1957 edition of his *International Economics,* the latter "are likely to be more expensive in more efficient countries." [31] On the other hand, international trade will tend to produce equality in the prices of tradable goods in the different countries after transportation costs and protective measures are taken into account.[32]

To further test Balassa's proposition, that the ratio of purchasing power parity to the exchange rate is an increasing function of income levels, within the Latin American area, the ratios suggested by him were computed by relating the ECIEL implicit rates for May 1968 to the corresponding official exchange rates (see Table 5). The ratios were calculated in terms of the Venezuelan bolivar, as no direct implicit rates with respect to the U.S. dollar were computed in the ECIEL study. Nevertheless, the results obtained would have been the same if the dollar had been taken as the base currency, because this would only involve multiplying the ratios for the different countries by the same set of constants.[33] The per capita income figures used are those published by the Inter-American Development Bank, as U.N. figures for 1968 have not yet been published. The ratios and income levels are

[31] Roy F. Harrod, *International Economics,* University of Chicago Press, p. 75.

[32] Although the results obtained in tables 3 and 4 tend to confirm some of the findings of Balassa, they are not consistent with other findings. For example, Balassa states in the article cited above that the relationship between purchasing power parities and exchange rates provides clues as to the degree of overvaluation or undervaluation of a currency. In the case of LAFTA countries this does not appear to be true. Almost all of these currencies were considered to be overvalued in 1968 at the official exchange rates indicated in Table 3. This is in direct contradiction to the situation suggested from the comparisons in tables 3 and 4. In this instance official exchange rates appear closer to equilibrium exchange rates than implicit rates.

[33] In this case the constant would be the ratio of the implicit rate of the bolivar with respect to the dollar to the official rate of exchange between these currencies.

TABLE 5

Ratio of Implicit Rates to Official Exchange Rates
Related to Per Capita Gross Domestic
Product, LAFTA Countries, 1968 [a]

(base country: Venezuela)

	Ratio of Implicit to Official Exchange Rates	Ranking of Countries by Ratios	Per Capita GDP in 1963 U.S. Dollars [b]	Ranking of Countries by Per Capita GDP
Argentina	.66	(9)	660	(1)
Bolivia	.84	(2)	135	(10)
Brazil	.80	(4.5) [c]	290	(6)
Chile	.94	(1)	360	(4)
Colombia	.69	(7)	280	(7)
Ecuador	.70	(6)	215	(8.5) [c]
Mexico	.82	(3)	470	(3)
Paraguay	.67	(8)	215	(8.5) [c]
Peru	.80	(4.5) [c]	300	(5)
Uruguay	.54	(10)	530	(2)

[a] Implicit rates are those calculated under the ECIEL program on the basis of private consumption expenditures.

[b] From figures presented in Inter-American Development Bank, *Socio-Economic Progress in Latin America*, Washington, D.C., 1969.

[c] In case of ties the countries are assigned rankings equal to the average of the rank they would have had if the tie had not occurred.

shown in Table 5, with the countries being ranked according to their values.

It is immediately apparent that no pattern emerges between these two sets of statistics. Argentina and Uruguay, the countries with the highest levels of income per capita among LAFTA countries (with Venezuela excluded) have the lowest ratios; Bolivia, with the lowest per capita income, has the third highest ratio. In fact, the rank correlation coefficient is very low and negative (-0.27).[34]

[34] Actually, the income variable should be expressed in real terms. However, this would not alter the conclusions. In fact, with the per capita incomes of Argentina and Uruguay being relatively larger in real terms, and the Bolivian one smaller, the hypothesis tested would appear to hold even less in real terms.

Since there are, in some of these countries, significant divergences between official and free exchange rates, additional testing was done on the basis of the ratios of implicit rates to free rates. The data are presented in Table 6 with the countries ranked as previously. The coefficient of rank correlation was again negative and quite small (−0.30). It appears that without further manipulation Latin American data are not consistent with the Balassa hypothesis and that therefore there are, in this respect, significant differences between the developing and developed countries which Balassa examined. The Balassa hypothesis might also hold in comparisons among broad groups of countries classified according to geopolitical area and level of economic development, but there is doubt that they would apply to countries within

TABLE 6

Ratio of Implicit Rates to Free Exchange Rates Related to Per Capita Gross Domestic Product, LAFTA Countries, 1968 [a]

(base country: Venezuela)

	Ratio of Implicit to Free Exchange Rates	Ranking of Countries by Ratios	Per Capita GDP in 1963 U.S. Dollars [b]	Ranking of Countries by Per Capita GDP
Argentina	.66 [c]	(8)	660	(1)
Bolivia	.84 [c]	(1)	135	(10)
Brazil	.71	(3)	290	(6)
Chile	.69	(4.5) [d]	360	(4)
Colombia	.69	(4.5) [d]	280	(7)
Ecuador	.57	(9)	215	(8.5) [d]
Mexico	.82 [c]	(2)	470	(3)
Paraguay	.67 [c]	(7)	215	(8.5) [d]
Peru	.68	(6)	300	(5)
Uruguay	.54 [c]	(10)	530	(2)

[a] Implicit rates are those calculated under the ECIEL program on the basis of private consumption expenditures.

[b] From figures presented in Inter-American Development Bank, *Socio-Economic Progress in Latin America*, Washington, D.C., 1969.

[c] For these countries the official and free exchange rates coincide.

[d] In case of ties the countries are assigned rankings equal to the average of the ranks they would have had if the tie had not occurred.

TABLE 7

Implicit Rates Calculated by ECLA, June 1960

(Peruvian sol = 1.00)

Argentina	3.08	Ecuador	0.68
Bolivia	0.44	Mexico	0.50
Brazil	0.01[a]	Paraguay	4.54
Chile	0.06	Uruguay	0.40
Colombia	0.29	Venezuela	0.29

SOURCE: U.N. Economic Commission for Latin America, "A Measurement of Price Levels and the Purchasing Power of Currencies in Latin America, 1960–62," mimeo, Santiago, Chile, 1963, p. 186.

[a] This figure has been adjusted to take into account the change to the new cruzeiro.

some of those groupings. Thus, the systematic relationship between implicit rates and exchange rates derived from Balassa's model does not appear to be generally applicable.[35]

Results of the 1960 and 1968 Surveys Compared

There have been sharp changes in implicit rates among LAFTA countries between 1960 and 1968 (compare tables 2 and 7).[36] With the Peruvian sol as point of reference, the implicit rate for the Brazilian currency was eleven times higher in 1968 than in 1960.[37] This means that the purchasing power of the cruzeiro relative to the sol was eleven times lower in 1968 than in 1960. Uruguay presents a similar situation. The currencies of Chile, followed by Argentina, have also depreciated considerably, although not as much as those of Brazil and Uruguay.

[35] Further work in this area would be quite fruitful. Balassa worked with a one-factor model. Christopher Clague and Vito Tanzi argue in a recent paper that the introduction of other productive factors is required to establish a relationship between implicit rates and exchange rates that would be applicable to different types of countries (see Christopher Clague and Vito Tanzi, "Human Capital, Natural Resources and the Purchasing-Power Parity Doctrine: Some Empirical Results," 1969, mimeo). Relaxing some of the assumptions of Balassa's model appears to be another promising avenue for research.

[36] This analysis is again based on implicit rates corresponding to private consumption expenditures. It is more convenient to take Peru rather than Venezuela as the base in this section because its experience from 1960 to 1968 can be considered as a representative average of all LAFTA countries. Venezuela, with a very stable currency, is an extreme case.

[37] Due to rounding in tables 2 and 7 the Brazilian currency appears to be only eight times higher between the two dates.

These countries have experienced the most virulent inflation in Latin America.

On the other hand, the implicit rates relative to the sol have become much lower for other countries. Thus, the purchasing power of the Mexican peso appreciated with respect to the sol. In the case of Bolivia, the rate improved from 0.44 to 0.32 pesos bolivianos to a sol. More pronounced was the change in Ecuador, going from 0.68 to 0.41 sucres for a unit of Peruvian currency. In the case of Paraguay the apprecia-tion was higher still. In 1960 the implicit rate of exchange was 4.54 guaranies per sol; by 1968 the purchasing power of the guarani had improved relatively and stood at 2.70 guaranies for one sol. The Vene-zuelan bolivar experienced the largest relative appreciation of all (from 0.29 to 0.15 bolivars per sol). These are the countries that have been most successful in controlling price increases throughout this period.

The only country whose implicit rate has not changed considerably with respect to the Peruvian sol has been Colombia. Both Peru and Colombia are in the middle tier of LAFTA countries with respect to the degree of inflation.

The radical changes in the implicit rates among the Latin American countries over time indicate the importance of recalculating these rates regularly.[38] Table 8 shows the set of implicit equivalences for different subcategories of private consumption, with Peru as a base, in 1968.

VII. PRICE RELATIONSHIPS AMONG LAFTA COUNTRIES

The ECIEL data have been used also to compute international price indexes. These have been calculated on the basis of the rates generally used by traders, that is, the official exchange rates. The indexes are shown in Table 9 in the form of a matrix, with every country presented alternatively as a base.

In Table 10 similar results are presented, but using the adjusted implicit ECLA rates as exchange rates. These rates have been estimated solely on the basis of private consumption expenditures and refer to May 1968.

[38] The Economic Commission for Latin America found that for LAFTA countries the rates changed significantly between 1960 and 1962. See ECLA, "Measurement," pp. 76–78.

TABLE 8

Implicit Equivalencies for Private Consumption Subcategories, 1968 [a]
(Peruvian sol = 1.00)

	Argen-tina	Bo-livia	Bra-zil	Chile	Co-lom-bia	Ecua-dor	Mex-ico	Para-guay	Peru	Uru-guay	Vene-zuela
Food	7.46	.33	.08	.18	.43	.43	.36	2.62	1.00	4.62	.15
Beverages	6.09	.31	.05	.17	.36	.45	.32	1.87	1.00	3.95	.17
Tobacco	11.06	.38	.09	.24	.21	.36	.23	3.04	1.00	9.81	.17
Clothing	8.71	.33	.09	.23	.40	.40	.41	2.74	1.00	5.65	.14
Rent	6.33	.39	.10	.26	.44	.41	.38	2.62	1.00	3.90	.17
Utilities	13.65	.19	.11	.23	.08	.33	.08	4.74	1.00	0.72	.09
Durables	8.12	.29	.06	.23	.33	.38	.30	2.86	1.00	5.94	.11
Non-durables	6.56	.37	.07	.16	.32	.40	.26	3.00	1.00	5.21	.11
Services	7.07	.26	.09	.19	.25	.34	.31	2.69	1.00	3.37	.15

[a] Same weights as in preceding tables.

In comparing the preliminary results presented in these tables, significant differences stand out. On the basis of the official exchange rates, Venezuela has the highest prices, Chile the second, and Bolivia the third highest. But if ECLA rates are used, these places are occupied by Chile, Mexico, and Colombia, in that order. The countries that rank lowest in intercountry price relatives based on official exchange rates are Uruguay, Paraguay, and Argentina in that order. With the ECLA rates, the lowest-priced countries are Argentina, Ecuador, Brazil, and Uruguay.

These comparisons reflect two basic facts. First, price differences will vary with the exchange rate used. In price (or cost) comparisons for an examination of prospective trade allocation the equilibrium exchange rates are the most appropriate. Depending on the purpose and assumptions of the comparison either the "actual" or the "free trade" equilibrium rates would be utilized. But if the objective is to utilize price advantages assuming that present policies are unchanged, then official exchange rates should be used, as in Table 9. On the other hand, for checking the extrapolation of international price indexes over time the implicit rates are most pertinent (see Table 10).

Second, the calculation of implicit rates on the basis of extrapolating benchmark calculations by using national price index information,

Role of the Price Structure

TABLE 9

Matrix of International Price Indexes for Private Consumption on the Basis of Official Exchange Rates, 1968 [a]

Denomi-nator	Numerator										
	Argen-tina	Bo-livia	Bra-zil	Chile	Co-lom-bia	Ecua-dor	Mex-ico	Para-guay	Peru	Uru-guay	Vene-zuela
Argen-tina	1.00	1.23	1.16	1.35	1.00	1.01	1.20	0.97	1.17	0.79	1.44
Bolivia	0.81	1.00	0.95	1.10	0.82	0.82	0.98	0.79	0.95	0.64	1.18
Brazil	0.86	1.05	1.00	1.16	0.86	0.87	1.03	0.83	1.00	0.68	1.24
Chile	0.74	0.91	0.86	1.00	0.74	0.74	0.89	0.72	0.86	0.58	1.06
Colom-bia	1.00	1.22	1.16	1.35	1.00	1.01	1.20	0.97	1.16	0.79	1.44
Ecuador	0.99	1.22	1.15	1.34	0.99	1.00	1.19	0.96	1.16	0.78	1.43
Mexico	0.83	1.02	0.97	1.13	0.84	0.84	1.00	0.81	0.97	0.66	1.20
Para-guay	1.03	1.26	1.20	1.40	1.03	1.04	1.23	1.00	1.20	0.81	1.49
Peru	0.86	1.05	1.00	1.16	0.86	0.86	1.03	0.83	1.00	0.68	1.24
Uru-guay	1.27	1.55	1.47	1.72	1.27	1.28	1.52	1.23	1.48	1.00	1.83
Vene-zuela	0.69	0.85	0.81	0.94	0.69	0.70	0.83	0.67	0.81	0.55	1.00

[a] The weights used are 1960 expenditure weights derived by Richard Ruggles from unpublished ECLA data. They are Latin American averages.

does not appear to be sufficiently accurate. If the updating of the ECLA rates were precise, all the entries in Table 10 would be close to 1.00. This follows by definition, given that the implicit rate between two countries is that which equalizes their prices or the internal purchasing power of their currencies.

In interpreting the results in this section it should be kept in mind that these comparisons are based on market prices rather than factor costs, under the assumption that the results would not differ significantly between them. Also, some of the goods priced in the different countries are imported, although to a very large extent the final goods for the consumer market are domestically produced in most of the countries (Bolivia, Paraguay, and Ecuador are the exceptions). Thus, in certain instances a price advantage might just be due to low-priced imports entering final consumption in particular countries.

TABLE 10

Matrix of International Price Indexes for Private Consumption on the Basis of Adjusted Implicit Rates Calculated by ECLA, 1968 [a]

Denomi- nator					Numerator						
	Argen- tina	Bo- livia	Bra- zil	Chile	Co- lom- bia	Ecua- dor	Mex- ico	Para- guay	Peru	Uru- guay	Vene- zuela
Argen- tina	1.00	1.19	1.04	1.41	1.26	1.03	1.40	1.05	1.14	1.04	1.21
Bolivia	0.84	1.00	0.87	1.19	1.06	0.87	1.18	0.89	0.96	0.87	1.02
Brazil	0.97	1.14	1.00	1.36	1.22	1.00	1.36	1.02	1.10	1.00	1.17
Chile	0.71	0.84	0.73	1.00	0.89	0.73	1.00	0.74	0.81	0.73	0.85
Colom- bia	0.79	0.94	0.82	1.12	1.00	0.82	1.11	0.84	0.90	0.82	0.96
Ecuador	0.97	1.15	1.00	1.37	1.22	1.00	1.36	1.02	1.10	1.00	1.17
Mexico	0.71	0.84	0.74	1.00	0.90	0.73	1.00	0.75	0.81	0.74	0.86
Para- guay	0.95	1.13	0.98	1.34	1.20	0.98	1.33	1.00	1.08	0.98	1.15
Peru	0.88	1.04	0.91	1.24	1.11	0.91	1.23	0.92	1.00	0.91	1.06
Uru- guay	0.97	1.14	1.00	1.37	1.22	1.00	1.35	1.02	1.10	1.00	1.17
Vene- zuela	0.83	0.98	0.86	1.17	1.04	0.86	1.16	0.87	0.94	0.86	1.00

[a] The weights used are 1960 expenditure weights derived by Richard Ruggles from unpublished ECLA data. They are Latin American averages.

Comparison Based on the Overall Price Indexes

One important conclusion can be drawn from a comparison of the results presented in Table 9, referring to 1968 and similar 1960 calculations based on ECLA data. Venezuela's 1964 devaluation, together with a low rate of price increase from 1960 to 1968, appear to have brought the price level in that nation much more in line with those of other Latin American countries. Given that the price comparisons presented here refer only to private consumer goods, Venezuela's heavy reliance on imports of producers durables at low nominal tariffs could bring down its general price level relative to other LAFTA countries even further.[39]

[39] This is under the assumption that Venezuelan prices for construction goods and public consumption goods bear the same relationship to Latin American averages as private consumer goods do.

In his recent experiment with 1960 ECLA data Richard Ruggles calculated the relationship between Venezuelan and Argentinian prices to be much higher than in the ECIEL study (compare tables 9 and 11). The indexes are shown with Argentina equal to 100 and are computed using Walsh's index with geometric expenditure weights. (This is also the formula used in the present study.)

In Table 11 the results obtained by ECLA using average Latin American quantity weights are also presented. Mexico is used as a base, and the results also refer to 1960. Venezuelan prices are 110 per cent higher than Mexican prices in the ECLA index. Following Venezuela, Chile has the highest prices. In 1968 (Table 9), Chile had the same ranking as in the ECLA calculations in Table 11, although Chilean prices have also experienced a decline relative to the rest of LAFTA. Bolivian prices seem to have risen faster in relation to changes in the exchange rates than prices in other LAFTA countries. In 1960 Bolivian

TABLE 11

International Price Indexes for Private Consumption on the
Basis of Official Exchange Rates, 1960

	ECLA (Mexico = 100)	Ruggles (Argentina = 100)
Argentina	90	100
Bolivia	99	99
Brazil	91	99
Chile	144	145
Colombia	112	118
Ecuador	100	102
Mexico	100	107
Paraguay	93	92
Peru	96	103
Uruguay	86	85
Venezuela	210	228

SOURCE: U.N. Economic Commission for Latin America, "A Measurement of Price Levels and the Purchasing Power of Currencies in Latin America, 1960-62," mimeo, Santiago, Chile, 1963, p. 191; Richard Ruggles, "Price Indexes and International Price Comparisons," in *Ten Economic Studies in the Tradition of Irving Fisher,* New York, 1967, p. 189.

prices were in the middle range for LAFTA countries, whereas in 1968 that country had the third highest price level.

Uruguay continued to be the lowest-priced country in Latin America in 1968, having widened somewhat its price advantage with respect to both Argentina and Mexico since 1960. Paraguayan prices declined further in relative terms reaching the second lowest position in 1968. Argentina, Colombia, and Ecuador follow in the 1968 survey, the three of them having very similar relative price levels. The most notable changes among the low-priced countries were in Colombia, whose international price relatives appear to have fallen considerably since 1960, and in Brazil, whose price relatives have risen.

Comparisons Based on Subindexes

Uruguay, Paraguay, Argentina, and Brazil had the lowest prices in food and beverages in 1968 as can be seen in Table 12. Venezuelan prices were high in these subcategories, with Chile, Bolivia, and Mexico being next. The ECLA results for 1960 for the low-priced countries were quite similar, as Table 13 shows. Again, Argentina,

TABLE 12

International Price Indexes for Private Consumption
Subcategories on the Basis of Official
Exchange Rates, 1968 [a]

(Peruvian sol = 1.00)

	Argentina	Bolivia	Brazil	Chile	Colombia	Ecuador	Mexico	Paraguay	Uruguay	Venezuela
Food	0.86	1.06	0.96	1.05	1.00	.91	1.11	0.81	0.73	1.07
Beverages	0.68	1.01	0.61	0.99	0.86	.95	0.98	0.57	0.61	1.44
Tobacco	1.24	1.24	1.06	1.41	0.49	.76	0.73	0.93	1.52	1.43
Clothing	0.98	1.06	1.14	1.32	0.96	.84	1.27	0.84	0.88	1.25
Rent	0.71	1.28	1.17	1.49	1.04	.88	1.19	0.80	0.60	1.42
Utilities	1.53	0.61	1.27	1.36	0.19	.70	0.25	1.45	0.11	0.80
Durables	0.91	0.93	0.78	1.36	0.78	.82	0.94	0.87	0.92	0.97
Non-durables	0.74	1.21	0.80	0.93	0.76	.85	0.81	0.92	0.81	0.99
Services	0.81	0.84	1.07	1.05	0.59	.73	0.93	0.83	0.53	1.23

[a] See notes to preceding tables.

Role of the Price Structure

TABLE 13

International Price Indexes for Private Consumption
Subcategories on the Basis of Prevailing
Exchange Rates, 1960

(Mexico = 100)

	Argen-tina	Bo-livia	Brazil	Co-lom-bia	Chile	Ecua-dor	Mex-ico	Para-guay	Peru	Uru-guay	Vene-zuela
Food	72	92	78	116	112	98	100	82	86	79	197
Beverages	79	150	66	159	112	120	100	108	98	81	270
Clothing	86	85	86	73	156	71	100	87	90	84	150
Rent	163	146	208	183	223	90	100	80	129	78	316
Transport, communication	133	92	142	139	122	141	100	114	113	94	237
Personal care	88	105	83	108	161	112	100	112	114	102	277
Recreation, entertainment	102	89	90	116	164	109	100	112	132	78	261

SOURCE: U.N. Economic Commission for Latin America, "A Measurement of Price Levels and the Purchasing Power of Currencies in Latin America, 1960–62," mimeo, Santiago, Chile, 1963, p. 198.

Brazil, Uruguay, and Paraguay had the lowest prices in food and beverages. The position of Venezuela as the highest-priced country was even more salient in 1960, and Chile was next. But in 1968 Colombia had been supplanted by Mexico as the third highest priced country in these subcategories.

In clothing and textiles, the cheapest countries in LAFTA in 1960 were Ecuador, Colombia, Uruguay, and Bolivia. In the 1968 comparisons Ecuador, Paraguay, and Uruguay were the cheapest, with Colombia a distant fourth. Chile and Venezuela were the highest-priced countries in 1960. This was true again in 1968, with Mexico also having high intercountry price relatives.

In rent, Venezuela had prices three times those of Mexico in 1960, while Chile's and Brazil's were twice as high. In 1968 Chile had the highest relative rent prices, followed by Venezuela, Bolivia, and Brazil (Table 12). Uruguay, Paraguay, and Ecuador had the lowest rents in 1960. In 1968 the ranking was Uruguay, Argentina, Paraguay, and Ecuador.

A comparison between the other ECLA subcategories presented in

Table 13, and the rest of the subcategories resulting from the present study, shown in Table 12, is not strictly possible. Nevertheless, even though in each subcategory there are slight differences in composition between the ECLA and ECIEL studies, taken together these subcategories cover more or less the same kinds of goods and services.[40] Thus it would seem that some global comparisons can be attempted. In general it appears that for these subcategories taken as a whole, Uruguay and Brazil are consistently lower priced in the ECLA 1960 results, with Colombia and Uruguay enjoying a similar position in 1968. Among high-priced countries, as usual Venezuela and Chile stand out in the 1960 ECLA survey. No definite pattern of high-priced countries appears in the 1968 survey.

General Conclusions Resulting from the Price Comparisons

Two basic general conclusions can be derived from these comparisons:

a. In relative terms the results of the 1960 and 1968 surveys bear a striking resemblance to each other. The high- and low-priced countries in 1960 generally were in the same position at the end of the period.

b. On the other hand, a definite contraction in the intercountry price relatives has occurred at both ends of the scale. The range of price variation within LAFTA has narrowed. In fact the coefficient of variation declined from 0.33 to 0.15 between 1960 and 1968. The drop in the coefficient is strongly influenced by the decline in Venezuelan prices relative to the Latin American average.

The first fact confirms the validity of the relative ranking of countries in both the ECLA and ECIEL surveys. The reductions in price dispersion apparent in 1968 might be partly due to the methodological innovations introduced in the ECIEL survey, and specifically to the collection of many more observations per product in 1968 than in 1960. However, there is reason to believe that most of the reduction in price dispersion can be attributed to more realistic exchange rate policies

---

[40] The subcategories in question here are durable consumer goods, nondurable consumer goods, and consumer services in the ECIEL classification; transport and communication, personal care, and recreation and entertainment in ECLA's classification. The ECIEL categories could be rearranged to fit the ECLA classification.

and/or wider and more effective use of monetary and fiscal policies in controlling the price level on the part of many LAFTA countries between 1960 and 1968. Increasing official and unofficial trade and migration in the LAFTA region probably has also been a contributing factor.

Venezuela is a case in point. While official par values have remained relatively fixed, more sophisticated use of policy instruments has been made for the control of inflation. In many countries, however, the exchange rate has been kept much more flexible, with the use of frequent (sometimes monthly and even bimonthly) devaluations to better relate internal to international prices. Finally, greater trade and economic contacts and competition in world markets also appear to have aided in bringing the price structure of these countries closer together.

Implications for Trade Among Latin American Countries

Within the entire LAFTA region, Uruguay, Paraguay, Argentina, Colombia, and Ecuador are the lowest-priced countries (Table 12). The River Plate countries (Argentina, Uruguay, and Paraguay) have a price advantage over Colombia and Ecuador in food and beverages, but higher prices in tobacco and durables, and similar price levels in clothing and nondurables. In relation to the other Andean countries (Bolivia, Peru, and Venezuela), the River Plate price advantage extends to all tradable subcategories with the exception of tobacco.

Brazil, Mexico, and Peru seem to be located in the middle tier of LAFTA countries with respect to price levels. Brazil has lower consumer durable prices than any of the other countries. Mexico does not have an overall price advantage in any particular subcategory, but has lower tobacco prices than any country except Colombia.

Important implications of the results of Table 12 concern the Andean Common Market countries, Colombia, Ecuador, Bolivia, Peru, and Chile, which as pointed out in an earlier section, show promise of greater dynamism in the Latin American integration movement. Venezuela is still considering becoming a member of the group. Her trade possibilities now appear much more promising than in 1960. If Chile, with high relative price levels, can compete with the other Andean countries, it would seem that Venezuela would also have as good a chance of gaining from Andean economic integration. This is especially true if it is noted that Venezuela has a definite comparative advantage in some intermediate petrochemicals and investment goods.

Colombia and Ecuador seem to be the countries with a price advantage in the Andean Group, as Table 9 shows, with Peru and Bolivia in an intermediate position. Their advantage holds throughout the different subcategories examined in Table 12. Some interesting patterns appear for the high-priced countries.[41] In food and beverages the Venezuelan prices are decidedly the highest, with Chilean prices being below those of Bolivia. On the other hand, Chile has the highest prices in clothing and textiles, with Venezuela the second highest, followed by Bolivia. Chile has a very high price disadvantage in consumer durables, while Venezuela and Bolivia are below Peru in this subcategory. In the nondurable consumer goods sector Bolivia has the highest prices, followed by Peru, with Venezuela and Chile next.

Trade is determined by comparative advantage rather than absolute price advantage. Money costs can be influenced by changes in the levels of factor payments and changes in efficiency. These factors operate in the medium and long run. However, government policy can affect money costs in the short run through exchange rate variation, subsidies, and protective measures.

The final purchasers' or retail prices used in this study include the costs of certain nontraded services. The appropriate prices to use in an analysis of possible trading patterns are potential f.o.b. export prices in each country rather than retail prices. Moreover, these calculations should be made in terms of value added and refer to factor costs rather than market prices. Nevertheless, given the obstacles involved in making such estimates, the patterns implied above are useful as an indication of potential trade relationships.

APPENDIX A. EXPENDITURE CLASSIFICATION

I. Private consumption
   A. Foodstuffs
      1. Meats: Beef, lamb, pork, poultry, various meats
      2. Fish and seafood
      3. Dairy products and eggs: Milk, dairy products, eggs
      4. Bread and cereals: Rice, corn, wheat, food pastes, bakery products, other cereals

[41] In the analysis that follows, Venezuela is considered part of the Andean Group.

5. Fruits: Citrus fruits, melons, other temperate fruits, other subtropical fruits, other tropical fruits, dried fruits, juices and canned fruits

6. Vegetables: Potatoes and similar roots, other root vegetables, beans and vine vegetables, head and stalk vegetables, dried beans, canned vegetables

7. Sugar and preserves: Sugar, preserves

8. Fats and oils.

9. Other foodstuffs: Prepared soups, baby food, hot beverages, spices and condiments, candy and other sweets, purchased meals.

B. Beverages: Nonalcoholic, alcoholic, purchased alcoholic beverages

C. Tobacco

D. Clothing and textiles

1. Men's and boys' clothing: Overcoats, suits, trousers, shirts, underwear, hosiery, fabrics and knitting materials, tailoring, other men's and boys' clothing

2. Women's and girls' clothing: Overcoats, suits and dresses, blouses and skirts, underwear, hosiery, sweaters, fabrics for dressmaking, dressmaking-seamstress, other women's and girls' clothing

3. Infants' clothing

4. Household textiles: Household fabrics, semidurable household textiles, durable household textiles

5. Sewing notions

6. Footwear: Men's and boys' footwear, women's and girls' footwear, infants' footwear

E. Rent

F. Fuels and utilities: Gas, electricity, water, other fuels

G. Durable consumer goods

1. Durable housewares: China and glassware, cutlery, cooking utensils

2. Furniture: Beds, chairs and tables

3. Large home appliances

4. Small home appliances

5. Radio and television

6. Tools

7. Automobile parts and accessories

8. Therapeutic appliances and equipment

9. Other durable goods

H. Nondurable consumer goods

1. Household supplies: Soaps and detergents, miscellaneous supplies

2. Toiletries and personal care: Cosmetics, toiletries, other personal care supplies

3. Pharmaceuticals

4. Educational and reading materials: Textbooks and notebooks,

books, newspapers and magazines, writing supplies, other educational materials
    5. Recreational materials: sporting goods, toys, other recreational materials
  I. Services
    1. Transportation: Public transportation, private transportation, school transportation
    2. Communications: Telephone, mail and telegram
    3. Health services: Physician's services, dentist's services, surgery and other services, hospital expenses
    4. Other professional services
    5. Domestic services: domestic help, laundry and dry-cleaning
    6. Personal services
    7. Educational services
    8. Recreation: Public entertainment, other recreational services
    9. Other services
II. Government consumption
  A. Purchases of current goods and services (by ministry): Foodstuffs, beverages and tobacco, clothing and textiles, rent, utilities and fuel, transportation and communications, other goods, other services
  B. Wages and salaries (by ministry): Administrative personnel, technical personnel
III. Gross fixed capital formation
  A. Construction
    1. Dwellings: Residential buildings, workingclass houses, other houses
    2. Nonresidential buildings
    3. Other construction and works
  B. Machinery and equipment
    1. Transport equipment
    2. Other machinery and equipment: Agricultural machinery, tractors, machinery for construction and mining, electrical machinery, motors, machine tools, other machinery, office equipment, office furniture
IV. Increase in stocks
 V. Exports of goods and services
VI. Less: Imports of goods and services

APPENDIX B. INDEX NUMBER FORMULAS USED

First there are binary-type formulas using alternatively the base country's set of weights and then the other country's weights. For international comparisons a base country replaces a base period and so the Laspeyres formulation in terms of price relatives and expenditure weights is:

(1) $$\Sigma(p_{jm}/p_{jl})V_{jl},$$

where the range of summation is from $j = 1$ to n; $V_{jl} = p_{jl}q_{jl}/\Sigma p_{jl}q_{jl}$, with the same range of summation; and p = prices, q = quantities, l and m = countries, and j = goods.

The Paasche formulation instead of using the base country's weights uses the other country's weights. The price relative formulation with expenditure weights is:

(2) $1/\Sigma(p_{jl}/p_{jm})V_{jm}$,

where $V_{jm} = p_{jm}q_{jm}/\Sigma p_{jm}q_{jm}$, and the range of summation is the same as in (1).

The Palgrave index, the reciprocal of the Paasche with countries reversed, produces results that are much closer to those of the Laspeyres index than are the Paasche results. This is because when prices change across countries, quantity weights are considerably affected while expenditure weights are not. The Palgrave formulation (over the range of summation $j = 1, \ldots , n$) is:

(3) $\Sigma(p_{jm}/p_{jl})V_{jm}$

These indexes will be used in the computation of implicit rates in a binary fashion, that is, for each pair of countries the implicit rates will be calculated first under the Laspeyres formulation and then under the Paasche formulation. The Laspeyres and Palgrave results will also be compared.

Yet, a set of unambiguous conversion rates is required for value comparisons. Fisher's ideal index, crossing the Laspeyres and Paasche formulations, provides a way of estimating such a set of rates:

(4) $\sqrt{[\Sigma(p_{jm}/p_{jl})V_{jl}]\,[1/\Sigma(p_{jl}/p_{jm})V_{jm}]}$,

where the range of summation is as in the foregoing formulations. So does the index suggested by Theil, based on a crossing of the Laspeyres and Palgrave formulations:

(5) $\Pi(p_{jm}/p_{jl})^{a}$,

where $a = (V_{jl} + V_{jm})/2$, and the range of Π is from $j = 1$ to n. These indexes satisfy the country reversal test, which means that the implicit rate of country A with country B as a base is the reciprocal of the implicit rate for country B with country A as a base. On the other hand, these indexes are not circular. The set of rates they produce is not consistent. If they were, the implicit rate for country A with country B as a base would coincide with the implicit rate resulting from the product of the implicit rate of country A with country C as a base and the implicit rate of country C with country B as a base [A/B should be the same as $(A/C) \times (C/B)$].

In order to satisfy the circularity test it is possible to compute a single consistent scale of implicit rates from the whole set of binary comparison rates. Theil "recommends that the geometric average of all binary comparisons between two countries be computed in order to produce a single scale." [42]

A less cumbersome alternative is to calculate the implicit rates by using the same set of weights for all the countries involved. This could be achieved by crossing the weights of the different countries, thus arriving at average weights for all countries included. The Walsh index provides such a formulation. The formula below is the geometric version of the index.

(6) $$\Pi(p_{jm}/p_{jl})^b$$

where Π is taken from $j = 1$ to n; and $b = V_{jy} = (\Pi V_{ji})^{1/s}/\Sigma[(\Pi V_{jl})^{1/s}]$, with Π taken from $i = 1$ to s and Σ taken, as before, from $j = 1$ to n. Here $l, m, i,$ and s represent countries, and y is the average of the countries included. This index satisfies both the circularity and country reversal tests.

There are other ways of producing a common set of weights applicable to the countries compared. First, the Walsh index can also be computed using an arithmetic instead of a geometric average of the weights corresponding to the different countries. Then an average of quantity weights for the countries involved could be used, following the market basket rather than the price relative approach. This was the formula used by ECLA in their study:

(7) $$\Sigma p_{jm}q_{jy}/\Sigma p_{jl}q_{jy}$$

where the range of the summation is from $j = 1$ to n and $q_{jy} = (1/s)\Sigma q_{ji}$, and the range of Σ is from $i = 1$ to s. These formulations also meet the country reversal and circularity tests.

The geometric variant of the Walsh index is the formulation utilized in this preliminary paper. However, Richard Ruggles has shown that the results obtained in using the approach suggested by Kloek and Theil are very close to those derived from the application of a common set of average weights, while the results obtained by different ways of calculating or applying these uniform average weights are very similar to each other.[43] One of the by-products of the ECIEL study will be the testing of some of these findings, using the data gathered in 1968.

APPENDIX C. LIST OF LATIN AMERICAN RESEARCH INSTITUTIONS PARTICIPATING IN THE STUDY ON INTERNATIONAL PRICE COMPARISONS

Argentina: Fundación de Investigaciones Económicas Latinoamericanas (FIEL)

[42] Ruggles, "Comparisons," p. 191.
[43] See *ibid.*, pp. 189–201.

Bolivia: Instituto de Investigaciones Económicas–Universidad Mayor de San Andrés

Brazil: Instituto Brasileiro de Economia–Fundação Getulio Vargas

Chile: Instituto de Economía y Planificación–Universidad de Chile

Colombia: Centro de Estudios sobre Desarrollo Económico (CEDE)–Universidad de Los Andes

Ecuador: Junta de Planificación y Coordinación

Mexico: El Colegio de Mexico

Paraguay: Centro Paraguayo de Estudios de Desarrollo Económico y Social (CEPADES)

Peru: Centro de Investigaciónes Sociales, Económicas, Políticas y Antropológicas (CISEPA)–Universidad Católica del Perú

Uruguay: Instituto de Estadística–Universidad de la República del Uruguay

Venezuela: Banco Central de Venezuela; Centro de Desarrollo de la Universidad Central (CENDES)

COMMENT
ROBERT M. WILLIAMS AND R. HAL MASON

While we are in sympathy with the desire to provide a vehicle for making intercountry price and value comparisons, we do find parts of the Grunwald and Salazar paper to be somewhat confusing. Early in their paper they review the work done by ECIEL. Unfortunately, one is left with the impression that Grunwald and Salazar are attempting to provide a valuation method which can be used in studies of comparative costs and locational decisions. This is not in fact the case. Their objective is much less ambitious, but it is not clearly stated. Their objective is simply to use a price parity approach to develop a set of conversion rates, so that various national account data can be compared from country to country on a uniform basis. They note that "it is important to point out that when strict cost or price comparisons are undertaken for the purposes of determining trade possibilities and trade patterns, the equilibrium rates of exchange, rather than implicit rates, should be used." They fail fully to disclose the usefulness of the implicit rates they have calculated. A strong statement on this point combined with several examples would have been helpful to the reader.

The study conducted by ECIEL is perhaps one of the most complete of its type to date. It nevertheless suffers from the same weaknesses all such studies inherently confront. These are, of course, the problem of which set of weights to use on the basic data, selection of sample cities in which to generate data, differences in government policies relative to different types of consumption, selection of a common bundle of goods and services for study, the shifting composition of gross domestic product, and the differing levels of development of the countries involved. The authors are aware of these difficulties and the problems of bias which attend this type of research. Again, it would have been useful had they drawn out in greater detail the difficulties encountered, so that future researchers could have the full benefit of their field experience.

To get around some of these problems several rather critical assumptions were made which can affect applications of the technique and be misleading if too much reliance is placed on these initial data. The authors point out that their assumptions will be tested in future work. However, it would be useful in a document of this sort to have a clearer understanding of the biases which could result if these assumptions are not met, so that other researchers do not misuse the data.

For the record we should like to indicate some of the potential pitfalls of using implicit exchange rates as calculated in this first effort.

Although the authors have conducted some tests, as a matter of expediency they selected either the capitol or the most important city as the site for collecting price data for the sample of common goods and services in each country. Insofar as the selected city is representative of urban consumption in general, they are probably on safe ground. However, we expect they will find that national price averages will diverge from single-city indexes and by amounts that differ from one country to another. In general, the prices of manufactured goods are lower and the cost of services higher in large cities than in smaller ones and in rural areas. Moreover, the LAFTA countries differ greatly in degree of urbanization and, therefore, in the extent to which prices in one city are representative of the national price structure. The more urbanized countries would tend to yield implicit rates which would make existing exchange rates appear to be overvalued in relation to those in less urbanized countries, when in fact they are not. Grunwald and Salazar argue that this is not a serious problem in Latin America, i.e., that there is little relation between the ratio of implicit to official exchange rates and level of development (which usually is a surrogate for level of urbanization).

When we rank their ratios, which reflect the extent of overvaluation, and correlate them with per capita product (their Table 5), we obtain a Spearman's rank correlation coefficient of 0.336. While this is not significant at the 0.05 level, it does indicate that the relationship is in the expected positive direction. In Table 1 we offer data which show a rather substantial range in the level of urbanization of the countries under study.

As might be expected, there also appears to be a strong relation between the level of economic development (as measured by per capita product) and the level of urbanization. We obtain a Spearman's rank correlation coefficient of 0.904, which is highly significant. This indicates that the more highly developed countries are more highly urbanized and hence that the major city may not be very representative of the consumption patterns and price relationships of the less urbanized ones. Thus, it may prove rather hazardous to make intercountry comparisons of value data without adjustment for differing levels of urbanization. We hope the authors will tackle this problem early in their continuing research.

Grunwald and Salazar present some basic data on international price comparisons in tables 12 and 13 of their paper, and these are followed by a section entitled General Conclusions Resulting from the Price

TABLE 1

Urban Population as a Percentage of
Total Population, 1968

Argentina	n.a.	Mexico	50.7
Bolivia	n.a.	Paraguay	36.1
Brazil	46.3	Peru	47.4
Chile	68.2	Uruguay	82.2
Colombia	52.0	Venezuela	67.4
Ecuador	35.8		

SOURCE: *Statistical Abstract of Latin America, 1968,* University of California at Los Angeles, Latin American Studies Center, 1969 (compiled from United Nations and national sources).

TABLE 2

A Comparison of International Price Indexes for
Consumption Goods in 1960 and 1968

	1960				1968			
Category	Lowest Value	Country	Highest Value	Country	Lowest Value	Country	Highest Value	Country
Food	72	Argentina	116	Colombia	73	Uruguay	111	Mexico
Beverages	66	Brazil	159	Colombia	57	Paraguay	101	Bolivia
Clothing	71	Ecuador	156	Chile	84	Paraguay	132	Chile
Rent	78	Uruguay	223	Chile	60	Uruguay	149	Chile
Transport, communications	92	Bolivia	141	Ecuador				
Personal care	83	Brazil	161	Chile				
Recreation, entertainment	78	Uruguay	164	Chile				
Tobacco					49	Colombia	152	Uruguay
Utilities					11	Uruguay	153	Argentina
Durables					78	Brazil & Colombia	136	Chile
Nondurables					74	Argentina	121	Bolivia
Services					53	Uruguay	107	Brazil

SOURCE: Grunwald and Salazar: 1960 data from their Table 13 (Mexico = 100), 1968 data from their Table 12 (Peru = 100); data for Venezuela are omitted in both years.

Comparisons. In this section they state that the two surveys, the first in 1960 by ECLA and the second in 1968 by ECIEL and Brookings (1) "bear a striking resemblance" in that the same patterns of high- and low-priced countries are observed, but that (2) the range of price variation within LAFTA narrowed from 1960 to 1968. As they admit, however, much of the reduced variation resulted from the sharp decline in the relative price level in Venezuela.

To focus attention on some aspects of their analysis our Table 2 summarizes the data in their tables 12 and 13. Our Table 2 lists the lowest and highest price index and identifies the country for each price category in 1960 and 1968. Venezuela, where the relative price indexes were extremely high in 1960, is omitted from our analysis. The two surveys are not strictly comparable in any respect, although four broad categories of goods and services are common to both. In these four categories the range of the price indexes is somewhat less in 1968 than in 1960, although it is still large, especially in the beverages and rent categories where government subsidies, taxes, etc., may be important price determinants. Similarly, the range of price indexes in 1968 is very wide for tobacco (49 to 152) and even wider for utilities (11 to 153). Moreover, it is interesting to note that Uruguay had the highest price index for tobacco (152) and the lowest for utilities (11).

While it may be true that there was some narrowing of the range of price indexes between 1960 and 1968 among the countries for which there are comparable data, it is also nevertheless true that there was significant alteration in the rankings of countries. This would seem to indicate either significantly different patterns of demand development or significantly different rates of price inflation or both. We suggest again that this is a problem which needs additional research. We need to have an assessment of the biases introduced by the shifting composition of demand and differential rates of price change across various consumption items under study.

In summary, we consider this a useful effort but one fraught with problems of sampling and statistical bias. We look forward to further research and suggestions for techniques designed to cope with these difficulties.

REPLY by Grunwald and Salazar

The three major points in the comment by Robert M. Williams and R. Hal Mason refer to the scope of our paper, and the representativeness and interpretation of the results. Regarding the scope let us restate the content of our paper in order to clear up any doubts. We discussed two ECIEL studies. In section II of our paper we briefly reviewed the first one, which has been completed and deals among other things with cost comparisons. In section III we outlined a technique used in that study for sensitivity analysis of rates of exchange in making international cost comparisons. The remaining sections, which make up the major part of our paper, deal with value comparisons and rely heavily on another ECIEL study which is still under way. Specifically, a technique is presented which is applied within the context of final expenditure comparisons (and in the paper only for private consumption expenditures). The implicit rates of conversion which derive from this technique make possible comparisons of consumption patterns, factors underlying living standards, investment, public expenditures, income, and other important variables in international studies.[1]

Regarding the representativeness of our findings, it is clear, as we indicated, that certain biases will be introduced if one wishes to generalize from the results of international comparisons of urban centers to relationships among countries in which the cities studied are located. While there seem to be significant differences in levels of urbanization among LAFTA countries as measured by the proportion of population living in places of more than 2,000 inhabitants, there are substantial discrepancies between data from different sources.[2] However, for the purposes of our study the relevant variable is not the proportion of urban population (which in LAFTA is generally high and increasing) but the proportion of urban expenditures in total expenditures. These ratios will tend to be even higher and have a lower dispersion than population ratios.[3] Therefore, we believe results from urban comparisons to be fairly good approximations of results that would be obtained

[1] Although we did not propose to use implicit rates for cost comparisons, they could be used as rough approximations.

[2] For example, Ecuador has the lowest urbanization rate in Table 1 of the Williams and Mason comment, 35.8 per cent (based on UCLA's *Statistical Abstract of Latin America, 1968*). Estimates by the United Nations Economic Commission for Latin America (ECLA) indicate a rate of 48.3 per cent ("Indicadores demográficos, sociales y económicos," in *Notas sobre la economía y el desarrollo de América Latina*, January 1971, p. 2). During the last decade the dispersion of urbanization levels has been diminishing considerably with the much more rapid movement of population from rural to urban areas in the poorer countries compared to the more developed countries in LAFTA.

[3] Urban per capita incomes are generally higher than rural per capita incomes in LAFTA countries. Using income as a proxy for expenditures, the urban expenditure proportion will be higher than the corresponding population ratios.

Per capita incomes originating in rural areas will tend to be higher relative to urban incomes in LAFTA countries with a relatively small rural population than in countries with a relatively large rural population. For example, in Chile and Venezuela, some high-productivity activities, such as copper and petroleum production respectively take place in rural areas but these countries have a relatively small rural population. Likewise in Argentina and Uruguay, also with relatively small rural populations, the productivity of agriculture (a rural economic activity) is higher in relation to services and manufacturing (urban activities) than in the poorer countries with a large rural population ratio. (See U.N. Food and Agricultural Organization, *Monthly Bulletin of Agricultural Economics and Statistics*, June 1967, Table 2, p. 3). These factors will tend to offset the dispersion of the urban population proportions among LAFTA countries.

from countrywide comparisons, but only further research can settle this empirical question.[4]

Regarding the comparisons of the data in our tables 12 and 13, we indicated that similar patterns of high- and low-priced countries can be observed between the two surveys (1960 and 1968). For example, in the food category, Argentina and Uruguay are relatively low-priced countries and Colombia and Mexico are relatively high-priced ones in both years. Similar relationships hold true for other categories examined.[5]

[4] According to Williams and Mason, "the more urbanized countries would tend to yield implicit rates which would make existing exchange rates appear to be overvalued in relation to those in less urbanized countries, when in fact they are not." The meaning of this statement is not clear, but in any case not much can be said about the bias in implicit rates and over- or undervaluation due to differences in urbanization levels unless much more is known than the relative price differentials indicated in the Williams and Mason Comment.

[5] We calculated the correlation of the country rankings between the two years for total private consumption and obtained a high positive relationship ($r = 0.69$).

Relative Prices in

Planning for Economic Development

GUSTAV RANIS

YALE UNIVERSITY

I

THE social significance of relative prices in traditional economic theory is closely related to the efficiency of resource allocation in a general equilibrium context. The heart of that relationship consists of ensuring optimality in the Pareto sense through the interaction of relative commodity and factor prices. Given production conditions and consumer preferences, general equilibrium theory aims to show how efficiency can be achieved in a market-oriented or capitalist system.

When a time dimension is added to the above we obtain the so-called dynamic general equilibrium model in which relative prices once again play an important role. The problem of resource allocation now takes on intertemporal as well as horizontal dimensions. Besides relative factor and commodity prices, we have an additional price to deal with, namely, the rate of interest, which affects the crucial decisions as between consumption and saving. The central interest of traditional theory remains: How does the market or capitalist system simultaneously bring about an efficient horizontal as well as intertemporal allocation of resources.

Another extension of our static general equilibrium theory in which relative prices play a prominent role is in the space dimension, usually called international trade theory. Now flows between countries are included and another relative price, the exchange rate, becomes relevant. But the basic social problem remains the same, i.e., to ensure maximum global efficiency, as both relative prices within countries and exchange rates between them are adjusted to take maximum advantage of the additional production opportunity called trade.

Thus the most important role of relative prices in the traditional classical and neoclassical literature has been in the achievement of efficient resource allocation extended to time and space. The relevance for practical planning or policy making is relatively slight. In fact, only one real policy conclusion can be drawn from the general equilibrium model as extended, namely, to let the price system function as freely as possible.

We know that the real world, even in the mature economies, does not always meet the implicit conditions which permit the general equilibrium system to operate to ensure Pareto optimality. Even if we should accept the efficient utilization of resources as "the" major social problem, certain essential conditions must be fulfilled if such a system is to be at all relevant to a real society and if planning based upon it is to make any sense. For one, we must assume the existence of a minimal set of price- and profit-sensitive entrepreneurs or other economic agents. For another, the society must be politically and ideologically ready to accept the capitalist system as a driving force. In other words, the relevance of the price system as an essential instrument to ensure optimality requires that there exist no economic necessity, e.g., because of scale or other reasons, for government to play a substantial role in the economy's directly productive areas, and moreover, that there exist no overriding noneconomic or ideological "necessity" to have the public sector play a more extensive role. Thirdly, we must assume the relatively full and free flow of information and resources, i.e., the absence of pronounced institutional constraints.

In the developing economy context, to which this paper is primarily addressed, the existence of a sufficiently large number of entrepreneurs sensitive to price and profit signals cannot be taken for granted. Secondly, there is customarily in evidence a shortage of those many social and economic overheads painfully built up over the centuries and taken for granted in what are now the mature economies. Moreover, in many of these societies, especially in the early stages after emergence from colonialism, there exist strong ideological reasons for not wanting to accept a market-oriented system, which is often identified with imperialism, as the driving force. Finally, neither the mobility of resources, nor the flow of information, nor the absence of other major institutional constraints, can be taken for granted. In fact, perhaps more than anything else, it is the absence of these features and the consequent inability to use the convenient ceteris paribus assumptions of traditional theory which lie at the heart of the development problem.

Under these circumstances, it is legitimate to ask whether or not the efficient utilization of available resources is, in fact, "the" major social problem facing the developing society. As it emerges from a frequently stagnant colonial agrarian situation, a developing country usually demands a reallocation of resources and is almost bound to make some use of prices and profits in helping to achieve that reallocation. The role of relative prices in this context is, however, very different from that envisioned in the dynamic general equilibrium system. While this system may be valid in the long run, i.e., once an economy is approaching economic maturity—with all the caveats we are familiar with even in those contexts—it does not capture the essence of the problem of development; consequently, the simple policy advice flowing from it is not really relevant.

If resource allocation across time and space is not "the" problem of major relevance for the developing economy, what is? Basically, it is the achievement of structural change via a broadening of the resources base, both human and material. The basic question, in other words, is not how to allocate given resources more efficiently, but how to introduce technological change, how to broaden participation, how to create entrepreneurs, how to create institutional change, and how to induce minimum mobility. If these issues lie at the heart of the problem, and if they can be addressed with the help of planning and policy making, relative prices can be viewed as taking on a new and quite different role. It is this role to which this paper is addressed. In section II, I describe the typical import substitution phase the newly independent developing economy is likely to pass through initially. In section III, I seek to outline the dimensions of the required transition from import to export substitution and the role of relative prices in planning for that transition. Finally, in section IV, this role is illustrated for the case of Korea and Pakistan.

In traditional theory, relative prices provide the information and the signals required for efficient static allocation as well as for moving the economy in the right direction dynamically. Prices serve as stimulants and propellants, but they cannot be expected, in any simple fashion, to help create the proper environment, or entrepreneurial capacity, *ab initio*. If there exists a shortage of entrepreneurs in a developing country, or if there exists the impediment of institutional barriers, planners or policy makers may well set shadow prices in such a way as to provide larger than normal profits to offset larger than normal risks. Over time, once such decision makers, given the benefit of experience, begin to improve at their task, and once institutions are gradually transformed in directions which accommodate rather than obstruct change, these extra price margins can be reduced and finally eliminated.

This idea is not a new and startling one, but it lies at the base of the infant-industry argument. It is essentially what Smith and List were talking about when they recognized the need for government intervention to affect relative prices in behalf of new industries. The infant-industry entrepreneurial argument is but another way of stating the same case—for the use of administered distortions in relative prices to permit learning-by-doing processes to assert themselves.

Newly independent governments with developing economies have, almost without exception, tried to replace traditional colonial patterns of production and trade—orchestrated mainly by the commercial interests of the mother country—by interposing themselves and taking direct action in the import-substituting direction. Typically, they first move to gain full control of the critical raw material export flows in order to prevent continued reinvestment of these flows for the exclusive benefit of that same sector, or for repatriation abroad—and to channel them into the domestic industrial and service sectors. Typically also, they see the world through early Prebisch eyes, as an unequal partnership between Center and Periphery, with anticipation of unfavorable demand patterns for traditional exports, coupled with a firm belief in the dynamic learning processes associated with import substitution. In virtually all cases, this leads to more or less clear notions of what the government must do directly and what it can induce or order the private sector to undertake.

Most import substitution efforts reflect a consensus that government must provide social and economic overheads, but there is much less consensus concerning the ideal division of labor between the public and private sectors in the directly productive sphere and least of all on how to organize or cajole what remains in the private sector. Here, of course, we have a wide range of choice, almost a continuous spectrum, between direct government ownership, on the one extreme, and something approaching textbook laissez faire, on the other. Most developing societies have, in fact, partly for economic and partly for ideological reasons, opted for a relatively expansive definition of what should be in the public sector—as well as for substantial direct controls over the private sector. The tools most frequently used are exchange controls, the compulsory surrender of foreign exchange, and the allocation of import licenses to socially desirable projects in overheads and industry.

This import substitution syndrome usually includes substantial government deficit financing accompanied by inflation and an increasingly overvalued exchange rate. Quantitative restrictions are preferred over tariffs, credit rationing at low interest rates over an approach to market allocation at higher interest rates, and the rationing of any critical materials, like cement, over excise taxes. In fact, the policy choice can often be characterized as one of trying to displace markets rather than attempting to work through them.

The system described obviously provides windfall profits for importers and tends to discriminate against exports, since a local producer can acquire more local currency by saving a dollar of imports than by earning a dollar of exports.

A second major concomitant of this distortion of relative prices consists, very often, of the neglect of agriculture. Typically this sector, instead of becoming a major propellant of overall development, turns out to be a drag, incapable of even keeping up with population growth, not to speak of freeing workers and providing savings for industrial growth. Food shortages consequently frequently inhibit further industrial growth as industrial wages tend to rise prematurely.

Thirdly, in the market for capital, the administratively controlled interest rate usually is far below the rate of return on investment. Interest rates are often kept at these levels in less developed countries (LDC's) mainly because it is believed that higher rates would discourage investment, as well as for so-called equity reasons, i.e., to help the small investor. Both arguments are defective. Most developing countries chronically suffer from an excess of intended investment relative to available savings; higher interest rates would not only improve the allocation of a given amount of savings, but more importantly, increase the total volume of savings. On the equity issue, the choice is really one between low interest rates which go to the favored large-scale borrower, and high interest rates at which all borrowers, large and small, new and old, have approximately equal access at a price.

The allocation of imports, of investment funds, for that matter of virtually every scarce commodity, is thus likely to be highly inefficient during the import substitution phase, since administered prices drawn up by bureaucrats are asked to bear the burden of determining output as well as factor input mixes. The price of industrial goods is usually pegged high relative to that of agricultural goods, not only via the exchange rate, but also via taxes and subsidies intended to protect the urban consumer; capital goods are often priced low relative to other industrial goods both because imports are undervalued and because the interest rate is kept artificially low. For all these reasons industrial production is likely to be capital- and import-intensive, in spite of the presence of surplus labor. Efficiency becomes irrelevant when receipt of an import license or of a loan per se bestows a sizable windfall profit and becomes a main objective of entrepreneurial activity.

The costs of maintaining this kind of system are patently large. Anne Krueger estimated, for Turkey, that import-substituting industries used 20–75 lira to save a dollar of imports, while export industries required 8–14 lira to earn a dollar of exports.[1] Johnson, for Chile, estimated that about 12 escudos were needed to save a dollar of imports at a time when the official exchange rate was only 2 escudos per dollar.[2] Stephen Lewis estimated that Pakistani manufactures received about 40 per cent more rupees per dollar than did agricultural goods in the early sixties.[3]

[1] Anne O. Krueger, "Some Economic Costs of Exchange Control: The Turkish Case," *Journal of Political Economy*, October 1966, Table 3, col. 5.

[2] Lelland J. Johnson, "Problems of Import Substitution: The Chilean Automobile Industry," *Economic Development and Cultural Change*, January 1967, p. 209.

[3] Stephen R. Lewis, Jr., "Effects of Trade Policy on Domestic Relative Prices: Pakistan, 1951–1965," *American Economic Review*, March 1968, Table I.

Moreover, in spite of its high costs, import substitution as a way of life may be difficult to abandon. Industrial importing interests become ever more entrenched and ever more used to making large windfall profits. The civil service enjoys not only its absolute power but also its ability to supplement its income as *sub rosa* payments grease the wheels of the disequilibrium system. Perhaps most importantly, any change in policy must be prepared to run the gauntlet of accusations of "giveaway" either to foreign or domestic private interests.

It should be remembered that this set of policies is basically a re-action to the real or imagined lack of indigenous industrial entre-preneurship. But it will fulfill its historical mission and thus possibly be worth the price only if the system can also be geared to a gradual reduction of these controls over time. Otherwise, the self-fulfilling prophecy of the "absent" entrepreneur forcing government into more and more direct actions may well constitute the most vicious of the many vicious circles we have heard about. In other words, the imposi-tion of a hothouse industrial sector can have the desired effect of creating sufficient entrepreneurial capacity for use at a later stage only if there are assured gradual reductions in the temperature over time. Only in this way will embryonic entrepreneurs have a chance to divert their energies from chasing slips of paper and subverting the control system to making some of the finer allocative decisions at the margin. Only if entrepreneurs become discouraged from trying to maintain the hothouse indefinitely or using their influence with government to have it maintained—and only if government in turn is willing to recog-nize the prohibitive costs of continued import substitution—can a transition to a more efficient stage of development occur.

The use of relative prices in planning for such a transition relates much less to the efficient allocation of known and given resources, and much more to uncovering additional resources and exploiting slacks in the system. In other words, the conventional wisdom about the main springs of growth undergoes gradual change. Emphasis must shift to the broadening of the resource base, the attempt to bring the economy closer to its full potential, mainly through the adoption of technologi-cal change; and an adjustment of relative prices is likely to be essential in effecting the necessary adjustments. While under the previous regime public and large-scale private enterprise were the beneficiaries in response to the actual or assumed shortage of domestic entrepreneurship, a lowering of the hothouse temperature really requires a restructuring of relative prices; that is to say, the role assigned to relative prices must increasingly be one of reflecting actual scarcities rather than facilitating, in a very passive sense, the government's directly allocative actions. The goal must now become a broadening of the development base in the attempt to harness a much larger proportion of the previously disenfranchised economic agents to the development effort. Especially if peasants and medium- and small-scale industrialists are to be mobilized, this broadening cannot be done effectively either by government ownership or by direct horizontal controls over resources allocation in the private sector—if for no other reason than the sheer impossibility of making all the millions of necessary decisions on a broad front, and even physically reaching all the agents concerned. Increasingly, therefore, as the economy moves out of its import substitution subphase and into the next phase of development, the catalytic role of government, through its influence on relative price signals, rather than through its direct control of resources captured and allocated, becomes the critical element.

III

The transition which a successful developing society must be prepared to negotiate is from a land- or raw material–based import substitution phase, as described above, to what may be called a labor and, later, skill-based export substitution phase. The role of relative prices in planning for such a transition is crucial. It can perhaps be best summarized as promoting growth by undoing the artificial distortions while preserving the gains of the earlier period. For example, distortions between the price of capital and of consumer goods may have led to high saving and low capital formation, as in the case of Argentina, or to relatively low saving and low capital formation, as in the case of Pakistan. Substantive inefficiencies within the industrial sector, characterized by high rates of excess capacity and capital intensity, result from the overvaluation of the exchange rate and artificially low interest rates. Stagnation in agriculture usually accompanies the artificial depression of that sector's terms of trade in the effort to assist the industrialization drive and keep vocal urban consumers under control.

All this is subject to change by tackling relative prices in the context of development planning. The terms of trade between agriculture and nonagriculture may be a prime objective. With agricultural activity still a preponderant feature of the landscape, the introduction of technological change in that sector usually remains a prerequisite for sustained growth—no matter how important the role of the foreign sector. But while new knowledge on miracle seeds, fertilizer, and other input combinations is clearly required for any major change in physical relationships to take place, it is likely to be relative price adjustments which are the *sine qua non* for the adoption of such new technology. As long as, either because of an overvalued exchange rate or because of forced procurement at artificially low prices, the farmer's terms of trade are stacked against him, the potential bounty made available through the courtesy of the International Rice Research Institute or Mexican wheat researchers is not likely to be realized. This certainly has been the comparative experience in India and Pakistan, where a time-phased relationship between changes in agricultural price policy and in the willingness to adopt the burgeoning new technology can be established. Relative price adjustments can, of course, also be used on the agricultural input side, especially when the new technology is sensitive to the use of a new input, such as fertilizer. Sensible planning which seeks to harness relative price changes for the promotion of structural change and growth may well call for temporary subsidization of that input, quite in addition to overall government support of the output price as an underpinning of the market for major food crops. Such relative price readjustments should, however, have time limits, since one would clearly not wish to move away from one set of distortions to perpetuate another. In other words, both on the input and output side, the government, in its growth-promoting role of adjusting relative prices away from previous levels of distortions, should be sensitive to the necessity, over time, of returning the economy as quickly as possible to international prices, both in terms of the support levels on major food crops and the restoration of input prices, such as fertilizer, to competitive levels, after the period of introduction.

Perhaps the most important relative price which needs to be adjusted during this transition period is, of course, the exchange rate, through which an indirect tax is levied on exports while importer-industrialists benefit from incentive-dulling windfall profits. Devaluations, either *de facto* or *de jure,* have been a major tool of the restructuring that began to take place in many of the developing countries during the latter half of the 1960's, especially where such devaluations were accompanied by import liberalization, i.e., the partial dismantling of the import quota and licensing system, permitting a somewhat more market-determined allocation of bottleneck inputs. As the economy tries to move away from its almost exclusive reliance on traditional exports and seeks to export more of its abundant labor power—and, somewhat later, its indigenous skills—a more realistic exchange rate permitting increased participation in the international economy becomes essential.

Similar comments apply to the relative price governing intertemporal choices between saving and consumption, i.e., the interest rate. In the typical situation, with official rates way below the scarcity price of capital, and a wide gap between it and unofficial curb rates, a move toward unitary official rates at a considerably higher level is likely not only to lead to a better allocation of investment, but also, and more importantly, to a substantial rise in the volume of saving.

There are, in other words, a large number of relative price adjustments which, in the context of planning, can promote growth through a restructuring effort. In order to determine, in any particular country, what role to assign to the adjustment of which relative prices, and in what sequence, we must first have a clearer picture of the type of economy we are talking about and the phase of development it finds itself in. For example, the growth promotion problem may not simply be one of enhanced participation of all the factors; there may be special problems of income or regional distribution which must be addressed if a political explosion is to be avoided—a consideration also relevant to growth. For another, the relative importance of the exchange rate is much greater in the case of a small economy than of a large one, and internal terms of trade much more crucial in the latter than in the former. If an economy has a strong and diversified natural resources base, with good expectations as to the future, the pressures for restructuring from land- to labor-based development are much smaller. In such cases, e.g., Malaysia, the attempt may well be made to skip the import substitution stage completely. And if the inherited human resources endowment is strong, the required length of that phase may be much shorter. In other words, any sensible assessment of the role of relative prices in planning cannot be independent of the type of economy we are talking about, e.g., its size, its land-labor ratio, its infrastructure, and its relative strength of human and natural resources, among others. Without an understanding of these elements as well as some historical perspective on where the economy has been (during its colonial period), and where it is now, the potential growth-promoting role of relative prices in planning cannot be fully realized.

The only really general statement that can thus be made, in summary, is that there may exist a unique role for relative prices in promoting growth via a planned restructuring of the developing economy's system—long before the promotion of efficiency in the more familiar general equilibrium context becomes relevant. Then, as distortions are gradually eliminated, these readjustments in relative prices can be the prime force in gradually moving the economy out of import and into export substitution, with the growth-promoting role of relative prices gradually yielding to the promotion of Pareto efficiency in the fully activated mature economy. This role of relative prices in the transition process is illustrated by a brief look at a couple of actual cases, South Korea and West Pakistan.

IV

At the time of initial attempted transition to modern growth the small dualistic economy of South Korea found itself with a fairly strong agricultural infrastructure and a fairly well developed indigenous entrepreneurial class. Nevertheless, in the aftermath of partition and war, Korea in the early 1950's turned toward a fairly conventional import-substituting set of policies, tending to favor industry and services through foreign exchange controls, with an increasingly overvalued exchange rate as domestic inflation made itself felt. As long as stabilization efforts are not successful and the economy continues to be subject to rapid inflation and inflationary expectations—as was the case in the 1950's and early 1960's—relative prices are unlikely to be effective either as growth-promoting or finely allocative devices. When such signals are obscured by massive overall inflation, and energies are concentrated on making quick profits, rather than on productive investment, there is very little chance to reap the full benefits of import substitution and move beyond it. During the period under discussion, Korea's growth rate was just about high enough to keep up with population growth, while saving rates were negligible—for some years, even negative.

By 1963 the back of the inflation was finally broken and, given the basically strong inherited human resource endowment, the first efforts to attempt a developmental transition via changes in relative prices became possible soon thereafter. In order to shift from what are essentially land-based food and raw material exports to the exportation of labor and, increasingly with time, domestic skills and ingenuity, Korea first had to achieve a more realistic relative price of foreign exchange, i.e., it could not, especially since it is small, continue to live behind artificial walls of protection without serious consequences for growth. As a result, in May 1964, Korea substantially devalued her currency and simultaneously unified a complicated multiple exchange system. Moreover, imports were liberalized, i.e., the licensing system was broadened through the widening of import quotas, the introduction of export retention schemes and, later, a quasi-automatic licensing system to cover an expanding volume of imports. The effects of a change in the signals via a change in this crucial relative price have been startling. Exports, which had grown at annual rates of less than 15 per cent during the 1958–62 period, have been growing at annual rates of 30 to 40 per cent since 1964. Moreover, this export boom has been especially pronounced in light industry, where value added in the form of pure labor could play an increasingly important role.

In 1965, relative prices in the sector complementary to the foreign trade sector, i.e., the credit sector, were changed dramatically. Interest rates, which had been kept at artificially low levels, were drastically raised in 1965, and the huge gap between the low official rates, actually available only to established prime borrowers, and the astronomically high rates facing ordinary people on the curb market was substantially narrowed. Interest rates on saving deposits doubled, and deposits responded by rising by more than 200 per cent between 1964 and the end of 1965, and by more than 700 per cent by September 1968. To indicate that this was not just a shift from one form of saving to another, we should note that the overall saving rate, which had been negative in the 1958–62 period and had stood at only 5.8 per cent as late as 1962–64, reached 13.6 per cent in 1968 and is currently about 15 per cent.

It can be said that the changes in these two relative prices, the exchange rate and the interest rate, more than anything else, have led to the spectacular turnaround in the performance of the Korean economy, summarized in Table 1. As a direct consequence, Korea was placed in a position to put her abundant high-quality human resources to use in an export-led rather than import-substitution-dominated industrialization effort. Increasingly also, domestic skill and innovative ingenuity could be incorporated with unskilled domestic labor as medium- and small-scale entrepreneurs had an opportunity, really for the first time, to gain access to resources and participate broadly in the development process.

That other relative price, the terms of trade between agriculture and industry, has not as yet in Korea been substantially modified from its distorted earlier levels. It is true that, in 1968, the Korean government adopted a price support policy which has tended somewhat to improve the terms of trade of the agricultural sector. Unfortunately, however, this price is announced at harvest rather than at planting time and thus serves more as an income redistributive rather than incentive device. Largely as a consequence, the adoption of better technology including double cropping, fertilizer, and lime use, etc., has been slow, and techniques for substantial agricultural productivity increases still

TABLE 1

Growth Performance of Korea, 1955–67

	Years	Per-centage
Average annual rate of growth of real per capita income	1955–60	1.6
	1960–65	3.7
	1965–67	8.3
Domestic saving rate	1958	−2.5
	1966	9.2
Average annual rate of growth of exports	1955–60	−0.8
	1965–67	39.3

wait to be harnessed. While many of the distortions of the import substitution regime have, in other words, been corrected through changes in relative prices, much yet needs to be done to activate the agricultural sector.

Pakistan adopted a classic set of import substitution policies soon after partition and independence. While inflationary pressures built up, rendering the exchange rate increasingly overvalued, the proceeds of the traditional raw jute and cotton export trade, supplemented by foreign aid, were reallocated, via exchange controls and licensing, to the construction of overheads and industry in West Pakistan.

The overall economic performance which resulted throughout the 1950's was little short of dismal. Agricultural production was barely able to keep up with population growth; exports were sluggish throughout the decade, actually declining in value. Only large-scale industry, much of it in the public sector, grew at a fast pace, i.e., in excess of 30 per cent annually. Domestic saving averaged around 5 per cent, and consequently, more than 50 per cent of the investment expenditures of the first Five Year Plan (1955–60) had to be financed from abroad.

In 1959 the first restructuring of relative prices was undertaken via a *de facto* devaluation of the exchange rate through the establishment of an export bonus system. This was followed by additional import liberalization, including an expanding open general license system and a "free list." By 1964 more than 40 per cent of imports was liberalized in one way or another. Industrial excess capacity declined from more than 50 per cent in 1960 to 18 per cent of a much larger industrial plant in 1965. Nontraditional exports rose by 89 per cent between 1959 and 1964 and accounted for 60 per cent of the total by 1964.

In 1961, moreover, the policy of forced procurement of major food crops at low prices was abandoned. Instead, prices were permitted to be market-determined, undergirded by government-guaranteed minimum price supports, with fluctuations reduced through the operation of buffer stocks. This reform, supplemented by fertilizer subsidies, constituted a marked improvement in agriculture's terms of trade. In this fashion farmers' incentives were realigned, culminating in substantial growth of agricultural productivity, especially in West Pakistan, even before the new miracle seeds became generally available. Once this more drastic change in input-output relations became possible, especially in wheat, farmers were ready to respond and, moreover, able to increase vital water inputs through the free importation of pig iron needed for the construction of tubewells. The realignment of the terms of trade thus made the 32,000 private tubewells which had mushroomed up by 1965 profitable, while readjustments in the exchange system made them possible. Food grain production, which had been growing at 1 to 2 per cent annually during 1950–60, spurted ahead at an annual clip of 4 per cent during 1960–65. By 1970–71 a wheat crop at 170 per cent of 1964–65 levels is expected; and agricultural surpluses, rather than the persistent deficits of the 1950's, are being contemplated.

Moreover, the substantial increase in agricultural productivity and the accompanying demand for pumps to power the tubewells led to the surprising development of engineering and other smaller-scale industries in West Pakistan. In this mutually self-reinforcing fashion, agricultural surpluses financed the growth of decentralized medium- and small-scale industries, many of which in turn provided the physical inputs and incentives for further agricultural productivity increase. Changes in crucial relative prices thus effected major growth-promoting changes in the economy. The change in aggregate performance for Pakistan, from negligible per capita income increases in the late 1950's to increases of better than 3 per cent annually on a sustained basis, in spite of war, aid declines, and drought, amply testify that the economy, in spite of its political problems, now seems to be moving on entirely different tracks. This is illustrated in Table 2.

In summary, the role of relative prices in planning for the transition from colonial agrarianism, through import substitution, to a more market-oriented and broadly based growth effort is a central one. In the typical situation, the attempt is made to achieve economic independence by cutting the colonial pattern and capturing the land-based resources for import-substituting industrialization; relative prices are administered and largely irrelevant, with resources allocated directly to what are considered socially desirable areas. Then, as the crazy quilt of administered pricing and controls begins to take its toll in terms of low efficiency and growth rates, structural change in the direction of a

TABLE 2

Growth Performance of Pakistan, 1955–67

	Years	Per-centage
Average annual rate of	1955–60	1.2
growth of real per	1960–65	2.9
capita income	1965–67	3.4
Domestic saving rate	1958	5.5
	1966	9.0
Average annual rate of	1955–60	2.5
growth of exports	1965–67	8.3

fuller participation of the society's peasants and medium- and small-scale entrepreneurs is considered increasingly essential. Such a transition, in keeping with the changing entrepreneurial capacity of the economy, requires major changes in relative prices. The ability to transform the economy so that, first, unskilled labor, and then, domestic ingenuity and skills can carry more and more of the essential burdens of growth is heavily dependent on the timely, well-planned adjustment of relative prices.

COMMENT
RICHARD RUGGLES

In the first section of his paper, Ranis discusses the significance of relative prices for the efficiency of resource allocation in the context of general equilibrium theory. He emphasizes that the central interest of traditional theory is in how the market or capitalist system simultaneously brings about an efficient horizontal and intertemporal allocation of resources. In this context relative prices include factor prices, commodity prices, interest rates, and exchange rates.

Ranis recognizes that in order for market-determined prices to produce efficient resource allocation in a Pareto-optimal sense, certain essential conditions would have to be met. For example, enterpreneurs would have to be exclusively profit maximizers; there would have to be full and freely available information; institutional constraints would not exist; and there would have to be no overriding economic or noneconomic reason for the government to play an extensive role. Ranis argues that although in developed countries these conditions may not be met, in developing economies their absence lies at the heart of the development problem. The basic question is therefore not how to obtain Pareto efficiency, but rather how to introduce technological change, broaden economic participation, create entrepreneurs, bring about institutional change, and induce mobility. This then is the question which Ranis addresses.

Although Ranis is sympathetic with the problem, his description of what developing countries actually do is quite the reverse. The import-substitution syndrome and the expansive definition of the public sector, he feels, result in a myriad of tools to accomplish their purpose. Thus, exchange controls, foreign exchange allocation, import licences, government deficit financing, inflation, overvalued exchange rates, neglect of agriculture, control of the interest rate, and allocation of investment funds are all part of the picture. The costs of maintaining such a system are shown to be large in terms of the inefficiency of import-substitution industries relative to export industries in Turkey, Chile, and Pakistan. It is not at all clear from the discussion that Ranis feels that the relative price distortions created by development policies accomplish anything but an increase in costs and inefficiencies. In fact, the main emphasis of the paper lies not on how relative prices may be used to shape economic development, but rather on how restoration of relative prices which reflect market conditions (both domestic and international) results in healthy economic growth. The final proof of the pudding, according to Ranis, is the examination of the cases of South Korea and Pakistan, where evidence seems to show that when more market-oriented prices were substituted for the crazy quilt of administered prices and controls, broadly based growth could take place.

From both a theoretical and empirical point of view the thesis which is presented at first glance seems quite plausible. Ranis admits that under conditions found in less developed countries relative prices as determined by market conditions may not be optimal. Such logic, he indicates, leads countries to adopt policies which distort the system and are inefficient and costly to maintain. The only bright spot on the horizon is that if such countries return to market-oriented prices, virtue will be rewarded by increases in efficiency and growth.

What makes me uneasy about such a presentation is the implication that although theoretically changes in relative prices can be used for development purposes, at best this is true only in a very temporary hothouse situation, and usually such interference is an impediment to healthy economic development. It is almost as if Ranis is saying that government interference with the market mechanism is inevitably arbitrary, clumsy, and irrational, and that sticking to the market mechanism is vastly superior. It is the unseen hand which best guides our destiny, and what governments should do is to help facilitate the market process rather than oppose or alter it for purposes of economic development.

In many ways this is the council of despair. What the market system produces we must like. By definition it is most efficient. Interference with it will produce chaos. People are not masters of their own destiny —the market system is. It is true that unwise decisions by governments often create undesirable situations. On the other hand, undesirable situations are also created by the market process. Extremes in income distribution, inadeqaute housing, lack of education and sanitation, and poverty all occur in market-oriented systems; their effects cannot be overcome by strict adjustment of relative prices to market levels. Specific policies which may interfere with relative prices must be developed.

The interest rate is a case in point. Ranis suggests that the rate of interest affects the crucial decisions between consumption and saving, and that higher interest rates not only improve the allocation of a given amount of savings, but also, and more importantly, increase the total volume of savings. In terms of equity, Ranis argues that the choice is really one between low interest rates which channel available savings to favored large-scale borrowers and high interest rates at which all borrowers, large and small, new and old, have approximately equal access at a price. It is true that higher interest rates do increase the total volume of savings, but they accomplish this not so much by affecting the consumption-saving decision as by affecting the distribution of the income flow in the economy. Interest is not so much a reward for current saving as it is a reward for having money. High interest rates increase interest income, and interest income accrues to the higher-income groups who are more likely to save it; they who have get more. Increased saving thus occurs at the cost of increasing the inequality of the income distribution. With respect to the allocation of investment funds, it is true that large and small, rich or poor borrowers alike have equal access at a price, but the result, given the price, is that investment funds are likely to be channeled into luxury housing, office buildings, or other investments which have been made profitable by the increase in income inequality and the affluence of the financial community receiving higher interest rates.

In similar manner free and open trade may permit much of a country's foreign exchange to be used for luxury consumption or to flow abroad. Merely because many governments make poor use of imports does not mean that market-determined use would be optimal or even superior to what some governments have done or are now doing.

The successes which Ranis cites might better be summed up by the mottoes "devaluation is a good thing" and "agriculture needs stimulation." The impact of devaluation, however, may not be through the shift in relative prices nearly as much as through the income effect of additional external demand and the shift from imports to domestic production. Thus I would maintain that the marked improvement which Ranis cites for Korea and Pakistan was primarily due to the income effect of devaluation which increased the absolute level of economic activity in the system, rather than to an increase in the efficiency of resource allocation which might have resulted from relative price changes. With respect to agriculture the problem is somewhat more complex. Relatively higher prices may encourage agriculture in some situations, but it may do so only at the cost of raising food prices in urban centers. If agricultural response is slow because of institutional or other factors, the price in real terms may be too high for the system to pay, and other methods of raising agricultural output may have to be tried.

I do not mean to say that irrational distortion of relative prices by governments is justified in the name of development planning, but by the same token I do feel that development planning will necessitate rational departure from the relative prices which would occur if the economic system were left to go its own way. In some instances market solutions are appropriate; in others they result in distributions of income or uses of resources which are not compatible with long-range economic development goals. The argument that the primary criterion in determining optimal relative prices should be efficiency of resource allocation stated in terms of the marginal conditions is naive, because it either ignores the fact that relative prices also determine the income distribution or it assumes that the income distribution can be altered without affecting the marginal conditions and thus the efficiency of resource allocation. In practice it is often not possible or politically feasible to alter an initial income distribution of an economic system significantly, and it may be easier and more efficient to adopt relative prices which may not be optimal in a resource allocation sense but which will result in an initial distribution of income that will provide greater welfare and be more socially acceptable. The role of the economist in planning is to analyze the impact which alternative policies can be expected to have on the economic system, rather than just to indicate that the only role of the government should be to facilitate the working of the unseen hand.

PETER ECKSTEIN, Center for Research on Economic Development, University of Michigan

The main thesis of the Ranis paper is that the development of a newly independent economy should occur in two phases. (Mercifully, he has abjured the term "stages.") The first is a "growth-promoting" phase in which there is a "planned restructuring" of the economy toward import substitution. Resource use is determined by direct government allocation or by administered prices that have been distorted away from the levels that prevail in world markets or that would provide domestic market equilibrium. The second is an efficiency-promoting phase in which relative prices are adjusted toward their equilibrium levels, undoing the "artificial distortions" of the earlier phase and shifting the economy toward export expansion.

I find myself able to agree with exactly 50 per cent of this argument, fortunately the half that describes the direction in which most under-developed economies should be moving today. Development economists have been increasingly recognizing the need to go beyond the phase of import-substituting industrialization,[1] and the Ranis paper is useful in marshaling many of the arguments and in illustrating them with two of the most persuasive case histories.[2] The most important contribution of the paper may be the suggestion from the Korean case that saving rates can actually be increased by dismantling a system of controls partly established for the purpose of stimulating saving.[3]

I find myself unable to accept even the qualified endorsement Ranis bestows on the distorted-price phase: that it is "worth the price," but "only if it is geared to a gradual reduction of controls over time." My own position is that there is far less conflict than he implies between the objective of basic growth and the objective of efficiency, and that what conflict exists does not justify the kinds and magnitudes of price distortions typically adopted to encourage import substitution.

[1] See, for example, Santiago Macario, "Protectionism and Industrialization in Latin America," *Economic Bulletin for Latin America*, March 1964, pp. 61–101; United Nations Economic Commission for Latin America (Raul Prebisch), *Towards a Dynamic Development Policy for Latin America*, New York, 1963, esp. pp. 6–8, 67–78; Bela Balassa, "Integration and Resource Allocation in Latin America," 1966, mimeographed; John H. Power, "Industrialization in Pakistan: A Case of Frustrated Take-Off," *Pakistan Development Review*, Summer 1963; Power, "Import Substitution as an Industrialization Strategy," *Philippine Journal of Economics*, Second Semester, 1966, pp. 167–204; and Henry J. Bruton, "Productivity Growth in Latin America," *American Economic Review*, December 1967, pp. 1099–1116.

[2] In our common zeal for the merits of a market system we should be careful not to exaggerate. When Ranis tries to establish for Pakistan "a time-phased relationship between changes in agricultural price policy and in the willingness to adopt the burgeoning new technology" of the Green Revolution, I fear he risks crossing this line. Mexican wheat and International Rice Research Institute rice were not introduced into Pakistan on a commercial scale until 1965 and 1967, respectively. Growth of acreage was spectacular, and improvements in market conditions undoubtedly made the new varieties more attractive. However, the profitability of adoption would have been high even without these improvements, and we cannot contrast this fast adoption with some earlier period in which the technology was available to Pakistani farmers but was not being applied. (For profitability figures, see Lester R. Brown, *Seeds of Change*, New York, 1970, p. 42.)

[3] It is not really clear, however, why "distortions between the price of capital and of consumer goods may have led to high saving and low capital formation" in Argentina but "to relatively low saving and low capital formation" in Pakistan.

THE RELATIONSHIP OF PROBLEM AND POLICY

The Ranis paper offers three economic bases for a conflict between growth and efficiency as an economy emerges from a state of dependency—a lack of price-responsive entrepreneurs, a shortage of overhead facilities, and the immobility of resources and information.[4] The policy implications of these deficiencies would seem to be straightforward. The "infant entrepreneurial argument" is one that favors subsidizing and supporting entrepreneurship in general—through schools of business administration, special training programs in entrepreneurial skill and motivations, and the widespread availability of business credit (raised, if necessary, through taxation) at equilibrium interest rates. A lack of market information suggests that government should supply it directly or encourage cooperation among competing firms to seek it out. Resource immobility and deficient infrastructure justify government action to subsidize or supply basic overheads in transportation, communications, and education. What is striking, however, is the contrast between such neutral policies and the pricing and allocation policies which Ranis defends as necessary to overcome the

[4] Ranis cites a fourth, noneconomic justification for the system of distorted prices: "strong ideological reasons for not wanting to accept a market-oriented system" and for having "the public sector play a more extensive role." I do not think the economist must mutely bow in deference to such "reasons." The ideologies in question rarely seek ends which are unattainable through a fairly close adherence to equilibrium prices; rather, they often introduce dogmatic misperceptions of the relationship between means and ends. The job of the economist is not to take such misperceptions as given, or to rationalize them into "necessities," but to point out how ignoring opportunity costs can cripple the attainment of any set of economic objectives and to devise less costly ways of translating ideology into policy. For example, if the state must play "a more extensive role," the economist can make the case that the entrepreneurial gap is wider and the expected social return to investment is higher in the agricultural infrastructure than in automobile assembly.

The notion that adherence to ideologically prescribed means can itself be a source of national welfare parallels the argument that no forms of habitual consumption can be decried as "wasteful," since the individual's preference for them is itself an indication of their utility. Veblen's reaction seems apt: "The question is . . . not whether, under the existing circumstances of individual habit and social custom, a given expenditure conduces to the particular consumer's gratification or peace of mind; but whether, aside from acquired tastes and from the canons of usage and conventional decency, its result is a net gain in comfort or the fullness of life." This way of posing the question is even more appropriate in examining development policy, which can often gratify the politician or bureaucrat who calls the tune, while detracting from the comfort of the taxpayer, worker, or consumer who must pay the piper.

same obstacles. He lists many of the typical elements of "the import substitution syndrome": the undervaluing and rationing of foreign exchange; tariffs and import controls that are more stringent for consumer goods than for capital equipment; subsidized interest rates to favored borrowers; price controls and rationing for some basic material inputs; and measures to turn the internal terms of trade against agriculture. To this list we might add several more items: governm.ent inducements for higher urban wages; the escalation of tariff structures by degree of fabrication; the conferring of astronomical levels of effective protection; and a systematic tendency to underprice government services and products.

The net effect of these distorted price and allocation policies is to induce economic decisions which ignore the opportunity costs of resources, as represented by world prices and domestic factor availabilities. In an economically arbitrary manner these discriminatory policies favor the production of import substitutes over exports, of manufactured goods over agricultural commodities, and of consumer goods over capital goods; [5] they stimulate so wide an array of industries that few can attain an internationally competitive scale of production; they encourage the use of imported inputs in the domestic assembly of final goods; they favor capital-intensive techniques over labor-intensive ones; and they create bottlenecks in the provision of overhead services that provide neither guidance for the direction of further expansion nor the means by which such expansion can be financed.[6]

Ranis accurately describes the costs of maintaining this system as "patently large," so it should be abandoned once it has had time to "do its job." The system he describes, however, is never well suited to the job he has assigned it, is never accurately aimed at "the heart of the development problem."

[5] Power ("Industrialization," pp. 192–97) argues that the bias toward the production of consumption goods itself entails a bias toward consumption expenditure.

[6] Ranis at one point characterizes his early phase as one of "land- or raw material–based import substitution" as against later phases of labor-based and then skill-based "export substitution." If (as appears in the discussion of Korea) he means to contrast the characteristic inputs to exports, this distinction seems useful. The import-substitution process, however, is itself rarely "land or raw material" intensive but, as he says elsewhere, typically "capital- and import-intensive," and this defiance of the law of comparative advantage is a major source of its excessive cost.

Governments do not need distorted prices to induce them to stimulate entrepreneurship, to provide information, or to undertake overhead investments. Rather, increased supplies of entrepreneurship, information, and overhead capital can make their greatest contribution to development only if they support directly productive activities that are planned or established in close response to real opportunity costs in the economy. Many overhead services to production will realize that contribution only if they are rationed by prices which reflect their actual scarcities.

By contrast, the system of price distortions does "its job" by creating "larger than normal" profit opportunities in some lines but not in others. It stimulates entrepreneurship in automobile assembly but not in fertilizer production; it creates flows of information about the domestic market for tires made from imported rubber but not about the world market for glass made from domestic silicates; it provides railway lines to mammoth steel complexes but few dirt roads to village craftsmen and vegetable growers; it provides transportation so cheap that the mills can locate far from their sources of coal but close to their sources of import licenses.[7]

EFFICIENT AND INEFFICIENT GROWTH

The important contrast is not between growth and efficiency but between efficient growth and inefficient growth. Both theory and history suggest that efficient growth in the early phase of economic independence is (1) faster, because it wastes fewer of the limited resources currently available in the economy; and (2) more sustainable, because it saddles the future with fewer social structures that resist change and fewer economic structures that have to be scrapped, subsidized, or artificially supported.

As to the greater speed of efficient growth, the case histories of South Korea and Pakistan are suggestive but not conclusive, since the period of negligible per capita growth under distorted prices may—as Ranis

[7] See, for example, Edward S. Mason, *Economic Development in India and Pakistan,* Cambridge, Mass., September 1966, pp. 8–9; Anne O. Krueger, "Some Economic Costs of Exchange Control: The Turkish Case," *Journal of Political Economy,* October 1966; John A. King, Jr., "Colombia: Steel," Case 30 in *Economic Development Projects and Their Appraisal,* Baltimore, 1967, pp. 505–27; and Alan Carlin, "Indian Transportation: A Sectoral Approach to Development Constraints," *Journal of Development Studies,* July, 1967.

implies—have laid some essential groundwork for rapid growth when price distortions were finally reduced. Fortunately, there are many examples of underdeveloped economies that have grown continuously and rapidly in the postwar years in a single phase of broad participation in the world market—the Central American republics, the Ivory Coast, Lebanon, Malaysia, Singapore, Hong Kong, and, to a great extent, Mexico and Peru.[8] Both Dudley Seers and Barend de Vries have provided cross-sectional evaluations of the strategy of inward-directed growth through distorted prices, largely for the Latin American economies, and have shown that only the largest of these have been able to maintain respectable aggregate growth. Thus, the South American pattern of development—what Prebisch has come to lament as "industrialization in watertight compartments"—has not taken Brazil, with a broad spectrum of resources and a sizable domestic market, nearly so far from the exploitation of comparative advantage and economies of scale as it has taken Paraguay and Uruguay.[9] Estimates of Chile's loss of current GNP through allocative distortions run from 2.5 per cent (Harberger) to 14 per cent (Balassa's upper limit).[10]

[8] The list includes none of the largest of the underdeveloped economies—not because the policy of growth through trade at world prices has failed for them, but because few (if any) have tried it. Reaching farther back into history, there are many explanations of the remarkable development of Japan, but it seems difficult to explain the pattern of that development without including the fact that for most of the Meiji period Japan was forbidden by treaty from levying import duties of more than 5 per cent ad valorem. (See, for example, W. W. Lockwood, *The Economic Development of Japan*, Princeton, 1954, p. 539.) Individual enterprises were established and temporarily subsidized by the government, but the main thrust of "structural change" took place in the context of world prices.

[9] Barend A. de Vries, "Importance of Size for the Orientation of Economic Policy," in David Krivine, ed., *Fiscal and Monetary Problems in Developing States*, New York, 1967, pp. 309–23; and Dudley Seers, "The Stages of Economic Development of a Primary Producer in the Middle of the Twentieth Century," *Economic Bulletin of Ghana*, 1963, pp. 57–69. This kind of reasoning and evidence tends to support Ranis's assertion that "the relative importance of the exchange rate is much greater in the case of a small economy than in that of a large one." Such assertions, however, should not overlook the effect of the distorted price policy in reducing the import share of GNP but making it more strategic for the continued functioning of the economy. The smaller tail is often more able to wag the dog. Witness, for example, stories of Pakistani coal mines being forced to close temporarily for lack of imported safety lamps, or 40 per cent of Indian tractors being out of commission in 1966 for lack of imported spare parts. On the latter, see Brown, *Seeds*, p. 60.

[10] Balassa, "Integration," pp. 3–8. Arnold C. Harberger, "Using the Resources at Hand More Effectively," *American Economic Review*, May 1958, pp. 134–55. Assume these resources to have been saved rather than wasted. From an historical (but

Inefficient growth is less sustainable than efficient growth because it achieves not only "a broadening of the resources base, both human and material," but also embeds that base in structures that continue to delay and inhibit the transition to a more efficient pattern of production. On the human side, entrepreneurs trained at "chasing slips of paper and subverting the control system" may bear no special qualification for chasing customers in world markets or subverting the mindless application of Western technology to domestic production.[11] "Entrenched" industrial and bureaucratic interests may use all their accumulated power to sabotage any tendency toward market rationing at equilibrium prices.

There is little evidence that the distorted price system serves to transform institutions "in directions which accommodate rather than obstruct change." All too often the corollary of "structural change" through distorted prices is structural resistance to restoring an efficient pattern of production. Significantly, the dramatic decontrol measures in South Korea and Pakistan were both decreed by strong governments that were born in military coups and had secure power bases independent of the bureaucratic and industrial interests.[12]

On the material side, the most pernicious legacy of an inefficient pattern of investment is not the abandoned cannery or the broad highway reverting to jungle, widespread though such examples may be. Such investments can be written off to experience while the economy

inefficient) Chilean capital-output ratio of 3.2, we can crudely calculate that the growth rate could have been higher by 0.8 to 4.4 per cent. Bruton, "Productivity," estimates "residuals" (annual growth rates of productivity) during the postwar period which are respectable for Mexico (above 2 per cent), low for Brazil and Colombia (about 1½ per cent), negligible for Chile, and negative for Argentina.

11 Presumably the spectacular business success of Captain Gohar Ayub in Pakistan over the period 1963–68—in automotive assembly, canning, and the distribution of imported tractors—was not entirely due to the applicability of his military training to entrepreneurship but bore some relationship to the fact that he was the son of the president of the republic.

12 It might be unfair to apply to a normative "phase" theory one of Simon Kuznets's requirements for a descriptive "stage" theory—that it identify "the major processes in the preceding stage that complete it and, with the usual qualifications for exogenous factors, make the next . . . stage highly probable" ("Notes on the Take-Off," in W. W. Rostow, ed., *The Economics of Take-Off into Sustained Growth*, New York, 1963, p. 24). If, however, as Ranis implies, movement out of the distorted-price phase is a requirement for its validity, then any useful normative theory must establish that the impetus for the transition is something more endogenous to the economy than the *deus ex machina* of a takeover by strong-willed and well-advised military leaders.

goes forward into more promising lines of production. Nor is it the government enterprise which, after a decade of operations, enjoys a profit rate only half that of comparable private firms. Rather, the heaviest burden on the future is created when inefficient enterprises must have their operating costs subsidized directly by the government (like the ubiquitous national airlines) or indirectly by the economy (like the Pakistani industries which, well into the "efficient" phase of economic development, were consuming raw materials worth more on world markets than the final goods they were producing).[13] An additional burden on the future results when new inefficient enterprises are created primarily to justify an original inefficient enterprise by providing its inputs (e.g., the parts for domestically assembled automobiles) or by purchasing its outputs (e.g., electricity or steel for which there is inadequate domestic demand).[14] While the cases of direct subsidization are more blatant and entail the extra cost of dissipating scarce government revenues, the many forms of indirect subsidization may ultimately do more to hamstring the growth potential of the economy.

CONCLUSION

I do not think we need to be so relative in our advocacy of economic efficiency as Ranis implies. I think it is perfectly possible to devise a

[13] While the extent of "negative value added" in Pakistan reported by Soligo and Stern, based on highly indirect evidence, was probably exaggerated, more detailed investigations still find examples of the phenomenon. Examples are not confined to import-substituting industries but spread to the export sector—e.g., cotton textiles in Pakistan, cocoa butter in Ghana—when export preferences are granted to manufacturing but not to agriculture. (See, for example, Richard Mallon, "Export Policy in Pakistan," *Pakistan Development Review*, Spring 1966, pp. 58–79; and Elliot J. Berg, "Structural Transformation vs. Gradualism: Recent Economic Development in Ghana and the Ivory Coast," 1969, azographed.) Of more quantitative importance may be the heavy outlays in domestic resources to save insignificant—but positive—amounts of foreign exchange.

[14] Specific examples of "linkages" used to subsidize inefficiency include the progressive "content-protection" regulations applied to automobile assembly in Latin America; action of the colonial government of Uganda to subsidize an abortive industrial estate near the site of the Owen Falls Dam; and tax exemptions granted by the Colombian government to users of steel from the Paz del Rio mill. See, for example, Leland L. Johnson, "Problems of Import Substitution: The Chilean Automobile Industry," *Economic Development and Cultural Change*, January 1967, pp. 202–16; Walter Elkan and Gail G. Willson, "The Impact of the Owen Falls Hydro-Electric Project on the Economy of Uganda," *Journal of Development Studies*, July 1967, pp. 387–404; and Richard C. Porter, "The Effectiveness of Tax Exemption in Colombia," 1969, multilithed.

general defense of the equilibrium exchange rate as the basic device for rationing foreign exchange and an equilibrium interest rate as the basic device for rationing capital and for price rationing in general as opposed to quantitative restrictions. I think it is possible to phrase that defense in ways that are independent "of the type of economy we are talking about" and the "phase of development" in which that economy finds itself, one which would be as relevant for Burma as for the United States. Equilibrium prices do not imply laissez faire, and such a defense need not preclude a substantial developmental role for government—in the areas of saving, investing in infrastructure, stimulating entrepreneurship, exercising monopolistic power in particular world markets, nurturing truly infant industries, regulating aggregate demand, and insuring some appropriate tradeoff between equity and the speed and efficiency of the growth process.[15] Nor need that defense deny that an efficient pattern of growth will entail substantial and continuing import substitution, particularly for a large economy. It should even recognize that administrative obstacles or distributional considerations may force a solution in which some individual prices are taxed or subsidized to draw them away from world or domestic equilibrium levels. But a general statement of development policy would hold that efficiency is always "relevant" and that no rational pattern of divergences from equilibrium prices would in any way resemble the systematic distortions and gross inefficiences typically introduced in the name of "structural change" through import substitution during the "growth-promoting phase" of economic development.

JAGDISH N. BHAGWATI

Ranis is in the happy position of having Ruggles support one half of his paper and Eckstein support the other half. Between the two

---

[15] The price that will bring about market equilibrium will, of course, depend heavily on the taxation, production, and purchasing decisions of the government. The dependence, for example, of the equilibrium interest rate on the level of government saving does not invalidate the principle of using the equilibrium rate to ration capital; it does, however, suggest the wide range of policies consistent with such a principle.

discussants, therefore, Ranis has full protection from damaging criticism!

The problems raised in this session are so wide-ranging that I shall have time to focus on only a few questions. I find myself in sympathy with what both discussants have said; but I think that they have not drawn the issues sharply enough.

Ruggles rightly questions whether we ought to continue thinking in terms of static allocative efficiency. He introduces the question of income distribution. He also raises the important question of the impact of the investment policies on the rate of savings. He is dead right. We certainly can argue, at an a priori level, that if savings are a function of the market-imputed distribution of national income, and if the allocation of investments is designed to maximize current output, the rate of growth of income might be less than if we reduced output with a view to increasing the rate of savings. This familiar second-best problem from the theory of optimal growth could conceivably be of great importance from the viewpoint of specific countries. However, we as economists have still to ask two more questions before we rush ahead and justify the observed departures from static efficiency in actual practice by resort to such arguments. We have to ask whether, in fact, the sectors to which we have redirected resources in search of higher savings actually have these higher savings rates; and next, we have to ask whether this shift was brought about in an optimal, least-cost manner. I would submit that, in my experience, neither of these two arguments is valid for many countries which are characterized by high short-run inefficiency although I am willing to be persuaded otherwise.

I also wish to join issue with Ruggles when he feels that the waste from inefficiency is small and has been shown by Harberger and others to be so. Let me say, for one thing, that the mythology has grown up, thanks to Harberger's paper, that an inherent property of inefficiency is that it must be small. Needless to say, you only get out of your exercise what you put in, and all such estimates are based on guesses at production functions, etc., which are by no means better than hunches of one kind or another. Secondly, the wastes vary with the nature of the distortions. Waste from monopoly, in a general equilibrium model, does not involve a consumption cost, but a tariff will: for this reason, Harberger's estimate of monopoly-induced waste is already an underestimate of what waste can and does occur in practice. Thirdly, Harberger cannot have estimated the loss that occurs from the kinds of distortions which result from lack of competition in sheltered markets: the waste that takes the form of unduly high costs, failure to improve the product in response to foreign competition that quantitative restrictions (QR's) imply, etc. Finally, there is a psychological point: Anything divided by national income looks small. A 2–3 per cent loss of national income is a small integer but a large absolute loss. Besides, in relation to important and critical magnitudes such as the annual increment in domestic investment, or marginal savings, or foreign aid, the loss is by no means small but indeed very large.

Let me now turn to Peter Eckstein's interesting comment. While I am in overwhelming agreement with his general description of where things tend to go wrong in the underdeveloped countries, I must state forcefully that the notion that import substitution is necessarily harmful is untenable. Economic philosophy swings from one end of the pendulum to another; we are now exhorting countries to go in for export promotion, and I predict that, in another two decades, we will be talking of desirable import substitution and excessive export promotion. In fact, we were doing that only a couple of decades ago, when import substitution began as a conscious strategy in many countries. "Fine tuning" is as much out of our grasp in the less developed countries (LDC's) as it is in the more sophisticated and expertise-endowed developed countries.

While it has become fashionable to denounce import substitution at the moment, let me remind ourselves that most LDC's do not live in a world where exports can be sold at given prices in indefinite amounts: We have surely heard of the textile quotas, the pending U.S. legislation on import restrictions, and such unpleasant things. The fact that we have gone around calculating effective rates, costs, and benefits of projects, etc., at international prices, pretending to ourselves that world prices are fixed, may itself have contributed to the general tendency to think that after all the world is indeed characterized by such fixity of prices and that LDC's who act contrary to such an assumption must be import substituting out of a burst of irrationality.

The really important criticism of the LDC's must be not that they have been import substituting but that (1) they have suffered from export pessimism and have carried import substitution too far in some cases, in consequence; and (2) they have gone in for indiscriminate, high-cost import substitution, either following the policy of letting domestic industrialization proceed under the impetus provided by exogenously imposed QR's and high tariffs or putting up industries indiscriminately under planned programs and making it profitable by adjusting trade policy so as to give the necessary protection to such industry. It has become increasingly obvious that the costs from both these sources, and especially from the latter cause, have tended to be very high in a number of countries; and the proper focus of debate would seem to me to be whether we can think of optimal policy frameworks in the area of both trade and domestic investment policies which would avoid such costs and increase the efficiency and pace of development in the LDC's.

WOLFGANG F. STOLPER, University of Michigan

There are a number of disagreements with Gustav Ranis's presentation of the problem but, to vary the French phrase, *l'accord vient en lisant.* In fact the paper seems to be written by two people. There is Ranis the statesman and apologist, the understanding father confessor. And then there is Ranis the economist, who really knows better, who knows that in fact *tout comprendre n'est pas tout pardonner,* and who realizes that the cost of nonsense is just too high. In a discussion, it is proper to stress the disagreements even though in fact the agreements dominate. The disagreements diminish with each section.

First, I regret that Ranis has in a sense prejudiced his discussion by equating a market-oriented with a capitalist economy, and by seeming to suggest that only in these do prices have a proper role. Even if we had a centrally planned economy, prices would of course be an essential planning tool—*vide* "Liebermanism"—though they would (ideally) reflect the planners' rather than consumers' preferences. Even there they would (ideally) reflect true scarcities of factors, which of course are affected by the planners' preferences for particular output mixes.

Prices are not an ideological phenomenon—though many countries believe they are, and act as if they could ignore them. No priceless economy of any complexity exists. What happens depends on what prices happen to be, and if they are irrational, irrational things happen. Why should the absence of a "large number of entrepreneurs sensitive to price and profit signals" make any difference? (Ranis). For one class of entrepreneurs, farmers, it is by now reasonably well established that they do react to price signals. But suppose there are no entrepreneurs, and the whole manufacturing and agricultural sector is controlled by the government. How would a planner decide upon a steel or textile mill or anything else without reference to cost and prices? And if he wants to increase the amount of goods available to the economy—whether for private consumption or public investment or education or social overhead—he still would want to avoid waste. How could that be done without prices?

Let us also agree that the conditions of Pareto—optimality in the static sense—are not entirely relevant, and in the dynamic sense not easily achieved. But let us then declare a moratorium on the necessity of such stringent conditions, let us forget the very artificial and indeed pernicious distinction between prices as an allocation and prices as a growth-promoting device, and let us settle for practical purposes on the necessity to use prices and to have prices reasonably (not perfectly) realistic (as defined above).

Ranis states:

the relevance of the price system as an essential instrument to ensure optimality requires that there exist no economic necessity, e.g., because of scale or other reasons, for government to play a substantial role in the economy's directly productive areas, and moreover, that there exist no overriding non-economic or ideological "necessity" to have the public sector play a more extensive role. Thirdly, we must assume the relatively full and free flow of information and resources, i.e., the absence of pronounced institutional constraints.

I find this almost totally unacceptable even where it is correct.

1. The supposed economic necessity for government to play a role refers, among others, presumably to economics of the public utility type, where "natural monopolies" make marginal cost pricing inapplicable. Now from a planning standpoint which deals with *future* investments, variable and fixed and hence marginal and total cost are the same anyway. But surely, the failure of marginal cost pricing (as

applied to a particular existing project) to give correct answers hardly justifies dismissing the use of prices as a planning tool. There are still more or less rational ways to do business.

2. Ditto for having a larger or smaller public sector. The real point is that "ideology" has been used to "subsidize,"—i.e., to justify—an uneconomic allocation, or to put it differently either (a) to justify the eating up of one's capital; and/or (b) to tax the productive sectors (usually agriculture) more and more in favor of supposed "dynamic" sectors or "socially desirable" ends. The fact, however, is, as J. R. Hicks remarked a long time ago, that the satisfaction of social needs quickly runs into the barrier of insufficient productivity. Or, as I have desperately tried to put it to a minister of finance: I understand that politics has priority over economics. I do *not* understand how you propose to meet political ends without economic means. Prices are nonideological, and the preference of ideology over economics is a confusion of ends and means.

Since these lines were written—and I have stressed this point for many years—*Le Monde* has carried a report of Le Duan's prescription for North Vietnamese planning. Le Duan stresses the importance of productivity and the weaknesses in project management (*gestion*). He stresses that there must be planning, of course, but *"dans quelle mesure utiliser les rapports de marché, et les leviers du crédit, des prix, des salaires, du profit?"* [1] I could go on quoting the first secretary of the North Vietnamese Communist party as a crown witness for my point of view. It suffices to stress that it is completely wrong to say, as Ranis does, that "the society must be practically and ideologically

---

[1] Jacques Decornoy, "M. Le Duan met l'accent sur 'la révolution technique' et la nécessité de rationaliser l'economie," *Le Monde* (Paris), June 21–22, 1970, p. 5. Decornoy summarizes with numerous quotations a 200-page North Vietnamese document. It is somewhat embarrassing for a capitalist American to quote the Chief Enemy. But I can think of nothing better to show that economic development is "really" a matter of economics and that prices belong to the *faits récalcitrants et têtus* of the economy than to do so. Since I have several times referred to the recalcitrant nature of economic reality and since this is a highly idiosyncratic use of the word, I wonder whether part of my royalties have come from Hanoi!

Le Duan's willingness to analyze his situation so objectively and to blame the neglect of economics rather than the Central Intelligence Agency or even the bombing for his troubles explains perhaps why North Vietnam has been able to cause us so much trouble! It would certainly be better for the United States if he preferred ideology to economics!

ready to accept the capitalist system as a driving force." I am aware that political scientists sometimes argue this way. But the problem is one of efficiency and not ideology; it is not whether an enterprise should be public or private, but whether it produces a net output or wastes resources.

3. Finally, the lack of information is desperately real. But the conclusion I draw is that planners must still use prices the best way they can. The presence of "institutional constraints" explains why things go wrong, not that one can do without prices.

Ranis has put his finger on an important shortcoming of planning models in general: the absence of government in influencing allocation. But this means not that prices are less important, but only that the models are irrelevant precisely in situations in which the government is given a crucial role in determining *how* resources are to be used against how many are to be used.

I do not therefore see just what Ranis is driving at in his implied assertion that an efficient utilization of available resources is not in fact "the" (his quotes) major social problem, particularly in the face of a "frequently stagnant colonial agrarian situation," and that such role as relative prices has does not capture the "essence" of the development problem; which is "basically . . . the achievement of structural change via a broadening of the resources base, both human and material. The basic question . . . is not how to allocate given resources more efficiently, but how to introduce technological change . . . ," etc. Precisely. Having defined the object of development to make sure that as the result of one's resource allocation I come out with more resources to allocate rather than less, and with more and better choices (in my *Planning Without Facts*) and being a student of Schumpeter, I have never understood the problem of resource allocation in a dynamic context to be anything else. The dichotomy made by Ranis does not exist (except possibly on the rarified level of purest mathematical static theory), any more than the idea that prices have something to do exclusively with a market economy. Ranis's section I, in other words, is a red herring.

It is a very dangerous red herring indeed. Perhaps Ranis has been seduced by the theory of stages. He discusses in his section II the import substitution phase through which newly independent countries are "likely" to pass. But again Ranis seems to me to contradict himself. Prices cannot be expected to create the environment for growth; therefore planners may have to use protection and subsidies to make production profitable. But this simply means that the price system is rigged in favor of certain activities. It is a kind of primitive shadow-pricing policy.

Countries try to get rid of colonial production patterns—and more power to them. But the colonial patterns were often (not always) maintained precisely by rigged prices—the French system of paying higher than world market prices is perhaps the best example—and rigged markets—again the French have offered protected markets to their colonies. It should be self-evident that underdeveloped countries having scarce resources must rationally allocate them to achieve their ends. Ranis's account shows that in fact the opposite has happened.

How did it happen? Ranis refers to Prebisch, and far be it from me to defend him. But those of us who had thought to bypass the pricing mechanism in favor of continuous subsidies or of decision making in physical terms bear a considerable guilt. We complain about techniques deemed too capital-intensive, yet rig low interest rates; we complain about misusing scarce foreign exchange, yet rig overvalued exchange rates; we complain about the absence of entrepreneurs, and let a bureaucrat produce steel with no economic sanctions and virtually unlimited access to the budget. We create institutions to break bottlenecks, and then make it impossible for them to achieve their end because we set up an irrational price system. To add insult to injury, this sort of nonsense is sometimes defended by reference to "learning by doing." Yet those of our colleagues who developed this idea never had in mind the abuse, any more than Arthur Lewis's *Industrialization of the Gold Coast* can possibly be used to defend what passes as an import substitution policy.

In short it is precisely the attempt to bypass prices as a planning device—or to console oneself perhaps that they are the dual of an input-output table—which has led to the absurd situation so well described by Ranis. There has been no "learning by doing" because the curriculum has been irrelevant in the absence of decent prices. Nor has there in all likelihood been any import saving.

Thus Ranis is obviously right that if the "hothouse" atmosphere of controls and wrong prices (leading to windfall profits instead of out-put), etc., is not abandoned, entrepreneurs cannot learn their business. But it remains quite unclear just how the creation of the hothouse atmosphere did any good in the first place. There is a Rasputin-like quality about the argument: the more you sin, the greater the salva-tion. But it really makes no more sense in economics than in theology, and it can ruin economies as well as empires, ministers of finance and planning as well as czars.

Ranis describes well what happens: ". . . under the previous regime, public and [very rarely—w.f.s.] large-scale private enterprises were the beneficiaries in response to the actual or assumed shortage of domestic entrepreneurship. . . ." Precisely. In the abstract, the "import substi-tution phase" is seen as a necessary period of economic violence, as it were, to break with the past and establish a base for the future which the next step (so well documented by Ranis as a substitution of price signals for direct controls) is to rationalize.

But in *actuality* what has happened and what Ranis has described is really nothing of the sort. If the colonial policies, as in British West Africa, have induced the development of a cocoa industry by small- and medium-sized farmers, it was to the benefit of the future country— and the absence of unjustifiable subsidies, of rigged prices, monopolies, milking of budgets and the rest, indeed laid a sound foundation for later stages. Where colonial policies were policies of rigged prices and guaranteed markets, of subsidies and exploitation, it did nothing of the kind. The policies of import substitution as practiced—not as envisaged by W. A. Lewis or Hirschmann—in fact continued the colonial pattern of exploitation, of freezing the economy in inefficient patterns, of preventing the emergence of entrepreneurs, whether private or public. What difference that the color and nationality of the exploiter changed? What difference the socialist rhetoric to which models of indifferent academic interest give some respectability? Nkrumah went through over $1.75 billion. It is impossible not to do *some* good while spending this kind of money. Yet the present Ghanaian government is after ten years of Nkrumah's "socialism" with-out foreign reserves, with a foreign debt of $1 billion, without working capital, with a dubious endowment of fixed real capital, and has to undo the damage of years, only to meet with snide sniper attacks.

Sukharno did the seemingly impossible: He did eat up practically all of his patrimony without noticeable benefits. In Latin America, the industrialization policies have aggravated revolutionary situations. The periods of import substitution had in fact not done what they were, theoretically, supposed to do, and they could not.

So my conclusion is that the very establishment of a base for growth, of an incipient entrepreneurial group—whether private or governmental is irrelevant—requires sound price policies. (Needless to say it requires a lot more than that, but this conference deals with price problems). So I agree with Ranis that the problem is to promote "growth by undoing the artificial distortions while preserving the gains of the earlier period," while insisting that if there were any gains at all in the "import substitution phase" they were accidental and not inherent in past policies.

Perhaps it would be good to add more specific uses of prices in planning. In project evaluation, the "correct" prices are evidently important. No great sophistication is needed. The truth is that investments will produce growth only if they are "really" profitable and if they do not swallow up resources as hidden or open subsidies. Hence it becomes important to estimate output prices and cost, but also timing problems, tax revenues and resources required, cash flows, etc. This links the projects also to budgets and hence to savings which, in most countries, are prominently made a task of the government. If the prices are reasonably correct, we can evaluate the project. If they are rigged by tariffs or subsidies, the project can be made to look good, but by working out the budgetary implications there is a check on whether the evaluation was reasonable. It is possible to make any individual project look good. It is not possible to make all of them look good at the same time.

Practically speaking it means that one should try to overestimate cost and underestimate revenues, and that one should be careful about when to accede to direct or indirect subsidies which hurt the budget and are therefore at the expense of alternate investments and/or other uses. It is precisely this neglect that leads in Ranis's import substitution phase to such waste.

Prices are not only signals. There must be a discipline. If prices are improper, say for "social" reasons, it will show in the budget. Example:

In Tunisia the railway proposes an economic tariff. The government may, for perfectly good reasons, prefer a different tariff and agree to compensate the railway. It is a legitimate use of governmental power. But the economist must point out that if the subsidy had been eliminated, savings would have been bigger (though perhaps by less than the subsidy reduction).

Or, if a steel mill gets the right price it will operate efficiently. If its prices are kept high, there will be a cost to other enterprises and/or the government. If it is too low, there will be subsidies, or else there will be borrowing for the wrong purposes. Instead of using resources to augment resources, instead of finding new resources, the wrong prices invariably reduce present and future resources. This is true no matter what the stage of development of the economy.

Prices may change over time. Hence if there is a lag between inputs and outputs, input prices must be current—I leave aside the problem of replacement cost—and output prices must be the best guess of the future. Again the stage of development is irrelevant. Some of the Ghanaian factories can be salvaged. As for the others, if the earth swallowed them, it would be the best thing that could happen. The annual operating subsidies in some cases I know of would pay for whole new factories, with a greater output and more employment!

I do not feel it necessary to discuss Ranis's last section. There is complete agreement as well as the awareness, shared by Ranis I am sure, that much more than prices are involved in the Korean or Pakistani performance, or that, for that matter, the last word on these experiences has not yet been spoken. I conclude that the distinction made by Ranis between growth-promoting and efficiency-promoting functions of prices is a red herring from the standpoint of development policy (whatever may be said for it from a purely theoretical standpoint). No one in his right mind has ever claimed that correct prices will automatically lead to development. Such a unicausal proposition is undoubtedly much better than explaining growth by the method of swaddling babies, but still insufficient. But there is no doubt in my mind that the ignorance of how prices work and the attempt to bypass them have in fact caused the very difficulties which are referred to as neocolonialism and which are much more the fault of domestic leaders of the Nkrumah-Sukharno type and their intellectual tutors than of such foreign scapegoats as are fashionable at the moment.

JACK BARANSON

The transition from Phase Two import substitution to Phase Three export orientation can prove to be difficult and painful, as the experiences of several developing countries in more advanced stages of industrialization already demonstrate. For example, in the automotive industry among countries of the Latin American Free Trade Association there is already nearly ten times the industrial plant that would be required under cost-competitive conditions.[1] Once national industries have been developed behind substantial protection walls, they are difficult to phase out from both an economic and political standpoint. The Japanese experience is often cited as a model of successful transition, but both the rapid growth in the size of the Japanese home market and the system of "administrative guidelines," which have carefully nurtured Japanese industry toward progressive improvements in industrial efficiency, are unique to Japan. Developing countries would do better to plan Phase Two and Phase Three industrialization jointly, with a view toward avoiding excessive and indiscriminate Phase Two import substitution.

REPLY BY RANIS

In responding to my main critics, Ruggles, on the one hand, and Eckstein and Stolper, on the other, I find myself in somewhat the unenviable position of the man in the childhood fairy tale caught between a crocodile and a lion; the only thing to do is get out of the way. Ruggles vehemently objects to the notion that a developing country may benefit substantially from trying to utilize the market mechanism in support of its development effort—especially during the second or export-substituting phase of development. Eckstein and

[1] See Jack Baranson, "Integrated Automobiles for Latin America?" *Finance and Development,* December 1968.

Stolper, on the other hand, just as vehemently disagree with the notion that some deviation from the market mechanism—such as in the first or import-substituting phase of development—may be necessary or desirable. I have tried to make my own position amply clear, on the basis of economic reasoning, not ideology or religious conviction. I believe that it makes sense to distinguish between these two phases, and that our judgment has to be sensitive to where the economy finds itself in historical perspective.

Let me also assure Stolper at the outset that I do not view "market-oriented" as synonymous with "capitalist"—witness the East European use of the market mechanism. What we are all concerned with is development in the institutional context of the so-called mixed, garden variety of developing economy which, as a Myrdal "soft state," is typically in danger of suffering from the worst of both worlds. Here I am afraid Stolper was looking for a straw man, since there is no disagreement between us. With respect to his more substantive criticism, however, i.e., his questioning of the need for any import substitution phase at all, I can only re-emphasize, as economist and not father-confessor, the possible need for temporary distortions while major structural change is being effected. The principal objective during this early postindependence phase is not necessarily to have more resources at that particular moment for immediate allocation, but to transform such resources, e.g., people, and to provide the necessary overheads, e.g., irrigation contours, so that the second phase of sustained growth can get under way. Stolper certainly would not say that the infant-industry argument or the infant-industry entrepreneurial argument is entirely invalid—or deny that the creation of overheads may be essential. Or would he? What would he really substitute in place of a period of import substitution after independence is reached? He says that "no one in his right mind has ever claimed that correct prices will automatically lead to development." But what do he and Eckstein really have in mind? Given the initial severe colonial distortions of the entire economy, with structure and infrastructure poorly designed for sustained domestically oriented growth, what would they advocate for the newly emerging developing society? Complete laissez faire? Eckstein asserts that the infant-industry entrepreneurial argument favors subsidization through schools of business, special training programs, and development of entrepreneurial skills. But what in fact is the best training program for previously commercial entrepreneurs or landlords who are having their first real experience in industrial activity?

Let me be very clear. I agree that whatever conflict between growth and efficiency may exist "does not justify the kinds and magnitudes of [the] price distortions typically adopted to encourage import substitution" (Eckstein). But that is different from reading all distortions out of the party. I would rather take my stand with Bhagwati, who pointed out that import substitution may be necessary but that it is a question of how far it is taken and when and how the structure is ultimately dismantled. Surely we can all agree that departures from the market are required to handle externalities, indirect returns, decreasing costs. Why then is it so difficult to conceive of a purposive deviation from efficiency to facilitate the emergence of industrial entrepreneurship and the creation of a domestic agricultural infrastructure? One suspects Stolper and Eckstein of failing to recall, whenever it is convenient, that earlier colonial policy had usually been one of rigged prices, lack of spillover, lack of involvement of domestic agriculture, and lack of generalized infrastructure beyond that required for the exploration of cash crops or minerals for export. Can they really fail to give any weight to the setup and learning costs of people moving into unfamiliar pursuits and the decline of cost curves according to the infant-industry entrepreneurial argument? We must also not forget, as Linder has pointed out, that comparative advantage may be acquired, at least in part, by first producing for the domestic market before one reaches international competitiveness. Eckstein's only advice seems to be equilibrium prices right off the bat and "independent 'of the type of economy' . . . and the 'phase of development' "—a prescription he calls "as relevant for Burma as the United States."

How would Eckstein go about nurturing truly infant industries with that prescription in mind? We can all join in our profound disapproval of many of the policies which have been followed in the name of import substitution. We can also agree that the neutral version of infant-industry protection has a better chance of separating the "men from the boys" over time than the crazy quilt of preferences for particular industries and particular individuals which we find all too often in the less developed world. But let us not confuse our distaste for the particular way in which import substitution has often been carried out in response to all kinds of vested interests—and continued in force long beyond the point of rational application—and the basic merits of the case, as put forward in my paper. All the countries cited by Eckstein as examples of possible continuous market-oriented growth as they emerge from colonialism into independence are either relatively small ones with an unusually strong entrepreneurial base and a small agricultural hinterland, e.g., Hong Kong and Singapore; or an unusually strong natural resource endowment, e.g., Malaysia; or they don't really fit his own description, e.g., Peru and Mexico.

All in all, I cannot avoid the uneasy feeling that Stolper's and Eckstein's views on the role of government intervention, regardless of the country, the time, and the quality and longevity of the tools applied, verge on the religious. My position, on the other hand, is not that the more you sin (in the early phase) the greater the salvation (in the later phase) but that the need for a basic postindependence restructuring usually requires government action. One can then distinguish between good and bad forms of intervention, e.g., I believe that indirect policies, working through the market, are better than direct policies that rely on administrative controls; that any distortions created should be as neutral and nondiscriminating as between industries as possible; and, most importantly, that they should have a built-in downward trend over time. In my view, it is just as sinful to believe that the invisible hand alone can solve all the problems of developing societies as it is to believe that the visible hand of enlightened bureaucrats can continue to manage their lives efficiently.

Turning now to Ruggles, near the other end of the spectrum, his criticisms are perhaps more difficult to meet, since he more or less ignores my import substitution argument and tackles only my views concerning the longer-run development pattern. While my Michigan friends see red at any mention of government intervention, Ruggles seems to have the same reaction at any mention of the market mechanism. All I can do is reiterate that I clearly do not believe in the unfettered market at work, but that the method of government intervention and the rules of the game established over time can make a good deal of difference. If market determination would lead to undesirable levels of luxury housing or luxury imports, which both Ruggles and I would object to, let us put appropriate taxes and tariffs into place. If the market yields undesirable distribution patterns, let us use tax and expenditure policies, including education, to ameliorate it; but let us not fall prey to the fallacy of trying to solve all problems directly, and thus getting ourselves into an unmanageable network of across-the-board interventions. Otherwise, even with the best intentions, the very people Ruggles is concerned about will usually get hurt.

A good example of this relates to his assertion that higher interest rates would favor the capitalist, a situation that would offend his egalitarianism. But the diagnosis is, in fact, wrong for all LDC's I am familiar with. The Ruggles-proposed low-interest-rate policy which, in fact, usually obtains, ensures that only the large, established capitalists can get loans, guaranteeing them substantial windfall profits in a disequilibrium situation. I am afraid I must also strongly reject, in this context, Ruggles' view of the West Pakistan and Korean success cases, which are cited in my paper, as simply related to devaluation. We have had lots of devaluations across the developing world over the past two decades, without similar results. What is esssential is the accompaniment of devaluation by such other measures as import liberalization, i.e., a freeing up of the foreign exchange market, thus providing more equal access to imports at closer to realistic prices.

It is not my position that the only role for government is to facilitate the "working of the unseen hand." In fact, government has many functions to fulfill. I am also not suggesting that the government should take its hands off and go back to a textbook laissez faire nineteenth century stance. Markets themselves are admittedly imperfect; private returns do not equal social returns. The time horizon of private entrepreneurs may be too short. The question rather is, What role should government play in lessening the impact of these imperfections without returning the society to colonialism or a rampant market mechanism? In my view, that role is one of trying to bridge the gap between social and private returns and of trying to perfect the markets just a little, by indirect rather than direct means. In other words, once it has decided, for one reason or another, what activities should be in the public sector, in affecting what goes on in the rest of the economy, it should attempt to work through taxes, tariffs, and subsidies, and as even-handedly as possible, e.g., through objective, uniform fiscal and monetary rules, rather than through the low-interest and overvalued exchange rates and the variety of other licensing packages which are bound to be inefficient, discretionary, and whimsical.

Just because it happens to be the conventional wisdom, there is no need to abandon our view that government must also provide the overheads, must see to it that markets operate better, must provide information to ensure that weaker elements in the market are not disadvantaged by monopoly or oligopoly power. It must provide information on new technologies, including intermediate technology; it must be in a position to provide technical assistance when entrepreneurs have little at their disposal but the blueprints of the advanced countries, and those made available by avid salesmen from abroad. Government cannot simply step aside and let the signals speak for themselves. It has a tremendous responsibility to direct the development effort. It is merely a question of what tools are more effective for that purpose.

It is a serious mistake to permit one's concern with the possible excesses of the market to lead one to an acceptance of across-the-board government intervention in its place. Neither the information nor the civil service capacities exist—not to speak of the possibilities for vested interests really to go to work once the rules of the game become completely absurd. If it is not considered economically or socially desirable to let certain industrial and civil service minority groups come into substantial power in the course of the import substitution phase, the best way to achieve that objective is not necessarily to implement a number of complicated direct controls on foreign exchange, housing, etc., but to set substantial tariffs and excise taxes while giving everyone equal access to the required resources.

The crucial question to be kept in mind in this discussion, it seems to me, is how the government can give direction to the economy while ensuring maximum participation of its economically disenfranchised actors, i.e., the farmer and the medium- and small-scale industrialist. A maze of direct controls is most likely to impede the emergence of all kinds of domestic innovative talents. Even if it is politically determined that a particular group is to be discriminated against, e.g., expatriate minorities in Africa or the Chinese in Southeast Asia, discriminatory taxes and subsidies are much to be preferred to abrogation of the market. The tail of unequal market power, in other words, should not be allowed to wag the dog of development.

Ruggles writes as if administrative talent and the knowledge of just what to do existed in ample supply among the bureaucracies of the developing world. My position is that neither the knowledge nor the ability nor the depth of talent is available. Consequently I would rather, in this second phase, let the government do what it is best at, i.e., set its controls in a vertical and impersonal rather than a horizontal and personal fashion, and thus induce the broadest possible participation of millions of dispersed decision makers and innovators in all parts of the economy.

Price and Cost Differences—
Industries and Commodities

International Price Comparisons of Selected Capital Goods Industries

BAREND A. DE VRIES

INTERNATIONAL BANK FOR RECONSTRUCTION

AND DEVELOPMENT

IN the past two decades developing countries have invested an increasing proportion of their resources in new industries and the infrastructure needed to support them. Many of the new industries have been light, simple, and consumer oriented. But a significant number of less developed countries (LDC's), mostly the larger and richer ones, have established heavy, more complex capital goods industries. Both sectors of industry have been largely oriented to the domestic market, although there are some LDC's which have succeeded in sharply increasing their industrial exports, mostly of light and simple products.

The absence of export success may in itself suggest the prevalence of substantial price differentials and cast a doubt on the efficiency and competitiveness of the new industries. The question has been raised in several quarters whether, in fact, the resources spent on industrialization have been well spent or whether the LDC's could have achieved more growth—in domestic product or export earnings—by a different design of industrialization or by more emphasis on other sectors. These questions are of special relevance for the newly established capital goods industries, because:

1. Several LDC's which have not yet, or hardly, begun with heavy industrialization are appraising the case for establishing capital goods industries.

NOTE: This paper is in part based on research undertaken in the World Bank but the views expressed are those of the author and do not necessarily reflect those of the bank. The author acknowledges comments received on an earlier version of this article by Bela Balassa, Ayhan Cilingiroglu, Vinod Dubey, and Bertil Walstedt.

2. The investment outlays for capital goods industries and their related infrastructure are substantial and may impose severe strains on the country's finances, leading to inflation and eventual impairment of industrial efficiency.

3. While the growth of exports of light industrial products has in some countries been promising, a breakthrough of exports from the *larger* LDC's (which have invested in heavy industry and had by and large the poorer industrial export performance) will require exports from the engineering and other capital goods industries. (See [5].) When competitive, these industries can obtain the large orders that will make for substantial and sustained export growth.

Questions about international price differentials and, more broadly, the competitiveness of industry in the LDC's and the success of import substitution as a development strategy have been extensively discussed in the professional literature. There is now a growing body of empirical material, in particular on Latin American and Indian experience, which can provide guidance to policy makers in these and other countries. This study adds to the empirical findings on international price differentials prevailing in selected capital goods industries and then discusses the main explanatory factors underlying the price difference between LDC's and industrial countries.

THE NATURE AND LEVEL OF PRICE DIFFERENTIALS

The difference between LDC prices and prices of comparable competing supplies is maintained with the help of a wide variety of measures in the importing countries. The measures include outright prohibition, quantitative restrictions, multiple exchange rates, and restrictions on procurement for public or infrastructure projects. One particular measure, common to many LDC's, is the requirement that no import license be granted for products which are also produced locally unless it can be demonstrated that the local product does not suit the purpose of the user. The particular *form* or *technique* by which price differentials are maintained may over time affect their magnitudes, i.e., have an impact on the competitiveness of industry. In this paper the differences in prices between imported and domestic products will be called "protection." Thus, the paper disregards the particular technique of protection, and instead focuses on the magnitude and possible economic causes of the price differentials.

It is now generally recognized that in calculating protection a distinction must be made between gross or nominal protection and net protection, i.e., protection of value added after allowing for the excess cost (over international levels) or material inputs ([1], [2], and [3]). These two measures make it possible to single out material input costs as one important cost-raising factor.

For the LDC producer let

p = price of final product
a = cost of imported materials
b = cost of domestic materials and supplies
c = value added

$p = a + b + c$ and $p' = a' + b' + c'$, the comparable prices and costs of a representative foreign producer, expressed in the same currency as p, etc., calculated at the applicable rate of exchange.

Gross protection is

$$T_1 = (a + b + c)/(a' + b' + c') - 1.$$

Protection, assuming imported inputs at international prices, is

$$T_2 = (a' + b + c)/(a' + b' + c') - 1.$$

Net protection is

$$T_3 = (a' + b' + c)/(a' + b' + c') - 1.$$

It will be noted that net protection is similar to "effective" protection T_4, a measure which has recently been widely used (e.g., [4]):

$$T_4 = (c/c') - 1 = (p'/c')T_3$$

When either T_3 or T_4 is negative, but T_1 is positive, the industry can be export-competitive if appropriate allowance is made for excess input costs.

The domestic resource cost per unit of foreign exchange saved, a concept used by Bruno [3], is defined as $(b + c)/(p' - a)$.

The differences of the first three measures of protection, all expressed as a proportion of the foreign price of the finished product, are:

$T_1 - T_2 = T_a$ and $T_2 - T_3 = T_b$, where $T_a = (a - a')/p'$ measures the excess of the cost of the import component of materials over international levels (i.e., the prices paid by a representative foreign producer). This excess may be caused by duties or other taxes or by imperfections in international prices or because purchases by LDC producers are on a smaller scale than those of their competitors. $T_b = (b - b')/p'$ measures the excess of prices of domestically produced material and supply inputs over comparable prices paid by producers in developed countries.

In testing the competitiveness of LDC capital goods industries one would like to have calculations for a wide range of individual products at different times and in different countries. Such results cannot be expected for some time, especially since these price data are not included in regular statistical series. Instead, one has to resort to a comparison of fairly broad aggregates which may cover up points relevant to certain policy decisions. An alternative would be comparisons over time even if these are possible for only few products. This paper presents price calculations for thirty products in four countries as of approximately the same time (1966).

Table 1 presents the observations of a, b, a/p, b/p, and the four measures of protection for products of the automotive, heavy electrical, and mechanical equipment industries in Argentina, Brazil, Mexico and Pakistan.[1]

Comparisons have been made between LDC prices of finished products and components and those prevailing in industrial countries (converted to a c.i.f.—cost, insurance, and freight—import basis). For the automotive industry, the comparison was between prices of home plants and/or international manufacturers and their subsidiaries. For the other industries, comparisons were made with import prices of finished products in the LDC's and material input prices of representative producers in the industrial countries (again often parent companies).

The data presented should be interpreted with care, considering in particular that:

---

[1] This section draws on findings from field visits undertaken by Jack Baranson, Ayhan Cilingiroglu, and José Datas-Panero, of the IBRD staff. Most of these will be presented in more detail in [7] and [8].

1. Price data from both developed countries and LDC's change over time. Most of the data presented here are based on information obtained in 1966.

2. The coverage is limited and uneven.

3. Firms may quote different prices for the same or nearly the same equipment, depending on their particular relations with the customer or country. Price indications may vary with the source of the information, e.g., as obtained from bid analysis or company interviews.

4. In practice, selection of a price for the purpose of comparison must allow for many factors, including delivery time, financing terms, quality, performance, maintenance costs, etc.

Subject to these reservations one may draw the following general conclusions:

1. The excess material costs account for a significant part of gross protection.

2. The protection rates, either gross or net (T_1 or T_3) show considerable variation within individual countries.

3. Eliminating the excess material costs reduces the extent of variation: the T_3 series has a smaller standard deviation (35.3) than the T_1 series (46.0).

4. Among the countries included, industry in Argentina has the highest protection rates, both net and gross.

The effect of commonly recognized cost-raising factors on the variation in protection rates is less obvious and straightforward. The next section discusses these factors in the light of the data and the experience obtained in collecting the data and discussing them with the firms concerned.

MAJOR COST-RAISING FACTORS

Start-up Costs

In its early years an industrial firm is bound to incur special costs associated with getting established. These costs include training of the production workers and of the technical, administrative, and supervisory force and management; expenses associated with the start-up of a new plant; the build-up of production volume to capacity level and

TABLE 1

International Price Comparisons of Selected Products

| Country and Product | Material and Supplies as % of Final Price [a] | | | Import Component [col. (3) as % of (1)] | Ratios: Domestic to International Price [c] | | Protection (% of foreign price) [d] | | | | Domestic Resource Cost (per unit of foreign exchange saved) |
	Total (1)	Domestic [b] (2)	Imported [b] (3)	(4)	Domestic Materials (5)	Imported Materials (6)	Gross (7)	Inputs at International Prices (8)	Net [e] (9)	Effective Protection [f] (10)	(11)
Small truck [g]											
Argentina	61	49	12	19.7	2.34	2.43	80	67	17	31	1.74
Brazil	57	53	4	7.0	1.54	2.25	28	25	2	3	1.26
Mexico	71	39	32	45.1	2.66	2.03	52	27	-10	-18	1.36
Small truck [h]											
Argentina	74	62	12	16.2	3.48	2.50	104	90	-1	-2	1.99
Brazil	72	68	4	5.6	2.32	2.50	50	46.5	-11	-20	1.48
Mexico	75	43	32	42.7	2.23	2.00	30	10	-20	-38	1.07
Mechanical industry											
Argentina											
Diesel engine 225/280 HP	37	22	15	40.5	2.43	1.09	99	97	71	132	2.35
Diesel engine 410/685 HP	40	22	18	45.0	3.30	1.12	133	129	93	200	3.07
Tractor deca A-55	47	42	5	10.6	3.44	1.11	207	205	114	233	3.38
Mexico											
Excavator	45	25	20	44.0	1.30	1.09	21	19	12	22	1.25
Crusher	28	8	20	71.4	1.32	1.07	24	22	20	28	1.29
Road Roller	41	24	17	41.5	1.57	1.11	43	41	29	50	1.52
Motor Grader	49	23	26	53.1	1.40	1.11	26	23	15	30	1.33
Boiler	40	24	16	40.0	1.40	1.11	40	38	28	51	1.48

Heavy electrical equipment

Argentina: generators											
2,109 KVA	39.0	15.3	23.7	61.0	2.13	1.49	150.0	131.0	112.0	260.0	4.95
4,000 KVA	33.5	15.3	18.6	55.0	1.68	1.42	81.0	71.0	59.8	100.0	1.83
Brazil											
Transformer 33 MVA 220/88 KV	51.8	12.6	39.2	75.7	1.28	1.64	17.0	-2.0	-5.9	-9.9	1.5
Generator 42 MVA 13.8 KV 100 rpm	45.9	11.6	34.3	74.9	1.38	1.09	46.0	42.0	36.5	77.0	2.0
Motor 700 HP 6.9 KV	19.3	12.5	6.8	35.2	1.65	1.00	50.0	50.0	42.0	44.0	1.6
Generator 1,500 KVA 380 V 900 rpm	50.3	25.7	24.6	48.8	1.56	1.37	6.1	-1.5	-11.3	-20.4	1.1
Mexico											
Transformer											
25/33 MVA 161/69 KV	80.6	40.2	40.4	50.1	1.61	1.16	20.0	13.0	-5.0	-17.6	1.38
12.5 MVA 115/6.9 KV	79.5	34.1	45.4	57.0	1.53	1.20	-10.0	-17.0	-27.6	-59.9	0.83
40/55 MVA 115/66/13.8 KV	80.9	25.7	55.2	68.4	1.30	1.34	40.0	20.0	11.1	78.4	2.77
92 MVA 230/13.2 KV	77.4	22.0	55.4	71.6	1.68	1.22	28.1	15.0	4.0	16.4	1.97
Switch panel 2,400 V 3-phase	78.9	29.2	49.7	63.1	1.25	1.39	25.0	16.0	8.6	43.2	2.06
Motor control panel 480 V 3-phase	73.9	60.3	13.6	19.5	1.47	1.08	45.0	45.0	17.3	54.3	1.56
Distribution table 2 sections	79.1	19.9	59.2	74.8	1.96	1.32	45.0	24.0	9.8	47.8	4.19
Current transformer	17.1	13.0	4.1	56.3	1.38	1.00	40.0	40.0	35.0	43.1	1.57
Pakistan											
Motor 20 HP 380/220 V	64.9	23.2	41.7	64.3	2.17	1.34	71.0	52.0	29.0	92.0	3.3
Transformer											
25 KVA 11/0.4 KV	46.6	26.8	19.8	42.4	2.48	1.15	48.8	45.0	21.2	36.0	1.81
50 KVA 11/0.4 KV	53.2	21.6	31.6	59.3	1.93	1.18	77.7	68.0	50.0	148.2	2.7

NOTE: The definitions of columns 7–11 are discussed in the text.

a Supplies include electricity, fuel, lubricants, office supplies, and rent.

b Including indirect, i.e., import component of domestic inputs and depreciation unless otherwise specified.

c Domestic prices include taxes unless otherwise indicated.

d International price (c.i.f., port of entry, unless otherwise indicated).

e I.e., assuming all material and supply inputs are valued at international prices.

f Defined as percentage premium of value added of domestic industry over that of representative international manufacturer.

g Foreign prices f.o.b. Foreign and domestic prices excluding indirect taxes.

h Prices c.i.f., and including indirect taxes.

adaptation of the production process to local conditions; the opening up of supplier industries.

After an initial in-training period for labor, management, and plant, a firm producing heavy equipment will gradually upgrade the size and quality of its product—at least part of this process may be regarded as a starting up of the plant.

In the LDC's start-up costs will tend to be higher and they may extend over a longer period of time than in advanced industrial nations. In some cases start-up costs may exceed the cost of fixed plant. The starting-up period cannot be defined with precision. It will vary with countries, industries, and even firms.

An argument can be made for treating start-up cost separately in calculating the cost of the industrial investment. Since much of this cost will be peculiar to the conditions in the LDC, it may also be argued that it should be treated somehow without being expressed in the price paid by final users or in the price used for comparison with import prices. Rarely, the start-up cost can be written off by the parent firm. Part or all of the cost may be absorbed by the LDC government, for example, in the form of an outright subsidy, exemption from taxes, a participation in equity, or a loan on concessionary terms. If no special arrangements are made, the start-up costs will increase the product's price during the early years of the firm: the protection in those years may be substantial.

The impact of start-up costs are difficult to trace in the data. Most of the firms presented are in the latter part of the start-up period, having been in production at least three or four years. Most of them are also receiving special financing to cover at least part of the start-up costs, e.g., tax holidays (e.g., Mexico) or financing at subsidized interest rates (e.g., Brazil). No comparative analysis was made of the arrangements for financing start-up cost. A substantial part was probably absorbed by the parent company which, however, will expect a return on its investment in later years.

Apparently Brazilian truck manufacturers received domestic inputs at better prices than their counterparts in Argentina or Mexico. The former were further ahead in the start-up period. In Hirschman's terminology there was more backward linkage in Brazil. The cost of establishing backward linkage is part of the start-up cost. Hirschman

[6] discusses some deep-seated social reasons for limited backward linkages, whose impact may stretch well beyond any reasonable start-up period and will keep input costs high. Additional reasons why input costs may be high will be discussed next.

Cost of Material Inputs

An important determinant of input costs $(T_a + T_b)$ may be the relative importance of the import component, since imports are often cheaper than domestic products. Even so, imported materials may be expensive when compared with prices paid by competing industries in developed countries. At times the smaller LDC firms may have to pay for smaller lots than their much larger counterparts in the industrial countries. International firms may control the price of their inputs and charge prices for industrial components which appear high when compared with the cost of the final product of which they are a part. The premium thus charged may be higher as the imported components are reduced.[2] At the same time, material cost will go up as domestic producers switch to domestic supplies. In some industries the cost differential rises sharply as the domestic content begins to include the more complex components. The size of the domestic component will vary with the availability of local raw materials and components but in many cases is pushed up regardless of cost consideration by government requirements. Thus, the excess of LDC prices over imports may be directly related to the size of the domestic component.

The relatively high cost of materials inputs in the truck industry makes for a sharp difference between gross and net protection. In some cases the latter is negative, suggesting that the industry can be competitive on export markets. In the production of trucks domestic costs become especially high after the import component falls below 35 per cent, both because of the deletion allowance and the excess costs of engine, driveline, and sheet metal, especially in Argentina.[3]

A striking feature is the high cost of imported inputs in the electrical equipment industry, caused by high ex-duty prices paid for raw material inputs (e.g., electrolytic copper).

It is conceivable that the high cost of inputs $(T_a + T_b)$ turns a low

[2] In the trade the premium takes the form of a "deletion allowance."
[3] Cf. [7].

net protection (T_3) into a high gross protection (T_1). As noted, this appears to be the case with the truck industry. But in a larger number of cases both T_1 and T_3 are high (or low) at the same time, or—put in another way—net protection and high input costs go together. The data suggest a high correlation between T_3 and T_1 and between T_3 and $(T_a + T_b)$.[4] It would seem that, in intercountry comparisons, singling out input cost as a cost-raising factor in a way begs the question. One suspects that in some situations the factors causing net protection to be high also operate on input costs. These factors might be volume of production, or exchange rate policy and the general level of protection, which are taken up next.

Volume of Production

Economies of scale, important for several products, are hard to come by in the relatively small markets of most LDC's. In many lines there are few plant and product designs which will make for efficient operations at low volumes. Export growth, a crucial way of widening markets, is often handicapped by excessive domestic orientation of industry. A comparison of the electrical equipment industries of Austria and Argentina is telling. Although these industries have markets of similar size in these countries, Austria exports two-thirds of the output of its industry but Argentina exports none. None of the firms from which data are presented exported to any significant extent.

The structure of the industry may further limit the volume of production of individual firms. In fact, some countries have far too many firms, all of them too small for efficiency. They began by providing home producers with heavy protection. Then they sought to obtain competition by permitting several firms under the protection umbrella. The final result has often been high production cost and low capacity utilization. An almost classic example is the Argentine automobile industry, in which there are 13 manufacturers producing 68 models.

Related to economies of scale is the better capacity of larger firms to adopt and assimilate advanced technology.

[4] The correlation coefficient between the T_3 and $(T_a + T_b)$ series is $R = .7018$; that between T_1 and T_3 is .922. While these are based on intercountry comparisons, it is noteworthy that Lewis and Guisinger found that for Pakistan a ranking based on gross protection would provide a reasonable approximation for one based on effective protection (cf. [10]).

It is well known that economies of scale are different for different products. Least affected are the more complex products that are made to specific order, such as heavy electric generators. Transformers are another example of a product which may have modest economies of scale. Because of the variety of products covered in the data, it is not possible to pin-point precisely the impact of volume.

In several industries the cost of fixed plant per unit of product was relatively low. Improvement in capacity utilization, frequently low, would reduce the capital cost. However, for many products this factor was outweighed by the impact of high (domestic and imported) material cost.

Exchange Rate Policy ·

The importance of appropriate exchange rate policy has been discussed extensively in the literature. From the viewpoint of making industrial products export-viable, it is the basic export rate of exchange which counts. Thus, the maintenance of an overvalued rate does not promote favorable cost competitiveness. This situation has tended to prevail in some LDC's which have emphasized heavy industrialization, either because overvaluation was pursued as a matter of industrialization policy (see, e.g., [7]), or the exchange rate lagged behind inflationary price increases which accompanied the industrialization efforts.

The exchange rate must, of course, be considered in conjunction with prevailing charges and subsidies on imports and exports. The general level of protection will depend on the level at which the exchange rate is fixed. In some cases the basic rate of exchange may be accompanied by surcharges or uniform duties applicable to broad import categories, while the basic rate applies to most exports. Such practices are not equivalent to maintaining a more depreciated basic rate and doing without some or all of the surcharge. In the former case the basic rate is lower and works as a penalty on exports. LDC's producing capital goods would be especially adversely affected, since in their present phase of development they are able to diversify by increasing exports of new products, both manufactured and agricultural, which may be particularly sensitive to a more favorable exchange rate.

A higher level of general protection may itself be a cause of industrial inefficiency. Protection, especially when exercised through quantitative controls, will shield industry from outside competition and give it an inward orientation. This may be reflected in the structure of industry, small production volumes, high profits, tardiness in adopting new techniques, etc.

Among countries considered, Argentina clearly had an overvalued basic rate at the time the data was collected. Subsequently, in 1967, it devalued by 41 per cent. This factor accounts for a substantial part of the high protection rates observed in Argentina. In Brazil, exchange rate policy was to adjust the rate to domestic price changes, but the policy was implemented stepwise (about every twelve months), while inflation proceeded at 25 to 40 per cent per annum; consequently, the "realism" of the exchange rate was bound to erode even in a period of months. On the other hand, as part of Brazil's stabilization efforts manufacturers attempted to keep their own prices stable even though the general trend was upward.

Other Factors

The impact of the factors enumerated thus far must be seen against the background of others which may have affected the observations to some extent.

Besides exchange rates and protection, LDC policies may influence costs through the impact of inflation and demand stability. LDC governments must often take measures to moderate the pace of expansion. These measures, affecting public expenditure or credit extension, impinge heavily on the demand for capital goods. LDC industries, confining their sales to the home market, are not able to offset domestic fluctuations with larger exports. Capital goods industries in the LDC's have probably been subject to more severe fluctuations than their counterparts in industrial countries. These fluctuations have aggravated the problem of excess capacity.

High protection rates (as defined in this paper) may be associated with (or cause) high profits per unit of product. There was some evidence of this in the cost breakdown underlying the data presented.

The cost of capital (per unit of output) varied greatly from country to country or product to product. It will depend on the capital intensiveness of the production process. The real interest rate in LDC's is, of course, at least as high as in developed countries. The amount of working capital required may be high in the LDC's because of the absence of a dependable raw material supply (both domestic and imported); its costs may be high particularly if the manufacturer—squeezed by inflation, with costs rising faster than finished product prices—must rely on outside financing. Furthermore, financing of finished products, indispensable for capital equipment sales, may be more expensive than in developed countries, if facilities for such financing exist at all.

The cost per worker of supervisory and production staff is generally below that in industrialized countries. But this advantage may be offset by higher labor requirements, so labor costs per unit of output may be close to or above those in industrial countries.[5] The share of wages (and sometimes also profits) in total costs may rise in the inflationary process—this may account for the relatively high nonmaterial component of the Argentine products on which observations were made.

It has not been possible to make a comparison of the share of wages in the total cost. The data available often pertain to firms which in turn have greatly different product mixes.

The LDC cost of selling and distribution (per unit of output) also is usually above (sometimes double) that in industrial countries.

CONCLUDING REMARKS

The price differential between LDC's and industrial countries is influenced by many factors. These factors or combinations of them apply in widely varying intensities. Consequently, there are wide differences in price differentials for individual products among coun-

---

[5] For example, following are data on direct labor requirements of three Brazilian items shown in Table 1 (cf. [8]).

	Man-hours Required in		
	Brazil	Industrial Countries	
	(1)	(2)	(1) ÷ (2)
Diesel generator, 1,500 KVA; 900 rpm	1,850	600	3.1
Transformer, 300 KVA; 220/88 KV	9,880	4,100	2.4
Water-wheel generator, 42 MVA; 13,820 V	28,000	16,000	1.75

tries or for various products in individual countries. No hard and fast rules seem to exist whereby countries or industries can be classified as to their competitiveness in the manufacture of capital goods.

Any new firm or industry must incur special costs in getting established. Most of these costs are commonly associated with *infant industries:* the training of labor and management, the working-in of the plant and adaptation of the production process to local conditions, opening of supplier and marketing channels, development of supplier industries, etc. In LDC's these costs are bound to be higher and may be stretched over a longer period than in industrial countries with whose products the LDC firm must compete. Unless special provisions are made to finance start-up costs, they will be reflected in the final price; the price differential between local and imported products will then often be substantial. The level and duration of start-up costs vary with the individual firm, industry, and country.

After an initial starting-up period the costs of establishing the industry will be eliminated or at least greatly reduced. The prices of the final product will become more in line with import prices. However, inherent in the basic conditions or prevailing policies of many LDC's are several factors which may work to keep their prices well above comparable import prices.

These factors fall into two broad categories. The first are those which may be influenced by appropriate changes in *government policy,* e.g., exchange rate adjustment, diminished reliance on direct controls, moderation in domestic content requirements, stabilization of public procurement and investment credit. Secondly, there are factors—associated with the hard-core infant-economy argument—which will change only as the economy becomes more developed: scarcity of skills, management, and capital; high cost of services, supplies, and material inputs; high-risk factors; lagging technology; low production volumes. There will be a gray area between these two categories, which may be narrowed by government policies, but which will also be affected by the attitude or actions of industry itself and the progress made in establishing the basic conditions for modern industry. A further consideration is the increasing efficiency of some industries in developed countries, reflected in falling prices during the past five to ten years.

As the start-up period is completed, infant-economy factors will tend to outweigh the factors associated with a particular infant industry. Moreover, factors considered *internal* to a particular firm may also reflect countrywide conditions and affect other firms and industries.

Generally, the more competitive LDC industries are those which have effectively incurred the initial costs of getting established, are located in countries where there is a reasonably realistic exchange rate and where the number of firms in the industry is not so large as to cause unduly low production volumes in individual firms. Even where this combination of favorable factors prevails, infant-economy factors may impinge on LDC competitiveness, and it is not uncommon to find price differentials up to 15–25 per cent.

Much empirical work currently in progress is based on industry aggregates. However, the data on individual products presented here suggest great variation within the industries. It is worthwhile to check the findings based on industry studies against those pertaining to individual products. Perhaps one ought to be more cautious about broad tariff policy conclusions based on industry aggregates. Certainly, proposals for individual tariffs must be based on studies of individual products.

The data in this paper make possible some intercountry comparisons for similar products. Although industry in the countries selected is in different stages of development, the differences in protection observed are caused also by other factors, such as the structure of industry and exchange rate policy. The conclusions should be substantiated further by studies of the development of industry or production of individual products *over a period of time*. After a five-year lapse it would be worthwhile to take a repeat look at the firms and products studied here.

The high cost of inputs is an important cost-raising factor for some (e.g., the automotive) but not all industries studied here. The data suggest a close correlation between net and gross protection and between the net protection of finished goods and the protection of inputs used in the production of these finished goods. This points to the importance of factors operating on the whole industrial sector or even the economy. This is particularly relevant to the formulation of "minimum conditions" which, as suggested above, should refer in part to conditions for the economy as a whole.

REFERENCES

1. H. G. Johnson. "The Theory of Tariff Structure, with Special Reference to World Trade and Development." In *Trade and Development*. Geneva, 1965.
2. ———. "Tariffs and Economic Development." *Journal of Development Studies,* October 1965.
3. Michael Bruno. "The Optimal Selection of Export-promoting and Import-substituting Projects." U.N. Interregional Seminar on Development Planning. Ankara, Turkey, September 1965.
4. Bela Balassa. "Tariff Protection in Industrial Countries: An Evaluation." *Journal of Political Economy,* December 1965.
5. Barend A. de Vries. *The Export Experience of Developing Countries.* World Bank Staff Papers No. 3. Baltimore, Johns Hopkins Press, 1967.
6. Albert O. Hirschman. "The Political Economy of Import-Substituting Industrialization in Latin America." *Quarterly Journal of Economics,* February 1968.
7. Jack Baranson. *Automotive Industries in Developing Countries.* World Bank Occasional Papers. Baltimore, Johns Hopkins Press, 1969.
8. Ayhan Cilingiroglu. *Manufacture of Heavy Electrical Equipment in Developing Countries.* World Bank Occasional Papers. Baltimore, Johns Hopkins Press, 1969.
9. Celso Furtado. "Industrialization and Inflation." *International Economic Papers XII,* 1967.
10. Stephen R. Lewis Jr. and Stephen E. Guisinger. "Measuring Protection in a Developing Country: The Case of Pakistan." *Journal of Political Economy,* April 1968.

COMMENT
DAVID FELIX

My initial reaction to de Vries's paper was, What is there for me to say? The two World Bank studies, *Automotive Industries in Developing Countries* and *Manufacture of Heavy Electrical Equipment in Developing Countries,* are chock-full of hard-to-get information on comparative prices and costs for carefully specified individual products of these two industries; consequently, one can only urge the bank's economics staff to exploit further its unique entree to individual firm data and give us more such valuable studies. De Vries's referral to these data is wrapped in appropriate warnings about their limitations as a basis for broad explanations of the difficulties that LDC's encounter in trying to move from industrial import substitution to industrial exporting. His analysis of those difficulties is equally qualified, cautiously incorporating most of the conventional explanations without seemingly committing himself on their relative importance. And to cap it all he concludes with a plea for more data. How to uncover grounds in all this blandness for some sort of scholarly confrontation?

I think I have found such grounds. It took some additional readings and a rather unfair stripping away of caveats and qualifications to uncover them, but unfairness is, after all, part of the style of confrontation politics. At any rate, it enables me to move from the uncustomary role of praise-singer to the more comfortable one of critic.

Ruthlessly and unfairly stripped of its qualifications, de Vries's rather optimistic diagnosis of LDC industrial exporting problems is the following.

1. Although unit costs and prices of most LDC industrial products are too high for profitable exporting, this is in part because the cost of final products is substantially increased by heavy duties on imported materials and high rates of protection of domestically produced materials.

2. Independently of import liberalization measures, however, domestic unit costs can still be expected to converge in time toward c.i.f. prices in the LDC's as

    a. High start-up costs are overcome and operative experience improves efficiency at the firm level;

    b. The growth of the home market permits greater exploitation of economies of scale and extensions of backward linkages;

    c. Physical and human capital and external economies accumulate *pari passu* with the further economic development of the LDC's.

3. The favorable cost-price trends can be hastened by adopting more "realistic" (i.e., lower) exchange rates and more liberal commercial policies, i.e., lower tariffs and fewer quantitative import controls. There is ample room for this, since the LDC's manifest a penchant for "overvalued" exchange rates and excessive protection and controls.

The first general point finds ample support in de Vries's Table 1. Although only one of the twenty-eight products has an LDC domestic price below the c.i.f. import price, the number would rise to seven if all material inputs could be obtained at the estimated c.i.f. prices (and provided, one should add, that the shift to foreign sources of materials would not require firms to hold substantially higher inventory levels).

There is, however, more in the table that is relevant to the diagnosis of export potential. For example, although for 15 of the 28 products the cost of imported materials is a higher percentage of final price than is the cost of domestic materials, lowering domestic material prices to c.i.f. levels would nevertheless reduce the cost of the final product much more than would lowering imported material prices to c.i.f. levels. In other words, the nub of the high materials cost obstacle lies in high protection of domestic rather than imported materials. All four LDC's seem in fact to have been pursuing the standard mercantilist strategy of keeping protection levels high for competitive imports and low for noncompetitive ones. This is indicated in Table 1 by the distribution of values for $(T_1 - T_2)/T_1$ and $(T_2 - T_3)/T_1$. In fact, Table 1 probably understates the ubiquitousness of the strategy, since

TABLE 1

Percentage Decline of Unit Costs of Products in de Vries's Table 1, with Imported and Domestic Materials at C.I.F. Prices [a]

	0–10%	11–20%	21–30%	Over 30%
	Decline with Imported Materials at C.I.F. Prices — $(T_1 - T_2)/T_1$			
Argentina	3	3	0	0
Brazil	3	0	0	1
Mexico	6	1	0	6
Pakistan	1	1	1	0
Total	13	5	1	
	Decline with Domestic Materials at C.I.F. Prices — $(T_2 - T_3)/T_1$			
Argentina	0	2	2	2
Brazil	0	2	1	1
Mexico	1	1	4	7
Pakistan	0	0	1	2
Total	1	5	8	12

[a] Excludes two products with negligible gross protection ($T_1 < 10$ per cent).

of the seven $(T_1 - T_2)/T_1$ items in the 30 per cent group, over six are heavy electrical equipment products whose main domestic buyers, the state-owned utilities, are generally constrained by law and political pressures to buy national.[1]

Table 1 thus suggests two reasons why the convergence of domestic and c.i.f. prices may be a more difficult accomplishment than is implied by de Vries's rather optimistic prognosis. The first is that the easier sort of import liberalization—the lowering of duties on noncompetitive imports—would contribute far less to convergence than would lowering protection on competitive imports, while the latter, though contributing more toward reducing costs, would also drastically disrupt industrial employment and output, at least transitionally, and hence would be a difficult feat to pull off politically. The second is that whatever contribution extending backward linkages may make to employment and foreign exchange saving, it appears to raise rather than lower production costs of final products. This is contrary to the implications of de Vries's analysis, although to be fair, he seems to be of two minds on this. This is further indicated by regressions of gross protection, T_1, and net protection, T_3, on the ratio of imported materials cost to total unit cost, a/p (columns 7 and 9 on column 3 in the de Vries's Table 1).

$$T_1 = 86.883 - 1.186 \quad (a/p) \qquad R^2 = 0.155$$
$$(2.280)$$

$$T_3 = 49.901 - 0.8895 \quad (a/p) \qquad R^2 = 0.153$$
$$(2.198)$$

The negative relationships are not strong, but are significant at the 95 per cent confidence level. As an added bonus, the similarity of the two regressions indicates that the net or effective rates of protection correlate fairly closely with the gross rates for the twenty-eight products.

The c.i.f. prices of de Vries's table have been estimated via the assumption that removing formal protection would suffice to lower the

[1] The main exceptions occur when the capital goods purchases of the utility companies involve foreign financing, either suppliers' credits or World Bank financing. In the latter case the bank requires competitive bidding, with only a maximum 15 per cent preference margin to domestic bidders.

prices of imported materials, intermediate products, and equipment to levels roughly competitive with those of producers in advanced countries. How justified is this assumption? Let me cite some contrary evidence from pre-World War II Argentina, from an era when, as we know, the right people, guided by the sacred tenets of economic liberalism, still ruled that country and the efficient Argentine price structure had not yet succumbed to the onslaughts of Peronist policies, that root cause of Argentina's poor postwar economic performance, according to the conservative devil theory of Argentine stagnation. Table 2 indicates that for at least four high-volume capital goods imports, tariffs, custom fees, and carriage costs explain only a modest fraction of the excess of the Argentine wholesale price over the U.S. wholesale price. The neoclassical revival, from which we are, hopefully, beginning to recover, has tended to blind us to the importance of differences in market structure and pricing strategies as causes of sustained differences in relative prices.

Further evidence on this is supplied by Table 3, which is a summary prewar comparative price information for an array of internationally tradable industrial commodities, some actually imported by Argentina and some home produced. The variance of Argentine from U.S. relative prices appears substantially larger than can be explained by transport costs, tariff duties, and differences in indirect taxes. Moreover,

TABLE 2

Ratios of Argentine to U.S. Wholesale Prices of Four
Argentine Capital Goods Imports, 1939

	Actual Ratio	Ratio Net of Argentine C.I.F. Costs and Import Duties
Automobile	1.62	1.35
Tractor	1.38	1.32
Combine (12-ft.)	1.56	1.46
Plow (2-bottom)	1.47	1.40

SOURCE: Armour Research Foundation, *Technological and Economic Survey of Argentine Industries*, Buenos Aires, 1943, Table XII.

TABLE 3

Ratio of U.S. to Argentine Purchasing Power of Cattle and Wheat
for Selected Commodities, 1937 and 1939

| | Terms-of-Trade Ratios, U.S. to Argentina [a] | | | |
| | Cattle | | Wheat | |
	1937	1939	1937	1939
Wool cloth	440	367	119	175
Cotton denim	—	582	156	269
Sulphuric acid	939	568	245	262
Caustic soda	551	564	144	259
Denatured alcohol	756	541	198	249
Kraft paper	402	250	193	194
Coal	836	757	219	249
Fuel oil	410	293	107	134
Gasoline	1,821	1,480	476	731
Steel rails	602	458	156	214
Electrolytic copper	541	501	143	232
Lumber	570	436	149	200
Cement	500	—	129	—
Automobile	—	412	—	306
Radio receiver	—	—	—	342
Tractor	—	580	—	273
Combine (12-ft.)	—	669	—	314
Mowing machine	—	906	—	416
Plow	—	611	—	281

SOURCE: Armour Research Foundation, *Survey*, Tables XIII and XV.

[a] For cattle: $(p_i/p_c)_{us} \div (p_i/p_c)_a$; for wheat: $(p_i/p_w)_{us} \div (p_i/p_w)_a$, where p_i designates wholesale prices of selected industrial products; p_c, the price of live cattle; p_w, the price of wheat; *us* refers to the United States; and *a* refers to Argentina.

one can detect in these prewar price ratios the main outlines—though with some deviations—of the Argentine relative price structure of the 1960's, the intercession of Peron and excessive import substitution notwithstanding.[2] Alternatively, there is little evidence of convergence

[2] For detailed 1960's relative prices see Economic Commission for Latin America (ECLA), "A Measurement of Price Levels and the Purchasing Power of Currencies in Latin America, 1960–62," mimeo, Santiago, Chile, March 1963.

between domestic and c.i.f. industrial prices in Argentina during the past three decades, learning curves and capital and skill accumulation notwithstanding.

Tables 2 and 3, however, also modify some of the negative implications of backward linkage suggested by Table 1. They suggest that the margin of maneuver for LDC industrialization strategy is probably much more circumscribed than is implied by the de Vries paper. The potential range of choice for industrial users is not between high materials prices under protection and "competitive" c.i.f.-level prices under free trade, but perhaps a much narrower range reflecting structurally embedded market imperfections. The prewar price tables may also help explain why indignation at the high relative prices of various import substitutes in the LDC's tends to be greater among visiting economists than among the local citizenry. The latter have been partly inured by high relative prices of the corresponding imports during the pre-import substitution years.

What about more "realistic" exchange rates as a means of hastening the convergence of domestic and c.i.f. prices? Facile references to "overvalued" or "unrealistic" exchange rates grossly overestimate, it seems to me, the ability of economic authorities to sustain a major alteration of the ratio of domestic to international prices by means of a few simple macropolicy devices. The evidence for Argentina—not untypical of industrializing LDC's at least in this regard—is that the short-term price elasticities of demand for imports and supply elasticities of agricultural exportables are very low, that the chief mechanism of adjustment has had to be sectoral income shifts combined with a drop in aggregate income,[3] and that domestic prices tend to rebound quickly,[4] unless special political conditions permit the preservation of the income shifts and/or the recession long enough for the sluggish long-run supply elasticities to take hold. The "realistic" 40 per cent devaluation, in March 1967, approvingly cited by de Vries, is a recent illustration of the last point. It did take until spring 1970 for Argen-

[3] Cf. Carlos Diaz-Alejandro, *Exchange Rate Devaluation in a Semi-Industrialized Country,* M.I.T. Press, 1965; Richard Mallon, "Exchange Policy—Argentina," in G. Papanek, ed., *Development Policy: Theory and Practice,* Harvard University Press, 1968, pp. 175–206.

[4] Arnold Harberger, "The Effects of Inflation on the Price Level," in W. Baer and I. Kerstenetsky, eds., *Inflation and Economic Growth,* New York, 1964.

tine wholesale prices to rebound the full 40 per cent, but this rebounding period, unusually long by previous Argentine experiences with devaluation, was elongated by a military regime that sat hard on money wages to the point of lowering real wages, until the social upheavals of May 1969 forced an easing of wage controls. And yet it seems doubtful that even a three-year rebounding period is enough to allow resource reallocations in Argentina to gain adequate momentum. Be that as it may, the essential argument is that since changes in relative prices also affect income distribution, the changes will, according to the organized strength of discommoded groups operating both in the market place and the political arena, set in motion countervailing price reactions to restore *status quo ante* price relationships. This may, in turn, thwart the desired reallocation, unless supply responses to relative price changes are quick and elastic, a behavioral characteristic for which LDC's are not widely noted.

The emphasis on the convergence of comparative production costs would suggest that LDC industrial exporting should originate and gain momentum from the relatively low-cost, low-technology, and low-capital-intensive side of the industrial product gamut, rather than from the high-technology side where the twenty-eight products of the de Vries paper are situated. The actual export pattern, however, seems more mixed. To illustrate let me summarize some paradoxical findings I have obtained from a study of Argentine nontraditional industrial exporting.[5] These are:

1. Around 60 per cent of these exports in 1963–66 originated in industries with above-average capital intensity, the percentage being similar for exports to the Latin American Free Trade Association (LAFTA) and for those to the rest of the world.

2. The industries originating these exports were in the upper half of the Argentine relative industrial price spectrum.

3. Multiple regressions showed the variance of nontraditional exports for 1955–66 to be unrelated to variations in exchange rates, whether lagged or unlagged (the exchange rates were adjusted to incorporate the differential tax subsidies applicable to various categories of nontraditional exports).

[5] David Felix, "Subsidies, Depression and Non-traditional Industrial Exporting in Argentina," Harvard University Development Advisory Service, Economic Development Report No. 107, September 1968.

4. Export variance, on the other hand, was significantly related to variations of excess capacity of the respective industries and to the establishment of LAFTA in the 1960's.

Spasmodic respect for comparative cost doctrine makes me skeptical that Argentina's destiny is to become an important exporter of high-technology and capital-intensive industrial products in the next few decades. The skepticism is reinforced by an awareness that marketing costs are especially high for this range of products, as are also the levels of marketing sophistication, research and development outlays, and risk required to compete effectively in high-technology production with producers in developed countries. Argentine nontraditional exporting was, after all, still a marginal activity—5 to 6 per cent of total exports— during the period covered by the study, and it is possible that after further shaking out, a quite different longer-run pattern may emerge than that manifested in the twelve years covered by the study.

The twelve-year pattern did conform, however, to the aspirations of the economic authorities and more interestingly, to the expectations of the Argentine business community in the 1960's. The industrial promotion measures of this period were strongly biased toward encouraging the export of sophisticated products of recently established industries, rather than the less technologically exacting products of longer-established ones. Similarly, Argentine trade association executives, when asked in a 1963 survey to predict the chief sources of future Argentine industrial exports, chose high-technology industries such as machinery, motor vehicles and tractors, and organic chemicals, citing as the main reasons for their choice, in order of frequency: (1) current excess capacity; (2) minimal production by other LAFTA countries; (3) future excess capacity; (4) progressive management. Cost competitiveness was virtually ignored despite the urging of the interviewer to give it major weight.[6]

The implications for LDC industrial export prognosis to be extracted from this limited Argentine evidence are: (1) Firms that progress from high-cost import substitution to import competitiveness—and many, of course, do not—need not therefore move on to exporting.

[6] José M. Dagnino Pastore, *Productos Exportables: Resultados de Encuestas* (Documento de Trabajo), Buenos Aires, Instituto Torcuato Di Tella, 1964.

(2) Firms that are tuned into well-established foreign market channels, whether as subsidiaries of international corporations or through other foreign ties, may export despite high unit costs, if exporting helps relieve excess capacity, or fits some short- or long-term international production or marketing strategy of the parent corporation. In general, the assumption that if the price is right exporting will follow may be a particularly unreliable basis for predicting industrial exporting patterns of LDC's.

It has become a commonplace to decry the inadequacy of the theoretical framework guiding analyses and policy prescriptions concerning LDC trade and economic development. The recurring balance-of-payments crises afflicting most LDC's, particularly the industrializing ones, have been seemingly impervious to long-run solutions via the orthodox trade and exchange policy prescriptions of economic liberalism. In just about all of the industrializing LDC's the industrial sector has substantially increased its share of GNP but not its share of employment. Mounting urban underemployment has become a key manifestation of new forms of socioeconomic dualism. I suspect that for Mexico, Pakistan, and Brazil—three of the four industrializing LDC's in the de Vries survey—the before and after income distribution pattern can reasonably be described by an intersecting pair of Lorenz curves reflecting little change in the Gini inequality index, as in Figure 1: The growth of the middle class and industrial worker cohorts are offset by a drop in the relative income status of the income recipients in the lower half of the distribution.

Let me conclude, however, on a positive note, by briefly suggesting a neglected aspect of trade and growth analysis that may indicate one of the paths toward a more relevant theoretical framework. There are two fundamental tenets on which the propositions of international trade theory have been erected. One is that countries can be viewed as decision making units writ large, with well-ordered and autonomously determined preference functions and sharing common and exogenously determined menus of goods and techniques. The other tenet is that trade is an engine of growth, a dynamic cultural force leading to the introduction of previously unknown goods, wants, and technology from without.

From the first tenet come all of the theorems of international trade,

FIGURE 1

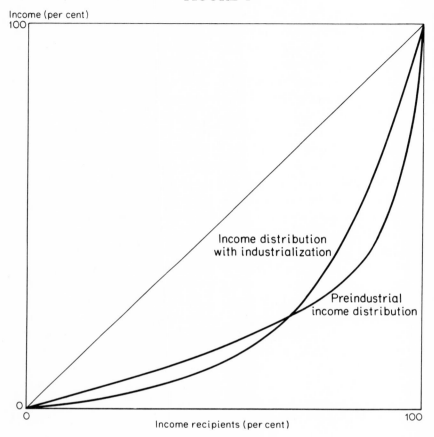

the welfare propositions and the policy prescriptions, whereas the second has mainly added rhetorical flourishes to international trade textbooks. Yet the analytic implications of the second tenet are profoundly disturbing for the theorems derived from the first. In effect, they could render many of them empirically irrelevant. For example, unless all goods are only gross substitutes—a proposition that would destroy the basis for aggregation—the introduction of new goods will alter the elasticity of substitution in consumption between older goods, so that before-and-after community indifference curves cross and judgments of the gains from trade have to rely on additional and more direct *ad hoc* measures of socioeconomic welfare to supplement flawed aggregate indexes like changes in GNP per capita.

We are increasingly aware of various forces affecting LDC trade and economic growth trends that have not been handled convincingly with our conventional tools of analysis, particularly as these are constrained in their use by widely shared if largely implicit behavioral and ideological assumptions about economic behavior. But we still try to comfort ourselves by pigeon-holing contradictory behavioral manifestations and persistent difficulties of the LDC's as "transitional." Something like this, I suspect, may underlie the optimistic tenor of de Vries's prognosis of LDC industrial exporting prospects. Yet when countries ranging from Pakistan, with less than $100 per capita income, to Argentina, with over $800 per capita income, are used to illustrate common industrial inefficiencies and exporting difficulties, the assumption that the difficulties dwindle away as income and productive capacity rise seems little more than an analytic copout.

The tendency has been to get around such difficulties by aggregating goods into broader classes, so that the auto and the oxcart lose their individuality in the category, transportation goods, and by assuming a symmetrical flow of influences between trading countries which does not affect the time-shape of preference functions. But aggregation buries as well as summarizes, and for some issues the buried information may be critical. Thus the fact that the auto is an import-intensive substitute for the oxcart could be quite important in analyzing employment and balance-of-payments problems in LDC's. As for symmetry of influence, it is obviously not inherent in trade and communication, but only one possibility.

Symmetry may not be an intolerable simplifying assumption for the analysis of contemporary trade between advanced countries, although the Vernon product cycle trade model suggests that the dynamics of industrial trade in a world of multinational corporations may be better explained by introducing asymmetrical influences. Possibly the analysis of nineteenth-century trade between the technologically advanced countries of that epoch can also be based on the simplifying assumption of symmetry of influence with only moderate damage to the relevance of the analysis. For despite British technological leadership, there was considerable technological interchange, and as the speed and volume of international communications grew, there was also a growing inter-change of consumer tastes, French consumption patterns being partly anglicized, British patterns somewhat gallicized, etc.

For LDC's, however, the influence flow has been patently one-way. The older export economy dualism models of the Myint type rest, for example, on asymmetrical technological and taste intrusions from without. But so also do the new forms of dualism associated with LDC industrialization. Import substitution can be viewed in this regard as a strategy of shifting the external technological and demand influences from the import structure to the productive structure of the industrial-izing LDC.

Confronted by accumulating evidence that LDC's are importing excessively labor-saving techniques, economists have tended to view the problem exclusively from the production function perspective. There ought to be a more labor-intensive least-cost way, they seem to be saying, of producing petrochemicals, motor cars, and TV picture tubes than the imported techniques actually employed. Yet the fact seems to be that both locally owned firms and foreign subsidiaries in the LDC find it more profitable and less risky to import packaged tech-nologies and product designs than to incur the costs and risks of doing indigenous R and D on production processes and of pioneering in indigenous product development; hence LDC producers of even high-technology products do very little of either.

If, however, we dispense with the notion that the changing final demand mixes in the LDC's reflect only autonomous forces that can be fully analyzed under the rubric of price and income elasticity, we may come up with a more persuasive explanation of the perverse choice of techniques by the LDC's. That is to say, the choice may be as much a demand mix as a production function phenomenon.

The regressions of the 1965 stock of TV receivers per 100 persons on per capita income for OECD and for Latin American countries, illustrate the point. Although the TV set is a more recently introduced artifact with a much higher relative price in Latin America than in Europe, the regression coefficient is similar for each group of countries and the intercept is considerably smaller for the Latin American group.

I suspect similar patterns illuminating the international demonstra-tion effect on LDC's can also be uncovered for other import and capital-intensive consumer items. We might also, perhaps, uncover significant differences among LDC's in the strength of the effect, and explore whether these differences correlate with the relative vigor of consumer indoctrination, as measured by the relative importance of foreign subsidiaries in the LDC industrial sector or the relative persuasiveness of Americanized sales promotion techniques, as indicated by the ratio of advertising outlays to sales, the uses of TV and radio, and similar indexes. For example, the much greater strength of these influence channels in Latin America compared to the Third World as a whole for equivalent per capita income classes may help explain why Latin American countries, although in the higher ranges of per capita income in the Third World, suffer with at least equal intensity from the new dualism with its inequalities, growing underemployment, and persistent balance-of-payments impediments to growth.

With these asymmetrical influences, liberal trading rules become double-edged. They do not merely promote a more efficient specialization of LDC's in the production of a subset of an exogenously determined menu of goods, but also maximize the channels through which the one-way international demonstration effect enriches the menu and twists preferences in indigestion-prone directions.

Given any double-edged situation, an economist instinctively thinks of some optimum trade-off. In this case, the trade-off could be a set of controls which selectively meters the influence flow so as to minimize unemployment and balance-of-payments distortions. This seems to be the direction toward which the economic policy of many LDC's, beset by these problems, seems to be tending. Crude and lurching though these policy trends may be, they may nevertheless have a more rational economic basis than conventional analysis has been willing to grant. Another possible arrangement could be one-way trade concessions by advanced countries to make amends for the vigor of their one-sided cultural impact on the LDC's. The growing popularity of this ploy among trade economists has to be viewed, so far, as a victory for benevolence over existing theology. We could, however, do the Lord's work with less theological *angst* if we would recognize that it is the theology, not the benevolence, which may be analytically inappropriate to the situation.

DOROTHY WALTERS, Economic Council of Canada

In respecting the constraint which time imposes on us this morning, I shall comment only briefly from some notes made during the conference. To begin with, I should like to express my regret that Barend de Vries was not able to be present at this session to discuss his interesting paper. Baranson has given us an admirable presentation; nevertheless one is left with the unsatisfied wish to "confront" the author himself.

Many participants at this meeting with experience in the collection and analysis of international price data will find it interesting to examine the tabular data on capital goods prices. The de Vries comparison of domestic and international prices allows us to look at the impact of prices of domestically produced and imported materials on gross price differences. The data for four countries and twenty-six items are too sparse to provide other than a rough indication of wide price differences among commodities and between countries. As de Vries pointed out, "the data should be interpreted with care" and "proposals for individual tariffs must be based on studies of individual products." It may be that the two forthcoming World Bank studies by Baranson and Cilingiroglu will provide a broader statistical base for more general policy conclusions.

In his discussion paper, Felix neatly summarized the data to highlight one not surprising conclusion—that price differences of domestically produced inputs are a more important factor in gross or final price differences than imported input prices. This raises a number of questions concerning productivity in the supplying industries, and the relative size of tariffs on the domestic materials industries compared to those on imported inputs. The special comparison raises questions of the relevance of the exchange rates for conversion. The Grunwald and Salazar paper deals particularly with the problem of evaluating competitiveness to take account of differences in price levels and equilibrium exchange rates in Latin America. Earlier this morning a comment by Ruggles reminded me of the Braithwaite-Dias price comparisons, which showed high prices in the Argentine and a number of other Latin American countries for capital compared to other goods.

There are other interesting points raised by these data, for example, the relatively high price of imported inputs for truck production. Does this reflect a peculiarity of the parent-subsidiary relationship which has wider relevance? Are the differences in the value-added prices related to labor or capital costs, or are they a function of efficiency, of market size, or of the degree of product specialization?

The data and the substance of underlying relationships would provide a better basis for understanding the price differences for capital goods which the de Vries paper sets out. But the whole thrust of the discussion around this point yesterday suggested that there may be serious limitations to drawing policy conclusions from this type of static price comparison about the effects of changes in tariffs or rates of exchange on scale, competitiveness, or resource allocation. Indeed, as the discussion between Balassa and Bhagwati suggested, there is still room for controversy about the relationship among productivity, prices, and exports.

De Vries has set out a short but comprehensive statement of the range of factors which affect price and competitiveness. As Baranson noted in his presentation, the next, but crucial, step is to assess the relative importance of these factors, before policy prescriptions become evident. Felix has already discussed some of the practical difficulties associated with the suggestion that tariff reductions provide a realistic answer to achieving a more competitive capital goods industry in the less developed countries. The paper by Ranis also emphasized the forces which act to preserve the established infant-industry "hothouse" environment.

Finally, I should like to re-emphasize a point already made by Felix. There is, among the less developed countries, a strong reversion to job creation as a prime goal of economic development. This may offend many economic sensibilities. But if it be true that the political, social, or economic circumstances require that employment become a priority goal, we should, perhaps, be evolving those "second-best" theories and prescriptions which take account of these realities and minimize the economic loss. It may be necessary to seek what Ranis has called "efficiency promotion" without abandoning the growth and commercial policy aspects of the infant-industry syndrome. As development policies become oriented to absorbing larger numbers of workers into the industrial mainstream, we may have to prescribe for what Bhagwati called "import substitution in an optimal way." We live in a world of multiple goals, and growing awareness of their conflict and interrelations may further constrain optimality and efficiency.

REPLY by JACK BARANSON FOR DE VRIES

1. On the point that the narrow sampling of individual industrial products does not give us an adequate basis for the conclusions drawn in the paper, I would agree that this is a legitimate criticism. As I pointed out in my presentation of the paper, there is a basic problem in making international cost comparisons. It relates to the comparability of items included and to the cost accounting systems used in different national environments. Using aggregated data for product groups runs the analyst into the difficult problems of comparing different baskets of goods (in terms of model variations, quality, or performance characteristics).

In the automotive products study, it was possible to get comparability among products manufactured in different national environments only by selecting near-identical vehicle models manufactured by a multinational firm with comparability among national accounting systems. Even within this common framework, adjustments had to be made for noncomparability in near-identical truck models, anomolies among accounting systems, and quality differences among national products.

2. Another criticism leveled at the paper is that the analysis does not tell us where the cost differences lie. These could be attributed to (a) differences in taxes and tariffs; (b) exchange rate anomalies; (c) varying operations. These differences are not articulated in the de Vries paper but have been dealt with in some depth in the automotive and electrical equipment studies cited there. The same applies to insights on the competitive position of capital goods industries, which are treated more definitely in the cited studies.

3. David Felix has questioned the paper's conclusion that tariffs

and overvalued exchange are the basic causes of high manufacturing costs. In a sense, we are dealing with a tautology, in that high costs are the creature of protection linked to an overvalued exchange rate, but the reverse is also true. It is true, as I indicated earlier in my remarks on the Ranis paper, that once industrialization under import substitution is carried to an extensive and excessive degree, cost efficiencies are undermined in other industries, including those that are export oriented. However, I do not believe that the prescription of "low-cost, low-technology" industries can be applied generally. The fact is that Argentina has exported $50 million to $100 million a year of fairly sophisticated industrial equipment, including machine lathes and IBM sorting machines. The chief disadvantages that manufacturing plants in developing countries face are scale and the dearth of supplier industries. If a plant manufactures at near-international scale, and if the country's trade policy allows a firm to import the high-cost range of materials and parts, a fairly broad range of manufacturing opportunities is feasible, including elements of the more complex engineering goods and capital equipment.[1]

[1] See Jack Baranson, *Manufacturing Problems in India,* Syracuse University Press, 1967, pp. 110 ff.

The Elasticity of Substitution as a Variable in World Trade

IRVING B. KRAVIS

UNIVERSITY OF PENNSYLVANIA AND

NATIONAL BUREAU OF ECONOMIC RESEARCH

AND

ROBERT E. LIPSEY

QUEENS COLLEGE AND

NATIONAL BUREAU OF ECONOMIC RESEARCH

PRICE changes, as well as income changes, play the major role in theoretical explanations of shifts in trade from one country to another. It has been natural, therefore, that economists have made many attempts to estimate the response of trade to price changes by calculating demand and substitution elasticities for individual countries' exports and imports. Our new estimates of international price levels and price changes, prepared as part of a recently published National Bureau study of price competitiveness in international trade,[1] provide an opportunity to carry forward this work on the basis of data which are in important respects more appropriate for the purpose than those previously available.

NOTE: The authors take pleasure in acknowledging helpful suggestions by Lawrence R. Klein. The computations were performed by Sultan Ahmad, Lorenzo Perez, and Jane Samuelson. The research reported on here is part of a National Bureau study of the role of prices in international trade, which is an outgrowth of the earlier work on international price measurement.

[1] Irving B. Kravis and Robert E. Lipsey, *Price Competitiveness in World Trade,* New York, NBER, 1971. See Chapter 6 for some earlier experimental calculations of elasticities on the basis of these data.

The main purpose of that study was to seek ways of improving the basic data on international prices for an important segment of trade in manufactured goods; machinery, transport equipment, and metal products.[2] The choice of this range of products was determined not only by their substantive importance in trade (about half of the exports of the main industrial countries) but also by the variety of competitive situations covered. They embrace all the stages of metal fabrication beginning with pig iron and its nonferrous equivalents and including differentiated products and custom-built goods as well as homogeneous products. Indexes were computed for 1953, 1957, and 1961 through 1964, for the United States, the United Kingdom, Germany, and, wherever possible, Japan. These indexes are distinguished from those used in other studies of international trade by several characteristics: (1) actual prices or price offers were used rather than unit values derived from trade statistics or domestic wholesale prices; (2) a uniform set of world trade weights (actually 1963 exports of member countries of the Organization for Economic Cooperation and Development) was employed in the aggregation of price indexes for each country, rather than the trade weights of the country itself; (3) country-to-country price relations for different points in time were used to aid in the establishment of intertemporal movements in price competitiveness; (4) price collection in terms of detailed preselected specifications was abandoned in favor of the collection of pairs of prices for specifications of the respondents' own choosing, each pair providing either a time-to-time or country-to-country price relative; and (5) regression techniques were employed to make international price comparisons for some commodity groups.

These data were used to prepare "indexes of price competitiveness" which measured the changes in relative prices for each pair of countries, usually at the four-digit SITC level.[3] In the present paper, how-

---

[2] SITC divisions 67 (iron and steel), 68 (nonferrous metals), 69 (manufactures of metals, n.e.s.), 71 (machinery other than electric), 72 (electrical machinery), and 73 (transport equipment).

[3] The index of price competitiveness is $[(P_t/P_{t-1})_F/(P_t/P_{t-1})_S] \times 100$, where P refers to prices, t to a time period, F to a foreign country, and S to the United States. It was usually formed by dividing time-to-time price changes for the foreign country by those of the United States, but in some categories it was derived from the change in the place-to-place price comparison, i.e., $(P_F/P_S)_t/(P_F/P_S)_{t-1}$. The latter method was employed particularly for custom-made goods for which place-to-place price comparisons could be obtained from bid data, but time-to-time data for any given country were difficult to obtain.

ever, we confine ourselves to aggregations of the price competitiveness indexes for two-digit categories. The potential number of observations on this level of aggregation for each pair of countries is 30
(5 periods times 6 categories) but in fact we have only 29 for the U.K.-
U.S. and for German-U.S. comparisons,[4] and only 10 for the Japa-
nese-U.S. comparisons owing to the paucity of data, particularly for
1953–57 and 1957–61.

A disadvantage of our data is that the observations cover only five
periods, and that estimates of substitution elasticities cannot be made
from time series in the usual way. While all five time periods have been
employed, data for the six different commodity divisions and three
different pairs of countries have been pooled in most of the calculations.

The basic form we have used in estimating price-quantity relationships relates the percentage change in relative exports (foreign to
United States) during a period to the percentage change in relative
prices (foreign to United States) including a constant term. That is,

$$(1) \quad [(Q_t/Q_{t-1})_F/(Q_t/Q_{t-1})_S] - 1 = a + b\{[(P_t/P_{t-1})_F/(P_t/P_{t-1})_S] - 1\}$$

where F represents the foreign country; S, the United States; Q, the
quantities exported; P, the international prices (export prices in the
large majority of cases, but domestic prices where exports of a particular category were nil or negligible); t, a reference year; and $t - 1$,
a preceding year.

The usual method of calculating demand or substitution elasticities
is to use as a price variable the ratio of one country's export price
index to another country's export or domestic price index or the ratio
of an index of import prices to an index of domestic prices. Since the
indexes used are usually not constructed specifically for these comparisons, the results do not represent the demand or substitution
elasticities they purport to. The indexes being compared may represent completely different collections of goods, or the same goods
with different weights, and the elasticities are then not own-price
elasticities, as they are intended to be, but rather a mixture of own-
price and cross elasticities. For example, more than one study has
produced a low estimate of the U.S. price elasticity of demand for

---

[4] For SITC 67, comparisons were made for 1961/1953 rather than 1957/1953 to avoid
the distorting effects of the Suez Crisis upon 1957 data.

raw material imports by comparing the movements of prices of imported raw materials with the price movements of domestically available raw materials—the former with large weights for crude rubber and raw silk, and the latter with small weights for these items and large weights for cotton and coal. Furthermore, since one or both of the collections of goods may be changing over time, there is little reason to expect the elasticities to be stable.

As already indicated, the prices used here for the estimation of elasticities of substitution have been collected specifically for the purpose of measuring changes in price competitiveness. Two assumptions, each related to the fact that we are dealing with four great industrial countries capable of producing a wide range of products, govern the way in which the prices have been used to form the relative price variable in equation (1):

1. The potential market of each country is represented by the aggregate of machinery and metal manufactures entering world markets. This means that the same set of weights, based on world trade, is used for aggregation for each country.

2. Price-induced substitutions favoring one of the countries as against another take place between products found within the same four-digit SITC code. It is German machine tools versus American machine tools, British trucks against American trucks, etc., that characterizes international competition. Of course, competition across four-digit categories such as British copper against American aluminum or British steam locomotives against American diesel locomotives can also be found, but an examination of the list of four-digit SITC categories led us to the judgment that such cases are much less important than those involving within-category competition.

In the results reported here we have confined our calculations to two-digit SITC divisions, and have ignored competition across the lines of four-digit SITC subgroups. However, it would be perfectly possible, using the data collected in the study, to use price indexes for one group in the explanation of exports in another group. For example, at a finer level of detail than we are presently reporting on, the change in U.S. exports of aluminum could be a function not only of income and relative prices of aluminum, but also of the ratio of U.S. aluminum prices to U.S. and foreign copper prices.

The relative change in export quantities, taken as the dependent variable in our equations, was derived by dividing the relative change in export values, $(X_t/X_{t-1})_F/(X_t/X_{t-1})_S$, where $X =$ export values, by the relative change in prices, $(P_t/P_{t-1})_F/(P_t/P_{t-1})_S$. The use of relative quantities rather than export values produces a higher coefficient of correlation and a higher elasticity of substitution. However, it should be kept in mind in interpreting these results that the elasticities of substitution derived by regressing relative quantities against relative prices are biased toward zero under certain circumstances.[5]

We begin by pooling all our data covering six two-digit groups, five time periods, and three pairs of countries. Using q's and p's to denote the measures of relative quantity and price change in (1),[6] we obtain

$$(2) \qquad q = 0.16 - 8.23p \qquad \bar{r}^2 = 0.29$$
$$ (2.5) \quad (5.3) \qquad S.E. = 0.53$$

The price elasticity of substitution is $-8\frac{1}{4}$. The positive value for the constant term may be interpreted as a trend toward a rise in foreign exports relative to those of the United States that is attributable to factors other than relative prices. These "nonprice" factors include the effects of changes in commercial policies, buyer preferences, supply availabilities (at fixed prices), and different rates of growth in various geographical markets, all of which may favor one country or another. They also include any effects on relative exports of the countries compared that are attributable to price changes in excluded countries.

If the constant term is interpreted as a trend, it must be trend per period. Since some of the periods were four years long and others only one, the idea of inserting a specific time variable to take account

---

[5] Cf. Guy H. Orcutt, "Measurement of Price Elasticities in International Trade," *Review of Economics and Statistics,* May 1950; G. D. A. MacDougall, "British and American Exports: A Study Suggested by the Theory of Comparative Costs," Part II, *Economic Journal,* September 1952; and Raymond E. Zelder, "Estimates of Elasticities of Demand for Exports of the United Kingdom and the United States, 1921–1938," *Manchester School of Economic and Social Studies,* January 1958, p. 34.

[6] q is the entire expression on the left side of equation (1), and p is the expression for which b is the coefficient.

of this difference suggested itself. The time variable, entered as "4" or "1," [7] can, in combination with the constant term, produce any combination of trends per year before and after 1961 that will best fit the data. Of course, it still is not possible to distinguish the effects of any change in trend over time from the effects of differences between one-year and four-year periods in general, since the two four-year periods make up the period before 1961. However, even if we cannot fully explain the cause of the differences, it is clearly preferable to take account of them rather than to ignore them as in equation 2.

When the time variable is added, the equation becomes:

$$(3) \qquad q = -0.14 + 0.14T - 6.22p \qquad \bar{R}^2 = .42$$
$$ (4.0) \quad (4.03) \quad (4.1) \qquad S.E. = .48$$

The time coefficient is significant and the elasticity is smaller. The implication is that the elasticity in the earlier equation was biased upward because it included part of the effect of a nonprice trend against the exports of the United States, a country which tended also to have adverse (relatively rising) price movements in the two four-year periods before 1961. The combination of the constant and the T coefficient in the present set of equations tells us that the foreign-to-U.S. quantity ratio tended to rise, owing to nonprice factors, by $10\frac{1}{2}$ per cent per annum $\{[-.14 + (.14 \times 4)] \div 4)\}$ before 1961 and to have no trend after that date $[-.14 + (.14 \times 1)]$.

An alternative possibility might be that the elasticities differed before and after 1961 simply because four-year periods provide more time for adjustments to changes in relative prices than do one-year periods. This can be tested by comparing the results for the two kinds of periods with each other and with those for the three-year period, 1964–61, within which the one-year periods all fall. Using the subscript "4" to refer to the 23 observations for 1957–53 and 1961–57, "3" to refer to the 15 observations for 1964–61, and "1" to refer to the

---

[7] In a few cases "8" was the length of the period. The effects of the formation of the European Economic Community, which began reducing internal tariffs in January 1959, and of the European Free Trade Association, which began cutting internal tariffs in July 1960, are among the many influences we have not tried to take specifically into account.

45 observations for 1962–61, 1963–62, and 1964–63, the equations
are:

(4) $q_4 = 0.37 - 11.11p_4$ $\bar{r}^2 = .34$ $S.E. = .81$
     (2.2)   (3.5)

(5) $q_3 = 0.07 - 5.03p_3$ $\bar{r}^2 = .38$ $S.E. = .24$
     (1.1)   (3.1)

(6) $q_1 = 0.01 - 2.22p_1$ $\bar{r}^2 = .29$ $S.E. = .11$
     (0.5)   (4.3)

The higher coefficient for p in equation 5 relative to equation 6
suggests that longer duration produces a higher observed elasticity
of substitution. However, it seems unlikely that the one-year difference between the length of the two periods before 1961 and the three-
year period after 1961 can account for the whole of the difference
between an elasticity of substitution of −11 and one of −5.[8]

This raises the question as to why the elasticity of substitution should
have been so high before 1961 and so low afterward. Alternatively,
the issue may be the difference in nonprice trends before and after
1961. In either case, the implication is that estimates of elasticity of
substitution have to be evaluated in terms of the historical context
from which the data for their estimation are drawn.

As a background for discussing this matter, it is useful to set out the
average percentage (unweighted) changes in the relative prices and
quantities for the four- and one-year periods (the former include
eight-year periods for SITC 67):

	p	q
Four-year periods	−1.3	+48.9
One-year periods	+0.5	−0.3
All periods	−0.1	+16.4

The small average decline in U.S. price competitiveness during the
four-year periods and the still smaller average increase during the
one-year periods cannot be regarded as the net results of widely dif-

---

[8] These coefficients differ from those reported in *Price Competitiveness in World Trade*
mainly because data for Japan are included here. The data excluding Japan yielded a
very low elasticity for the three-year period.

fering changes in relative prices for different two-digit categories and periods. The changes in relative prices were generally small, only three out of the 68 having been greater than 10 per cent and only seven others greater than 5 per cent. The changes in relative quantities showed much greater dispersion, nearly half being in excess of 10 per cent.

We turn now to some possible explanations for the apparent differences in the elasticity of substitution before and after 1961. This search for explanations for the particular differences we have found will serve also to call attention to some of the various kinds of influences that, in general, affect observed elasticities of substitution.

1   The Recapture-of-Shares Explanation

It is conceivable that the large quantity changes at a time of small relative decreases in foreign relative prices may have represented the final stages of the restoration of trading relationships that were disturbed by the war. Indeed, immediately after the war, West European countries were relying so heavily upon the United States as a source of supply that one of the important aims of the Marshall Plan was to increase intra-European trade. We selected 1953 as the starting date for our study because the recovery of Europe could be regarded as substantially completed by that date, but it is not unlikely that the process of recapturing lost market positions continued into the 1953–61 period, particularly for Germany and Japan.

If this were the explanation, it would be interesting to know more about the mechanism through which the recapture of former markets worked. Perhaps small declines in relative prices were associated with large increases in relative quantities simply because of the re-establishment of old customer loyalties or the reassertion of the advantages of location or of banking and distribution skills. It is more likely that this awaited or was facilitated by the recovery of supply capacities in the war-devastated countries.

Explanations along these lines have underlying implications concerning domestic and export price policies during the periods of scarcity. In perfectly free markets, optimizing firms would have charged high export prices during the period in which their exports were limited by supply scarcities. If, however, they were limited in their freedom to raise export prices by price levels set by the United States, and they preferred to supply the home market even at lower prices or were pressed to do so by their governments, improving supply conditions might have produced the observed results.

Further light could be thrown upon the recapture-of-shares hypothesis by a study of pre- and postwar shares for particular product groups in particular markets.

2 *Supply Elasticity Explanations*

The recapture-of-shares explanations may be regarded as a subgroup under a more general category of the effects of supply elasticity differences. The calculated substitution elasticities may reflect not only measurements derived from shifts in supply along the demand curve but also differences in supply responses to the same change in demand (i.e., differences in the slopes of supply curves) even when there are no shifts in supply curves.

It is, of course, difficult to estimate supply elasticities for exports, and recent work has fallen back on the use of activity variables (growth of GNP, extent of idle capacity, etc.). It is reasonable to suppose that supply elasticities are related to domestic economic activity, but it is not easy to say what the relationship can be expected to be. In the short run, growth in production to near-capacity levels should result in low observed supply elasticities. In the longer run, however, growth in production and capacity reflect high observed supply elasticities. Capacity is increasing, the economies of long production runs become attainable for more and more product variants, and productivity is rising on other accounts. In addition, expansion may bring new product variants which were not available for export before. These favorable consequences depend, however, on a situation in which the growth of demand is not outstripping the growth of aggregate supply. If aggregate demand is excessive it will lead to shipment delays, diversion of potential exports to domestic purchasers, and, depending on economic conditions abroad, possibly to relative inflation and thus to price disadvantages for exports.

It is not easy to sort out these matters, but for the products and times covered in our study the periods of rapid expansion in foreign exports relative to those of the United States were marked by rela-

tively rapid foreign growth, as shown by the table below, which gives
annual rates of growth in real product: [9]

	1953–61	1961–64
U.S. (GNP)	2.4	3.9
U.K. (GDP)	2.9	3.7
Germany (GDP)	7.0	3.5
Japan (GNP)	11.5	9.8

The data are thus consistent with the hypothesis that rapid growth
gives a significant export advantage as long as it is not accompanied
by a relative increase in prices, but they do not, of course, prove it.

3 Absolute Differences in Prices

It is possible that relative price levels (P_F/P_S) as well as changes in
relative prices (p) affected the changes in relative quantities. If the exchange rates that were established at the end of the war caused
foreign price levels to be lower than U.S. price levels, some relative
rise in foreign exports could have been expected even without a
further relative decline in foreign prices; the response to a decline in
foreign relative prices might therefore appear to be very great.

When a variable L is added to measure the effects on q of the percentage difference in the foreign and U.S. price levels,[10] we obtain:

(7) $\qquad q = 0.17 - 8.22p + .05L \qquad\qquad \bar{R}^2 = .28$
$\qquad\qquad$ (1.6)$\quad$ (5.2)$\quad\;$ (.06) $\qquad\qquad\quad$ S.E. $= .53$

(8) $\qquad q = -0.20 - 6.25p - 0.43L + 0.15T \qquad \bar{R}^2 = .41$
$\qquad\qquad$ (1.2)$\quad$ (4.1)$\quad\;$ (0.6)$\quad\;\;$ (4.06) $\qquad$ S.E. $= .48$

(9) $\qquad q_4 = -0.03 - 12.56p - 4.88L \qquad\qquad \bar{R}^2 = .36$
$\qquad\qquad$ (0.09)$\quad$ (3.8)$\quad\;\;$ (1.34) $\qquad\qquad$ S.E. $= .79$

(10) $\qquad q_1 = -0.03 - 2.17p - 0.29L \qquad\qquad \bar{R}^2 = .32$
$\qquad\qquad$ (1.1)$\quad$ (4.3)$\quad\;$ (1.7) $\qquad\qquad\quad$ S.E. $= .11$

A small or insignificant coefficient for L may mean that the difference in price levels at the beginning of a period, if any exists, repre-

---

[9] Based on data in the United Nations *Yearbook of National Accounts Statistics, 1966
and 1968.*
[10] $L = (P_F/P_S)_{t-1} - 1.$

sents an equilibrium situation. Such differences did exist in each of the five periods, and for the average of all included goods, changed very little, the U.K.-U.S. ratio varying within the 91–94 range and the German-U.S. ratio varying between 90 and 93. The coefficients for *L* suggest that, while there was probably a tendency for foreign relative quantities to rise more when foreign price levels were low, this influence was not a powerful factor. The failure of *L* to exert a greater influence and the persistence over eleven years of a situation in which U.S. prices were 6 to 10 per cent above those of its main competitors may, incidentally, have some adverse implications for the contention that the dollar was overvalued during this period.[11]

In any case, the difference in the calculated elasticity of substitution before and after 1961 does not appear to be explicable in terms of a rapid or gradual adjustment of relative exports to differences in beginning-of-period price levels.

4 Higher Price Elasticities of Demand for Foreign Goods

The fact that foreign relative prices were decreasing in 1953–61 and slightly increasing in 1961–64 might yield different estimates of elasticities of substitution for the two periods if the exports of the foreign countries had higher price elasticities of demand than U.S. exports. There are indeed a priori reasons for believing that this difference in price elasticities exists: More than for other large industrial countries, U.S. exports depend on technological sophistication, special-purpose uses, and speed of delivery.[12] However, if this were an important explanatory factor the behavior of foreign and U.S. prices over time, each taken separately, rather than the movement of foreign prices in relation to U.S. prices would be the appropriate independent variables. Equations using the time-to-time movement

---

[11] Of course, the difference in price levels we have found may have been offset by opposite differences in the types of goods not covered in our study. Also, while the overall U.S. trade surplus did not show a downward trend during the period, it may be claimed that U.S. needs for foreign exchange for purposes other than commodity imports required a larger or expanding trade surplus. However, if attention is confined to the trade account and if there were not offsetting differences in prices for other goods, the evidence would weigh against the claim that the dollar was overvalued. See Kravis and Lipsey, *Competitiveness,* Chap. 2, for a brief discussion of the factors that might have made the price level difference referred to in the text sustainable.

[12] Cf. *ibid.*

of foreign (P_F) and U.S. (P_S) prices are as follows:

(11) $q_4 = 4.05 - 16.70P_{4F} + 13.22P_{4S}$ $\bar{R}^2 = .35$
                  (1.3)   (3.6)   (3.5)   S.E. $= .80$

(12) $q_1 = 1.51 - .01P_{1F} - 1.50P_{1S}$ $\bar{R}^2 = .04$
                  (0.8)   (.5)   (0.8)   S.E. $= .13$

Neither equation can be regarded as an improvement over equations (4) and (6) in which changes in *relative* prices were used as the independent variable. The coefficients for the four-year periods [equation (11)] conform to expectations with respect to signs and a higher impact for changes in foreign prices than for changes in U.S. prices. For the one-year periods the results are much worse; the sign of P_{1S} is wrong and the relationship is not statistically significant ($F_{2,42} = 1.93$). In neither equation is the difference between the two coefficients statistically significant.

Different coefficients for P_F and P_S would imply lack of complete success in our effort to compare foreign and U.S. price changes for directly competitive goods. Also, were these two coefficients not equal, one of the underlying theoretical requirements for the valid measurement of the elasticity of substitution would not be met. The required condition is that $\alpha_F + \beta_F = \alpha_S + \beta_S$, where $\alpha =$ the price elasticity of demand and $\beta =$ the cross elasticity with respect to the good of the other country.[13]

5   Differences in Income Elasticities of Demand

World incomes rose more in the four-year periods than in the one-year periods. If the varieties of goods exported by the foreign countries were marked by greater income elasticities than the varieties exported by the United States, the omission of an income term from equations (4) and (6) would bias the estimate of price elasticity in (4) upward relative to that in (6).

When the relative change in export quantities is related to changes in world income as measured by the U.N. series on world gross

[13] Cf. E. E. Leamer and Robert M. Stern, *Quantitative International Economics*, Boston, Allyn and Bacon, 1970, Chap. 3; and Zelder, "Estimates."

domestic production,[14] the results are as follows:

(13) $\qquad q = -0.19 + 0.04G - 6.11p \qquad \bar{R}^2 = .44$
$\qquad\qquad\quad (1.9) \quad (3.4) \quad\ \ (4.2) \qquad\quad S.E. = .47$

(14) $\qquad q_4 = -0.57 + 0.05G_4 - 8.00p_4 \qquad \bar{R}^2 = .38$
$\qquad\qquad\quad (0.9) \quad (1.5) \quad\ \ (2.2) \qquad\quad S.E. = .79$

(15) $\qquad q_1 = 0.13 - 0.02G_1 - 2.03p_1 \qquad \bar{R}^2 = .29$
$\qquad\qquad\quad (1.2) \quad (1.2) \quad\ \ (3.8) \qquad\quad S.E. = .11$

where G stands for the percentage change in real-world GDP and the other symbols have the same meanings as in the earlier equations.

It can be seen that equation (13), which includes all observations, is not substantially different from equation (3), in which a time variable was used in lieu of G. The reason is that the annual percentage rates of growth in world gross domestic product did not vary much from one period to another and were almost equivalent to a scaled version of the time variable: [15]

	Time	Per Cent Increase in World GDP
1957–53	4	16
1961–57	4	17
1962–61	1	5
1963–62	1	4
1964–63	1	6

If growth in real world income really were the true explanation, rather than some other unspecified factors subsumed under T in equation (3), we should obtain significant coefficients for G within the two four-year periods and within the three one-year periods. In fact, the G coefficient is significant for neither set of periods [equations

[14] *Yearbook of National Accounts Statistics, 1968,* Vol. II, p. 119.

[15] We experimented with both industrial production and world manufactures export volume as alternatives to gross domestic product. The export series was more variable from one period to another, but its explanatory power was smaller than that of GDP, the $\bar{R}^2$ for the equation analagous to (12) being 0.37. Industrial production did better $(\bar{R}^2 = .40)$, but neither industrial production nor exports has a superior theoretical claim to priority over GDP for this purpose. In any case, all three yield elasticities of substitution in the range from −6.4 (industrial production) to −6.9 (exports).

(14) and (15)], and in one of the cases [equation (15)] the sign points to higher income elasticity for U.S. exports.

The test may be unfair in view of the small variation in income changes between the two four-year periods and among the three one-year periods. On the other hand, the growth rates are hardly atypical of what we may expect in the future; it would take great economic success to raise the one-year rates a few percentage points above 6 per cent and great economic calamity to drive them down a few points below 4 per cent. The fact that the coefficients of *G* are not larger or statistically significant is therefore ground for rejecting the hypothesis that differences in the response of foreign and U.S. exports to income growth accounted for the differences in the elasticities of substitution before and after 1961.

As in the case of the price elasticities of demand, the finding of a substantial impact of income growth upon relative exports would reduce our confidence in our success in having compared prices for identical or at least directly substitutable products. Theoretically, a zero coefficient for *G* is another of the conditions for the validity of elasticity-of-substitution measures.[16]

6   The Effect of Market Shares upon the Elasticities

The difference in response of relative quantities to price changes before and after 1961 may be related to another finding from the price competitiveness study, namely, that there was an asymmetry in the response to relative price changes between cases of increases and decreases in U.S. price competitiveness. The response to the latter was much greater than to the former. The two time periods can be distinguished by the fact that declines in U.S. price competitiveness predominated in the early period, while improvements were more frequent in the later years.

One explanation for these asymmetries might be that the response of quantity changes to price changes is not uniform under all circumstances and that it may be sensitive, in particular, to the market share of each country included in the comparison.

The smaller the share of the market a country has, the larger the

---

[16] Leamer and Stern, *Economics*. In our equations q plays the same role as q_1/q_2 in theirs.

potential benefit it can reap from a decline in its relative prices. If its share is large, the export expansion it can expect from a price decline may be small in relative terms, because it cannot gain much at the expense of other sellers and finds its expansion limited by the market price elasticity (see curve labeled "$P_{F/S}$ declining" in Figure 1). When prices are rising (price competitiveness declining), a country with a high share is vulnerable to losses and therefore has a high elasticity of substitution. The relation of elasticity to market share is less easy to predict when prices are rising for a country with a low market share. It is possible that it is already relying only on those markets in which it is entrenched, and thus has a low elasticity. That is the relation suggested by "$P_{F/S}$ rising" in the figure. But it could also be argued that large percentage reactions can most easily take place where exports (and export shares) are small; this would, for example, be the case if a country with a small share were knocked out of the market completely by a rise in its relative prices.

In any case, the elasticity of substitution may be asymmetrically related to market shares, changing differently for falling and rising relative prices. [Were the U.S. relative share plotted on the horizontal axis, the diagram would be similar except that the identity of the

FIGURE 1

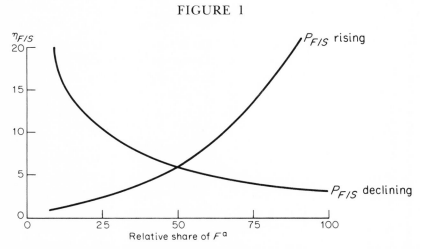

a Actual numbers on axes are used solely to make the diagram more tangible, and are not meant to convey the quantitative relationships.

curves for rising and falling relative prices ($P_{F/S}$) would be reversed.]

Average (unweighted) market shares for the six two-digit SITC categories were as follows:

	U.S.	U.K.	Germany	Japan	OECD
1953	30	20	14	2	100
1957	29	23	18	6	100
1961	21	16	21	6	100
1962	22	15	22	6	100
1963	21	14	20	7	100
1964	21	13	19	7	100

It can be seen that the United States did in fact have high shares at the earlier dates and that by 1961 the U.S. shares were lower and not much different from those of Germany.

The range of export shares among two-digit groups, the relevant consideration for this discussion, is considerably wider. Japan accounts for most of the very low export shares, particularly in the early years; and the United States, the highest proportion of the large export shares, again concentrated in the beginning of the period.

In seeking to test the expectations of asymmetries associated with shares, we make the coefficient b in equation (3) dependent on relative shares and the direction of price movement:

$$b = f(S_S, S_F, S'_S, S'_F)$$

where subscripts have the same meanings as before and S stands for the share of each country in OECD exports, the primed figures for the cases in which foreign prices were rising relative to those of the United States, and the unprimed figures for the cases in which foreign relative prices were falling.[17] The estimating equation for q may then be taken as

$$(16) \qquad q = \alpha + \beta p + \gamma S_F p + \delta S_S p + \epsilon p' + \theta S_F p' + \lambda S_S p'$$

where the p' represent the product of p and a dummy variable which takes the value of 1 for observations in which p is positive (i.e., foreign prices are rising relative to U.S. ones), and 0 for observations in which p is negative. The results, first for all periods and then separately for

---

[17] That is, p or $\{[(P_t/P_{t-1})_F/(P_t/P_{t-1})_S] - 1\}$ was positive for the S' figures and negative for the S ones.

the four- and one-year periods are as follows:

(17) $q = -.05 - 15.23p + 1.37S_Fp - 0.83S_sp$
      (.6)   (2.2)   (3.0)   (3.7)

$$+ 11.34p' - 1.49S_Fp' + 1.11S_sp'$$
$$(1.2) \qquad (2.3) \qquad (3.3)$$

$$\bar{R}^2 = .53 \qquad S.E. = .43$$

(18) $q_4 = .11 - 36.46p_4 + 2.64S_Fp_4 - 0.68S_sp_4 - 79.15p'_4$
      (.5)   (2.2)   (2.5)   (1.4)   (0.7)

$$+ 1.99S_Fp'_4 + 1.25S_sp'_4$$
$$(0.4) \qquad (1.3)$$

$$\bar{R}^2 = .53 \qquad S.E. = .68$$

(19) $q_1 = .01 - 11.52p_1 + 0.42S_Fp_1 + 0.26S_sp_1 + 9.50p'_1$
      (.5)   (5.2)   (3.0)   (2.3)   (3.4)

$$- 0.59S_Fp'_1 - .12S_sp'_1$$
$$(3.3) \qquad (.8)$$

$$\bar{R}^2 = .49 \qquad S.E. = .09$$

In these equations, the coefficients of the unprimed variables refer to the cases in which foreign prices are falling relative to U.S. prices. The coefficients for the primed variables in the equation show the amounts by which the coefficients for rising foreign prices differ from those for falling foreign prices. The t ratios for the p' terms refer to the significance of the difference, and not to the significance of the relationship between quantity change and price change when foreign prices are rising. Essentially the same analysis may be performed by estimating separate equations for the cases of falling and rising prices. For example, such equations corresponding to equation (17) are:

Foreign prices falling ($p < 0$)

(17a) $q = -.05 - 15.24p + 1.37S_Fp - 0.83S_sp$
               (.4)   (1.6)   (2.1)   (2.8)

$$\bar{R}^2 = .50 \qquad S.E. = .60$$

Foreign prices rising $(p > 0)$

(17b) $\qquad q = -0.04 - 4.01p - .11S_Fp + 0.28S_Sp$
$\qquad\qquad\quad (1.0) \quad (1.7) \quad\; (.7) \qquad\; (3.1)$

$$\bar{R}^2 = .22 \qquad S.E. = .16$$

In general, the coefficients conform well to the model set out in the diagram. When foreign prices are falling relative to U.S. prices [equation (17a), "$P_{F/S}$ declining" in Figure 1, and unprimed p in equations (17) to (19)], the coefficient for the product of the foreign share (S_F) and negative p should have a positive sign if a high foreign share acts as a deterrent to the relative expansion of foreign export quantities, and the coefficient for S_Sp should have a negative sign if a high U.S. share facilitates the expansion of relative foreign exports. The first expectation (positive coefficient for S_Fp) is satisfied in all three equations and the second in the first two. When foreign relative prices are rising [equation (17b), "$P_{F/S}$ rising" in the diagram, and p' in the equations], the sum of the coefficients for S_Fp and S_Fp' in equations (17)–(19) should be negative and the sum of the coefficients for S_Sp and S_Sp' should be positive. The corresponding two conditions for equation (17b) are that the coefficient of S_Fp should be negative and that for S_Sp positive. The first of these conditions is found in equations (17), (17b), and (19), and the latter in all the equations. Although equations (17), (17a), and (17b), which cover all periods, pass all tests, the equation for the four-year periods has the wrong sign for S_Fp' and the equation for the one-year periods has the wrong sign for S_Sp. In each of the two latter instances the variance of the shares was low relative to the variances for the situations in which the same coefficients conformed to the model.

These equations make the elasticity of substitution a variable, the size of which depends upon the shares in trade and the direction of the price change. Taking some illustrative shares on the basis of the unweighted observed averages given in an earlier text table, the elasticities of substitution derived from equation (17)[18] are as follows:

[18] In terms of equation (16) the elasticities for $P_{F/S}$ falling (η_p) and rising ($\eta_{p'}$) are:

$$\eta_p = \beta + \gamma S_F + \delta S_S$$

and

$$\eta_{p'} = \beta + \epsilon + (\gamma + \theta)S_F + (\delta + \lambda)S_S$$

	$P_{F/S}$ Declining	$P_{F/S}$ Rising
$S_F = 15,\ S_S = 30$	-19.58	$+2.71$
$S_F = 15,\ S_S = 20$	-11.88	-0.09
$S_F = 20,\ S_S = 20$	-4.43	-0.69

Even though the coefficients are significant and have the correct signs, the equation produces elasticities for rising $P_{F/S}$ that have to be rejected. We are unable to explain this result other than to point to the imperfections in the market share and quantity data, particularly the improper inclusion of domestic markets, mentioned below. Perhaps more data will improve the result or a different specification of the relationship, particularly that involving the shares, may be needed.

When other variables discussed above such as T, T and L, or L and G are added to the variables in equation (17), they do not greatly alter the coefficients of the p and Sp variables; the coefficients of the added variables usually have t values between 1 and 2 and do not affect the $\bar{R}^2$ very much either. This can be seen in the following equation in which T and L have been added:

$$(20) \quad q = -0.27 + 0.10T - 14.78p + 1.54S_F p - 0.79S_S p$$
$$ (2.4) \quad (2.6) \quad\ (2.2) \quad\ (3.5) \quad\ (3.5)$$

$$+ 12.80p' - 1.76S_F p' + 1.00S_S p' - 0.81L$$
$$(1.3) \quad\ (2.8) \quad\quad (2.9) \quad\quad (1.2)$$

$$\bar{R}^2 = .58 \quad\quad S.E. = .41$$

The equations described thus far involve the assumption that changes in relative quantities depend not only on changes in relative prices, but also on certain other variables, particularly shares. The pooling of the data for different commodity groups and for different countries implicitly assumes that the relationships are not affected by differences in commodity or country. Since the commodities range from standardized metals to complex machinery, with probably different price behavior and different degrees of response to price change, the assumption that relationships do not differ among commodities is a hazardous one. However, it is not clear how one should expect the quantity-price relationships of various groups to differ.

One would expect that where there is product differentiation along national lines, as is at least partially true, for example, between U.S. and German automobiles, quantity responses will not be as great as, say, in metal products, where there is a greater degree of standardization. It is conceivable, however, that the true quantity responses may be unobservable for highly standardized products because similar export price changes are imposed in all the countries by market forces. We have some evidence [19] that export price movements are more alike than domestic price changes, and trade shifts for standardized goods could come about principally through the operation of domestic supply elasticities in countries with declining competitiveness.[20]

The number of observations on the two-digit commodity level is small, and we have therefore divided the commodities into only two groups which we shall call "metals" (M) and "equipment" (E). The former includes iron and steel (SITC 67) and nonferrous metals (SITC 68); the latter, metal manufactures (SITC 69), nonelectrical machinery (SITC 71), electrical machinery (SITC 72), and transport equipment (SITC 73). The results, based on 21 observations for M and 47 for E, are:

For "metals":

$$(21) \qquad q_M = .09 - 8.96p_M \qquad \bar{r}^2 = .30$$
$$ (.6) \quad (3.1) \qquad S.E. = .68$$

$$(22) \qquad q_M = -0.24 + .16T - 4.63p_M \qquad \bar{R}^2 = .40$$
$$ (1.1) \quad (2.0) \quad\ \ (1.4) \qquad S.E. = .63$$

$$(23) \quad q_M = -0.85 - 0.2T - 7.66p_M + 1.67S_F p_M - 1.24S_S p_M$$
$$ (1.7) \quad (1.1) \quad (0.4) \quad\ \ (1.4) \quad\quad (1.1)$$

$$- 23.95p'_M - 1.59S_F p'_M + 3.61S_S p'_M - 4.07L$$
$$(0.6) \quad\quad\ (1.0) \quad\quad\ (1.7) \quad\quad (2.0)$$

$$\bar{R}^2 = .42 \qquad S.E. = .62$$

---

[19] Kravis and Lipsey, *Competitiveness*, Chap. 8.

[20] See Robert M. Stern and Elliot Zupnick, "The Theory and Measurement of Elasticity of Substitution in International Trade," *Kyklos*, 1962, Fasc. 3.

For "equipment":

(24)
$$q_E = 0.19 - 7.73 p_E \qquad \bar{r}^2 = .25$$
$$(2.8) \quad (4.1) \qquad S.E. = .46$$

(25)
$$q_E = -0.13 + 0.15T - 7.50 p_E \qquad \bar{R}^2 = .41$$
$$(1.2) \quad (3.6) \quad (4.4) \qquad S.E. = .41$$

(26)
$$q_E = -.04 + 0.10T - 15.43 p_E + 2.47 S_F p_E - 1.09 S_S p_E$$
$$(.5) \quad (2.7) \quad (2.0) \quad (5.7) \quad (3.6)$$

$$+ 20.46 p'_E - 3.03 S_F p'_E + 1.24 S_S p'_E + 0.87 L$$
$$(1.6) \quad (4.4) \quad (2.5) \quad (1.4)$$

$$\bar{R}^2 = .73 \qquad S.E. = .28$$

Simple relationships [equations (21), (22), (24), and (25)] as well as those involving the share variables [equations (23) and (26)] are shown. In the latter equations, the coefficients of the S_p and $(S_p + S_{p'})$ variables all have the correct signs. However, both equations yield elasticities that are positive for a number of realistic S_F and S_S combinations, particularly when foreign relative prices are rising.

The same variables used in separate equations for the 29 U.K.-U.S. observations (K/S) and for the 29 Germany-U.S. observations (G/S) produce results as follows:

$$q_{K/S} = -0.10 + 0.03T - 14.78 p + 1.40 S_F p - 0.58 S_S p$$
$$(1.9) \quad (1.3) \quad (1.8) \quad (1.5) \quad (1.4)$$

$$+ 21.67 p' - 3.10 S_F p' + 1.44 S_S p' - 28 L$$
$$(2.1) \quad (2.4) \quad (2.8) \quad (.6)$$

$$\bar{R}^2 = .58 \qquad S.E. = .15$$

$$q_{G/S} = -0.41 + 0.17T - 32.43 p + 2.48 S_F p - 0.46 S_S p$$
$$(2.0) \quad (2.0) \quad (2.0) \quad (2.1) \quad (1.1)$$

$$+ 32.37 p' - 3.45 S_F p' + 0.92 S_S p' - 5.10 L$$
$$(1.7) \quad (2.0) \quad (1.3) \quad (1.9)$$

$$\bar{R}^2 = .59 \qquad S.E. = .46$$

Both the U.K.-U.S. and the Germany-U.S. equations have coefficients with signs that conform to the a priori expectations set out above [as does equation (17)].

It seems likely that the high U.S. share at the beginning of our period helped to explain the large responsiveness of relative quantities to declining relative foreign prices. The share and other variables we have introduced do not, however, fully explain the observed differences in the elasticity of substitution before and after 1961 or its asymmetry for declining and rising relative foreign prices.

However, the share variables perform well enough to suggest that the usual procedure of seeking a single measure of the response of quantities to price changes is invalid, and that this responsiveness is itself a variable dependent on other factors.[21]

We have at this stage hardly done more than identify some of these factors. The results reported here represent an early stage in our planned exploration of quantity-price relations in international trade. The market share variable itself is not properly applied to the world market as a whole, since conditions of competition, and therefore the response to price change, may differ from one market to another. A country may have reached a ceiling on its exports to one area while its share is still low in the world market as a whole. We plan to analyze the response to price changes in several divisions of the world market both for these reasons and also to eliminate the domestic markets of competing countries which tend to distort the results reported here because each country's sales on its own domestic market are omitted.

A further extension of this work will be the analysis of price-quantity reactions on a more detailed commodity breakdown, as far as that can be carried out within the limits of the trade statistics. The results so far must be affected by the heterogeneity of the two-digit SITC divisions which combine many products not linked by any competitive relationship.

[21] Mention might also be made of the difference in the measured elasticity that may be produced when observations are based on changes in individual prices rather than on the broad changes in $P_{F/S}$ that result from a devaluation. If there are significant cross elasticities of demand between two exports of one of the countries, the elasticity of substitution between the exports of the two countries will differ for the two types of price change. Cf. Zelder, "Estimates."

COMMENT
ROBERT M. STERN, University of Michigan

The appropriate starting point for my comment may be to ask why one wishes to measure the elasticity of substitution in world trade. Historically speaking, the main reason was that ordinary least squares analysis of import and export demand functions, based mainly on interwar data, frequently yielded price elasticities that were so low as to cast doubt on the efficacy of the international price mechanism. The elasticity of substitution was a conceptual alternative that apparently yielded empirical results more in accord with a priori presumptions concerning relatively high price elasticities. More recently, this concept has been prominent in models designed to explain relative export performance.

In pursuing the measurement of the elasticity of substitution over the years, it has too often been overlooked that its theoretical foundation is rather shaky. Let me elaborate briefly.

THEORETICAL FOUNDATION [1]

In terms of utility analysis, the elasticity of substitution is rigorously defined with respect to movement along a single indifference curve. However, since the value of this elasticity will depend upon the particular indifference curve selected as well as upon relative prices, it is necessary to impose the assumption that there be equal proportional responses of the quantities of each good to changes in the levels of all other variables, chiefly income and the prices of other goods. All of this presumes, furthermore, that the two goods are not identical, since if they were, the indifference curves would be straight lines and the analysis would be trivial.

NOTE: The preparation of this comment benefited materially from discussion with Edward E. Leamer, J. David Richardson, and other members of the Research Seminar in International Economics at the University of Michigan.

[1] This section draws upon the discussion presented in Edward E. Leamer and Robert M. Stern, *Quantitative International Economics*, Boston, Allyn and Bacon, 1970, especially pp. 57–63.

In order to clarify matters further, suppose now that we move from a utility framework to conventional demand analysis, and write the following export demand functions:

$$(1) \qquad q_1 = f(p_1, p_2, y, p_n)$$

and

$$q_2 = g(p_1, p_2, y, p_n),$$

where q_1 and q_2 and p_1 and p_2 refer to the quantities and prices of the respective goods; y, to money income in the importing country; and p_n, to the general price level in this country of goods other than 1 and 2. Assuming constant-elasticity approximations to equation (1), we can then write:

$$(2) \qquad q_1/q_2 = (a/b)[(p_1^{\alpha_1-\beta_1})/(p_2^{\beta_2-\alpha_2})]y^{\alpha_y-\beta_y}(p_n)^{\alpha_n-\beta_n}$$

where the α's and β's refer to the elasticities of the respective variables. Holding money income and other prices constant, it is evident from equation (2) that q_1/q_2 will be functionally related to p_1/p_2 in terms of the elasticity of substitution (e) only if the exponents of the price variables are equal:

$$(3) \qquad e = \alpha_1 - \beta_1 = \beta_2 - \alpha_2, \text{ or } \alpha_1 + \alpha_2 = \beta_1 + \beta_2$$

Equation (3) asserts that the sum of the direct and cross elasticities of demand be the same for each commodity. With respect to money income and other prices, it also follows from equation (2) that the income elasticities and cross-price elasticities must be comparable, that is $\alpha_y = \beta_y$ and $\alpha_n = \beta_n$. Now whether or not the foregoing equalities hold is a question of fact rather than theory. This suggests that the proper test of their validity and thus of the concept of the elasticity of substitution is a regression of the form:

$$(4) \qquad \log(q_1/q_2) = a + b_1 \log p_1 + b_2 \log p_2 + c \log y + d \log p_n.$$

The hypothesis represented by equations (2) and (3) could then be examined by testing whether $-b_1 = b_2$ and whether $c = d = 0$.

MEASUREMENT

In their equations (2)–(6), Kravis and Lipsey (K-L) have imposed the a priori assumption on the data that $-b_1 = b_2$ and that $c = d = 0$.

Their apparent justification for this stemmed from the way in which their data were gathered. Since their success in data gathering could not be assured in advance and if equation (4) above is granted, the K-L regression results presented in their equations (2)–(6) are, strictly speaking, not acceptable. Their most meaningful results are, in contrast, contained in equations (11) and (12) in which the changes in foreign and U.S. prices are entered separately, and in equations (13)–(15) which contain a world income variable. Despite the authors' contention that the separate price coefficients in equation (11) do not differ from one another statistically speaking, it is nevertheless conceivable that the elasticities of −17.11 and 13.08 may be economically different, particularly if the significance tests are not interpreted literally. The authors do not place much stock in their equations (13)–(15) especially since the income variable was highly correlated with their trend variable in equation (3). Again, economic logic would dictate that the income variable is more meaningful than the trend variable, which is usually a catchall and therefore difficult to interpret. It would have been preferable of course if the income variable had been included with the separate price variables in K-L equations (11) and (12).

A related matter of logic concerns the authors' aggregation of the four-digit SITC data to the two-digit level. In carrying out this aggregation, it was in effect assumed that the elasticity-of-substitution relations noted held at the four-digit level. As argued in the preceding discussion, there is no a priori basis for such an assumption.

Leaving aside for a moment the question of the appropriate form of the model, there are some troublesome points that arise when we take K-L on their own ground. These concern mainly (1) the derivation of the export quantity indexes; (2) the disregard of cross effects involving the United Kingdom, Germany, and Japan; and (3) the adjustment lags.

To obtain export quantities, the authors divided current value figures by a price index based upon 1963 weights. The resulting quantity index is unfortunately difficult to interpret since it involves variable weights. Rather, what they should have done was to construct a quantity index that reflected the same weighting pattern as their price index. This might admittedly be a difficult undertaking because of data problems, but it would be worthwhile to determine if the results were materially affected by using a different quantity index.

In focusing only on the substitution relations involving the United States vis-à-vis the United Kingdom, Germany, and Japan, the possibility exists that substitutions among these latter three countries might be attributed erroneously to substitution vis-à-vis the United States. Suppose, for example, that the pattern of specialization at the four-digit SITC level differed substantially and that substitutions occurred among the three countries that were different from those that occurred vis-à-vis the United States. It is conceivable therefore that the K-L measure may overstate the responsiveness of foreign export quantities relative to the United States.

On the matter of adjustment lags, it is noteworthy that the authors obtain quite different results for the two four-year periods from 1953 to 1961 in equation (4) as compared to the results for the period 1961–64 in equations (5) and (6). On the face of it, this is not really surprising since there could be differential time lags involved in the different classes of manufactured goods. Thus, part of what may appear to have been a change in the structure of the relationship is perhaps attributable to the time units chosen as they relate to the nature of the adjustment lags.

Let us turn next to the question of the variability of the elasticity of substitution with respect to market shares and the asymmetry of declining and rising relative prices. It is evident from the space allotted that the authors consider their findings here to be interesting and important. Now it is true that a country's existing market share will influence what it can gain or lose in this respect as its prices decline or rise. It does not necessarily follow, however, that the elasticity of substitution need be variable. This can be seen from the following expression for the elasticity of substitution defined in terms of market share, e_g: [2]

$$(5) \qquad\qquad e_g = (e + 1)(1 - g),$$

where e is the conventional elasticity of substitution and g is the market share. Thus, e_g will vary with g, but e can nevertheless remain constant.

[2] See *ibid.*, pp. 178–79, n. 9.

IMPLICATIONS FOR FURTHER RESEARCH

One of the obvious extensions of this research is to disaggregate not only by commodity categories but also by importing regions. The authors can do the former since their price indexes were based upon the four-digit SITC classification. Unfortunately, they cannot effectively disaggregate by importing region. This is because their price indexes refer to exports to all regions and there is no reason to believe that the same price is applicable throughout.[3] Further research may also be hampered by the fact that the authors' indexes stop in 1964. It would be desirable if these indexes could be kept current and differentiated by importing region.

If disaggregation is to be pursued, a more comprehensive pooling procedure might be employed. Particularly to be recommended is the procedure used by Ginsburg, in which separate allowance is made for the effects of commodity composition, regional composition, time, and curvilinearities in the relative price influences.[4]

However, before substantial additional resources are expended on further research, it seems fitting to ask why it is that we want to measure the elasticity of substitution in international trade. If the answer is to obtain better estimates of price elasticities of demand, then why not approach such estimation directly rather than in a roundabout way. This same conclusion holds even when we are seeking to explain export-market shares, especially since most implications for policy can be stated more readily in terms of the directly estimated rather than the substitution elasticities.

REPLY BY KRAVIS AND LIPSEY

Stern raises several theoretical points, on which we disagree almost completely, and makes a number of suggestions, some of which we plan to carry out in future work and some of which we would follow if the

---

[3] See Alan L. Ginsburg and Robert M. Stern, "The Determination of the Factors Affecting American and British Exports in the Inter-War and Post-War Periods," *Oxford Economic Papers,* July 1965, p. 267.

[4] See Alan L. Ginsburg, *American and British Regional Export Determinants,* Amsterdam, North-Holland, 1969.

required data were available. Our main disagreement relates to the meaning of the price variable. Stern treats it as a relation between prices of two different commodities and we consider it to be a comparison of the price in two countries for the same commodity. The divergences of our views regarding both the use of individual-country prices rather than price competitiveness and the importance of income variables stem mainly from our differences in the interpretation of the price measure.

With respect to the use of substitution elasticities, as opposed to demand elasticities, Stern's objection seems to be to the use of relative prices, in place of an individual-country price index, in the denominator of the elasticity measure. This is not really an objection to the substitution elasticity because the same objection can be made to demand elasticities, many of which are calculated using relative, rather than absolute, price as the independent variable. In fact, there is not, as Stern claims, any economic logic which requires the use of the separate price indexes. There is nothing in the underlying theoretical formulation applying to comparisons between commodities, summarized by Stern at the beginning of his comment, that dictates the order in which our equations should be presented. Since we consider relative prices to be the appropriate variable, we start with them. We run the separate country price equations that Stern advocates [(10) and (11)] to see whether we have successfully matched commodities between exporting countries. In any case, the question of which measure provides the better explanation of trade flows is one to be answered empirically, and we found relative prices superior in this respect.

In some products or industries we could go further and say that the single-country price index, which Stern advocates, has little meaning. Competition takes place through successive place-to-place comparisons by buyers, as in international bidding for heavy electrical equipment. The time-to-time index is an artificial construction which we have put together to produce a comprehensive price index, but it does not represent the buyer's view of the market.

Stern asks why the elasticity of substitution should be calculated at all. Its virtues are pointed out by Leamer and Stern themselves, in their book. It avoids the need for including a large number of variables that would be required for explaining the level of exports. These variables, such as income in the importing country, canceled out, as we expected, when we focused on the explanation of export shares instead.

Professor Stern suggests that our export quantity index, which is derived from the value of trade and the price index, is difficult to interpret because it involves changing weights. The problem is a very old one. The only observable event is the change in the value of trade, and we wish to analyze this event by factoring the change in value into price and quantity elements, which are analytical categories, not observable values. Since the price index is a Laspeyres (fixed weight) index, the corresponding quantity index that factors the value change is a Paasche (current weight) quantity index. It is true that the elasticity measure calculated in this way will differ from that derived from Paasche price and Laspeyres quantity indexes, or from Fisher indexes for both price and quantity. The latter form would meet Stern's preference for price and quantity indexes of the same type. His suggestion of fixed weight price and quantity indexes, on the other hand, would not factor the value change. The conditions under which there will be bias, and the factors determining the direction of bias with each type of index, have been discussed elsewhere.[1]

One question Stern asks is whether the difference between our results for the four-year periods before 1961 and those for the one-year periods afterward is a consequence of the length of the period alone, since one might well expect longer-run quantity responses to be greater than the short-run ones. We calculated an elasticity coefficient for the period 1961–64 as a whole and found it to be higher than the one-year coefficient, but still considerably below the four-year coefficients for earlier years.

Another suggestion is that it would be useful to disaggregate by importing regions, but that our data are not suitable for this purpose because we calculate a single index for exports to all countries. There are two issues involved. One is that there may be differences in price behavior in exports to different regions and the other is that there may be regional differences in response to the same price changes. We cannot deal with the former question, although we wish we had the data for it. We can and will test the latter possibility and we think there

[1] See, for example, Robert E. Lipsey, *Price and Quantity Trends in the Foreign Trade of the United States,* New York, NBER, 1963, Chap. 3.

may be significant differences in response to a U.S. price change be-tween say, the EEC countries and Canada.

To say, as Stern does, that there is no reason to believe that the same price movements are applicable to different regions is an exaggeration. One would not expect large differences for most commodities. How-ever, there are at present no data with which to answer this question. Given the limitations of price data, it is completely unwarranted to assume that differences in unit values represent regional price differ-ences, as the comprehensive pooling procedure used by Ginsburg and approved by Stern would require.

Several of the other points Stern raises we have no disagreement with. Some of the suggested analyses are part of our future program; others are beyond the limits of our data. We do plan to disaggregate by both commodity and region and we will test country and commodity cross elasticities, although we do not expect them to be significant be-cause we believe that our commodity matching was successful in elimi-nating most of them. We wish the data covered a longer period but we will leave that job to others. Our plans do include, however, an attempt to interpolate and extrapolate our indexes using domestic price data for each country, reweighted to form indexes with a single set of international trade weights.

Index